The Unfolding Life

The Unfolding Life

Counseling Across the Lifespan

Radha J. Horton-Parker and Nina W. Brown

BERGIN & GARVEY
Westport, Connecticut • London

Library of Congress Cataloging-in-Publication Data

Horton-Parker, Radha J., 1936–
    The unfolding life : counseling across the lifespan / Radha J. Horton-Parker and Nina W. Brown.
      p. cm.
    Includes bibliographical references and index.
    ISBN 0-89789-915-6 (alk. paper)
    1. Counseling. 2. Developmental psychology. I. Brown, Nina W. II. Title.
  BF637.C6 H66 2002
  158'.3—dc21   2002020848

British Library Cataloguing in Publication Data is available.

Library of Congress Catalog Card Number: 2002020848
ISBN: 0-89789-915-6

First published in 2002

Bergin & Garvey, 88 Post Road West, Westport, CT 06881
An imprint of Greenwood Publishing Group, Inc.
www.greenwood.com

Printed in the United States of America

The paper used in this book complies with the Permanent Paper Standard issued by the National Information Standards Organization (Z39.48-1984).

10 9 8 7 6 5 4 3 2 1

To my father, PAYNE, *who taught me to love and always look up*
To my husband, SKIP, *who makes the journey of life wondrous for me,*
and,

IN MEMORIAM,

To my aunt, MARGUERITE, *who taught me how to open my arms to life,*
and to my mother, KATY, *who gave me the gift of laughter.*

—R.H-P.

To my husband, WILFORD, *who has been with me the majority of my life,*
and has been a major influence on how it unfolded.

—N.W.B.

Contents

Chapter One

Setting the Stage

W HAT IMAGES COME TO MIND when you think of an unfolding life? A flower gradually unfolding as it opens to the sun? Peeling an onion? Unwrapping a present? Watching a child grow and change? A stage drama? There are many such images that can be triggered as you reflect on an unfolding life.

This concept, the unfolding life, is a major premise for this book and is intended to present material to guide your understanding of how people grow and develop. It is not possible to present everything that influences human growth and development, the varied impact of these factors on individuals, or how each person responds to these influences. We can only give you an overview of some of the major factors.

Another premise for the unfolding life concept is that clients gradually present their lives and self to you, the counselor and therapist, and it is one of your major responsibilities to accept that you must be patient and allow the process to unfold. Each client will differ in significant ways, and you must understand that some material is masked, hidden, sensitive, and not easily accessed or understood by either you or the client. Further, your expertise, personal growth, and experience will enable you to understand some things that clients do not, and may not even be aware of or know.

Read the following cinquain and reflect on the course of your life and how it unfolded:

Life
Unfolds
My existence
Happy
Gift.

A cinquain is a poem in five lines that follows a sequence for what appears on each line, and the number of syllables on each line. The sequence is (Brown, 1996):

- ◆ Line 1—names the image.
- ◆ Line 2—describes the image.
- ◆ Line 3—tells its use.
- ◆ Line 4—describes your feelings.
- ◆ Line 5—renames the image.

The number of syllables also follows a sequence that starts with the number of syllables in the first line. Line 2 doubles the number, line 3 doubles the number of syllables in the second line, line 4 returns to the number for line 2, and line 5 has the same number of syllables as does line 1. When constructing a cinquain, try to use descriptive words but not sentences. Now try writing a cinquain about the image that comes to mind when you think of your unfolding life.

As you reflect on your life, tune in and heighten your awareness of how you feel about it, especially as it is today. You may have experienced trauma, disappointments, failures, successes, love, happiness, and despair to arrive at where you are today. You may continue to have, and be influenced by, family of origin issues and unfinished business. So too, are your clients with their lives. You and your clients have hidden material, shaming secrets, fears, fantasies, and yearnings. You are alike and yet you differ in significant ways. The places where you touch each other can connect you in meaningful ways and allow trust, safety, and rapport to build. This is the cornerstone for effective counseling and therapy.

The material presented in this book seeks to deepen and expand your self-understanding, and to guide you to better understand how your clients' lives unfolded, even when clients are unable to verbalize many of his or her experiences.

Where Counselors Work

Counselors work in a variety of settings with a variety of clients who have a vast array of presenting conditions. While, at one time, counselors worked primarily, or only, with school-age children, the current situation is that counselors are to be found conducting counseling and therapy in every mental health treatment group or facility, from inpatient to support and psychoeducational groups. Thus, counselors must be prepared to deal with human growth and development issues across the lifespan, from preschool to later life, and to treat or provide learning experiences for the many and varied conditions that clients encounter.

This book is designed to provide students with both theories and applications that can be helpful whomever their clients are, and whatever the conditions. While it does not present in-depth information on either, it does provide a macro framework for understanding counseling across the lifespan. Following is an overview of the material presented in this book.

Chapter 1 begins with a discussion of the Lifespan Counseling Model developed by the authors that tries to capture and categorize the vast array of presenting problems, issues, and concerns across the lifespan. There are five categories: *life transitions, family of origin issues, situational concerns, serious physical and/or emotional disorders,* and *existential issues.* There can be overlap among categories, but every attempt is made to have them be as discrete as possible. The model will serve as a framework for the applications chapters for children, adolescents, and adults. The model gives us an opportunity to see the different situations and conditions for each age group, and to understand the pervasive effect throughout life for some events, conditions and, situations.

This chapter also presents current delineations among psychoeducation, counseling/therapy, and psychotherapy. The Standards of Practice for counselors is summarized, and the section ends with a table of examples of psychoeducational, counseling/therapy, and psychotherapy activities and interventions applied to children, adolescents, and adults. Chapter 1 concludes with a discussion of some basic and fundamental guidelines for conducting counseling across the lifespan. This section provides a review of skills, treatment planning, and basic therapeutic factors that have application to the array of presenting conditions and problems of children, adolescents, and adults. Specific strategies and techniques for each developmental level of clients (e.g., children) are presented in the chapters on "applications."

Chapter 2 presents information on becoming a culturally sensitive therapist. Given that the vast majority of clients will differ from their therapist in significant ways, the chapter focuses on increasing awareness of personal biases, stereotyping, and prejudices, as well as understanding cultural differences and diversity. Some differing definitions for multicultural, cross-cultural, and diversity issues are presented together with three models for counseling culturally different and diverse clients.

Chapters 3 through 5 present developmental theories on

♦ life stage tasks

♦ cognitive development

♦ moral development

♦ social development

- ◆ gender identity development
- ◆ psychological development.

Highlighted are the theories of Havighurst, Erikson, Adler, Piaget, Kohlberg, Gilligan, Fowler, Freud, Klein, Winnicott, Mahler, and Kohut. These theories highlight the range and complexity of human development and emphasize the many variations it can take.

Chapters 6, 7, 8, 10, 12, and 14 present the expected life-stage development for infants, children, adolescents, and adults. The Lifespan Counseling Model is applied to the specific life stage to conceptualize major developmental tasks that are expected to be accomplished, situations and events that promote or retard successful accomplishment, how the theories apply to the specific life stage, and prevalent problems encountered. Clinical cases and other examples are provided as illustrations.

Chapters 9, 11, and 13 focus on counseling applications for children, adolescents, and adults. Specific guidelines and instructions are given, as are descriptions of useful techniques (e.g., play therapy).

Lifespan Counseling Model

Table 1.1 presents the overall categories and examples for problems and issues across the lifespan. The categories are:

- ◆ Life transitions
- ◆ Family of origin issues
- ◆ Situational concerns
- ◆ Serious physical and/or emotional disorders
- ◆ Existential issues.

Life transitions are those developmental tasks usually encountered or that individuals are expected to complete. The specific concerns that arise at each stage of development are different, as are the tasks, but there is an underlying expectation for each stage that provides the basis for meeting individual, familial, and societal expectations that is termed "life transitions."

Family of origin issues can be the etiology for many problems and concerns encountered by individuals throughout their lives. For example, a 40-year-old man is suffering from depression, abusing alcohol, and has a mother who is dying in the hospital, but he refuses to see or talk with her because she failed to protect him from abuse by his father and his stepfather. The long-lasting and pervasive effects of family of origin issues are described more fully in the chapter on psychological development.

Situational concerns are those that are time-bound and that may be out of the person's control (e.g., the economy that affects employment), but that have a significant impact on current functioning. The contributing

TABLE **1.1**

Examples of Intraindividual Determinants, Environmental
Determinants, and Responses

Intraindividual Determinants

Personality

Character traits

Cognitive ability

Biology (e.g., genetics, gender)

Temperament

Environmental Determinants

Social class

Minority versus majority status

Country of origin

Educational and employment opportunities

Recreational/sports/hobbies

Parenting

Society's caring and concern

Economic situation of country

Spiritual opportunities

Civic opportunities

Responses

| Coping ability | Resilience | Optimism |
| Self-esteem | Self-efficacy | Self-confidence |

situation may actually consume little time, but the reactions can linger and affect other parts of the person's life.

Serious physical and/or emotional disorders are chronic, and can become acute, in addition to being chronic. These disorders affect the person's quality of life and can be detrimental to all aspects of his or her life (e.g., the ability to secure and perform a job).

Existential issues, while not always conscious, are pervasive throughout one's life. Events, situations, and self-reflection can be the means by which these issues come to the conscious forefront of our thoughts, and can exert considerable unconscious influences on decisions, relationships, and functioning.

It is not easy to conceptualize and capture the breadth, width, and depth of all the issues, concerns, and problems people encounter, or may encounter, throughout their lives. Indeed, the literature on any one stage of life is voluminous and too extensive to summarize. When the task is to have an overview for the entire lifespan, it is daunting. This is one of the main reasons for the development of this model. The model is an attempt to conceptualize and categorize the extensive nature of life, with a focus on developmental tasks, physical, psychological, and mental and their underlying bases.

Intraindividual and *environmental* determinants interact with each other and with lifespan concerns to produce individual responses. Table 1.1 presents the list of characteristics and actions associated with each determinant, and examples of responses.

INTRAINDIVIDUAL DETERMINANTS

These are the characteristics that have a genetic base (nature) interacting with nurture, such as personality characteristics, temperament, and cognitive ability. Intraindividual determinants are internal and unique to the individual, with infinite combinations. These determinants are not under the individual's conscious control, but do exert significant influences on how the individual behaves and on his or her attitudes and beliefs. The reactions and responses to life experiences are determined, in a major way, by these intraindividual characteristics.

ENVIRONMENTAL DETERMINANTS

There are external events and characteristics that are out of the direct control of the individual but that can exert significant influences on his or her growth and development. Events such as the quality of nurturing or parenting received and characteristics such as race are examples of environmental determinants. Race is classified as environmental, as it is not race in and of itself that exerts the influence, but is instead the responses of the people in the culture and environment that impact a person. Environmental determinants play a very important role in how individuals perceive and respond to events in their lives. They interact with intraindividual determinants in reaction to lifespan concerns to produce unique and individualized responses.

Counseling and Psychotherapy

At one time there was a clearer distinction among guidance, counseling, and psychotherapy. However, there is more overlap for these categories today, with guidance becoming psychoeducation, and counseling including working with clients on issues rooted in family of origin concerns (e.g., victims of domestic violence). Psychotherapy has incorporated elements of psychoeducation as part of treatment. This blurring of distinctions among education, development, and remediation calls for a higher level of understanding for counselors that work in all settings and who will work with children, adolescents, and/or adults who have a variety of problems. That is, counselors cannot expect to be effective when using psychoeducational strategies, programs and techniques without having a deep understanding of psychological and developmental factors that underlie the problems being addressed.

This discussion will use the following basic definitions (Gazda, 1989; Ivey, Pedersen, & Ivey, 2001):

- *Psychoeducation*—the more structured form of counseling and therapy in which there are also specific educational goals and objectives. This includes programs that are designed to focus on a specific problem (e.g., anger management). These may also be developmental (i.e., providing information and skills to foster successful completion of stage-appropriate developmental tasks such as career exploration). An example of psychoeducation for therapy would be the informational components in support groups for chronic conditions (e.g., bibliotherapy for depression).

- *Counseling/therapy*—usually of shorter duration than psychotherapy; can be developmental (e.g., managing difficult emotions or divorce) and tends to be more narrowly focused than psychotherapy.

- *Psychotherapy*—focused on remediation of problems, the exploration of family of origin issues as the underlying etiology for current problems and concerns, and is of longer duration than psychoeducation and counseling/therapy.

Another consideration for what is presented is the mode for education, counseling, and therapy. That is, will the mode be individual, group, or family? Each mode has strengths and weaknesses, and the nature and condition of the client will play a role in choosing the mode.

Table 1.2 presents some examples of the different ways in which psychoeducational, counseling, and psychotherapy activities can be applied to children, adolescents, and adults. There are some topics and conditions that apply to all, or almost all, life stages but will be handled differently both because of strategy chosen (e.g., psychotherapy) and because of the needs and abilities of clients at that stage. For example, career-development and social-skills training could continue across the lifespan, as would treatment for depression and substance abuse. However, the same strategies would not be used with children, adolescents, and adults.

The Role of Theory

The theories presented in this book are focused on physical, psychological, spiritual, moral, and cognitive development. Counseling and therapy theories are only briefly discussed, usually in reference to appli-

TABLE **1.2**

Examples of Counseling Strategies for Basic Tasks and Problems

Life Transitions

Psychoeducational

- Provide needed information
- Establish personal priorities
- Teach and provide practice in communication and relating skills
- Clarify personal goals and objectives

Family of Origin

Psychoeducational/Cognitive-Behavioral

- Show how to manage difficult emotions
- Provide communication-skills development
- Deal with conflict behavior and teach conflict resolution

Counseling/Therapy

- Provide interpersonal learning
- Address intimacy concerns
- Instill hope
- Allow practice in new ways of behaving and relating

Psychotherapy

- Facilitate catharsis
- Illuminate influence of early experiences and early relationships
- Foster psychological growth and development (e.g., separation and individuation, healthy narcissism)

Situational Conditions

Psychoeducational

- Provide mediation (e.g., divorce)
- Teach parenting skills

Counseling/Therapy

- Explore and cope with feelings around loss and grief
- Cope with feelings of helplessness when faced with adversity (e.g., illness)

Psychotherapy

- Facilitate understanding of personal reactions
- Promote deep change for feelings and reactions

continued

TABLE 1.2 *(continued)*

Support Groups
- Reduce isolation
- Provide information and guidance

Serious Physical or Emotional Illnesses and Disorders

Psychoeducational/Cognitive-Behavioral
- Provide needed information about condition
- Teach new skills for coping
- Prevent relapse
- Provide social-skills development

Counseling/Therapy
- Increase awareness of personal style of behaving and relating
- Reduce shame and guilt
- Encourage empowerment

Psychotherapy
- Promote understanding of the role that early experiences played in establishing personal reactions and behavior
- Facilitate catharsis leading to interpersonal learning

Support Groups
- Provide needed information
- Reduce isolation and alienation
- Provide encouragement and support
- Provide a needed outlet for "venting"

cations. The authors assume that readers have a firm grounding and understanding of theories that guide their counseling and therapy styles and strategies.

The authors also assume that the different human growth and development theories have different applications at different levels. General assumptions across theories are that

- ♦ establishing the relationship is critical,
- ♦ setting goals and objectives with clients is a collaborative process,
- ♦ personal growth for the therapist is not only encouraged, but should be continual, and
- ♦ the welfare of the client has priority over other concerns.

Regardless of preferred theory, the client's education, counseling, and treatment should be geared to his or her needs and abilities. There is evidence that suggests that the therapist plays a more significant role in successful therapeutic outcomes than does the theoretical approach used.

Ethics and Standards of Practice

Ethics are a fundamental expectation for all mental health professionals and should receive more attention than just being placed in the appendices of books. These standards are fundamental, critical, and of the utmost importance for the legal and moral protection of the client and of the counselor. They are intended to protect the client from harm, and as a guide for therapists to ensure that their actions do not compromise client safety. Presented here is an overview of the general Standards of Practice (American Counseling Association, 1995) that guide counselors and that are similar for other mental health professionals. Chapters 9, 11, and 14 will discuss ethics and standards that have particular application for specific age groups. Readers are also encouraged to learn the legal requirements and restrictions that apply in their state.

THE COUNSELING RELATIONSHIP

Standards 1 through 8 describe the expected attitudes and behaviors that are associated with therapeutic relationships. These are intended to protect clients and the public from harm that could emerge during counseling. Specifically forbidden are sexual intimacies with clients, and dual relationships are to be avoided.

1. Non-discrimination—respect diversity.
2. Inform clients—disclose the counseling process to be used, preferably in writing.
3. Dual relationships—avoid, whenever possible.
4. Sexual intimacies with clients—forbidden.
5. Protection in groups—protect group members from physical or psychological harm.
6. Explain fees—prior to beginning counseling, explain costs and payment options.
7. Ending counseling—refer clients for additional counseling when needed and/or hold follow-up sessions.
8. Inability to help—refer clients elsewhere when unable to provide services.

Standards 9 through 16 present the responsibilities and limitations on maintaining client confidentiality. There are circumstances in which confidentiality should not and/or cannot be maintained or guaranteed. Emphasized are the counselor's responsibility to inform clients in advance of limitations on confidentiality, to secure their permission to share personal information when necessary or appropriate, and to understand that the same responsibilities and limitations apply to the client's family, to the counselor's subordinates, and to other mental health professionals.

9. Maintain confidentiality—confidentiality is mandated, except when disclosure is "in the best interests of clients, for the welfare of others, or is required by law" (ACA, 1995, p. 10).

10. Confidentiality and subordinates—counselors have the responsibility to have subordinates keep client information confidential.

11. Confidentiality and group work—inform group members that confidentiality cannot be guaranteed.

12. Confidentiality and family counseling—information about a family member cannot be revealed to another family member without permission from that person.

13. Confidentiality and records—records created, stored, transferred, or destroyed must be kept confidential.

14. Recording or observing—clients who are recorded or observed must give prior permission.

15. Third-party disclosures—clients must give permission to reveal or transfer their records, except as noted in standard 9.

16. Anonymity—when using clients' data for research, training, or publication, their identities must be disguised.

Standards 17 through 28 refer to the counselor's professional responsibilities and cover a wide range of topics. Forbidden is sexual harassment, recruiting clients from one's personal work site where a salary is paid, and exploitative relationships with supervisees, students, or staff. Highlighted is the counselor's need for continuing education, the understanding of self-limitations and of possible personal impairment, and appropriate ways to represent himself or herself professionally.

17. Competency limits—practice only within personal competency limits.

18. Continuing education—maintain professional competence through continual educational experiences.

19. Impairment—to be avoided. Defined as intrusion of personal problems or conflicts that could be harmful to clients or others.

20. Advertising—accurately advertise your services and credentials.

21. Recruiting for private practice—soliciting clients from one's work site or institutional affiliation is prohibited.

22. Claims for credentials—credentials presented either directly or indirectly must be accurate, and any misrepresentations by others must be corrected.

23. Sexual harassment—forbidden.

24. Misuse of professional position—do not use position to seek or receive unjustified personal gains, sexual favors, unfair advantage, or unearned goods or services.

25. Notifying other mental health professionals—when the client consents, others working with that client can be notified.

26. Negative work environment—employers must be notified if policies or conditions are damaging or have the potential to impair the counselor's professional responsibility or are harmful to clients.

27. Selection of staff—refers to competencies, skills, and assigned responsibilities of staff.

28. Relationships with subordinates—do not engage in exploitive relationships with those you supervise, evaluate, or instruct.

RELATIONSHIPS WITH OTHER PROFESSIONALS

Standards 29 and 30 refer to relationships with other professionals (i.e., it is forbidden to accept referral fees, or charge fees to the client when the counselor receives a salary from the organization or agency).

29. Fees—extra fees must not be accepted from clients when the agency or institution employs the counselor.

30. Referral fees—forbidden.

EVALUATION, ASSESSMENT, AND INTERPRETATION

Standards 31 through 35 are intended to guide counselors in assessment in counseling. Covered are the appropriate text selection, use, interpretation, and reporting of results. Also addressed are topics such as who receives results, and counselor competence.

31. Competency limits—perform only those procedures for which you are competent and ensure the same by those under your supervision.

32. Appropriate instrument use—use assessment instruments only as intended.

33. Explanation to clients—clients must have the purpose, kind, and proposed use of assessment explained prior to administering that assessment.

34. Interpretation of test results—clients should receive accurate and appropriate interpretations of test results.

35. Obsolete tests and outdated test results—decisions, interventions, or recommendations should not be made using either.

TEACHING, TRAINING, AND SUPERVISION

Standards 36 through 43 address issues for counselor educators, students, and supervisors. Protection of students and supervisors is emphasized, as is the necessity for counselor educators who supervise to have appropriate coursework.

36. Sexual relations with students or supervisees—forbidden.

37. Credits for students—students and supervisees are to be given credit for their contributions to research and scholarly projects.

38. Supervision—counselors offering supervision must be trained and prepared in supervision methods and techniques.

39. Evaluation—supervisees are to be provided in advance what their expected competency performance is and what the assessment methods and timing are. During supervision, supervisees should receive periodic assessment feedback.

40. Peer relationships—the rights of peers should be maintained when students and supervisees are assigned to lead groups or provide supervision.

41. Remediation and dismissal—students and supervisees who need remediation should be assisted in obtaining it. Those who are unable to provide competent service should be dismissed.

42. Self-growth experience—students who participate in self-growth experiences must be informed of ethical obligations and rights, and are not to be graded on their nonacademic performance.

43. Standards—students and supervisees must abide by the Code of Ethics and Standards of Practice.

RESEARCH AND PUBLICATIONS

Standards 44 through 48 set forth the expectations of counselors when conducting research and reporting results. Care should be taken to ensure accuracy, eliminate misrepresentation, and to give appropriate credits to others who contribute.

44. Avoiding injury—avoid causing physical, social, or psychological harm or injury to research subjects.

45. Confidentiality—information about subjects should be kept confidential.
46. Research outcomes—all variables and conditions are to be reported.
47. Accuracy of results—results should not be distorted, misrepresented, fabricated, or biased.
48. Publication—credit should be given to those who contributed to the research.

RESOLVING ETHICAL ISSUES

Standards 49 through 51 present the performance, reporting, and investigation expectations for counselors. Emphasized is the avoidance of making unwarranted accusations of ethical violations.

49. Expected behavior—counselors are expected to take appropriate action when there are reasons to believe that a mental health professional is acting in an unethical manner.
50. Unwarranted complaints—do not initiate, encourage, or participate in filing complaints that are unwarranted.
51. Cooperation with the ethics committee—expected.

Relationship and Therapeutic Factors

There are some relationship and therapeutic factors that are helpful whether the mode used is psychoeducation, counseling/therapy, or psychotherapy for individuals, a group, or a family. The relationship factors are based on core conditions such as the following (Carkhuff & Berenson, 1967; Corey, 1991; Egan, 1990; Ivey et al., 2001; Rogers, 1986; Thompson, 1996):

- Acceptance, warmth, and caring
- Positive regard
- Empathic responding
- Genuineness
- Tolerance and respect
- All the attending and listening skills.

These conditions and skills are fundamental and are more dependent on your "being" than they are on actions that can be learned. Certainly, some can be learned (e.g., the nonverbal behaviors that indicate attending). However, most are a function of who you are (i.e., your "being") and have to be developed through self-reflection and self-exploration. Hence, there is considerable emphasis in this book on your continual personal development.

Failure to develop a therapeutic relationship almost guarantees that little or nothing will be accomplished. Clients have to feel safe, trusting, and valued before they are willing to disclose significant personal material, explore painful unfinished business or long-standing issues, or to accurately hear and understand your interventions. Everything of consequence in therapy rests on the foundation and quality of the therapeutic relationship.

You are encouraged to engage in personal development with a therapist, and to work through the personal development exercises in this book. It could also be helpful for you to write in a journal as you read the chapters, and to record your feelings, personal associations, memories, and so on.

The therapeutic factors are similar in many respects to the therapeutic factors that Yalom (1995) describes as helpful for group therapy and group psychotherapy. Some are helpful across the board, while others would be of greatest benefit for a particular mode (e.g., psychoeducation). The therapeutic factors to be discussed are

- ◆ reduction of loneliness, isolation, and/or alienation
- ◆ imparting information
- ◆ encouragement and support
- ◆ fostering the appropriate emotional expression
- ◆ modeling
- ◆ strength building
- ◆ modifying the effect of lingering family of origin concerns
- ◆ addressing existential issues
- ◆ teaching more effective ways of behaving and relating.

REDUCE LONELINESS, ISOLATION, AND/OR ALIENATION

Reduction of loneliness, isolation, and/or alienation is helpful for all clients. They can feel different, weird, off-beat, and in some ways cut off from others. They can be so mired in their problems and concerns that they truly feel isolated. They may be alienated because of their feelings about being different or they may feel that way because of how they are responded to or treated by others. Whatever the reason, any reduction of these feelings can foster connections of reaching out to both give and receive help and begin to promote empowerment (Yalom, 1980).

Recognizing that these feelings are present is the first step. Clients do not always openly and directly express them. They may say things like "Nobody likes me" (a child); "I don't have any friends" (an adolescent); "Am I crazy?" (an adult); or "Nobody understands me" (any age). These are disguised ways of expressing loneliness, isolation, and alienation.

Once these are recognized, steps can be taken to reduce the feelings.

Your acceptance, understanding, and listening can foster your client's connection with you. Once that is accomplished, other strategies can be introduced to enhance other interpersonal relationships.

IMPARTING INFORMATION

There is a vast difference between *giving information* and *giving advice*. Information leaves the person space to make decisions and judgments, and is empowering. Giving advice is telling the person what he or she should or ought to do, and the unspoken expectation is that the person is expected to follow the advice, because the advice-giver knows what is best for the other person. Advice-giving is limiting, judgmental, and puts the receiver in a dependent position. It is important to understand the distinction between these two in order to make constructive use of this factor.

Imparting information means to correct misinformation that is generally factual in nature, to provide missing information, and to clear up ambiguous terms. The receiver is left free to accept what part, if any, is useful or will be used, and is not pushed to act on it either by an open demand or by covert means (e.g., guilt and shame). Skillful imparting of information is often very helpful and enlightening.

Advice-giving is risky even when requested by clients. You are *not* the other person and cannot fully understand all the factors in the situation, especially those that are personal to the person such as values and aspirations. Your advice may seem appropriate from your perspective, but may appear wildly inappropriate from the client's perspective. Additionally, there is always the spoken or unspoken possible outcome of the client saying, "I told you it would (or would not) work."

ENCOURAGEMENT AND SUPPORT

Demonstrating confidence that the client has the power to make desired changes, grow and develop, problem-solve, make decisions, and contribute to his or her treatment is therapeutic. Clients can "catch" your confidence and understand that you are being encouraging and supportive. Many clients will not have and other such supportive relationships.

Do not confuse encouragement and support with praise and compliments. Although praise and compliments have their uses, encouragement and support are different in that they are not just words, but a heartfelt conviction that the person has the needed resources and ability to actively engage in treatment and make changes.

Encouragement is also building on strengths. Many clients are so focused on their weaknesses and flaws that they fail to recognize and capitalize on the strengths that they do have. Many also continue to focus on how much more needs to be done and their setbacks and failures, rather than noticing what progress has been made or what has been accomplished. It is much more helpful and motivating to recognize progress, and it is the counselor's job to also provide this dimension.

Encouragement is one of the means by which you can instill hope; and without hope that the situation can be improved or that problems can be solved, clients can become despairing and give up. It can be important to convey hope, but care should be taken not to exaggerate or inflate expectations. What is needed is *cautious* hope. Cautious hope implies that if the client works on himself or herself, perseveres, and is determined then he or she can effect changes that can make the situation better—not necessarily get what is wanted.

FOSTERING THE APPROPRIATE EMOTIONAL EXPRESSION

Many clients will not be in touch with their feelings, and/or will be unable to express them in constructive, appropriate ways. "Appropriate" and "constructive" means that individuals choose the words accurately, describe the feelings, communicate the level and intensity of the feelings, achieve some relief (catharsis) from expressing the feelings, and obtain some degree of intra- or interpersonal awareness or learning. Inappropriate expressions include:

♦ attempting to bully or intimidate

♦ trying to manipulate the other person

♦ expressing narcissistic rage

♦ demanding that the other person change or provide what is wanted

♦ indirectly expressing feelings

♦ masking the level and intensity of feelings

♦ throwing tantrums

♦ sulking.

A very common practice is for people to confuse *thoughts* with *feelings* and to express their thoughts as if they were feelings by adding phrases such as: "I feel _____"; "My feelings are _____"; "You are _____"; or "I wish you would _____." Saying that you feel a thought does not make it a feeling. Examples include: "I feel we are getting off the track"; "I am feeling that this is a losing cause"; or "You are wonderful." These are not *feelings*, but are instead *thoughts*. The receiver is left in doubt regarding how or what the person is feeling.

Helping clients to be more precise in phrasing their feelings, to become more aware of gradations of feelings, and to increase their willingness to openly express important feelings are major tasks for therapy. The outcomes will have an impact on not only clients' personal growth, but also on the quality of their other interpersonal relationships.

MODELING

A therapeutic factor that is very beneficial to clients is *modeling*. You, as the counselor, are the model for desired behaviors and attitudes. You show clients how to relate, communicate, and be willing to receive feedback. You demonstrate the characteristics that foster interpersonal relationships (e.g., warmth and caring), and these can be carried over to clients' other relationships.

You will need to achieve a good level of personal growth, understand and work through many of your personal issues, and know that your "being" is under observation if you are to be a good model. Clients will react more to *who* you are than to *what* you say you are or do. Therefore these qualities will have to be internalized to the point that you are not consciously aware that you need to demonstrate something (e.g., respect), but you just automatically do it because that is who you are.

STRENGTH BUILDING

Just as with encouragement and support, *strength building* is therapeutic, because clients may not have previously received it. The tendency is to focus on weaknesses and flaws, rather than on strengths. However, it is the person's strengths that will enable him or her to achieve the desired changes.

Start to focus on strengths. At first, you will find that you are looking for what needs "fixing," and not on what resources the person has to do the "fixing." That is not to say that nothing needs to be "fixed," as everyone has problems and behaviors that need to be changed. These problems are also worthy of examination and focus. However, identifying strengths is most effective because this will encourage the person that he or she can indeed do something to help himself or herself.

One way of identifying strengths is to find them embedded in criticisms, either self-criticisms or those made by others. Most criticisms have a strength. For example, a strength for being stubborn is having the courage of one's convictions. Another example are the strengths in indecisiveness—that is, perceiving the complexity of a situation, being able to view both the positives and negatives, and having the desire to make the best possible decision. Begin to look for strengths in every behavior or personality characteristic that is perceived as negative.

FAMILY OF ORIGIN ISSUES

A very positive therapeutic factor is the modification of lingering *family of origin issues*. These issues include perceptions, feelings, and situations that the client has carried within for years that are related to events and people in the client's family of origin. Some will relate to psychological growth, such as those described in chapter 5 on "Psychological Development." Family of origin issues are buried very deep in the person's psyche and have a complex impact on his or her present functioning and relationships. Many current problems can be traced to unresolved family of origin issues.

If you are not conducting psychotherapy, you may wonder how family or origin issues may relate to your counseling, or just how they can be incorporated. The most important thing is for you, the counselor, to understand the importance of family of origin issues and behave in a manner that allows some of them to be corrected. The critical point to emphasize is that these unresolved issues can be corrected.

For example, if a client was expected to "read his or her parent's mind" (i.e., know what the parent wanted and give it to him or her without being asked), then you would need to be very clear and direct in your interactions with the client. This would reduce any perception that he or she was expected to read your mind.

Another example would be a situation wherein the expectation in the client's family of origin was that negative feelings would not be openly expressed, or that the consequences and retaliation for expressing them were severe. You would work to encourage the expression of negative emotions, and be receptive to that expression, even when you were attacked. Allowing the expression of such negative emotions would be corrective for this particular client.

EXISTENTIAL ISSUES

Existential issues are concerned with the basic human conditions that persist throughout life and are common to all of us. Some clients will not have had an opportunity to explore existential issues, some will not recognize their universality, and many will not understand that the answers today may not be sufficient for other times—they are looking for definitive answers where none exist. It is your responsibility to be aware of and identify existential issues and themes, such as

- ◆ responsibility and freedom
- ◆ isolation and alienation
- ◆ loneliness
- ◆ despair
- ◆ purpose and meaning
- ◆ existential anxiety
- ◆ death.

Most often these issues appear in disguised form, which implies that your expertise will be quite valuable as you point out to the client that the themes and issues are existential in nature, common to all humans, and incapable of being resolved. Existential concerns can only be understood in the context of the person's being and circumstances for the present.

This awareness can be very comforting and therapeutic, since it reduces the need for the person to blame himself or herself for not immediately understanding or resolving the issues (Yalom, 1980, 1995).

EFFECTIVE WAYS OF BEHAVING AND RELATING

The final therapeutic factor to be discussed is that of teaching more *effective ways of behaving and relating*. Clients arrive for counseling because what they are doing is not working, either for their own benefit or for their relationships. They may be seeking ways to make other people change rather than looking for needed personal changes, but they nevertheless want to become more personally and interpersonally satisfied.

Teaching clients more effective ways to relate, communicate, and behave will be of immeasurable benefit. As clients change their behaviors and attitudes, others change their perceptions of them and begin to relate to them in more satisfying ways. The client thereby increases his or her self-esteem and self-confidence, and the goals for counseling are somewhat achieved.

Teaching is accomplished through modeling, direct instruction, and behavior rehearsal. Many conditions respond to social-skills training, assertiveness training, management of difficult feelings, and communication-skills training. Psychoeducational activities, instruction, and groups are extremely useful for this purpose. They can allow for all modes of learning and can be a component for counseling as well as a stand-alone mode. This therapeutic factor is more structured and direct than are most of the others, but its importance should not be underestimated.

Exercises and Activities

There are exercises and activities throughout the book to promote personal growth and personalize some of the information. It is important for counselors to understand how their lives unfolded to this point, their important influences, how their beliefs and values developed, their areas of unfinished business, their level of narcissistic development, and their lingering family of origin issues. Understanding your "self" and how that self developed is key to understanding your clients. These exercises and activities are one way to increase your awareness and understanding.

Completing most or all of these exercises and activities can be compiled into a "Book of Self" at the end, and they are designed to give a rounded and holistic review of who you are. Readers are encouraged to think in terms of completing this book. Directions for the Book of Self follow.

The materials needed will be a loose-leaf binder or memory book with blank pages. Do not get a bound notebook because you will want to insert materials throughout, and you may want to move some from place to place. You will also need tabs or some way to divide the book into "past," "present," and "future," and a glue stick, crayons, felt markers, or colored pencils. You will make considerable use of magazines and catalogs, so it is suggested that you begin saving these. Other materials will be described for each exercise or activity.

The procedure is: Each exercise and activity will either focus on you as you are today, as you were in the past, or what you envision you will be in the future. However, you are free to place the product wherever you choose—it's your life! As you complete an exercise, place the product in the desired part of the book. Your products will include written material, drawings, collages, and photographs. Directions for these are given for each exercise.

EXERCISE **1**

The "Now" of My Life

Objective: To position yourself in the present and become aware of current experiencing and relationships.

Materials: You will need a photograph of yourself taken during the past year. If you do not have a photograph, get a disposable camera and have someone take one of you. You will also need magazines, catalogs, a glue stick, a sheet of memory-book paper, a sheet of regular writing paper, and a writing instrument.

Procedure: If the photograph is a special one for you, copy it on a color copier or from a scanner on the computer. This way you can save the original. Glue the photo in the center of the memory-book paper. Cut out symbols from the magazines and catalogs to describe:

- ◆ your greatest achievement
- ◆ a disappointment
- ◆ your values
- ◆ relationships that are important for you today
- ◆ hobbies
- ◆ a wish or wishes for the future.

Glue these symbols around your picture. Try not to cut out words, because symbols can be more graphic.

Once you have your collage, use the sheet of paper and writing instrument to describe what the symbols mean. Write a summary paragraph about yourself as you are today. Place the collage and write-up in the Book of Self.

Chapter Two

Becoming a Culturally Sensitive Therapist

THE 2001 U.S. SURGEON GENERAL'S supplemental report, *Mental Health: Culture, Race, and Ethnicity*, describes why cultural sensitivity is so important for counselors. It says that (p. 6)

♦ culture and social factors contribute to mental illness

♦ ethnic and racial minorities face greater exposure to discrimination, racism, violence, and poverty, which contribute to emotional distress

♦ racism and discrimination place minorities at risk for severe disorders such as clinical depression

♦ the cultures of racial and ethnic minorities alter the type of mental health services needed.

All mental health professional organizations recognize the importance of formal cultural and diversity training for mental health practitioners, and the need for understanding the needs of an increasingly diverse populace (American Psychological Association, 1993; American Counseling Association, 1995; American Group Psychotherapy Association, 1991). However, it is not easy to sort out and understand the complex interactions of race, ethnicity, diversity, social class, and other related topics such as racism and bias; nor is there a consensus about what the terms mean or how they are used in counseling.

For example, Hays (1996) reports that "despite distinct differences in their meanings, the terms race, ethnicity, and culture continue to be used interchangeably" (p. 333). Pedersen (1991) notes that "the phenomena of racism, sexism, ageism, and other exclusionary perspectives make the mistake of overemphasizing the culturally unique perspective while neglecting those common-ground universals and within-group differences that are shared across cultures" (p. 6). The Surgeon General (2001) notes that "the Federal Government created these broad racial and ethnic categories" (p. 3). Ivey, Pedersen, and Ivey (2001) assert that "we are all multicultural human beings" (p. 1).

Although there is increasing attention and research on cultural and diversity issues, there are still major gaps in our knowledge and understanding. Behancourt and Lopez (1993) and Clark, Anderson, Clark, and Williams (1999) provide examples of how research on ethnic minorities' perspectives is lacking and has yet to be integrated into training and practice. Hays (1995) found that nonethnic minority cultures such as women and people with disabilities tend to be separate from one another, and from the general multicultural counseling literature. It becomes increasingly evident that there are no definitive definitions or guides to becoming a culturally sensitive counselor, and it is a vast undertaking to try and understand what is needed for counselors to prepare for helping these clients. In this chapter, we attempt to increase your awareness of your personal need for knowledge, understanding, and sensitivity regarding counseling culturally diverse clients.

The following scale (table 2.1) is designed to heighten your awareness of diverse culturally determined behaviors. Assume that you are the counselor and are meeting the client for the first time. The client was born

TABLE **2.1**
Culturally Sensitive Behaviors Scale

Client's Country of Origin	Counselor's Behavior
Belgium	Giving the client a chrysanthemum
France	Making the ok sign of the thumb and index finger in a circle
Germany	Keeping your hands in your pockets as you talk
Spain	Addressing an older client by his or her first name
Hungary	Calling a client by her first name
Brazil	Speaking Spanish
Columbia	Addressing the client by his or her last name (e.g., Mr. Smith)
Egypt	Pointing with your left index finger
Saudi Arabia	Sitting in the figure 4-legged position with the bottom of your shoe facing the client
China	Asking the client to make "I" statements
Japan	Asking the client to make and sustain eye contact

in another country or is a first-generation U.S. citizen. If the behavior or action is culturally sensitive for the client from the identified country, answer *yes*. If it is not culturally sensitive, or is offensive, answer *no*.

All of the behaviors in the table are considered offensive, rude, and contrary to the particular culture's norms. Many of them are not considered so in the culture of the United States, and indeed some are encouraged in therapy. This highlights the need for you to become as culturally sensitive as possible, because many of your clients will not have been born in the United States, while others will be first-generation U.S. citizens whose country of origin's cultural expectations will not be the norm here. Others will not be from what is generally called "mainstream" U.S. cultural norms (Acuff, 1993).

Cross-Cultural, Multicultural, and Diversity

There are not clear definitions for the terms *cross-cultural*, *multicultural*, and *diversity*. Some authors use the terms interchangeably, while others try to make some distinctions between them (Baruth & Manning, 1991; Neukrug, 1999; Pedersen, 1991; Hays, 1996). It is beyond the scope of this book to try and construct definitions and/or to make distinctions, because the whole subject is much too complicated. What is done here is present some guidelines for therapist's expected competencies, a model for therapy, and a partial list of characteristics that make up the categories for cross-cultural, multicultural, and diversity.

Fukuyama (1990) presents the following categories for defining *multicultural*:

+ race
+ ethnicity
+ language
+ gender
+ religion
+ spirituality
+ sexual orientation
+ age
+ physical issues
+ socioeconomic status
+ other delineations.

Others, such as Gladding (1997), add

+ intellectual ability
+ physical, mental, and emotional disabling conditions.

In short, there are many characteristics that categorize people as multi-cultural, cross-cultural, and diverse. Trying to capture the identifying characteristics for just culture alone is very complex, let alone those for individuals. Suffice it to say that being culturally knowledgeable, sensitive, and skilled are essential for counselors and therapists, regardless of their work-setting.

Ivey et al. (2001) note that there are a variety of contextual issues around issues of diversity and these, together with Fukuyama's (1990) description of multiple categories, point out the need for counselors and therapists to be open and accepting of clients as they present themselves, for the extent of their diversity may not be apparent at first. Not knowing the cross-cultural, multicultural, or diversity identifications, categories, and the impact of these on the client can present the potential for making culturally insensitive assumptions, interventions, and remarks that will have a negative impact on the ability to establish a therapeutic relationship. Since this relationship is the foundation for counseling and therapy, a critical and important component will be missing; hence the needed outcomes will have little or no chance of being attained. Some clients may leave and not return.

Becoming Culturally and Diversity Sensitive

There are some attitudes, knowledge, and skills that can be developed and/or enhanced that will promote the needed sensitivity for cultural diversity. Attitudes include being aware of stereotyping, biases, and preconceived notions, whether conscious or unconscious. Knowledge refers to an understanding of how individuals are affected by discrimination, the sociopolitical climate and life experiences, as well how these may affect their ability to participate in therapy. These skills are derived from basic counseling competency and experience with an overlay of realization of cultural differences and needs (Atkinson, Morten, & Sue, 1993; Cass, 1979; Cross, 1991; Helms, 1990).

Most of the growth and development is internal and personal for the therapist. Thus it cannot be monitored or assessed but must rely for compliance on the person's dedicated commitment to the ethics and professional standards of his or her profession.

Further complicating matters is the unconscious. New research is being conducted on the "act of categorizing people" and is finding that the amygdala (a cluster of nerves located deep inside each brain hemisphere that is involved with strong emotions, memory, and learning rules) reacts to things that are emotionally significant such as racial differences (*Virginian-Pilot*, November 15, 2000). The article also reports on a study by Phelps and Banaji that demonstrated that when White subjects were shown pictures of young Black men, their amygdalas showed increased activity and excitement. The same subjects also scored higher on two other measures that assessed unconscious feelings about Blacks. Another study used an MRI scanner to map changes in the amygdala when Black and White subjects were shown pictures of Black and White faces. Both groups showed changes when looking at a picture of a Black face. These two studies suggest that the brain reacts to racial differences, and that the reaction will most likely not be a conscious one. While these studies were focused on racial differences, it is possible that researchers may find similar outcomes for other differences, even for those that are not obvious.

The importance of studies like these lies in their findings, interpretations, and/or suggestions that the role of the unconscious is important and that a conscious examination of deeply held values, attitudes, and beliefs may not be enough to overcome early learning experiences that lie in an inaccessible part of the brain. This, if true, would mean that therapists would have to be eternally vigilant and aware of possible biases, prejudices, and stereotyping.

In addition to increasing their personal awareness, therapists must also develop a knowledge base about cultural differences, including

- the effects of discrimination, stereotyping, and bias on physical, psychological, emotional, education, employment, and interpersonal relationships;
- differences that are important to consider in therapy such as communication style, lifestyles, values, beliefs, and limiting factors; and
- how varying life experiences, cultural heritages, sociopolitical backgrounds, and multiple cultural and diversity identities can affect clients.

Suggested strategies for learning include

- formal educational experiences,
- reading research on the subject,
- consulting with knowledgeable people, and
- becoming actively involved with culturally different people.

The Multicultural Models of Ramirez and Ivey

Ramirez (1991) developed a multicultural model for psychotherapy and counseling that has the following components:

- respect for the clients' origins,
- awareness of personal ways of thinking and communicating,
- learning to accommodate other ways of thinking and communicating,

♦ encouraging self and clients to grow multiculturally, and

♦ encouraging clients to become active community-change agents.

This model places considerable emphasis on cognitive strategies for

♦ building awareness of the impact of the larger culture on clients' functioning,

♦ developing coping strategies tailored to the clients' multicultural needs, and

♦ the necessity for therapists to remain in touch with both their personal experiencing of clients and clients' culturally determined reactions to therapists.

Ivey's (1997) model emphasizes a continual attention to the multiplicity of multicultural and diverse categories to which individuals may belong, and not try and fit them into any one category nor react to them on the basis of only one or two categories. Examples for members with multiple categories follow:

♦ A Jewish female, age 40, with multiple sclerosis who has been married to a Catholic lawyer for twenty years. They have three children, one of which is an adopted daughter of mixed Vietnamese and African-American heritage.

♦ An Irish-American gay man who has a long-term relationship with a Hispanic man of Mexican heritage. He is a very successful screenwriter.

♦ An adolescent male, age 16, who is learning-disabled. His parents are biracial. His mother is of Puerto Rican and Black heritage, and his father is of Black and Asian (Chinese) heritage. The family attends the Unitarian Church. Each parent had a previous marriage to white partners and each has a child from that marriage who is now part of the blended family.

Your perceptions, past experiences, and unconscious biases and prejudices will play a major part in determining which characteristics you feel are most important to give attention to, which to ignore, and which you will respond to, as well as how you will choose to respond.

Cultural Sensitivity in Action

Most of what was presented in the prior discussion addresses what a therapist can do to better prepare himself or herself to be a culturally sensitive counselor or therapist. The next discussion turns attention to specific actions to take when meeting with and treating culturally diverse clients. Much of the information presented in this and the prior discussion has the following assumptions:

- all clients will differ from you in one or more significant ways
- you will have a commitment to being culturally sensitive and will continue to enhance your knowledge and skills in this area
- clients will have multiple categories of culturally important characteristics
- it is not possible to anticipate or prepare in advance for all client variations that will be encountered.

There are four major steps for applying cultural sensitivity for specific clients:

1. do not jump to conclusions based on visible evidence
2. determine how the client self-identifies
3. stay in touch with your reactions, attitudes, and beliefs
4. obtain needed information about cultural characteristics that have relevance for therapy.

It is important that the therapist not jump to conclusions based on visible evidence. For example, skin color is not always an infallible guide to race or how the client self-identifies. The same is true for gender. There are females who have many masculine features, and vice versa. Just because a client *appears* to be female does not mean that that person *is* female. You can note visible characteristics, but reserve any conclusions until you have more information.

Regardless of visible evidence, it is much more important to understand how the client self-identifies. This is the point where you can determine what multiple categories are relevant to the client, his or her self-perception, and even where there may be some underlying problems and concerns. For example, if the client visibly appears to be of Asian heritage but self-identifies as Black, it would be important for the therapist to respect that self-identification, regardless of the client's physical appearance. There may also be a myriad of life experiences that the client has encountered because of the variance between his or her visible appearance and self-identification.

It can be crucial to obtain information about cultural and diversity characteristics, and even more important to determine the relative importance of these characteristics for the client. Do not assume that because *you* consider something to be important, that it is also important for the client. Basic information to be gathered includes

- education/occupation
- socioeconomic status—current and during childhood and adolescence
- religious affiliation and/or spiritual beliefs
- racial identity

- ethnic identity
- gender identity and any conflicts (e.g., a male dressing as a female).

Although it is assumed that you will have done considerable personal work on your attitudes, beliefs, biases, stereotypes, and prejudices, it is just as important for you to stay aware of your attitudes, assumptions, and expectations for this particular client. You will need to constantly monitor your inner experiencing and be self-reflective about your reactions. It may be difficult with some clients to sort out personal reactions that have transference or other personal associations as a basis, and the reactions that may be a part of your unconscious biases, prejudices, and/or stereotypes.

The final basic step is to obtain information when encountering a client with cultural and/or diversity characteristics about which you know little or nothing. Moreover, this situation may occur often. Information can be obtained by researching the literature, reading other materials, and/or consulting with someone knowledgeable about the culture, condition, or diversity. This may seem to be an overwhelming task at first, but there are probably resources more readily available than you realize. For example, where would you go to find out about cultural factors for a female immigrant from Bosnia who is a Muslim, is 30 years of age, married, and is being physically abused by her husband? The Internet could be a valuable resource, and a local university would be likely to have someone knowledgeable about the culture.

There are several specific points about which you would want to obtain information to guide your relationship building, goal setting, and expectations. These include the client's

- relationship with and attitude toward authority
- affective-response pattern
- societal context—that is, whether the society of origin is collectivistic or individualistic
- language and nonverbal behaviors taboos
- familial factors
- role of class and status in the culture of origin.

PERCEPTIONS OF AUTHORITY FIGURES

You, as the counselor, will be perceived by the client as an authority figure. Your age, credentials, and position all play into their perception of you and must be considered. For example, you could make a mistake in perceiving that a client agrees to something and will follow through when, in fact, what he or she is doing is showing respect for your perceived authority, because his or her culture teaches that one should never openly disagree, and must always appear to agree, with authority figures. Lots of valuable treatment time could be lost because of this misunderstanding. In the United States, it is generally expected to be okay to openly voice disagreement with an authority figure. Noncompliance could be resistance for the usual U.S. client, but even U.S. citizens who are foreign-born or reared in the expectations of their family's culture may give a culturally determined response to authority figures. Deviations from the expected response to authority figures would also provide valuable information to guide diagnosis and treatment.

CULTURALLY DETERMINED AFFECT EXPRESSION

It is very important to understand the culturally determined affective-response pattern. Some questions you may need answered are:

◆ Is it acceptable to openly express or display feelings?

◆ Are there feelings (e.g., negative feelings) that are expected to be suppressed or not verbally expressed?

◆ Can feelings of distress be expressed, either verbally or non-verbally?

◆ Are there feelings that should never be revealed to authority figures?

The role played by knowing the culture's expectations is illustrated in the following example:

A member of my process group at the American Group Psychotherapy Association's conference was from Africa. He spoke of how feelings are not openly displayed or expressed in his country and that people did not identify feelings, only saying "I'm okay" or "I'm not okay." Saying "I'm not okay," however, would not bring more explanation, probing, or identification of what the person was feeling. Thus, a counselor with a client from that country could become very frustrated at the client's inability or resistance to expressing feelings, when not expressing them is expected in the client's culture. The reverse would be true if the counselor was from that country. He or she would have to adjust to a U.S. client who did openly express and display feelings.

INDIVIDUALISTIC OR COLLECTIVIST SOCIETY

Knowing whether or not the culture has a collectivist or individualistic society is also helpful. The United States is an individualistic society in which the individual's concerns take precedence over the group's concerns, and these are protected by the government and culture. The U.S. culture also values individualism, and considerable time and effort are expended to highlight individuality and uniqueness. However, not all cultures value individualism. Some value adherence and commitment to the group, whether the group is a tribe or an entire country. In the collectivist culture, individuality is discouraged. You would not understand why a client was unable to act in his or her best interests if you did not realize that the client came from a society that considered individuals to be subservient to the group.

LANGUAGE AND NONVERBAL BEHAVIOR TABOOS

The importance of knowing language and nonverbal taboos cannot be overestimated. There are words, phrases, and gestures that are insulting, offensive, demeaning, and threatening to people *from* all cultures, but these are not common *to* all cultures. When the counselor is unaware of these taboos, he or she will unknowingly be offensive. Clients may even terminate without any explanation. Examples of some taboos include:

♦ use of the word "bloody" (Great Britain)

♦ eating or drinking in the presence of someone of the Islamic faith during Ramadan (Islamic countries)

♦ exposing the bottom of the foot to someone (Saudi Arabia)

♦ putting feet on a desk or chair (South Korea)

♦ using the left hand to eat (Middle East).

What is not often realized is that verbal and nonverbal taboos are mostly so internalized that people act and react to them without conscious thought. They are a part of the culture, and everyone assumes that everyone else in existence knows of them, and that when someone violates the taboo, they do so with conscious intent. Conscious intent therefore increases the offensiveness of the act.

FAMILIAL INFLUENCE

Familial influence refers to the role of the family in making decisions for individual family members. That is, are clients free to make decisions, or are they guided, supported, and encouraged by their families to the extent that the family has to be involved in all decisions? These clients cannot make independent decisions. For example, decisions about careers, college majors, or possible partners for marriage are not considered to be a personal decision for clients whose families fit the above description. The family, or parents, will decide on any or all life-transition issues, and the client will not be free to deviate from the family's decision.

The culture is very important in determining the role of the family and can produce considerable conflicts for your clients who are torn between family expectations and the expectations of the U.S. culture that promotes more individualism. This conflict is seen quite often in immigrants' children and in first-generation U.S. citizens who are still deeply influenced by the culture of their country of origin. You will also see the same kind of conflict in U.S.-born clients who come from families that function more as "tribes," in which individual members can only make decisions after consultation with others and are expected to abide by the collective decision.

ROLE OF CLASS AND STATUS IN THE CULTURE

The role of class and status is important in all cultures, including that of the United States. This is another area in which it is possible to be unintentionally offensive by not recognizing the particular culture's view of class and status. For example, there are cultures in which any work using the hands is considered proper only for people of low status. The bank president who tinkers with his automobile (e.g., restoring an antique car) would be applauded by most people in the United States. In other cultures, however, the man's industrious behavior would be frowned on as not being acceptable for someone at his or her status level. There are cultures in which even a suggestion that the person has a career or hobby working with his or her hands is offensive.

It is also important to reserve conclusions about a client's class and status designation, even when the client has been a U.S. citizen for several generations. For example, many people seem to assume that all Black college students are first-generation college attendees. This is not true for a considerable number of students whose grandparents or great-grandparents attended colleges developed for Black students (e.g., Howard University, Hampton University, and Virginia State University). These students could be fourth- or fifth-generation college attendees. It is always best to gather information before reaching conclusions.

Role and status are also closely tied to gender. There are cultures in which females

♦ are not expected to be educated beyond elementary school

♦ are not allowed to drive cars

♦ are not expected to work outside the home

♦ have arranged marriages

♦ are involved in other situations that are at variance with the expectations of the larger U.S. culture.

It should also be remembered, however, that there are groups in the United States who have role and status expectations based on gender. It is important that the therapist not make assumptions about U.S. clients' gender-influenced roles and status based on the therapist's own personal experiences.

Diversity Concerns

The discussion to this point has focused on culture. We now turn to basic strategies to use in order to become a more diversity-sensitive therapist. Diversity, for this part of the discussion, will be defined as intraindividual characteristics that set the person apart from most everyone else (e.g., learning disabilities), being acquired at birth (e.g., a developmental disability) or acquired after birth (e.g., a chronic disabling condition), and result in discrimination for personal characteristics that are not under the client's control. Examples of diversity include gender, age, developmental disabilities and handicapping conditions, socioeconomic status, and sexual orientation or lifestyle.

It is important that culturally sensitive therapists gain knowledge and information about common diversity issues (e.g., sexual orientation) from the literature. For example, therapists should be aware of the impact of all of the aforementioned conditions on individuals. While they may be unfamiliar with the specific situation for any particular client, general knowledge and awareness are helpful in establishing the relationship and reducing the potential for offending. These diversity factors may be compounded when there are also cultural factors (e.g., race/ethnicity) that play a major role.

Some diversity situations are readily visible (e.g., developmental disabilities), while others can be masked or hidden (e.g., sexual orientation). This is another reason why an extensive intake interview can be important. You may want to develop a habit of asking something like: "Do you have any conditions that have had a negative impact on your ability to form relationships, be accepted by your peers, or in achieving life-stage tasks (for example, school achievement)?" You will also want to ascertain the client's description of his or her diversity (i.e., what it feels like to him or her), and to estimate what contributions to therapy the person can make.

Information gathering will continue throughout therapy and can be allowed to emerge. The more emotionally intense aspects, impact, and feelings will be relatively simple to obtain. However, some of the deeper, more narcissistically wounding and repressed reactions will be more difficult to access, and some may never be known.

What cannot be overemphasized is the need for counselors to be self-reflective about their attitudes toward diversity and to become knowledgeable about different conditions. While knowing and understanding are helpful, they do not tell you some important things about the particular client, such as

- ♦ his or her readiness for counseling/therapy
- ♦ his or her life aspirations and goals
- ♦ the quality of his or her interpersonal relationships
- ♦ his or her personality characteristics
- ♦ his or her personal environment
- ♦ his or her commitment to change.

Your knowledge and understanding will allow you to be more sensitive to the particular characteristics of your clients' worlds as they experience them. You will be better able to empathize, rather than merely sympathizing. In therapy, empathy is considerably more powerful than sympathy.

Two Models for Culturally Sensitive Therapy

Hays (1996) presents the ADRESSING model for culturally sensitive therapists. This model includes what was previously discussed in the chapter as multicultural. What is categorized differently by Hays is race, which is included with ethnicity and not as a separate category. Ethnicity is defined as "shared language, beliefs, norms, values, behaviors, and institutions" (p. 334). She notes that the concept of race did not appear until late in the eighteenth century. New findings on DNA and other factors point to the greater physiological similarities for humans than the existence of physical differences such as skin color and hair texture. Further, the attempt to categorize by race does not take into account the increasing numbers of biracial and multiracial individuals. What Hays *does* include in her model are:

A   *age*

D   *disability*

R   *religion*

E   *ethnicity*

S   *social status*

S   *sexual orientation*

I   *indigenous*

N   *national origin*

G   *gender.*

This model highlights the complexity of multiple cultural and diversity influences, as well as introducing the consideration for the client's indigenous and national origin characteristics. Indigenous refers to the client's status in the present country, usually the United States (i.e., whether the client and generations of his or her ancestors were born in the country or were immigrants). This concept of indigenous is unique in the way it is phrased, but less so when you consider how young the United States is compared to many countries in the world. Most of its native-born citizens, except for Native Americans and some Hispanics, can trace their ancestors in the United States for a maximum of only about 200 years. In contrast, citizens of Korea have documents that can trace their genealogy for more than two thousand years. However, the current situation for clients (e.g., immigrants for one or two generations versus U.S.-born for the same period of time) can be important when conducting culturally sensitive therapy.

The country of origin is also more complex than it appears on the surface. When you note that many U.S. citizens hyphenate their national designation (e.g., Irish-American, Asian-American, and African-American), you realize that the ancestral country of origin appears to continue to be of importance to individuals and may have made significant contributions to their life experiences in this country.

Another complication is the designation of "American," as citizens of other countries in the hemisphere such as Canada, Mexico, and Brazil also consider themselves to be American. These people can become very offended when referred to as "South American," for example, especially when there appears to be an unconscious assumption that only U.S. citizens are "American."

The other side of the issue is that the client's country of origin can be an essential piece of information to understanding the person, and hence as a guide to therapy. This is especially true for first- and second-generation immigrants to the United States. You will want to gain more knowledge about their country of origin's culture and mores, because these most likely are continuing to influence them in many ways.

Hays (1996) emphasizes the following two points in her model for therapy: 1) increasing the therapist's awareness of personal bias, and 2) considering all salient multiple cultural influences. Her model again highlights the need for therapists to engage in self-reflection and self-exploration of possible biases, stereotypes, and prejudices. The additional point is that it is important to remember that clients seldom, if ever, have just one culturally different characteristic, and that the therapist must take into account all of the client's personal cultural characteristics that have relevance. Many times, it is not possible to guess which characteristics have relevance for the particular client, since these guesses are most likely projections on the part of the therapist.

The second model is the one developed by the authors to guide culturally sensitive counseling. It has three components: 1) recognize, 2) respect, and 3) reduce. *Recognize* means to become aware of personal biases, stereotypical thinking, and prejudices, and to accept the need for continual self-reflection. It also refers to understanding the need to be culturally sensitive and to prepare to deal with multicultural and diverse clients through education, consulting with knowledgeable people, and becoming actively involved with people who differ from you in significant ways.

Recognition is not limited to you, the therapist. It also applies to your clients. You must recognize the multiple cultural and diversity characteristics that each client possesses, and that these characteristics have played a significant role in his or her life experiences, and will continue to play a role in his or her self-identity, self-concept, and self-esteem. Recognition means a heightened awareness of self and of clients.

Respect grows out of your knowledge, understanding, and self-reflection. It refers to accepting and valuing differences between and among clients. It is a firm conviction that *different* is not considered as being wrong, limiting, alien, inferior, rejecting, or isolating. It is to be accepted as "different," explored, understood, and viewed as a source of strength and vitality. Respect means that you will take the perspective of looking for strengths in differences rather than assuming that being different is a weakness or substandard attribute. Another component for respect is your willingness to seek alternative ways to assist clients within the content of their differences. For example, if the client's culture demands that decisions be made collectively by the family, you would not push the client to make an individual decision. Another example would be modifying your reactions and assumptions about eye contact if the client's culture does not support the use of eye contact in this relationship.

Reduce refers to establishing a therapeutic relationship, promoting safety and trust, identifying commonalties by reducing the preponderance of differences, and enhancing similarities. This in no way is intended to suggest that differences be ignored, minimized, or suppressed. Cultural and diversity factors are very important. Reducing, in this discussion, means to acknowledge and understand differences, but also to focus on reducing the perceived differences between you and the client. The client also has some preconceived notions about you based on visible evidence and your position. It would not be unusual for clients to have biases, stereotypes, and prejudices, and to be unaware that they have them. Thus you will also be working to reduce these preconceptions and assumptions. Some clients will need to perceive or feel that there are important similarities with you in order to feel safe, disclose important personal information, and work on painful material.

What are your personal feelings about:

♦ Interfaith marriages?

♦ White couples adopting other-race children?

♦ Interracial dating/marriage?

♦ Mixed-race children?

♦ People with disabling conditions (e.g., mental retardation)?

♦ Gay couples?

♦ Lesbians?

♦ Avowed Wiccans?

♦ Fundamentalist Christians?

♦ Catholics?

♦ Orthodox Jews?

♦ Racial/ethnic minorities?

Don't be too quick to say that you have no problems with people in any of these categories. You really need to be self-reflective and answer the following:

◆ Do you know any people in each of the categories?

◆ Do you interact or socialize regularly with people in each category?

◆ What is your gut level reaction when meeting these people?

◆ Would you be friends with people in each category?

You probably will have at least one or two categories that give you pause to consider. You may consider yourself open and accepting, but would really prefer not to be confronted with having to interact with some people in some categories. That feeling would be usual and is to be expected. However, if you find that you are biased or prejudiced, you will want to work hard to overcome these perceptions and feelings on your way to becoming a culturally sensitive therapist.

Pretend in the following scenarios you are the counselor encountering the described client. Assume a culturally sensitive stance for your answers and do not be concerned about assessment and diagnosis. The intent is to increase your awareness of the need for cultural and diversity sensitivity.

1. A 13-year-old Kurdish girl comes to you for counseling and announces that she will be married in a week to a 28-year-old man selected by her parents. What other information would be important for you to gather from the girl? Is there other information needed and/or people to be consulted?

2. A couple comes for counseling because their son in unmanageable. He is 17, white, and will only associate with what the parents term as "lower-class African Americans." They are seeking your advice on how to "get him back where he belongs," that is, with white upper-middle-class friends. The father is a lawyer who was raised as a Catholic but does not regularly attend mass. The mother is a physician and a member of the Jewish faith. Her religion is very important to her, and the son had a bar mitzvah. What other information do you need? Who is your client?

EXERCISE 2

"My Cultural Competence"

Materials: Paper and a writing instrument.

Directions: Respond to each of the following:

1. Make a list of your family, friends, and close associates—for example, people with whom you socialize.
2. Put the following column titles at the top of the page: *Race/Ethnic Group, Religion, Country of Origin, Socioeconomic Level.*
3. Place an "X" by each person's name under each column for each difference from you. For example, a friend of a different race or ethnic group would receive an "X."

Reflection Questions:

1. Do you associate with people who are culturally different from you? If so, what similarities and differences are there between you? If not, what prevents you from having these kinds of associations?
2. What do you need to do to develop your cultural competence? Make a list of possible actions you can take.

Chapter Three

Social Development

H AVE YOU EVER WONDERED HOW you became the unique individual that you are today? Have you ever considered what factors entered into making us all the magical, mysterious, and sometimes perplexing creatures that we are?

This chapter will begin our exploration of how individuals grow and change throughout their lives. First, we will present an overview of developmental issues by focusing on Havighurst's theory of development stages and tasks. We will then consider Erikson's psychosocial theory of development and discuss the major issues that require resolution at each life stage. Finally, we will present Adler's model of the family constellation and examine the influence of birth order on personality development.

This chapter is designed to provide an overview of the various theories that will set the stage for issues that we will address in later chapters. It is a beginning that we hope will stimulate you to think about where you are in your development and how you have become who you are. Now let us embark on this exciting journey that we call "development."

Richard Havighurst's Theory of Developmental Tasks

When (if ever) do old dogs become incapable of learning new tricks?

Although the old adage might lead us to believe that at some point we stop learning and simply live out our lives using our prior skills, research suggests that we never stop growing and changing. Developmental psychologist Richard Havighurst coined the term *developmental task* to describe an expected task that must be accomplished at a given stage of life. New tasks arise at each stage of life and require that individuals acquire new skills to master them. Developmental tasks are sequential and build upon those of previous stages, so greater mastery of a given developmental task will likely lead to more positive outcomes with future tasks. None of us are born knowing how to deal with each new issue that confronts us, but instead we must *learn* how to approach the task and gradually master it. For example, few of us know how to be perfect parents, although we may think we do until we actually have children. Yet most of us can become better parents as we discover—sometimes through trial and error—what works with children. Thus it is accurate to say that we literally learn our way through life (Havighurst, 1972). Fortunately, the world presents almost infinite opportunities for learning, although we may not prefer some of the lessons that life offers.

Although developmental tasks vary from culture to culture, within a given society the tasks are fairly uniform. Successful mastery of developmental tasks leads to acceptance by others and personal happiness for the individual, while failure to master tasks at the appropriate time results in societal disapproval and unhappiness for the individual. Problems can occur when individuals fail to master developmental tasks at the appropriate times or when unresolved issues from previous stages make mastery of new tasks difficult. Consider a child who does not learn to read at around age five or six. Although this can be quite embarrassing during the childhood years, the problem is only accentuated and the humiliation intensified if the individual reaches adulthood and remains illiterate and becomes unable to find employment.

When developmental deficits occur, education can help individuals master the tasks with which they are struggling and empower them to achieve future success. Developmental counseling, which is primarily educational in nature, is both proactive and preventive, because it provides assistance in mastering current developmental tasks and prepares individuals for those tasks that can be expected to arise in the future. Through an awareness of developmental tasks, we can conceptualize our clients' issues and plan strategies for helping them acquire the skills necessary for mastery of both present and subsequent tasks, often making later remediation unnecessary. As mentioned earlier, few of us are born knowing how to be outstanding parents; however, most of us could learn to be better parents and would benefit more from learning effective parenting skills to address our toddlers' tantrums than to deal with our teenagers' delinquency. The ultimate goal of developmental counseling is therefore to help individuals excel in life rather than to simply cope with it.

Developmental tasks (see table 3.1) begin in infancy and continue to emerge throughout life. In early childhood (ages birth–6), children's first developmental tasks consist of learning important fundamental skills such as taking solid foods, controlling bodily elimination, walking, and talking. In addition, young children learn sex differences and acquire sexual modesty. In these early years, children begin to develop a conscience,

TABLE **3.1**

Havighurst's Developmental Tasks

Stage	Age	Tasks
early childhood	birth to 6 years	eating solid foods controlling bodily elimination walking talking learning sex differences forming a conscience distinguishing between right and wrong acquiring language forming concepts
middle childhood	6 to 12 years	learning to get along with peers becoming more independent developing basic skills in reading, writing, and math learning concepts necessary for living understanding gender-appropriate social roles acquiring democratic attitudes developing a personal set of values
adolescence	12 to 18 years	achieving more mature peer relationships preparing for a career gaining increased independence from parents continuing to develop personal values and an ethical ideology achieving socially responsible behavior
early adulthood	18 to 30 years	forming an intimate relationship learning to live with a partner starting a family raising children managing a household getting started in a career finding a congenial social group achieving civic responsibility
middle adulthood	30 to 60 years	helping adolescent children become independent learning to again relate to one's partner as a person, rather than as a parent of one's children caring for the older generation coping with the illnesses and deaths of parents and other friends and family members maintaining satisfactory career performance assuming a leadership role in civic activities developing appropriate leisure activities adjusting to physical changes associated with aging

continued

TABLE **3.1** (*continued*)

Stage	Age	Tasks
later adulthood	60 and beyond	adjusting to decreased physical strength and sometimes chronic health problems achieving satisfactory physical living arrangements adjusting to retirement dealing with the death of a partner staying connected and maintaining social relationships facing one's own mortality and accepting one's life

and begin learning the difference between right and wrong. Children start to form concepts in this stage and develop the ability to use language to describe their physical and social realities.

As children move into middle childhood, the period from ages 6 through 12, developmental tasks begin to focus on activities related to peers. Children shift their primary emphasis from the family outwards to classmates and friends; they begin to participate in work and games and start to understand the world of mental representations, including logic and simple concepts. Developmental tasks of this stage consist of learning to get along with peers, becoming more independent, developing basic skills in reading, writing, and math, and learning the concepts necessary for living, such as roundness and hardness. Children also begin to learn appropriate masculine and feminine social roles, and to develop democratic attitudes and a personal set of values during middle childhood.

During the adolescent years, 12 through 18, learning continues and typical tasks consist of achieving more mature relationships with individuals of both sexes, preparing for a career, and gaining increased independence from parents. With greater freedom comes more responsibility, and adolescents must further develop their values and construct an ethical ideology that will guide their personal behavior. Adolescents must learn to first desire and then achieve socially responsible behavior if they are to be successful later in life.

Early adulthood, comprising the years between 18 through 30, offers tremendous opportunities for learning, as individuals tackle some of the most important and challenging tasks of their lives.

For most young adults, these tasks include selecting a partner, learning to live with that "significant other," starting a family, raising children, managing a household, and getting started in a career. In the early adult years, individuals must find a congenial social group as marriage, parenting, and career moves may necessitate breaking old ties and forming new ones based on similar interests, social status, or geographic location. Young adults are also expected to accept civic responsibility and to become involved in community activities such as the PTA, church groups, and neighborhood improvement projects.

During the middle adult years, ages 30–60, individuals are considered to be at their peak of performance and are presented with massive amounts of responsibility. Middle-aged adults are often referred to as "the sandwich generation," because they are frequently squeezed between caring for their own teenage children and meeting the needs of their aging parents. Tasks of this stage include helping teenaged children become responsible and happy adults, caring for the older generation, reaching and maintaining satisfactory performance in one's career, and assuming a leadership role in civic activities. As teenaged children leave home, individuals must learn to once again relate to their partners as persons, rather than as the parents of their children, and must develop appropriate leisure activities as retirement approaches. Middle adulthood is also accompanied by physical changes to which individuals must adjust: these include menopause, diminished muscular strength, decreased sexual activity and interest, wrinkled skin, the need for reading glasses, and the inevitable girth around the middle that seems to never go away no matter how much one exercises.

In later adulthood, which spans the years from age 60 until the end of life, individuals must adjust to decreased physical strength and sometimes chronic health problems such as arthritis or heart disease. Because of such physical limitations, some older adults choose to change their living arrangements in order to avoid the physical exertion required to climb stairs or do yard work. It is, however, inaccurate to assume that most older adults reside in nursing homes or with their children; the majority of elders continue to engage in active and independent lives throughout their later years.

Later adulthood brings other challenges that can be quite formidable. Retirement requires that older adults establish new routines and adjust to changed roles. For some, this may mean a dramatic loss of prestige and even identity. In addition, the decreased income that accompanies retirement can be significant if individuals have not set aside substantial retirement funds throughout their working years.

The death of a spouse is another expected challenge that is often thought to be the most stressful of all life changes. The loss of a life partner may involve not only intense grief and loneliness, but also a reduction in financial resources and a need to independently make decisions and manage a household. After years of togetherness, this new, involuntary autonomy can seem both frightening and overwhelming.

In order to adapt to the changes of later adulthood, older adults must learn to stay involved in the world by assuming flexible social roles and developing interests that will bring joy to themselves or contribute to the welfare of others. By establishing an affiliation with other seniors as well as with younger friends and family members, older adults can both give and receive valuable support and find ever-widening sources of meaning to enrich their lives. The later years can thereby become truly "golden" and comprise a culmination of all that individuals have strived to become, as wisdom replaces frivolity and contemplation replaces haste.

Erik Erikson's Psychosocial Theory of Personality Development

In addition to mastering developmental tasks, individuals must also resolve a major psychosocial issue at each life stage. Similar to Havighurst, Erik Erikson believed that individuals continue to grow and change from birth through later adulthood. Although Erikson considered the first six years of life to be very important, he differed from Freud in that he did not assume that early childhood experiences ultimately determined the individual's later development, but they could certainly be influential.

According to Erikson (1963), a major psychosocial issue arises at each stage of development. These issues, which involve individuals' interactions with others in the social environment, must be resolved. The outcomes can be positive or negative, contingent on the degree of resolution achieved, and can impact on the mastery of subsequent issues. Although an issue may not be completely resolved in a given life stage, a higher degree of positive resolution is likely to lead to greater success with subsequent issues. For example, a neglected infant whose needs are not met will probably not develop a sense of trust in his or her primary caregiver and may have extreme difficulty trusting others in the future. When this person reaches adulthood, the scars of childhood may impede the development of intimacy and he or she may have to struggle with accepting love from anyone. Fortunately, however, individuals are amazingly resilient and can often work through issues that were not positively resolved earlier in life, and it is almost never too late to try.

Table 3.2 shows Erikson's stages of psychosocial development. The first psychosocial stage, *trust vs. mistrust,* arises in infancy and lasts to age 1. If an infant's physical and psychological needs are consistently met, he or she will develop a sense of trust in the world and a sense of security in himself or herself. Even in the temporary absence of the caregiver, the infant will not feel undue anxiety or fear that the caregiver will not return, because the infant has learned to trust that the caregiver will always be there when new needs arise. On the other hand, if these needs are not met satisfactorily or in a timely manner, the infant may view others and the world with mistrust, fear abandonment, and doubt his or her own worth. The foundation of trust that is laid in the early years is critically important, because it provides the necessary springboard for resolving all of the subsequent issues that occur throughout life.

TABLE **3.2**

Erikson's Stages of Psychosocial Development

Stage	*Age*	*Tasks*
trust vs. mistrust	birth to age 1	developing adequate trust in the world to assume that it is a safe place
autonomy vs. shame and doubt	ages 1–3	developing control over one's actions and a sense of being an independent person
initiative vs. guilt	ages 3–6	acquiring a willingness to try new behaviors and to assume responsibility for one's own actions
industry vs. inferiority	ages 6–12	developing confidence in one's own abilities and the ability to get along with peers
identity vs. role confusion	ages 12–18	achieving a strong sense of self by trying out many possible identities
intimacy vs. isolation	young adulthood	developing the ability to form a lasting and committed intimate relationship
generativity vs. stagnation	middle adulthood	assisting the younger generation in getting started in the world
integrity vs. despair	older adulthood	accepting one's life as having been meaningful and satisfactory

The second psychosocial stage, *autonomy vs. shame and doubt,* occurs between ages 1 through 3. During this time, the child is developing a sense of control over his or her own behaviors and a sense of self-reliance. Toddlers actively explore the world and attempt to achieve autonomous action, even though they have little understanding of the danger they may encounter by putting their fingers in electric sockets or pulling dogs' tails. Although it can be a tremendous challenge to childproof a home, parents should nonetheless find ways to ensure children's safety as they energetically express their autonomy: For if children are not allowed the freedom to explore and make mistakes, dependency and self-doubt may result.

Between the ages of 3 to 6, children are in the third stage, *initiative vs. guilt.* Children continue to attempt to understand the world by exploring it through their actions, but can also ask questions as they try to form concepts. If children are not given opportunities to take initiative and do things for themselves or to receive informative answers to their innumerable "why?" questions, they may become guilt-ridden and assume a passive stance toward life.

In the middle childhood years, ages 6 through 12, children are in the fourth stage, *industry vs. inferiority.* Peers become increasingly important as children shift their focus from home life to school activities. Children learn to set goals and to develop the competencies necessary for school success and acceptance by their peers. If children are not able to attain their goals or easily make friends, a sense of inferiority may result that can have long-acting effects. The painful memories of being called names or of always being the last one picked to be on any sports team at recess still linger with some of us today.

Puberty marks the beginning of the fifth stage, *identity vs. role confusion*, which lasts from ages 12 through 18. Adolescents routinely test limits and experiment with various possible identities, sometimes shocking their parents and others of the older generation in the process of their own self-discovery. As adolescents join cliques and "fall in love," they attempt to define their emerging identities by seeing their own images projected onto others and then reflected back to them. Adolescents typically spend enormous amounts of time talking to friends about mundane details that seem trivial enough to make their parents scream, such as whether to wear jeans or a skirt to an event. Yet it is through the reactions of peers to their own ideas that adolescents figure out who they are and what they believe. If adolescents do not have opportunities to experiment, they may fail to develop a personally meaningful identity and suffer the resultant role confusion that can impact later relationships. It is important, however, for adults to attempt to provide some measure of safety for adolescents who are likely to find themselves engaged in risky behaviors. Thus it is a wise parent who hands over the car keys and warns a teenaged son not to drink, but offers to come and pick him up if he ever does, knowing that a drunken child is preferable to a dead one.

At the conclusion of adolescence, the sixth stage, *intimacy vs. isolation*, begins and spans the early adulthood years, from ages 18 through 35. Young adults face the challenge of forming intimate relationships and making a commitment to a partner. Intimacy can be an especially tricky issue for young adults, because it requires that individuals who have just forged their own identities now fuse those identities with their partners. Intimate relationships necessitate that "you" and "me" thinking becomes transformed into "us," and the ability to compromise becomes a skill necessary for daily survival. Failure to establish intimacy can lead to isolation and loneliness.

Midlife brings the stage of *generativity vs. stagnation*, which spans the years from ages 35 through 60. Just as children depend on adults for care, adults depend upon youth to stay vibrant and engaged. Generativity refers to establishing and guiding the younger generation to help them find their place in the world. Midlife adults, who are at the peak of their professional and personal lives, have both the opportunity and responsibility to assist the next generation in becoming established. Failure to productively engage in helping their own children move out into the world or in mentoring younger colleagues can result in stagnation for midlife adults.

The final stage, *integrity vs. despair*, occurs after age 60. Older adults reflect on their lives and accomplishments. If there are few regrets, a sense of integrity will be achieved. Failure to accept that life cannot be lived over, or that there is too little time left, may result in despair, bitterness, hopelessness, and guilt. Yet for those adults who can look back and feel satisfied with the lives they have lived, a sense of integrity will prevail and inspire those who follow. As Erikson (1963) stated, "healthy children will not fear life if their elders have integrity enough not to fear death" (p. 269).

Adler's Theory of Personality Development

While Havighurst and Erikson highlighted the developmental tasks and psychosocial issues that emerge throughout life and impact development, Alfred Adler focused on the role of early childhood experiences within the family as a factor influencing personality formation. Although Adler did not believe that individuals' personalities were determined in the first years of life, he did assume that children's impressions of their place within the family strongly contributed to their development.

In his work with families and children, Alfred Adler discovered that no two siblings experienced the family in exactly the same way. Children's perceptions of the family seemed to be based on their psychological position within the family, so Adler (1958) developed his model of the "family constellation" emphasizing the role of birth order in personality development.

Within the family constellation, Adler identified five basic psychological positions that children hold based upon their birth order in relation to siblings (Corey, 2001). The positions are listed in table 3.3 and consist of *oldest child, second child, middle child, youngest child,* and *only child.* Each position has unique characteristics, challenges, and strengths that may be evident in how the child relates to others. The early perceptions that individuals form of themselves in relation to siblings can persist and continue to shape adult interactions and patterns of relating to others throughout life.

The *oldest child* initially occupies a highly favored position in the family, since he or she has the undivided attention of parents and no other siblings with whom to compete. Because this child spends much time in the company of adults, he or she is likely to mature quickly, work hard, and be highly responsible. The oldest child loses the position of "reigning monarch" in the family when siblings are born, however, and becomes "dethroned" when a younger brother or sister becomes the focus of parental attention. Oldest children may feel jealous of the younger siblings and nostalgically long for the past. As adults, oldest children may be high achievers but experience guilt and insecurity.

The *second child* never holds the position of power that the oldest child once possessed, for he or she always has an older sibling who is a rival

TABLE **3.3**

Adler's Family Constellation

Birth Position	Characteristics
oldest child	early maturity achievement-oriented and conservative dependable and responsible nostalgic of the past may experience guilt and insecurity
second child	competitive often strives in direction opposite of oldest child optimistic
middle child	may think life is extremely unfair feels squeezed out often skilled in negotiation and manipulation very aware of politics and family dynamics
youngest child	the "baby" of the family may be pampered and spoiled may excel if encouraged may become dependent on others may find it hard to compete in the adult world
only child	may be spoiled and indulged may find it difficult to compete, cooperate, or share often more comfortable with adults than peers may exhibit traits similar to oldest child or youngest child may become easily discouraged may be able to easily handle solitude often highly imaginative and creative

for parental attention. Because the older sibling is always slightly ahead of him or her, the second child is likely to be fiercely competitive and to behave as though in a race with the first child. The second child will typically find areas in which the older child has not excelled in which to compete, often striving in directions opposite those of the older sibling. Thus if the older child is academically inclined, the second child may pursue athletics. As adults, second children tend to be competitive and optimistic.

The *middle child* may feel that he or she is in a most unfavored position in the family, for he or she lacks both the power of the oldest child and the attention focused on the youngest. Middle children often feel "squeezed out" and may become the focus of the family's attention by exhibiting behavior problems. Middle children have a keen awareness of family dynamics, however, and may become skilled in both negotiation and manipulation.

The *youngest child* often receives attention and pampering from most members of the family. He or she may be considered the "baby" of the family even into adulthood and continue to reap the benefits of being the youngest. A youngest child may receive much encouragement from other family members, who are all ahead of him or her, and therefore excel. On the other hand, youngest children may become dependent on others and be easily discouraged when attention is not focused on them automatically.

The *only child* holds an extremely unique position in the family, for he or she never has siblings with whom to compete for parental attention or material possessions. Only children may exhibit traits similar to those of both oldest and youngest children and thus may be highly responsible and achievement-oriented or else pampered and dependent. Only children often find it easy to relate to adults, but more difficult to cooperate with peers and share. As adults, only children may find it difficult to compete and become discouraged if their efforts are not recognized by others. Because only children typically spend much time alone in childhood, however, they may develop their imaginations and become highly creative adults who are comfortable with solitude.

While all of the birth positions have their distinct characteristics, it is critical to note that the individual's perception of his or her place in the family is more important than the actual position he or she holds. For example, the child's impression of the family constellation may be affected by the gender of the children, the span of time between births of the children, and whether it becomes a blended family. The family constellation can, however, serve as a useful guide for making tentative hypotheses about family dynamics and individual psychology.

Scenarios

How would you conceptualize the following cases, and how would you suggest helping these individuals?

1. Jeanette feels like a failure and is considering dropping out of college in her sophomore year. Upon discovering that her love-interest was seeing someone else, Jeanette immediately ended their relationship and became seriously depressed. Although she easily excelled in high school with little effort, Jeanette is finding college to be much more challenging and demanding. Since she chose to attend a large college five hundred miles from home, she has had infrequent contact with her parents or siblings (an older brother and sister). Jeanette especially misses her mother, whom she describes as "a saint who did everything for me." Although Jeanette e-mails her parents and siblings every day, she misses having home-cooked meals and being tucked into

bed at night. She detests the "cold and uncaring" atmosphere of college and wants to go home.

2. At age 15, Mark is angry much of the time and is verbally abusive to both his mother and 17-year-old sister. He tends to bully his younger brother and has little interest in maintaining a relationship with his biological father, who recently remarried but wants to spend time with him—now more than ever before. Mark has never done exceptionally well in school, but lately his grades have dropped dramatically. Mark's mother found marijuana in his room and grounded him for two months, but he continues to sneak out at night and return home with alcohol on his breath. Last week, Mark's mother received a call from the school informing her that Mark had been cutting class and was seen "hanging out" on the street corner with some older boys who had dropped out of school the previous year. When Mark's mother questioned him about his behavior, he angrily replied, "Get out of my face, you sorry excuse for a human! I hate you all!"

Chapter Four

Cognitive, Moral, and Spiritual Development

T HIS CHAPTER WILL CONTINUE our exploration of how individuals grow and change by considering several models of cognitive, moral, and spiritual development. First, we will present Piaget's theory of cognitive development and examine how children's thinking evolves over time. Closely linked to cognitive development is moral development, so we will next venture into the realm of moral reasoning and discuss the theories of Piaget, Kohlberg, and Gilligan. Finally, we will explore spiritual development and how individuals develop faith and make meaning as they go through life.

Once again, we encourage you to think about where you are in your own development and how you arrived at this point. We hope you will find the ideas presented in this chapter to be thought provoking and illustrative of how we become who we are.

Piaget's Theory of Cognitive Development

In order to successfully master the developmental tasks that arise, individuals must think and use cognitive processes to understand the world and how to live in it. Swiss psychologist Jean Piaget proposed a theory of cognitive development to explain how cognitive abilities change as a result of maturation and interaction with the environment. By carefully observing his own children and designing simple experiments to test their conceptual understanding and its changes over time, Piaget charted the course of cognitive development from birth through adolescence.

Piaget considered children to be like little scientists who exert tremendous effort to discover how the world works. As they actively explore their surroundings, children construct theories and test their hypotheses in an attempt to gain conceptual understanding. For example, a young child may delight in realizing that a spoon will fall to the ground and make an interesting sound when he or she accidentally knocks it off the table. The child may then attempt to see if a cup of milk will follow a similar course when it is intentionally pushed from the table top. While parents may be less than enthusiastic about the child's natural experimentation, especially if it occurs as they prepare for a busy day at work, the child gains a rudimentary awareness of gravity during the course of a meal. As a result of such interaction with the objects that comprise their worlds, children begin to form concepts and to understand logic.

Piaget (1952b) believed that children, like all organisms, strive to achieve *equilibrium*—a balance of organized motor, sensory, or cognitive structures that provides effective ways of interacting with the environment. The process of acquiring knowledge involves actively achieving and re-achieving equilibrium as the child encounters new information from the environment that must be interpreted and understood. Knowledge begins with *schemas*—coordinated patterns of actions that arise as the child interacts with his or her environment. Schemas are the precursors of concepts.

As the child interacts with the environment, adaptation requires that two cognitive processes occur. These processes are:

♦ *Assimilation*, in which the child incorporates new information into existing cognitive structures based upon previous learning (e.g., a young child sees a long-haired man and calls him a "lady" because his flowing tresses resemble those of female family members).

♦ *Accommodation*, in which the child modifies his or her existing cognitive structures to incorporate new information based upon a change in understanding (e.g., the child discovers that this particular long-haired person has a hairy face and deep voice, and so a new category inclusive of the male gender is formed—perhaps that of "cool dude").

According to Piaget (1963), cognitive development occurs in four stages. Although the ages at which children move through the stages can vary based upon culture and other environmental influences, the stages are sequential and no stages can be skipped. These stages are listed in table 4.1.

In the *sensorimotor stage*, which lasts from birth to age 2, infants understand the world mainly through immediate action and sensation in the present moment. There is no sense of object permanence—things only exist for infants when being experienced in the here-and-now. Infants ini-

TABLE **4.1**

Piaget's Stages of Cognitive Development

Stage	Age	Characteristics
sensorimotor	birth to 2 years	Infants experience life in the here-and-now, and use reflexes and simple motor skills, such as looking and grasping, to explore the world.
preoperational	2 to 6 years	Young children use symbols and language to represent things in their world and are able to form simple concepts. Their understanding is egocentric and animistic, and they have difficulty with logical operations such as classification, seriation, and conservation.
concrete operations	7 to 11 years	Children are able to think logically about concrete objects and events, and can understand logical operations. They cannot yet grasp hypothetical concepts.
formal operations	12 years and beyond	Adolescents can think logically about abstract and hypothetical concepts and can consider possibilities of what could be, rather than just what is.

Source: Based on Piaget (1963).

tially respond to the world with reflexes that are present at birth (e.g., sucking, grasping).

In the *preoperational stage*, ages 2 through 6, children rely on perception and how things appear, rather than logic, to make sense of the world. Piaget's *conservation* experiments showed that children fail to understand that the quantitative aspects of objects remain constant even though the objects may change in form (e.g., a child will say that two identical balls of clay contain the same amount of substance, but that one has more when it is rolled into a snake-like shape). In this stage, children use language as though they understand concepts, when in reality they do not (Elkind, 1991). For example, a child may say, "Grandma died and I went to her funeral," and later ask, "When is Grandma coming back?" Children's thought is *egocentric*, and they assume that others share their sensations and experience the world just as they do (e.g., a child may say, "My tooth hurts. Can't you feel it?"). Also, children's understanding of the world is *animistic*, and they attribute life to inanimate objects (e.g., a leaf blowing in the wind is thought to be alive). Children in this stage have difficulty with *classification* (i.e., knowing what to include in a category) and *seriation* (i.e., being able to put items in order from first to last).

In the stage of *concrete operations*, ages 7 through 11, children become able to think operationally. *Operations* are thoughts or mental representations of actions. Children can now solve conservation problems, and their understanding of the world is no longer dominated by how objects appear. However, children's thinking is still bound to concrete objects, and they are unable to think hypothetically about abstract principles.

The final stage of cognitive development is *formal operations*, which occurs at around age 12 and lasts throughout life. In this highest stage of development, adolescents can reason hypothetically and manipulate abstract ideas. With their thinking no longer limited to what actually *is*, they can fantasize about what *could* be. This new ability can lead to adolescents developing extreme idealism and immense frustration with the older generation, who may seem to be hopelessly pragmatic and out of touch with the inspired vision of youth. In this stage, adolescents can also use inductive logic to generalize their understanding to new situations. It is important to note, however, that some individuals never reach this stage and do not progress beyond thinking concretely about what actually exists in the world as they know it.

Piaget's model of cognitive development has had a profound influence on educational practices and has important implications for counseling. To be effective, therapeutic interventions must take into account the way the client thinks and understands the world. Techniques appropriate to clients' developmental levels will be discussed in later chapters.

Moral Development

As individuals encounter life situations, moral dilemmas arise that require choosing between various options to achieve what is believed to be the best course of action. Several researchers have studied how moral reasoning begins in childhood and develops in stages as individuals mature. In this section, we will consider the theories of Piaget, Kohlberg, and Gilligan in an attempt to understand the process of moral development.

PIAGET'S THEORY OF MORAL DEVELOPMENT

Piaget studied children's moral development by asking them to judge the goodness or evil of characters in stories. Based upon their responses, Piaget found that children's beliefs about guilt evolve and that their moral sense occurs in two stages. Piaget therefore postulated a two-stage model of moral development and assumed that moral development reflects cognitive development, with the higher stage requiring the ability to think abstractly. Piaget's stages of moral development are as follows:

♦ *Heteronomous moral reasoning* (birth through ages 9 or 10): Children judge guilt by the objective consequences of the act, rather than by intentions (e.g., a child who accidentally breaks three cups while helping her mother wash dishes is deemed more guilty than a child who breaks one cup by deliberately throwing it at a sibling. The former child broke a larger number of cups and would therefore be considered more culpable). Acts are judged by their potential to be punished or rewarded by outside authorities such as parents, rather than by abstract principles of goodness or badness. In this stage, children consider rules to be concrete, immutable entities that require rigid adherence. For this reason, young children are not usually pleased when adults try to bend the rules of games to help give them a greater chance of successfully competing. Although the adults' intention may be to level the playing field, children may consider the modifying of rules to be an egregious example of foul play and exclaim "But that's not fair!" even though they would have little hope of winning without being given some extra advantage by their older playmates.

◆ *Autonomous moral reasoning* (ages 9 or 10+): Children become more likely to judge the motives behind an act, rather than rigidly adhering to concerns about objective consequences. Greater independence of thought occurs and increased attention is paid to ideals and principles. Rules are considered to be social contracts that can be cooperatively changed, and so older children often agree to modify the rules of games to make them more interesting, stimulating, or fair. Autonomous moral reasoning is similar to the relativistic reasoning of adults in which more than one perspective can be taken on a given situation.

KOHLBERG'S THEORY OF MORAL DEVELOPMENT

Lawrence Kohlberg, who was greatly influenced by Piaget, conducted a twenty-year longitudinal study of moral reasoning in males by having them respond to hypothetical moral dilemmas. Based upon this research, Kohlberg found that moral development evolves through three major levels, with each level consisting of two stages. Kohlberg's moral-reasoning model is presented in table 4.2 (Kohlberg & Wasserman, 1980). Kohlberg believed that moral development reflects cognitive development, and higher levels of cognitive development are essential, but not sufficient, for higher levels of morality. In Kohlberg's model the stages are considered to be sequential; no skipping of stages is believed to occur; and the reasoning in a given stage has been found to be remarkably consistent when an individual is presented with various moral dilemmas.

In Level 1, *preconventional moral reasoning*, acts are judged in terms of their ability to bring punishments or rewards for the actor. In describing Level-1 reasoning, Kohlberg (1967) states that "Moral value resides in external, quasi-physical happenings, in bad acts, or in quasi-physical needs rather than in persons and standards" (p. 171). Preconventional moral reasoning is comprised of the two following stages:

TABLE **4.2**

Kohlberg's Model of Moral Development

Level	Stages	Ages
Level 1: Preconventional	Stage 1: Punishment-and-Obedience Orientation	ages 5–7
	Stage 2: Instrumental-Relativist Orientation	ages 8–12
Level 2: Conventional	Stage 3: Interpersonal Concordance or Good Boy–Nice Girl Orientation	ages 13–16
	Stage 4: Law-and-Order Orientation	ages 16+
Level 3: Postconventional	Stage 5: Social-Contract Legalistic Orientation	adult
	Stage 6: Universal-Ethical Principled Orientation	adult

Source: Based on Kohlberg & Wasserman (1980).

♦ Stage 1—*punishment-and-obedience orientation*—acts are considered to be bad if they can be punished, and good if they are likely to be rewarded. Children are primarily concerned with the negative consequences of acts and the power of authorities to punish, with little awareness of the values that provide a foundation for rules and authority.

♦ Stage 2—*instrumental-relativist orientation*—acts are judged by their potential to produce hedonistic outcomes for the actor. Children reason pragmatically and think in terms of "If you do something for someone else, that person will do something for you."

In Level 2, *conventional moral reasoning*, moral judgments are based upon conforming to the expectations of others, maintaining social approval, and complying with the mandates of external authority. Regarding Level 2, Kohlberg (1967) states that "Moral value resides in performing good or right roles, in maintaining the conventional order and the expectancies of others" (p. 171). Conventional moral reasoning consists of the following stages:

♦ Stage 3—*interpersonal concordance or good boy–nice girl orientation*— acts are considered to be moral if they elicit the approval of others and help to maintain good relations. Adolescents are strongly influenced by peers and make moral decisions based upon peer norms. They also become able to judge acts in terms of the intentions of the individual who performed the act, rather than strictly in terms of the consequences of the act.

♦ Stage 4—*law-and-order orientation*—acts are judged in terms of adherence to rules, laws, and external authority. Adolescents respect social order per se, and attempt to abide by rules out of a sense of duty.

Finally, in Level 3, *postconventional moral reasoning*, morality is based on broad principles of individual rights and is not motivated by the need to adhere to societal expectations or to receive personal reward. To describe Level 3, Kohlberg (1967) states that "Moral value resides in conformity by the self to shared or sharable, standards, rights, or duties" (p. 171). This highest level is not reached before adulthood, and many adults never reach it at all. Postconventional moral reasoning includes the following stages:

♦ Stage 5—*social-contract legalistic orientation*—morality is based on preserving social contracts that support cooperative collaboration. Adults respect the relativistic nature of personal values and attempt to achieve consensual agreement regarding appropriate behavior, rather than assuming the existence of absolute right and wrong as in the previous stage.

♦ Stage 6—*universal-ethical principled orientation*—morality is based on individual conscience and universal ethical principles. In this highest stage, adults make decisions based upon their own personal ethics coupled with universal considerations of equality, justice, reciprocity, and the dignity of all individuals.

GILLIGAN'S THEORY OF MORAL DEVELOPMENT

Carol Gilligan found Kohlberg's research to be flawed because it included only males, and the subjects were presented with hypothetical, rather than real, moral dilemmas. In her study of female moral development, Gilligan interviewed women at a counseling clinic who were faced with deciding whether to have an abortion. Gilligan found that women reasoned differently from men, in that they responded more from an ethic of care, rather than relying on abstract principles of justice. Women were more concerned with how their actions might affect others, and tended to move more toward interdependence than autonomy.

Gilligan (1977) found that women moved through the following stages of moral development:

♦ Stage one—*selfish concerns dominate*. Women think primarily of their own needs, with little regard for how their actions will impact others. For example, a woman decides to have an abortion and gives as her reason, "I don't want a baby—I want to go to school."

♦ Stage two—*responsibility to others* is the primary concern and little attention is paid to one's own needs. Women make moral decisions based upon what they consider to be their obligations to others. For example, a young woman, explaining why she is having an abortion even though having a baby would make her feel like a real woman, states: "It wouldn't be fair to the child since I'm not really mature enough to be a good mother."

♦ Stage three—*morality of care and compassion* prevails and there is concern for both oneself and others so that the greatest good is done for all. Women balance the needs of others with their own, and the focus shifts from being self-sacrificing and "good" as defined by others, to being honest and intentional in choosing the best moral action. For example, a woman faced with having a second abortion ponders and assesses the negative impact that continuing the pregnancy would have on her life, her relationship, and the ultimate quality of life for the child, and weighs that against the other alternative of ending the incipient life of her child and suffering the accompanying guilt.

Gilligan found that women's moral reasoning seemed to revolve around construing moral dilemmas in terms of conflicting responsibilities. In summarizing her conclusions about women's moral development, Gilligan (1977) stated that "The development of women's moral judgment appears to proceed from an initial concern with survival, to a focus on goodness, and finally to a principled understanding of nonviolence as the most adequate guide to the resolution of moral conflicts" (p. 35).

Fowler's Theory of the Development of Faith

Throughout life, individuals are faced with *ontological* concerns—that is, issues pertaining to ultimate reality. Individuals often formulate and answer these questions differently at various stages of life. Thus, a young child may wonder if a beloved family pet will go to heaven and be with Grandma, while an older adult may ponder the gravity of having "lust in one's heart" or of committing sins of omission. James Fowler's empirical studies of how individuals grasp basic meaning when presented with existential questions led to his model of faith development. It is important to note that Fowler does not use the term "faith" to refer to a particular belief or religion, but rather to have trust in and loyalty to a transcendent center of value and power.

In his model, Fowler (1981) proposed that faith development is closely related to psychosocial development and that it occurs in stages similar to the cognitive and moral developmental stages of Piaget and Kohlberg. Fowler's structural-developmental model of faith development includes the following assumptions: The potential to develop faith is a universal capacity that all individuals possess from birth; the stages of faith are hierarchical, with the latter stages building upon previous stages; and not all individuals reach all stages.

Fowler believed that all humans have the innate ability to develop faith from the moment of birth. This capacity for faith development is universal and is present in all people across all cultures. Whether an individual develops faith, however, depends upon his or her environment and the social interactions that he or she has. Faith is shaped by community, language, ritual, nurture, and human experience, as well as by transcendent forces.

In this model, the stages of faith are hierarchical, with the latter stages building upon previous stages. Fowler (1981) describes faith development as occurring in a spiraling pattern in which each subsequent stage "marks the rise of a new set of capacities or strengths in faith. These add to and reconceptualize previous patterns of strength without negating or supplanting them. Certain life issues with which faith must deal recur at each stage; hence the spiral movements in part overlap each other, though each successive stage addresses these issues at a new level of complexity" (p. 274). Fowler adds that "[e]ach stage represents a widening of vision and valuing, correlated with a parallel increase in the certainty and depth of selfhood, making for qualitative increases in intimacy with others' self-world" (p. 274).

Not all individuals reach the higher stages, however, and some adults never move out of the stages of childhood or adolescence. Movement from one stage to the next can be painful and protracted, and individuals can get stuck in any of the stages. Arrested development is especially likely to occur if individuals are not in a given stage at the right time of their lives, as each stage has "its proper time of ascendancy" (Fowler, 1981, p. 274). Fowler's stages of faith are presented in table 4.3.

In this model, the *Pre-stage: Undifferentiated faith* occurs in infancy and corresponds to Erikson's psychosocial crisis of trust versus mistrust. Infants, who have not yet developed a sense of self separate from others, are totally dependent upon their caregivers. If an infant's needs are met in a timely and caring manner, he or she will feel a sense of safety and security that will provide the foundation for the later development of trust and faith. Whenever the infant's perceived needs are not met as quickly or completely as desired, however, a sensed threat of abandonment will emerge that can undermine trust and faith in the years ahead. In this period, which precedes the acquisition of language, the infant's mutual relationship with his or her primary caregiver shapes his or her preimage of God. Just as the infant is separate from, but totally dependent upon, this immensely powerful "other" who knew and loved the infant from the infant's first consciousness, so will the preimage of God be one of a benevolent, all-powerful caretaker who will provide love and expect love in return.

As children move into early childhood and acquire language, the first stage of faith begins. *Stage 1: intuitive-projective faith*, which spans the years from 2 through 7, is a time of growing self-awareness and tremen-

TABLE **4.3**

Fowler's Stages of Faith Development

Stage	Age	Characteristics
Pre-stage: Undifferentiated faith	infancy	Foundation for later faith development Seeds of trust, hope, and courage compete with fears of abandonment
Stage 1: Intuitive-Projective faith	early childhood	Self-awareness emerges Intuition guides grasp of relationship to ultimate reality Imagination fills in conceptual gaps in understanding Terrifying fantasies of death and sex may arise from limited knowledge and misconceptions about society's cultural taboos
Stage 2: Mythic-Literal faith	middle childhood	Reality is interpreted literally Symbols are one-dimensional Rules are considered to be real and concrete Ultimate reality is understood through anthropomorphic characters in cosmic stories
Stage 3: Synthetic-Conventional faith	adolescence	Ultimate reality is structured in interpersonal terms with images of unifying value and power derived from qualities experienced in personal relationships Beliefs are those of the dominant group Personal identity is rooted in belonging to the group
Stage 4: Individuative-Reflective faith	young adulthood	Self-identity and worldview become more differentiated from others Own interpretations of ultimate reality are formed Critical reflection and awareness of complexity of life arises Disillusionment with previous beliefs may occur
Stage 5: Conjunctive faith	mid-life and beyond	Unrecognized issues from past become integrated into self Past is reclaimed and reworked to arrive at new meaning and deeper awareness Heightened spiritual revelations are possible
Stage 6: Universalizing faith	rarely achieved	Extreme lucidity and compassion May involve martyrdom for faith and being more greatly appreciated after death

Source: Based on Fowler (1981).

dous curiosity about how the world works. Young children ask many "why" questions as they intuitively attempt to understand their relationship to the ultimate conditions of existence. As Piaget described, preoperational thought is characterized by magical and egocentric thinking, so a four-year-old girl may believe that her misbehavior caused God to make Grandma die. Gaps in children's conceptual understanding are filled in by their imagination as they attempt to understand the world. Children's fantasies may produce terrifying images as they begin to learn about sex, death, and the cultural taboos of society from the important adults in their world. Stories that adults tell children—whether from the Bible or fairy tales—create powerful and long-lasting images that can continue to influence individuals into adulthood. Thus an adult may harbor secret fears of burning in hell that emerge in dreams, even though he or she can think of no rational reason for having such disturbing images.

Stage 2: mythic-literal faith arises in middle childhood during the school years. During this stage, which corresponds to Piaget's concrete operations, children's imaginative grasp of the world yields to a literal interpretation of reality. Children develop their own stories to form a narrative of their lives. Because children cannot yet think abstractly or hypothetically, their symbols are viewed as being one-dimensional, and rules are taken literally. From these rules, children construct a set of moral standards based upon a sense of fairness and reciprocity, so that a child might assume, "If you want to go to heaven, you'd better be good all the time." Children understand ultimate reality through cosmic stories and narratives with anthropomorphic characters. Thus a child may consider heaven to be a place in the sky where God lives (and, of course, God has a long white beard).

In adolescence, *Stage 3: synthetic-conventional faith* emerges. As adolescents enter Piaget's stage of formal operations, they become able to think hypothetically and to imagine what is possible, rather than just what exists in the concrete world. It is also at this time that adolescents are attempting to define who they are, and interpersonal relationships become critically important in the process of identity development. Adolescents seek peer approval and define themselves based upon the reactions of their friends as they experiment with new social roles and behaviors. With the ability to think hypothetically, adolescents can imagine and long for relationships in which they can be totally and unconditionally accepted for who they are, and that this love can reach inexhaustible depths. Based upon the ideal of a rich and mysterious transcendent love, adolescents structure ultimate reality in interpersonal terms, with images of unifying value and power derived from qualities experienced in their personal relationships. Their beliefs are strongly influenced by those of the dominant group to which the adolescents belong, and their personal identity is rooted in belonging to the group. Because belonging to the group is so critical to adolescents' sense of identity, questioning or criticizing group values will be considered to be a threat to their being and will bring a fierce defense. Many adults never progress beyond this non-analytical stage and remain unable to question any of the teachings of their faith communities or to tolerate the values of others that differ from their own.

For those who are able to move beyond the conformity of synthetic-conventional faith, *Stage 4: individuative-reflective faith* emerges in young adulthood. Self-identity and worldview now become more differentiated from others, and individuals form their own interpretations of ultimate reality as they question their earlier assumptions. Critical reflection occurs and disillusionment with previous beliefs may arise as individuals realize that life is more complex than they once assumed. Individuals also question the meanings behind religious symbols, and may no longer tacitly accept the symbols as representative of the sacred as they did in the previous stage. Some adults do not reach this stage in young adulthood, but only later in their thirties or forties when they experience changes in primary relationships, such as divorce or the death of parents.

Stage 5: conjunctive faith rarely arises before mid-life and is often not achieved at all. In this stage, unrecognized or suppressed issues from the individual's past become integrated into his or her self and outlook. The past is reclaimed and reworked to arrive at new meaning and a deeper awareness. An openness to new depths of religious experience makes heightened spiritual revelations possible, and there is an inclusive acceptance of other spiritual traditions.

Stage 6: universalizing faith is the highest stage in the model and is extremely rare. It is achieved by those who are more lucid, simple, and fully human than others—individuals who tirelessly strive to achieve the ideals of absolute love and justice and transform present reality into transcendent actuality. Their universalizing compassion makes them heedless of their own pain and suffering. Gandhi and Mother Teresa of Calcutta are excellent examples of universalizing faith. Such self-actualizing individuals sometimes become martyrs for their faith and are often more deeply appreciated posthumously.

Because spirituality is now considered to be an important area to address in counseling, Fowler's model can be quite helpful as we work with clients. Understanding how individuals conceptualize spiritual issues can be instrumental in helping them work through and resolve them.

Chapter Five

Psychological Development

MOST THEORIES OF PSYCHOLOGICAL DEVELOPMENT are derived from the psychoanalytic, object-relations, and self-psychology perspectives. These attempt to explain how the psychic life of the person develops from birth, the major influences on this development, and how problems in adolescence and adulthood have their roots in the person's early experiences. Covered in this chapter are overviews for Freudian, object-relations, self-psychology, and adult-attachment theories. These are very brief summaries that present some major concepts and terms but do not go beyond that. Readers are encouraged to read about each of these theories in depth for a better understanding.

Freud

Sigmund Freud is recognized as the founder of psychoanalysis, the theory about (Thompson & Rudolph, 1983):

♦ psychological and mental development
♦ instinctual drives
♦ external environmental influences on psychological development
♦ importance of the family on psychological development
♦ impact of the attitudes of society.

Although Freud developed his theory from his clinical work with adults, he recognized that the first five years of life were critical to adult personality development. Freud divided this development into psychosexual stages: oral, anal, phallic, latency, and genital. Freud (1949) felt there were

TABLE **5.1**

Freud's Psychosexual Stages

Characteristics	Main task(s)	Location of libidinal pleasure	Adult manifestations "fixated"
ORAL (BIRTH–1 YEAR)			
oral erotic	weaning	mouth	smoking, eating,
oral sadistic	chewing food	mouth	drinking, gullibility, dependency (erotic), sarcasm (sadistic)
ANAL (1–3 YEARS)			
anal expulsive	bowel control	anus	generosity, messiness,
anal retentive		anus	stubbornness, stingi-ness, orderliness
PHALLIC (3–6 YEARS)			
sexual and aggressive feelings and fantasies	attitudes toward members of same and opposite sex	genitals	aggression, fetishism
LATENCY (7–13 YEARS)			
friends; activities	developing same-sex friends	relationships	
GENITAL (12–14 YEARS)			
	developing hetero-sexual relationships	genuine relationships with others	

important tasks at each stage of development, and when an individual fails at a task (i.e., does not receive the gratification that is the responsibility of the parents to provide), he or she remains "fixated" at that stage of development. Table 5.1 gives an overview of psychosexual stages, characteristics, main tasks to accomplish, locations of libidinal pleasure, and adult manifestations when the individual does not entirely complete the task or is not gratified, and thus becomes fixated.

STRUCTURE OF THE "SELF"

Basic to Freudian theory are the concepts of the structure of self—the *id, ego,* and *superego.* The *id* is the part of self that attends to needs and drives or instincts. It determines if the person responds to internal or external stimuli through impulsive motor activity or through image formation. The *ego* is the part of self that is most in touch with objective reality and operates as a balance between the demands of the id and those of the superego. The *superego* has two components: the "ego ideal" and the "conscience." Both combine to form the person's moral standards. When the id, ego, and superego are in harmony, the person fulfills his or her basic needs and desires, and has satisfying relationships and efficient interactions with his or her environment. If these components are not in harmony, the person is not satisfied with self or the environment and, if disharmony is extreme, maladjustment occurs.

DEVELOPMENTAL CONCEPTS

Freud presented three developmental concepts that have implications for understanding psychological development, the impact of early influences on development, and the role of the unconscious. The three concepts are: *identification, displacement,* and *defense mechanisms.*

Identification occurs as an imitation and/or resonating with the part or the whole of another person. You can identify with a trait, or with several traits, or with the entire person as you perceive him or her. Freud (1900) considered identification to be important in the development of the ego and superego. He noted that the process was not simple imitation of something experienced in the external world, as that is only a part of identification. There is also a part that is within the individual that combines with the external, and both remain in the unconscious.

Displacement is used to protect the cherished object by directing negative feelings to another object (person or thing). It is used as a defense against anxiety when the ego feels threatened with frustration, the potential loss of the desired object, or of being overwhelmed. A substitute is found for the original cherished object and energy is funneled to the replacement (Walrond-Skinner, 1986).

Defense mechanisms are used by the ego as protection from perceived potential threats. Defenses can be mounted when threats are perceived on the conscious, preconscious, or unconscious levels. That is, the perceived threat may be something of which you are aware (conscious), or the threat may be of something that you sense but are not able to verbalize or be fully aware of. With a little effort, you may become aware of who or what the latter threat is (preconscious). The unconscious holds the material of which we are not aware and cannot easily access, or maybe never access. However, even if the material in the unconscious cannot be easily accessed, the material influences our conscious life (i.e., feelings, attitudes, thoughts, and actions). Much attention is given to making the unconscious material conscious in psychoanalytic theory. Threats may be internal (e.g., memories, ideas, feelings) or external (e.g., an event, person, or situation). The twelve defense mechanisms listed by Thompson and Rudolph (1983) include:

- ◆ Repression
- ◆ Reaction formation
- ◆ Rationalization

- Denial
- Projection
- Fantasy
- Withdrawal
- Intellectualization
- Regression
- Compensation
- Undoing
- Acting out.

Projection and fantasy (phantasy) will be discussed in the section on object-relations.

Repression. Repression occurs when a threat is forced into the unconscious, and a barrier is raised to it becoming available to the conscious or preconscious. Victims of trauma can repress memories of the traumatic event, because the event is too threatening to the ego's equilibrium or its existence to be allowed to become conscious. Repression can also be a defense against experiencing personally unwanted thoughts and feelings.

Reaction Formation. Reaction formation occurs when someone develops attitudes or traits opposite to those that were repressed. For example, the child who hates the abusive parent represses the hatred and avows love for the parent. It is too threatening to the child to allow the hatred into the conscious and it is repressed, while love for the parent is put in its place.

Rationalization. Rationalization is employed to justify one's behavior. The person provides reasons why he or she acted as he or she did, justifies the behavior, and approves of the behavior. There can also be the desire or expectation that others will also approve. For example, the group member who always arrives late gives the reason that he or she has so much to do that it is not possible to ever be on time, and expects others to accept the reason as a valid one.

Denial. Denial is not a simple disagreement with what is being charged. Denial is a refusal to allow unpleasant anxiety-producing material into the conscious. The person has repressed this material, and will not allow it out of the unconscious. This denial is an unconscious defense mechanism, and not a conscious act.

Withdrawal. Withdrawal, as a defense mechanism, reduces involvement by distancing the ego from threatening material. Phasing out, becoming quiet, changing the topic abruptly, being shy, or acting passive are examples of withdrawal.

Intellectualization. Intellectualization is employed to defend against experiencing intense affect—either the person's affect (internal) or someone else's affect (external). The discussion or behavior switches to more cognitive material (e.g., asking a question, posing a hypothesis, requesting that a logical approach or explanation be used, or changing the topic).

Regression. Regression takes place when the person retreats to an earlier stage of development, usually one that is more immature, has greater dependency needs, and/or calls for more nurturing by others. Current demands are perceived as too threatening or overwhelming, so the best way to take care of the ego is to become more needy by resorting back to an earlier stage of development.

Compensation. Compensation can be seen when a weakness is hidden by enhancing a strength or when gratification that cannot be obtained from one source is sought after from another. Compensation takes many forms, some of which are constructive (e.g., academic achievement to overcome athletic deficiencies).

Undoing. Undoing occurs in reaction to immoral or bad behavior in which the person tries to atone for what was done. The bad, or wrong, is attempted to be wiped out by an act of atonement.

Acting Out. Acting out occurs in order to reduce anxiety aroused by forbidden desires by expressing them, either verbally or nonverbally. For example, when the adolescent wants to challenge the father but cannot do so directly, he or she commits some act that is an indirect challenge (e.g., taking the car without permission or "accidentally" cutting down the father's just-planted tree).

While modern psychoanalytic thought has moved beyond some of Freud's concepts, many are still viable regardless of theoretical orientation.

Object-Relations Theories

DEFINITION

Object-relations theory is really a collection of theories that have many similarities, but also have some distinct differences. These theories have their roots in psychoanalytic theory, but have taken some of the original concepts, expanded them, integrated them, and found empirical evidence for modifications.

"Object-relations" refer to relations with others, whether the relationship is internal or external, real or fantasized. How and when these object-relations develop, or fail to develop, determine the quality of relationships and functioning throughout one's life, and are reflected in current relationships. Thus, it is important for us, as counselors, to understand the development of our own psychic life in order to make counseling/therapy more effective.

Object-relations have both an objective real-world component, and a subjective inner component that is the mental representation of the other person or part of him or her. The internal mental representation may share some of the characteristics of the objective real-world person, but may also contain some characteristics of persons from previous relationships (e.g., parents). The internal mental representation is usually on the unconscious level, there being little or no awareness of its existence. Mental representations are formed from birth and continue throughout life. They influence and impact all other relationships, and the development of these inner mental representations can be thought of as psychological growth and development.

GENERAL ASSUMPTIONS ACROSS THEORIES

Object-relations theorists assume that crucial psychic development begins at birth and continues throughout life. They all agree that the quality of nurturing received, interactions with the caregiver (who is usually the mother), and the extent to which needs are fulfilled are the major variables that contribute to constructive and healthy psychological development. When any of these are missing, incomplete, or inadequate, psychological development is usually impaired, and because much of this crucial psychological development happens during infancy, memories of actual events and people are flawed. Only the effect of events, lingering affects, and impressions are left, so the reality has to be inferred. Further, passage of time can distort memories and can lead to misunderstandings or even incorrect interpretations of how present behaviors and emotions are related or connected to events occurring during infancy. There is really little or no evidence of what memories infants can record, nor how to translate them.

However, it is assumed by object-relations and self-psychology theorists that the first few years of life are important and that conditions such as borderline and narcissistic disorders have their etiology in this preverbal period.

MELANIE KLEIN

Melanie Klein (1882–1960) was one of the first to focus on object-relations as a way of understanding psychic development. She specialized in therapy with children and much of her theory is based on her clinical experiences and observations. The major concepts described here are splitting, projection, introjection, phantasy, and inner objects.

Splitting refers to what happens when there is an inability to integrate or synthesize incompatible experiences or feelings. Because they are incompatible, they are kept separate and one is split off. For example, it is difficult for the infant to accept that mother can be both nurturing and frustrating. Thus, one of the feelings is split off, leaving the infant with only the one that is most acceptable at that time. Mother is then seen as either all good, or all bad. When the development of the ability to integrate polarities, or opposites, is impaired, this impairment can be carried into adulthood and others will then be perceived and reacted to as totally positive or totally negative. Healthy development requires that one be able to see polarities and resolve conflicting thoughts, ideas, emotions, and perceptions by merging or synthesizing the polarities. Splitting can be either horizontal or vertical (Cashden, 1988). When the split is horizontal, the split-off piece is repressed (i.e., put in the unconscious where it is no longer available to the conscious). When the split is vertical, the unacceptable piece is projected onto another person.

Projection is a concept to describe the process by which an undesirable aspect or piece of self is unconsciously given to another person, and the person is reacted to as if he or she indeed had the split-off aspect, trait, or feeling. For example, someone who is anxious but cannot tolerate or accept that he or she is anxious can split off the anxiety, project it onto the other person, and then begin to treat the other person as if he or she were anxious. Projection is one means by which people, from infants to adults, get rid of uncomfortable feelings.

Introjection is the reverse of projection in that one takes into the self a trait, feeling, or attitude of another person. It is the process by which we become acculturated and understand expectations for behavior. We incorporate introjects on an unconscious level. An example of introjection would be when a child understands that something is disgusting by the look on a parent's face. Whatever is leading to the disgusted look may not be, in and of itself, disgusting, but because the feeling of the parent is one of disgust, the child introjects it and becomes disgusted also. Many patterns of adults' reactions and behaviors can be traced to introjections from their early years.

Klein (1957) defined *phantasy* as the inner mental representation of instinctual drives such as hunger. That is, the infant has certain instinctual drives that are experienced and/or controlled by the infant through mental imagery. The infant cannot, at this point, distinguish between reality and fantasy. This inability to know what is real and what is not leads to the infant's assumption and conviction that every discomfort or frustration is a personal hostile attack (St. Clair, 1989).

Sequence of Development. Klein was among the first to focus on the quality of nurturing received by the infant as being crucial for healthy psychological development. Her emphasis was on the kind and extent of the relationship developed from birth with the nurturer, who was usually the mother. How infants perceived the relationship and constructed *inner objects* greatly influenced their phantasies, and outcomes of these phantasies (e.g., the extent to which they felt discomfort and perceived it as a hostile attack from frustrating outside forces).

At first, the image of the nurturer is split into good and bad. To the extent that the infant's needs are met, the mother is "good," but whenever the infant is frustrated or distressed in any way, the mother is "bad." These images are incompatible for the infant and must be kept apart, hence the split. This was termed the *paranoid-schizoid position*. This position lasts from birth to approximately four months of age. During that period:

- ◆ tolerance of frustration is low
- ◆ the infant seeks to preserve and gratify self
- ◆ the infant exhibits extremes of emotions
- ◆ the infant wants to destroy persecutors, defined as anyone or anything who frustrates him or her
- ◆ there is no ability to distinguish between inner objects and external, or real-world, objects.

Gradually, the infant assumes what Klein terms the *depressive position*. This happens around the fourth or fifth month. The infant is able to tolerate both good and bad images of the major caretaker. Klein also proposes that it is during this period that

- ◆ the infant has guilt for previous destructive thoughts
- ◆ will act out of primitive impulses
- ◆ has the capacity to relate to part and whole objects
- ◆ can be concerned that the "good" object is in danger from the infant's destructive thoughts
- ◆ identifies with the "good" object.

Other theorists consider the mother–child relationship to be of major or crucial importance for the psychological development of the child. However, Melanie Klein was the first to develop a theory out of her systematic clinical observations. She was able to provide documentation of behavior that led to the development of her theory.

W. R. D. FAIRBAIRN

Fairbairn (1954) also considered the mother–child relationship to be of primary importance in the psychological development of the child. He felt that a maturational sequence focused on stages of developing "objects" was of more importance than Freud's proposal of psychosexual stages. Fairbairn's maturational sequence involved three stages: the early infantile-dependency stage, the transitional stage that can be a lifelong process, and the mature relational stage that involves mutual interdependence.

Early Infantile Dependence and Transition Stages. Splitting is also a very important concept in this theory, as Fairbairn proposes that splitting is the mechanism used to deal with an inconsistent and sometimes ungratifying world. The infant considers himself or herself and mother to have merged at first, which is Fairbairn's early *infantile-dependency stage*. The infant is dependent and must rely on someone else to meet all needs, and this person is usually the mother. Mother and self are merged and hence considered to be both gratifying and frustrating.

Although the infant is still dependent in the *transitional stage*, he or she is aware that mother is somewhat separate. Mother is split into both the "bad" and "good." The "bad" mother is perceived as an exciting object and/or a rejecting object, depending on the infant's internal state. She is an exciting object when she teases or tantalizes the child, thereby producing frustration and emptiness. An example of teasing for the child is when she or he is hungry and that hunger takes time to be satisfied rather than being immediately so. The mother is not engaging in teasing behavior as adults understand it since it is not deliberate, nor is the intent to frustrate or cause discomfort. Mother is a rejecting object when she is hostile or withdrawing, leading the child to feel unloved and unwanted. While an extreme example of rejection is easily understood, a possible milder version is not usually understood as such. For example, if a mother is ill or not feeling well and the child is demanding, or when the child's normal needs require more attention or energy than the mother has readily available, this can produce an attitude or behavior in the mother that the child perceives as rejecting. Parents who just want a good night's sleep provide another example of an unintentional attitude that could be perceived as rejecting. Mother becomes an ideal object when she makes the child feel desirable and loved.

Evidence of adults continuing to relate to others from the early infantile-dependence stage can be observed in the quality and quantity of dependency needs they show, as well as in their tendency not to relate to others as they are in real objective terms, but only in terms of "part objects." Fairbairn considered the transitional stage to continue throughout life and to lead to the development of ego stages. This stage can be seen when adults relate or perceive others as exciting, rejecting, or ideal in terms of how much the other meets their needs. Their needs continue to be of paramount importance in all relationships.

Mutual Relational Stage. Fairbairn's third stage is termed the *mutual relational stage*, in which there is mutual interdependence and the capacity to perceive and give to others according to their needs, not just one's personal need for acceptance and approval. Although he does not directly term it as such, altruism is a primary characteristic of this stage. Many adults usually have a foot in both stages. They never fully complete the transitional stage, but they do move into the mutual relational one.

DONALD WINNICOTT

Winnicott (1960) built on Klein's theory by accepting the importance of early nurturing relationships, and adding to it the importance of the surrounding environment. He proposed several concepts that are used extensively today: hallucination of omnipotence, good-enough mother, true self and false self, and transitional object.

Hallucination of omnipotence refers to the infant's belief that he or she controls the external world and causes things to "be" or "happen." The infant becomes hungry and as if by magic, he or she is fed. The inner fantasy is that the infant satisfies his or her own needs and brings the satisfying agent into existence.

Another concept coined by Winnicott is *just-good-enough mother* (1962). The meaning is that the parent, usually the mother, provides that which is sufficient for the child's needs at that stage of development. In other words, the mother anticipates, adapts, and changes in providing for the infant and child as he or she develops. When she does this, the infant begins to develop awareness of the external world and to relate to it. Winnicott (1971) notes that meeting the minute-to-minute needs of the infant calls for a high level of healthy identification with the infant; however, identification must not be tantamount to morbid preoccupation.

True self–false self is Winnicott's expression for that described by others as the "observing ego" (Winnicott, 1951). The assumption behind the concept is that good-enough mothering allows the "real self" to gradually become aware of and be in contact with reality. When there is an absence of good-enough mothering, the "false self" protects the "real self" and the external world is perceived and interacted with in a distorted way that builds false relationships. The "real self" allows individuals to be genuine and authentic in relationships.

Transitional objects are the first not-me thing or possession. Winnicott used the term to denote the infant's acceptance of a symbol. Examples of transitional objects are the mother, the infant's thumb, a blanket or toy (Winnicott, 1951).

MARGARET MAHLER

Mahler (1975) built on the object-relation theories of Klein, Winnicott, and others. She, however, focused on describing the psychological birth and development of the individual, describing three developmental stages of psychological development: normal autism (birth to 2 months), normal symbiosis (2 months to 5–7 months), and separation–individuation.

Normal autism describes the infant's customary state after birth. Everything is perceived in terms of self. The infant cannot distinguish between self and not-self and, in that way, is autistic. *Symbiosis* refers to "being one with the mother." The infant has begun to recognize that there is a need-satisfying object in his or her world (usually the mother), but considers the object as one with self (i.e., fused). Good-enough mothering gradually introduces the infant to external reality by providing necessary and satisfying functions.

Separation and Individuation. Table 5.2 presents an overview of separation and individuation subphases. Interruption or failure to complete the developmental tasks at any point during the separation and individuation phase is thought to be the root of psychological problems that appear in later life, such as borderline and narcissistic disorders. Separating and developing individuation are parallel developmental phases. Separation

TABLE **5.2**

Overview of Separation and Individuation Subphases

Category	Ages	Psychological Development
SEPARATION–INDIVIDUATION PHASE		
Differentiation	4th–8th months	Initial attempts at separation; frequent checking back to mother
Practicing	9th–18th months	Increased temporary separation from mother; increased exploration
Rapprochment	18th–24th months	Conflict between independence; wants to be with mother but fears engulfment
Individuality and emotional object constancy	24th month+	Permanent sense of self; permanent emotional and mental representations of others

refers to psychological differentiation from the mother and includes physical as well as psychological distancing, and disengagement. Individuation is an inner sense of independence from the symbiotic relationship. St. Clair (1989, p. 117) writes that

> Borderline and narcissistic disorders seem to result from traumas and disturbance of developmental processes during the separation–individuation phase. Some of the symptoms of narcissism and borderline pathology that involve omnipotence, splitting, and grandiosity are behavioral manifestations of developmental tasks that were disturbed or not completed.

Heinz Kohut and Self-Psychology

Heinz Kohut developed self-psychology as an outgrowth from object-relations and psychoanalytic theories. His books *The Analysis of the Self* (1971) and *The Restoration of the Self* (1977) present the framework for the theory. Both these books and his other writings focused on narcissism as a separate developmental line paralleling object-relations development, instead of the usual way of conceptualizing it as a part of object-relations development (Stone, 1992). Orestein (1978) and Orestein and Kay (1990) considered this development of self-psychology as the fourth-leading theory in psychoanalytic theories, along with id psychology, ego psychology, and object-relations theory.

Kohut (1977) considered the self to be "a unit, cohesive in space and enduring in time" (p. 99), and to be "the center of the individual's universe" (p. 311). The self is a psychological structure or organizer of experiences, and an existential agent or initiator of action (Stone, 1992).

SEQUENCE OF DEVELOPMENT

Development, for self-psychology, is not a progressive sequence of steps. Rather, it is viewed in terms of the relationship of the self to *selfobjects*: "Selfobjects are real people whereas self-objects are imaginal representations" (Cashden, 1988, p. 21). Kohut viewed the parents, or the other person, as distinctly separate individuals in the child's life as selfobjects when they were incorporated into the child's self.

He proposed that the infant is born without a self, and gradually develops one through the quality of relationships with selfobjects in his or her world. The quality of relationships with selfobjects referred to by Kohut is similar to Winnicott's just-good-enough mother and holding environment in which the infant's needs are met. Development is viewed in terms of the self in relation to selfobjects—not as a progressive sequence of steps. However, Kohut does propose that there is a sequence where the nuclear self, the rudimentary self, and cohesive self are formed. This sequence is not age-related, but is instead relationship-related. The definitions and sequence follows.

THE "SELF"

The *nuclear self* forms and is composed of the *grandiose-exhibitionistic self*—everything pleasant and good is a part of the infant, and everything frustrating and bad is not a part. The grandiose self is established by relating to a selfobject that empathicly responds to and mirrors the child's grandiose self. The other component of the nuclear self is *idealization*—the attempt to assign to the parent absolute power and perfection (imago) to maintain the original perfection, bliss, and omnipotence experienced in the womb before birth.

The *rudimentary self* forms by including and excluding psychological structures. The *cohesive self* emerges. This is the period in which organization and strengthening of the cohesive self occurs. Established are boundaries for "what is me" and "what is not me." The idealized parent image becomes the superego.

The nuclear self then incorporates the rudimentary self and the cohesive self and becomes a "self." The grandiose self becomes channeled into realistic pursuits, and the transformed and integrated grandiosity becomes energy, ambition, and self-esteem (Kohut, 1971, p. 107).

NARCISSISM

Kohut and Wolf (1978) describe psychopathology as resulting from *narcissistic* injuries. Narcissistic injuries are wounds to the essential self and occur from birth onwards. The individual responses to narcissistic injuries range from mild (e.g., discomfort) to intense, in which the person's inner experience is one of fragmenting and disintegrating. Attempts to restore the "self" include withdrawal and expressions of anger. When narcissistic injuries are repeatedly experienced, the individual can develop symptomatic responses (e.g., fetishes, obsessive-compulsive behaviors) or syntonic or dystonic character formation, such as alcoholism, delinquency, sexual perversions, or chronic depression (Stone, 1992).

Kohut focused on narcissism to understand the development of the self. In self-psychology, narcissism is considered to be different stages of maturity with varying expectations for just what constitutes healthy narcissism at each stage. He proposed that normal adults continue to have transformed needs for mirroring of the self by selfobjects. Adults' transformed mirroring needs are not the same as the normal infant's, child's or adolescent's needs. Narcissism changes across the lifespan and the healthy adult version is characterized by creativity, humor, and empathy (Kohut, 1977).

GOTTSCHALK'S PRIMARY NARCISSISM

Gottschalk (1988) presents an overview of narcissistic development through successive life stages, beginning with definitions for *narcissism*, *normal narcissism*, and *pathological narcissism*. The term *primary narcissism* was presented by Freud (1914) as being normal for the developing child (0–5 years). Primary or normal narcissism is characterized by:

♦ *megalomania*—the person experiences exaggerated feelings of greatness

♦ *omnipotence of thought*—the person feels that his or her thoughts are all-powerful

♦ *magic*—the person believes that he or she personally causes the outside world to perform as desired.

Gottschalk (1988) describes this period as ranging from months to years in which the child considers others as extensions of self, under his or her control, and existing to fulfill the child's desires and needs. He writes: "This state of inner satisfaction, self-confidence, omnipotence, infallibility, consummate entitlement prevails for several years" (p. 65). Table 5.3 presents an overview of Gottschalk's description for life tasks and life situations, and their effects at different stages when influenced by inadequate parenting and/or other circumstances from the person's life or the larger culture. His description highlights the long-term, wide-ranging, and lasting effects for the failure to develop healthy narcissism.

Gottschalk proposes that failure to develop age-appropriate narcissism is the root cause for disorders and conditions that children, adolescents, and adults exhibit. This developmental failure is tied to inadequate parenting at the stage of primary narcissism (0–5 years) where such effects follow the person throughout life. There are life situations that can promote inadequate parenting, and some of these are not under the control of the parent. Situations such as parental illness, parental depression,

TABLE 5.3
Causes and Outcomes for Failure to Develop
Age-Appropriate Narcissism

Age/Stage/Tasks	Life situations	Potential outcomes
BIRTH TO 5		
Freud's primary narcissism	parental illness sibling birth family move child's illness parental depression attending school death of a parent	anxiety phobias depression sleep disorders hypertension
5–10 YEARS		
acculturation; healthy, realistic appraisal of self-worth	divorce family size	same as birth–5 low concepts of self-worth self-defeating, self-destructive thoughts and actions
11–20 YEARS		
peer-group identification sex-role identification career, vocational selection self-identity developing relationships belief system	same as birth–10	suicide
21–50 years		
attaining a job pairing for intimate relationships decisions regarding children maximize skills community position parenting functions	nonsuccess at life tasks illnesses economic conditions	alcohol and drug abuse susceptible to physical ailments depression impaired relationships
51–80 years		
providing economic support caring for children and/ or parents college/training costs postparental period retirement eventuality of death	physical and/or mental decline reduced social-support system	depression chronic illness

and death can result in situations where the parent is not good enough for the developing child's needs. Gottschalk felt that this inadequate parenting leads to anxiety, phobias, depression, and sleep disorders in children and could persist into adulthood. He also suggests that these early experiences with inadequate parenting could lead to adult behavior such as criminal acts, alcohol and substance abuse, early pregnancy, child abuse, and other such conditions and activities. Thus, the pattern and basis for who adults are and how they behave are closely tied to, if not a direct result of, the parenting they received that influenced the development of age-appropriate narcissism.

THE REVERSE SELFOBJECT EXPERIENCE

A major disturbance for developing age-appropriate healthy narcissism occurs when the child has a reverse selfobject experience (Kohut, 1984). The reverse selfobject experience is when the child is expected to care for and nurture the parent, instead of the usual situation in which the parent nurtures the child. The child, in the reverse selfobject experience, becomes responsible for the parent's emotional needs and, in some cases, is expected to care for physical needs as well. The child can then develop an arrested grandiose self (Lee, 1988). This arrested grandiose self leads to adult behaviors such as (Kohut, 1977):

♦ inappropriately trying to control others' behavior
♦ considering others to be an extension of one's body, and hence to be amenable to control and manipulation
♦ engaging in sadistic behavior in personal relationships
♦ ruthlessly seeking power
♦ needing excessive admiration
♦ having an exaggerated sense of responsibility
♦ being hypercritical of others
♦ having excessive feelings of guilt
♦ always putting others' needs first
♦ having feelings of entitlement
♦ showing a lack of empathy
♦ engaging in interpersonal exploitiveness.

The adult is then trying to cope with an arrested self and the impoverished self that failed to adequately develop. This outcome affects interpersonal relationships, self-esteem, and self-efficacy in many and varied ways, usually leading to underlying feelings of dissatisfaction. When excessive, this can be a destructive narcissistic pattern (Brown, 1998), closet narcissism (Masterson, 1993), or pathological narcissism (Kernberg, 1995).

Adult-Attachment Theories

The theory of how and why adults make emotional and romantic connections, or why they are unable to do so, has received much attention in the years since Bowlby (1979) proposed it. Numerous research studies were and are conducted to further our understanding of adult attachment. Bowlby (1979) asserts that "There is a strong causal relationship between an individual's experiences with his [her] parents and his [her] capacity to make affectional bonds" (p. 135, my brackets). This theory proposes that the adult's ability to form and maintain meaningful relationships, especially those of a romantic nature such as love, have their roots in the quality of the parental relationship. Most often, the parental relationship that receives the most attention in studies is the maternal–child relationship. Consideration is also given to the basic personality and temperament of the child, but these are thought to be a part of the interaction with the parent and contribute to the complexity of this early nurturing relationship.

Experiences with others also seem to play a role in adult attachment. Bowlby (1979) says that the expectation an adult has for meaningful and satisfying relationships stem from his or her childhood experiences that determine if he or she has a secure personal base or not. This secure personal base has two factors: an internal representation of others as available, nurturing, and caring; and an internal representation of the self as valued, loveable and worthy (Bowlby, 1988).

INTERNAL REPRESENTATION OF OTHERS

Adult attachment capitalizes on the work done by object-relations theorists such as Klein (1955), Mahler et al. (1975), Winnicott (1951), and Fairbairn (1954), who developed theories of how mental representations emerge and are affected by the quality of the nurturing parent's relationship with the child. These theories used clinical experiences as well as psychological and laboratory studies in their development. Although each theorist has a different perspective, they all seem to be consistent in the assertion that early nurturer–child experiences play a major role in the child's, adolescent's, and adult's capacity for intimacy, and in his or her ability to form and maintain meaningful relationships. There is no one encompassing object-relations theory, but are instead a collection of theories that try to explain how and why mental representations develop as they do by focusing on the preverbal stage of development (i.e., infancy and childhood). Since infants and children do not have the verbal skills to relate or explain their inner experiencing, these object-relations theorists have to use observations, extrapolations, interpretations, and intuitions. Since much of this is subjective, there can be no definitive conclusions.

However, there does seem to be considerable evidence that people who perceive others as available, nurturing, and caring are better able to form and maintain meaningful relationships. In contrast, adults who had unsatisfactory parental relationships do seem to have difficulty forming and maintaining satisfactory and intimate relationships. For example, children who had one or more narcissistic parents are prone to fit this description (Brown, 2001; Donaldson-Pressman & Pressman, 1994). Other examples include adults who suffered trauma and/or deprivation, had alcoholic parents, or experienced parental abandonment.

There is considerable evidence from studies on resiliency that children do not necessarily have to continue to suffer the effects of trauma, neglect, and other distressing experiences (Davis, 1999). Something in some children's basic personality and temperament seems to allow them to overcome or moderate the negative effects of these experiences. One additional factor that seems to play a role is the early maternal–child relationship in which a positive, caring, and empathic relationship from parent to child helps build inner resources that assist the child in more effectively coping with negative experiences. This is one more reason why the quality of early mental representations of others is so important, both for the infant and child, and for his or her positive growth and development throughout life. This is especially important for adults seeking to establish intimacy and other positive relationships.

Mental representations of others as being available and caring develop from the kind and quality of nurturing, empathic responding, and unconditional positive regard provided to the infant and child by the mother or primary nurturer. When the infant's needs are met in a timely manner, and the personalization and holding and just-good-enough mothering described by Winnicott (1951) are available, the infant and child derive a secure base that persists throughout life. Experiences alter the mental representations along with healthy narcissistic development to allow the person to not expect that everyone is available, but to be able to select and choose whom to desire and expect to fulfill these functions. However, the secure person has a core belief and conviction that others are reliable, available, trustworthy, caring, and can be called on in times of need.

THE SELF

The other part of a secure personal base is the internal belief that one is worthy, loved, and valued. This belief also seems to be related and dependent on the quality of the maternal (nurturer)–child relationship from birth onwards. The object-relations and self-psychology theorists all assert that one's internal self develops from this relationship, and that many disturbances of the self can be traced back to an inadequate maternal (nurturing)–child relationship (Kohut, 1977; Masterson, 1993). There are several life stressors and personal conditions that can cause a disruption in this relationship, which result in the mother's being unavailable to meet the infant's and child's needs. Examples of stressors and conditions include

- maternal depression
- incarceration
- military deployment
- chronic or acute illnesses
- addiction
- poverty
- ignorance
- unemployment
- destructive narcissism.

Many of these on the list, if not all, are not under the conscious control of the parent, who himself or herself may have received inadequate parenting.

When the self fails to adequately develop, the result is a lack of a cohesive self that is secure and confident. This gets played out in adults who have insufficient self-esteem, underdeveloped or destructive narcissism, an inability to form and maintain deep and satisfying relationships, and, in extreme cases, borderline and narcissistic personality disorders.

ADULT-ATTACHMENT CATEGORIES

Hazan and Shaver (1987) categorize insecure adult attachment as *Insecure-Avoidant* and *Insecure-Ambivalent*. The avoidant adult

- is uncomfortable when close to others
- finds it difficult to trust others
- takes pride in not depending on others
- becomes anxious at the thought of intimacy
- is careful not to show signs of distress
- minimally self-discloses or does not self-disclose at all.

This person is a loner and uncommunicative, does not socialize well or doesn't at all, is very well defended and stoic, and although desiring intimacy, is terrified when anyone approaches him or her. This person both yearns for connection, and pushes it away.

The *Insecure-Ambivalent* adult is very much the opposite of the *Insecure-Avoidant* one. Instead of fearing closeness, this person is so desirous of merging with others that he or she seeks enmeshment and becomes too close for others' comfort. This is the person who

- ◆ demands a total and exclusive commitment from others
- ◆ clings to others
- ◆ constantly wants unqualified affection and attention
- ◆ does not respect boundaries or that others may be different
- ◆ has considerable emotionality and affect intensity.

This person can too easily trust others in their yearning for fusion, total and complete acceptance, and unconditional love. He or she is very dependent, giving rise to the description of being a "clinging vine," which brings forth the image of a vine that cannot grow, thrive, or be upright without something on which to cling. Vines can also smother the host and prevent it from receiving the light, water, and nutrients it needs. This is similar to what can happen in Insecure-Ambivalent adults' relationships, in which they try to be so close that others feel suffocated.

According to Hazan and Shaver (1987), Insecure-Ambivalent adults have developed this form of insecure attachment because of an inconsistent attachment figure in early life (e.g., the mother). True, the mother was present and took care of the infant's and child's needs, but she was not consistent in her emotional reactions, empathic responding, personalization, and handling. Examples of maternal conditions that contribute to inconsistent parenting include:

- ◆ mental and emotional disorders
- ◆ expectations that the child to take care of the parent's emotional needs (the reverse selfobject experience)
- ◆ addiction
- ◆ chaotic family situation
- ◆ abusive males, and other adverse circumstances.

It is easy to see that early maternal deprivation can set up a deep need to try and attain the longed-for closeness from adult relationships that was absent during infancy. The need is so deep that the person remains unaware that he or she is seeking the deprived closeness. What generally happens is that Insecure-Ambivalent adults do not get what they want because others push them away or are not responsive, so that they remain unfulfilled. They can never find a person who is willing to tolerate the kind of closeness (i.e., fusion) they desire.

Summary

Modern analytic thought continues to consider early relationships as being crucial in the development of self, personality, and character and thus focuses on these. While the movement has broken away from a sole emphasis on psychosexual development, many other Freudian concepts continue to be of importance. Indeed, even the cognitive theorists are increasingly paying attention to early development and early relationships (Beck, 2000). This information about early experiences seems critical for understanding how the self develops and how individuals come to be as they are.

There is also some therapeutic attention being paid to the *corrective emotional recapitulation of the family of origin* that has been shown to be a therapeutic or curative factor in group therapy (Yalom, 1995). Not only does it play a part in group therapy, the focus on unresolved family of origin issues plays an important role in self-understanding, personal development, and individual therapy. It can be especially important for mental health professionals in preventing the negative effects of countertransference from harming the therapeutic relationship.

Chapter Six

Conception, Prenatal Development, Birth, and Infancy

HAVE YOU EVER CONTEMPLATED what a miracle you are? If not, you may begin to do so as you consider how your amazing human life began. In this chapter, we will examine the mysterious process that starts with conception, develops in the tiny space of the womb, bursts forth at birth, and leads to the discovery of a new and strange world of sights and sounds in infancy. We will also consider issues that confront parents as they move into their new roles of being mothers and fathers.

In the Beginning . . . There Were Genes

Life begins with the union of two cells—the male *sperm* and the female egg or *ovum*. The sperm and the ovum each contain 23 *chromosomes*—half the number of chromosomes within the other cells of the body—and each chromosome is made up of thousands of genes. *Genes*—the basic units of heredity—are lengths of DNA that form the "double helix" molecule that gives a chemical code for development. The union of the sperm and ovum produces 23 pairs of chromosomes that comprise the individual's complete genetic endowment.

Both members of a chromosome pair influence the same trait in the individual. Genes also work as pairs to influence specific characteristics. Genes, however, do not necessarily give the same direction for the characteristic, as gene pairs may be either *homozygous* or *heterozygous*. In homozygous pairs, both genes give the same direction for the trait (e.g., two dominant genes paired together or two recessive genes paired together). In heterozygous pairs, the two genes give different directions for the trait (i.e., a dominant gene paired with a recessive gene). Dominant genes prevail over recessive genes; thus when a dominant gene is paired with a recessive gene, the dominant characteristic will manifest itself in the individual, but the recessive trait may be passed on to the person's children. Consider the genetic code for hair color. Dark hair is dominant and blonde hair is recessive, so a person with two dominant genes will have dark hair, while a person with two recessive genes will have blonde hair. On the other hand, an individual who has one dominant gene and one recessive gene will have dark hair, but may pass a recessive gene for blonde hair on to his or her child. If the child receives a recessive gene from the other parent, he or she will have blonde hair.

Most serious birth defects and genetic diseases (e.g., sickle-cell anemia, cystic fibrosis, hemophilia, Tay-Sachs disease) are carried on recessive genes. Therefore such disorders may not appear in the individual, but could be passed on to the person's children. If a man and woman both have a recessive gene for a serious genetic disorder, genetic counseling may assist them in deciding whether to conceive.

Most pregnant women now receive some form of prenatal genetic screening, including alpha-fetoprotein analysis for spina bifada, neural tube defects, and Down syndrome (Schimpf & Domino, 2001). If disorders are suspected, more invasive procedures can be conducted such as amniocentesis or chorionic villus sampling. However, the ability to detect prenatal genetic disorders has far outstripped the ability to treat the conditions, so typically the only option available is to decide whether to terminate the pregnancy.

Although most chromosomes are similar in males and females, the 23rd pair—the *sex chromosomes*—are distinct. These chromosomes are especially important because they determine the sex of the child. While males produce both X and Y chromosomes, females produce only X, so it is the father's genetic contribution that ultimately determines the sex of the offspring. An X-Y chromosome pair results in a male child, and an X-X pair results in a female.

Genotype refers to a person's genetic makeup, while *phenotype* refers to the trait that actually appears in the person. Having a genotype for a given trait does not mean that it will automatically arise, because the environment also plays a role in the trait's development. For example, although an individual may have a genotype for high intelligence, without the proper environmental stimulation and learning conditions the person's phenotype might be far from impressive.

Nature versus Nurture

The relative influences of nature versus nurture on development have been debated throughout history. *Nature* refers to an individual's genetic inheritance, while *nurture* refers to every other factor that impacts a person's life. Nurture is therefore an extremely large category that includes family variables, education, nutrition, drugs, diseases, life experiences, and all other environmental influences. Because nature and nurture cannot ordinarily be isolated from one another, twin studies offer the best method of studying the respective contributions of each on development.

Twins are of two types: identical or *monozygotic* twins result when a fertilized egg splits in two to form two identical embryos; fraternal or *dizygotic* twins result when two eggs are produced and fertilized by two separate sperm. While identical twins have 100 percent of their genetic inheritance in common, fraternal twins are no more similar than ordinary siblings, except that they share the womb together and are born at approximately the same time. Because of their identical genetic makeup, monozygotic twins separated at birth offer the most valuable means of studying nature versus nurture: any physical or psychological differences being necessarily due to nurture.

The term *heritability ratio* refers to the proportion of all the variance in a trait within a large group of people that can be linked to genetic differences among those individuals (Sigelman, 1999). High heritability ratios exist, showing the strong contribution of nature for traits such as introversion, extroversion, schizophrenia, obsessive-compulsive disorder, and bipolar depression. Even social attitudes and job satisfaction have been found to be influenced by genetics.

Conception

Conception begins when a sperm and an egg unite. Usually this occurs when a sperm fertilizes an egg that has left the ovaries and traveled to the fallopian tubes on its way to the uterus, during the phase of the woman's menstrual cycle called *ovulation*. The union of sperm and egg may also occur in a laboratory dish with an extracted egg and a donated sperm; however, most people still seem to prefer the less technically advanced method of bringing new life into the world.

Prenatal Development

PERIOD OF THE ZYGOTE (OR GERMINAL PERIOD)

After fertilization occurs, prenatal development progresses through three stages. The first stage, the *period of the zygote* (also called *germinal period*), occurs in the first two weeks following conception. At this time, the *zygote* (i.e., fertilized ovum) moves from the fallopian tubes to the uterus. The zygote divides rapidly while making the journey and firmly attaches itself to the uterine wall at the end of the trip.

PERIOD OF THE EMBRYO

The second stage of prenatal development, the *embryonic period*, begins when the zygote, now called an *embryo*, is implanted in the uterine wall. This stage, which lasts until the eighth week after conception, is a time of tremendous growth for the embryo, because all the major organs and body structures will be present by the end of this period. This period is also a time of great risk for the embryo, because it is the period that can be most adversely affected by *teratogens*—any medications, chemicals, diseases, or environmental agents that might interfere with the development of the fetus or result in the loss of a pregnancy, a birth defect, or a pregnancy complication (Health on the Net, 2001). Examples of common teratogens and their possible effects include the following (Berk, 1993; Health on the Net, 2001; Sigelman, 1999):

- ◆ Social drugs:
  - alcohol—fetal alcohol syndrome, mental retardation, facial abnormalities, and slow physical growth
  - tobacco—prematurity, low birth weight, miscarriage, impaired breathing, and death
  - heroin and cocaine—prematurity, low birth weight, physical defects, respiratory difficulties, drug addiction, convulsions, and death
  - marijuana—premature delivery, low birth weight; and respiratory problems
  - caffeine—premature delivery, miscarriage, and newborn withdrawal symptoms such as vomiting and irritability
  - aspirin—low birth weight, poor motor development, and lower intelligence

- ◆ Medications:
  - thalidomide—severe deformities in arms and legs
  - other drugs (e.g., Dilantin, Tegretol, Accutane, chemotherapy, lithium)—effects vary based upon the specific drug ingested

- ◆ Environmental agents:
  - lead—premature delivery, low birth weight, and brain damage
  - mercury—mental retardation, abnormal speech, and lack of motor coordination

- radiation—spontaneous abortion, slow physical growth, underdeveloped brain, malformations of the skeleton and eyes, and childhood cancer
- PCBs—premature delivery, low birth weight, deficiencies in short-term memory, and lower intelligence

♦ Maternal diseases and health conditions:

- Rubella (German measles)—malformations of the heart, eyes, and brain, blindness, deafness, liver, spleen, and bone-marrow problems, mental retardation, and retarded growth
- Chicken pox—spontaneous abortion, slow growth, and premature delivery
- Cytomegalovirus—neurologic and developmental problems, dental abnormalities, life-threatening infections, poor weight gain, hepatitis, and lung problems
- genital herpes—premature delivery, encephalitis, and severe rashes
- syphilis—miscarriage, blindness, and mental retardation
- AIDS and HIV—impaired immune system, frequent infections, and death
- toxemia (high blood pressure)—death
- anoxia (oxygen deprivation)—mental retardation, cerebral palsy, and delayed motor and cognitive development
- maternal age—older age associated with greater likelihood of Down's syndrome
- stress—premature delivery and infant irritability.

Teratogens are more likely to do major damage if they occur in larger doses for an extended time, or in a critical period when rapid development for a given body structure is taking place (e.g., the embryonic stage is especially sensitive for most organs and body systems), or in combination with other teratogens (e.g., smoking cigarettes and drinking alcohol). The adverse effects of teratogens also depend upon the genetic makeup and particular vulnerability of the mother and child.

THE PERIOD OF THE FETUS

The *fetal period* begins two months after conception and continues until birth. During the embryonic period the organs and body structures were formed. In this stage, the development of the *fetus* (formerly the embryo) consists primarily of rapid increases in overall size and further maturation of the organs.

Birth

After approximately 37 to 42 weeks of pregnancy, the birth process begins with the dilation and thinning of the cervix. The woman knows that labor is starting when the placental sac breaks and contractions begin. As the contractions occur more frequently and with greater intensity, birth is getting closer. The process, however, can be lengthy and painful, as labor can last 10 to 18 hours for the first baby, and somewhat less for later births. The delivery may be done either vaginally or, if complications occur, via a cesarean section.

Women have various options for pain relief during the delivery, including analgesics, regional anesthesia, and general anesthesia. Because drugs dull the awareness of the baby as well as relieving the pain of the mother, many women choose natural childbirth without medication to ensure that the infant will be alert and responsive immediately after birth. The father (or significant other) can play an important role in coaching and comforting the mother through the birthing process. For some women, a natural childbirth approach incorporating music, relaxation, breathing exercises, and a bathtub of warm water makes giving birth a wondrous experience.

Infancy

SENSORY DEVELOPMENT

From the moment of birth, infants are born ready to encounter the world. Although their senses are not yet fully developed, infants are aware of their surroundings and are constantly taking in sensory information. A *neonate* (newborn) has visual acuity between 20/200 and 20/600 and can see best at distances no greater than eight to fourteen inches, which is about the distance from a mother's arms to her eyes (Health on the Net, 2001). By the end of the third month, the infant's distance vision will dramatically improve and he or she should see quite well by the age of eight to twelve months. In addition, neonates can hear well and will turn their heads in the direction of a parent's voice and react to loud sounds. Neonates can taste, preferring sweet to bitter flavors, and are assumed to be able to smell. They are sensitive to touch and respond positively to stroking, while reacting adversely to pain.

REFLEXES

In addition to their sensory capabilities, babies are born with a variety of reflexes that enable them to respond to the world. If these responses are not present, a physician may suspect problems in the neonate. Newborns' innate reflexes include the following (Health on the Net, 2001):

♦ Blinking—closing eyes in response to a flash of light or puff of air

♦ Babinski—fanning out toes and twisting foot inward when the sole of foot is stroked

♦ Grasping—grasping tightly when palms are touched

♦ Moro—startling, which includes throwing back the head, arching the back, throwing out the arms and legs and then pulling them rapidly in toward the body in response to a sudden stimulus, such as a loud noise

♦ Rooting—turning toward the source of stimulation, opening the mouth and beginning to suck when the cheek is stroked or side of mouth is touched

♦ Stepping—moving the feet as if to walk when being held upright, with feet touching the ground

♦ Sucking—sucking automatically on any object touching the mouth

♦ Swimming—making coordinated swimming movements when placed facedown in the water.

In addition to the reflexes listed above, neonates have a less perceptible but equally innate response that is valuable to researchers who wish to study infants' awareness. The *orienting response* consists of an organism's tendency to respond to new stimulation by becoming more alert; in other words, to respond to the new stimulus by *orienting* or attending to it (LeFrancois, 1993). The orienting response, which is measured by changes in pupil size, heart rate, and galvanic skin response, only appears when the infant is exposed to a novel stimulus. Thus if an infant no longer shows the orienting response when exposed to a given stimulus, it can be assumed that the infant recognizes the stimulus as something familiar that he or she has experienced before. This measure provides an important indication of learning in infants and an understanding of their sense of object permanence, as well as clues regarding their ability to distinguish between familiar persons and strangers (e.g., if the infant could speak, he or she might say, "Hey, that picture isn't new; you just showed it to me a few seconds ago!" or "That's the face of my mother, but I don't know this other woman!").

COGNITIVE DEVELOPMENT

Piaget referred to the first period of intellectual development as the *sensorimotor stage*. This stage, which begins at birth and lasts until approximately age 2, is a time in which children use their senses and rudimentary motor skills to learn about the world. At first, children's motoric movements will be mainly responsive and consist primarily of reflexes. Later in this stage, children will assume increased ability to intentionally control their movements to achieve desired goals. In describing the importance of the sensorimotor stage, Piaget (1967) wrote:

> The period that extends from birth to the acquisition of language is marked by an extraordinary development of the mind. Its importance is sometimes underestimated because it is not accompanied by words that permit a step-by-step pursuit of the progress of intelligence and the emotions, as is the case later on. This early mental development nonetheless determines the entire course of psychological evolution. . . . At the starting point of this development the neonate grasps everything to himself—or, in more precise terms, to his own body—whereas at the termination of the period, i.e., when language and thought begin, he is for all practical purposes but one element or entity among others in a universe that he has gradually constructed himself, and which hereafter he will experience as external to himself. (pp. 8–9)

Piaget (1952b) divided the sensorimotor period into the following six sequential substages that map infants' cognitive development in the first years of life:

- *Reflexive activity* (birth–1 month): The infant's actions involve using reflexes in response to external stimuli (e.g., blinking, rooting, sucking).

- *Primary circular reactions* (1–4 months): Actions are simple, repetitive, and center on the infant's own body (e.g., grasping and ungrasping hands, sucking thumb, smacking lips).

- *Secondary circular reactions* (4–8 months): Actions are still repetitive, but are used to make interesting sights and sounds in the surrounding world (e.g., shaking rattle, dropping spoon).

- *Coordination of secondary circular reactions* (8–12 months): Several actions are combined to intentionally achieve a goal (e.g., pulling a blanket to uncover a hidden a toy and then grabbing the toy). Stranger anxiety occurs when the child sees unfamiliar people, and separation anxiety arises when the infant is separated from the primary caregiver.

- *Tertiary circular reactions* (12–18 months): Actions are used to explore the properties of objects by experimenting on them in novel ways (e.g., dropping a toy from different heights to see how it falls; dropping two different toys to see how their falls compare).

- *Mental representation* (18 months–2 years): Events and objects are mentally represented before actions are employed (e.g., Piaget's "matchbox" experiment). This substage marks a significant transition, because it represents the beginning of symbolic thought.

Piaget (1952b) discovered this transformation in mental representation in children's cognitions one day while playing with his daughter, Lucienne. After hiding an attractive watch chain in a partially opened match-box, Piaget made the following observations of Lucienne's behavior:

> I put the chain back into the box and reduce the opening to 3 mm. It is understood that Lucienne is not aware of the functioning of the opening and closing of the matchbox and has not seen me prepare the experiment. She only possesses two preceding schemes: turning the box over in order to empty it of its contents, and sliding her fingers into the slit to make the chain come out. It is of course this last procedure that she tries first: she puts her finger inside and gropes to reach the chain, but fails completely. A pause follows during which Lucienne manifests a very curious reaction. . . . She looks at the slit with great attention; then, several times in succession, she opens and shuts her mouth, at first slightly, then wider and wider! [Then] . . . Lucienne unhesitatingly puts her finger in the slit, and instead of trying as before to reach the chain, she pulls so as to enlarge the opening. She succeeds and grasps the chain. (pp. 337–338)

According to Piaget, throughout the sensorimotor stage children acquire a progressively greater understanding of *object permanence*, which refers to the child's understanding that objects continue to exist even when they are not being perceived. When infants acquire a sense of object permanence, the game of "peek-a-boo" loses its ability to enchant, because there is no more wide-eyed surprise when a toy is pulled out from under a blanket. Piaget believed that the sense of object permanence would not be fully complete until the substage of mental representation, but current research suggests that children may develop this understanding earlier.

Issues Facing Parents

Although the birth of a child is usually considered a joyous event, issues can sometimes arise that produce challenge and pain for families. The transition to parenthood is not always easy, nor do all infants survive. In this section we will examine some of the issues that can occur and factors that may impact individuals in the process of bringing new life into the world.

TRANSITION TO PARENTHOOD

Pregnancy, childbirth, and parenthood constitute a life transition marked by many changes for both men and women. For women, these include major physiological changes in the body and in appearance, as well as in social relationships, role demands, life structure, and thinking. For men, the changes are less pronounced but may still require a significant reorientation in both thinking and social roles. The transition to parenthood also requires both men and women to revise personal goals.

During pregnancy, women progress through a sequence of interdependent and qualitatively differential phases (Gloger-Tippler, 1983).

These phases suggest the woman's psychological preparation for entry into motherhood:

- *Disruption* (conception–12 weeks)—dramatic changes occur on biological, psychological, and social levels that may involve giving up some parts of the woman's previous identity, while integrating other new elements of being a mother.
- *Adaptation* (13–20 weeks)—adjustment is made to the initial disruptions, which reduces the cognitive dissonance experienced in the previous period.
- *Centering and anticipation* (21–32 weeks)—gradual reconceptualization of the child as an independent being occurs as the woman begins to anticipate what is to come.
- *Preparation* (33 weeks–birth)—active preparation is conducted for the birth and the woman's new life situation as a mother.

Perhaps because their bodies do not change as a result of conception, men's transition into parenthood begins more slowly and tends to focus on the parental role of being a provider. As the birth approaches, women's emphasis shifts toward the home and nurturing, while men become more oriented to work and the financial requirements of supporting a child (Cowan et al., 1985). The divergent trajectories of male and female transition into parenthood become even more pronounced as both new parents tend to assume more traditional gender-specialized arrangements of family tasks.

As men and women transition into parenthood, personal goals must be revised to allow the restructuring of lives that inevitably occurs with the arrival of children. Again, there are gender differences in how personal goals are reconstructed. Salmela-Aro, Nurmi, Saisto, and Halmesmaki (2000) found that women's goals related to motherhood increased continuously during pregnancy, while their goals of earlier transitions (e.g., achievement) decreased during this time. Also, women's goals related to the child's health and birth increased before the birth and decreased after it; with postnatal goals being more related to family. Although the degree of goal reconstruction was greater in women who were expecting their first child, it also occurred in those who already had children. Similarly, men revised their personal goals throughout the prenatal period and expressed concerns about the health and birth of the child; however, they mentioned more goals related to achievement and property than did women.

The transition to parenthood is not without stress. One-third of divorces occur within the first five years of marriage (National Center for Health Statistics, 1991), which may be related to the entry of children into the relationship. Studies have shown that when couples become parents, marital conflict dramatically increases, positive marital interchanges dramatically decrease, and marital satisfaction significantly declines (Belsky & Kelly, 1994; Cowan & Cowan, 1992). In a longitudinal study comparing childless couples with those who had children, Shapiro, Gottman, and Carrere (2000) found that marital satisfaction declined for wives in both groups during the first four-to-six years of marriage. Wives who became mothers, however, had significantly sharper rates of declining marital satisfaction than those who remained childless. Although there were not significant differences in marital satisfaction for husbands, those with children tended to be less satisfied than those who remained childless.

Although the transition to parenthood is undoubtedly stressful, there are buffers that can protect the relationship of the couple. Shapiro et al. (2000) found such protective buffers to include the husband's fondness and admiration toward his wife, the awareness or cognitive room the husband allocated to the wife and their relationship, and the awareness and cognitive room the wife allocated to the husband. In contrast, factors that damaged the couples' relationships included disappointment in the marriage, negativity toward the spouse, and perceived chaos in the lives of the partners. To assist couples in navigating the rocky path to parenthood, intervention programs should help partners nurture the protective factors of marital friendship, while simultaneously reducing their vulnerabilities (e.g., feeling that changes are out of the couple's control).

Like other major life transitions, the birth of the first child creates a period of disequilibrium and reorganization that requires the integration of new cognitions and behaviors. New parents must mobilize their resources to handle the stress and cope with the demands of parenthood; however, fathers and mothers differ in the manner in which this coping occurs. Levy-Shiff (1999) found that compared to mothers, fathers appraised parenthood as less stressful, less challenging, less self-controllable, and less threatening. Fathers less frequently employed coping strategies to deal with daily hassles and parenting issues, were less involved with their infants, and experienced less parental burnout after a year. The transition to parenthood appears to be less stressful for fathers than mothers, perhaps because fathers are more likely to relate as playmates to their infants than as primary caregivers.

Furthermore, gender differences exist in the coping strategies that are employed to deal with the stress of new parenthood. Levy-Shiff (1999) found that mothers were more likely to seek social support as a coping mechanism, while fathers were more likely to rely on their own problem-solving strategies. It is therefore likely that men experience a sense of personal competency as being more important than social support as a stress buffer, while women may find social support to be more beneficial. For both genders, however, viewing parenthood as a challenge rather than as a stressful situation was associated with more positive adjustment.

To assist with the transition to parenthood, educational programs should be designed to enhance new parents' skills in appraising and coping with daily parenting tasks and in obtaining social support (Folkman, Chesney, McKusick, Ironson, Johnson, & Coates, 1991; Levy-Shiff, 1999). Parenting programs should focus on two processes: a) *cognitive appraisals*, which focus on the meaning of parenthood and parenting tasks, as well as on parents' emotional responses, and b) *coping*, which enables the person to alter or manage the situation, as well as the fit between appraisal and coping. Fathers may find the educational component of working with cognitive appraisals to be more effective, while mothers may achieve more benefits from having social support in a group setting. Both mothers and fathers, however, should benefit from learning about gender-related differences in parenting dynamics and in developing strategies for clear communication to enhance mutual understanding. If parents begin to feel empowered through acquiring coping skills, they are more likely to view parenting as a challenge that can be managed, rather than as a stressful situation beyond their control.

COPING WITH THE DEATH OF A CHILD

Some believe that the death of a child is the most severe loss a person can experience, and a sudden, unexpected death may make the loss even more traumatic. When a *perinatal loss* occurs—that is, the death of a fetus or infant due to miscarriage, stillbirth, Sudden Infant Death Syndrome (SIDS), or other causes—parents may have to endure a particularly painful grieving process. A perinatal death can be especially devastating, because parents often have little or no time to prepare for the loss and may receive inadequate support after it occurs.

SIDS, the leading cause of death in infants from birth to six months, strikes healthy infants without warning. The victims of SIDS simply stop breathing and are unable to be resuscitated. Although the cause of the condition remains mysterious, it frequently occurs in infants who are sleeping on their stomachs. For this reason, a national educational campaign with the slogan "Back to Sleep" was established to remind parents to place infants on their backs in their cribs to reduce the likelihood of SIDS.

Upon experiencing a perinatal death due to SIDS or other causes, parents are propelled into a grief process that can last for years. When such a loss occurs, individuals must accomplish certain tasks of mourning in order for equilibrium to be reestablished and for the process of mourning to be completed (Worden, 1991). Individuals' abilities to get beyond the pain and to eventually achieve a sense of well-being will depend upon how well these tasks are accomplished. The tasks of mourning include:

♦ To accept the reality of the loss
♦ To work through the pain of grief
♦ To adjust to an environment in which the deceased is missing
♦ To emotionally relocate the deceased and move on with life.

If the tasks of mourning are not accomplished, normal grief may become pathologic grief, as is the case for the mother below:

> It's been eating at me for the last three years. . . . It gets worse everyday. It gets harder to deal with it more everyday. And I always felt like, you know, everybody said, "Okay, well just give it some time. Give it some time." And I'm like, "Damn, how much time does it take?" . . . I keep telling myself [that] one of these days I'm hoping that I'm going to wake up and feel better and I'm not going to feel like this. I'm not going to feel like getting up and blowing my brains out one day, and then I have to stop and realize, "I've got kids. I can't do this." (Oliver & Fallat, 1995, p. 304)

In interviews with grieving parents who had lost a child, Oliver and Fallat (1995) found similarities among those who were recovering from normal grief and those whose grief had become pathologic. All of the parents reported that their child's death was the most difficult and devastating experience that had ever confronted them, and because of that, their own fear of death had decreased because they had already faced the worst possible human suffering. They also all feared that their child would be forgotten, but the two groups dealt with this fear differently. The normally grieving parents kept their child's memory alive by having conversations with supportive persons, but the pathologically grieving parents, who lacked social support, kept their grief locked inside themselves. Finally, all of the married parents indicated that the death had put a severe strain on their marriage, with some reporting that they felt cold towards their partners years after the death had occurred. It seemed, however, that the couples either moved through the grief together, or became stuck in the grief together; with some marriages ending in divorce and others becoming stronger.

Although there were similarities, Oliver and Fallat (1995) also found three major differences between the parents who were recovering from normal grief and those whose grief had become pathologic. First, although all the parents were tempted to withdraw from others, the normally grieving parents had a multifaceted support network (e.g., friends, church members, therapists, support groups) that mobilized to care for them. The pathologically grieving parents did not have a support network beyond their immediate family. The second difference was that the recovering parents actively talked, cried, and expressed emotions with the members of their support network, while the other parents avoided the pain and hoped that time would heal their wounds. The latter group often attempted to anesthetize their pain by using alcohol, street drugs, and nonprescription pain relievers. Finally, the parents who were healing from their grief viewed God as being friendly, kind, and benevolent, while the other group saw God as being either distant or against them. The parents who were successfully moving through the grief process believed that their child's death was accidental and that God was with them; while the group experiencing debilitating grief felt that God had taken their child for some unimaginable reason, which caused them great anger.

When an infant dies, a factor that complicates the parental grieving process is that mothers and fathers typically experience incongruent grief—that is, they work through their grief in different ways or at different times (Menke & McClead, 1990). Male and female gender roles may enable women to express their grief more openly through crying, while men may be expected to remain stoic and strong. Fathers may also be expected to fulfill responsibilities requiring stability and strength (e.g., supporting the mother physically and emotionally in her anguish, informing relatives and friends of the death, and making funeral arrangements), which will influence how they grieve and that may actually facilitate their movement through the grieving process (Middleton & Quirk, 1990). Fathers often return to their jobs sooner and immerse themselves in their work, perhaps as a way of coping with the pain (Stierman, 1987).

In addition to gender differences, parents have incongruent bonding with the child—that is, the attachment process differs for fathers and mothers—that impacts their grieving when a perinatal death occurs (Peppers & Knapp, 1980; Wallerstedt & Higgens, 1996). Mothers usually identify with the fetus earlier than fathers and develop an emotional attachment with the child that grows stronger through the pregnancy and birth. On the other hand, fathers are more likely to have an intellectual prenatal attachment to the child, so a perinatal death may be more of an intellectual loss for fathers and an emotional one for mothers. Studies suggest that when a perinatal loss occurs, mothers express higher levels of grief, are more preoccupied with the loss, and grieve longer than fathers (Feeley & Gottlieb, 1988–1989; Klaus & Kennell, 1982; Menke & McClead, 1990). Such incongruent grieving can place tremendous strain on the partners' intimate relationship, because fathers may grow impatient at the mothers' sustained grief, while mothers may view fathers as callous and insensitive for getting over their own pain so quickly.

In spite of the differences in their grieving, both parents are usually deeply affected by the perinatal loss of a child. The pain can be so intense that it has been compared to losing an arm or having an aching pain in a phantom limb (Wallerstedt & Higgens, 1996). When grieving parents desperately need support, however, well-meaning relatives and friends may be less than helpful. As one grieving mother said to this author:

> When I lost my three-month-old daughter to SIDS, people would say things to me like, "Well, at least you hadn't had time to get too attached to her," or "You can try again," or "It was God's will." Their remarks really hurt because I was incredibly attached to her, I didn't want to try again, and I couldn't imagine why God would take her away from me. Other people were so uncomfortable with the idea of an infant death that they avoided the subject entirely and acted like I had never had a child. After a few

months, even my husband treated me as though I should just get over it. I felt alone in my grief.

To assist parents in perinatal grieving, Wallerstedt and Higgens (1996) offer the following suggestions:

- ◆ To foster open communication, show empathy for what each parent is experiencing by reflecting feelings and paraphrasing.
- ◆ Distinguish gender differences and facilitate grieving between the mother and father by making statements such as "Some mothers have said or felt . . ." or "Some fathers have said or felt . . ." or "Tell me how you feel about this, Stan, since Marge has expressed her feelings of . . ."
- ◆ Validate and confirm the existence of the infant by using the baby's name, encouraging the parents to preserve keepsakes and pictures, and listening to each parent talk about his or feelings toward the infant. It may also be helpful to ask open-ended questions such as "How is it for you, as a mother or father, in learning to live without your child?"
- ◆ If possible, recommend to parents that they hold the dead child and have a funeral or memorial service.
- ◆ Discuss gender differences in grieving, share information about the mother's stronger prenatal attachment, the intensity of a mother's grief, and give fathers permission to grieve.
- ◆ Inform parents that they may experience somatic sensations, such as aching arms, the fetus kicking, or the sound of their child's cry. Let them know that these normal feelings may be felt by either parent but tend to occur more often with mothers. Encourage parents to talk about their feelings and sensations to facilitate the grieving process.
- ◆ Advise parents that the father's grief process may be shorter than the mother's but that grieving takes time, so time limits should not be placed on either parent.
- ◆ Involve and educate extended family members and significant friends as much as possible. Provide information about the grieving process, gender differences, normal emotions, and how to include both parents in their care (e.g., asking the father how he is doing, rather than just inquiring about the mother).
- ◆ Discuss how to talk about the death and include siblings in the grieving process. Suggest ways to involve siblings, such as giving them a picture of the infant, allowing them to hold the dead child, encouraging them to attend the funeral, and helping them plant a tree in memory of the deceased child. Recommend age-appropriate books on grief and loss.

To conclude, although the grieving process can be long and arduous, parents can eventually heal from the pain of losing a child. Given time and adequate support, individuals can move on with their lives, and their marriages may even grow stronger. As one grieving father stated, "It is like I lost my right arm, but now I am learning to live as a one-armed man" (as cited in Wallerstedt & Higgens, 1996, p. 390).

EXERCISE 6

"My Life"

Materials: Sheet of paper 18″ × 24″ or larger (note, butcher paper, white wrapping paper, and newsprint are suggestions for paper), crayons or felt markers, writing paper, and a writing instrument.

Directions: Sit in silence and reflect on the course your life has taken from the time you were born until the present. Feel the progress of your life as it unfolded. Allow ten or more events that shaped your life.

- List the 10+ events on one side of the writing paper.
- Use the crayons or markers to draw a line on the large paper that depicts the course of your life. The line can ramble, change direction, cross back on itself, or take any shape you desire.
- Draw a symbol for each event you listed.
- Write a summary of what emerged about the course of your life.
- For each event, note the age you were when it happened.

Reflection Questions

1. What came to mind as you reflected on the course of your life? Did you change, eliminate, or edit anything? If so, record this.
2. Look at your list of events. What period of time is most clustered (e.g., a number of entries for early childhood)? What was happening in your family at that time? Write a brief paragraph that describes the cluster and related family events.
3. Review your cluster again and record the feelings you remember and those aroused as you reflect on the events.
4. Give your "life" picture a title.

Chapter Seven

Early Childhood
Development and Theories

A S CHILDREN LEAVE INFANCY and enter the stage of childhood, a myriad of changes occur. With a developing sense of autonomy and increased cognitive and motor skills, children become able to mentally represent and actively participate in their expanding worlds. With the rapid acquisition of language and increased opportunities for social interaction, children discover others' perspectives and develop the rudiments of empathy and cooperation that serve as a foundation for successful relationships later in life. As they form concepts about themselves and their experiences, children begin to understand gender roles, internalize parental values, and distinguish between right and wrong. In this chapter, we will consider the vast physical, cognitive, social, and personality changes that characterize the stage of childhood, and how counselors can facilitate children's growth and development.

Introduction

Three-year-old Timmy, pretending to be a Mighty Morphin Power Ranger, climbs up on the kitchen counter in a secret mission to capture a big cookie that was stolen by mutants from outer space. As he grabs the cookie (which he had been admonished by his earthling parent not to touch), Timmy accidentally knocks over his mother's favorite vase and watches it tumble off the counter. Retreating back to his home base on the floor, which is now surrounded by tiny, sparkling mountains of shattered glass, Timmy sits happily munching the cookie until he hears maternal footsteps quickly approaching. Fearing that punishment is soon to follow, Timmy closes his eyes so tightly that his face scrunches up. By

blocking out every ray of light and everything he sees, Timmy believes that he
will immediately become invisible and escape the wrath of a horrified Mom.

Childhood, which spans the approximate years of 2 through 5, is often
called the "age of play." Using the vehicle of play, children actively and
imaginatively explore the world to learn about the wonders it holds and
to acquire understanding about themselves. In the magical realm of early
childhood anything is possible, and the child's experiences constitute
ultimate reality for him or her. Whether it's an imaginary friend, a monster in the closet, or being able to fly like the wind, the contents of the
child's imagination are as real to him or her as credit-card bills are to us
(and sometimes just as scary!). In the egocentric mind of a young child,
personal sensations are not recognized as being private to the individual,
but are believed to be felt by all. It is not until later that children learn that
closing one's eyes won't make one invisible and that imaginary friends
won't come to one's rescue. (Yet how often have we as adults wished that
such fantastic feats could really occur?)

As we discuss the early childhood years, try to remember what you
experienced when very young. How did the world look to you at that
time? What was most important? What made you laugh, and what made
you cry?

Physical Growth and Motor Development

A child's appearance and physical capabilities change dramatically in
early childhood. During the years from 2 to 6, individual differences in
growth within our culture are far greater than gender differences. An
average girl increases from approximately 34 to 45 inches in height and
from about 27 to 44 pounds in weight, while an average boy increases
from approximately 34 to 46 inches in height and from about 28 to 46
pounds in weight (Centers for Disease Control and Prevention, 2000).
Both sexes lose their babyish appearance as the thick layers of fat that
afforded protection during infancy gradually disappear, and both experience significant changes in bodily proportions. Head-size decreases in
proportion to the rest of the body from the fetal period through adulthood. While young children's gains in height and weight may not seem
impressive, their *gross motor skills*, or large body movements, appear to
develop at an extraordinary rate. The awkward gait and clumsy gestures
of the toddler quickly turn into running, jumping, hopping, climbing,
throwing, and skipping, as the child explores the world with abundant
enthusiasm. Parents, often wishing that they themselves had the tremendous energy of their preschooler, find it necessary to take extra precautions to protect the safety of both the child and the home. It is critical that
the child be given the freedom to engage in exploratory activities, however, because early sensory experiences lay the foundation for later cog-

nitive development. As children make contact with the world through their senses, they begin to form concepts and develop understanding about themselves and the impact of their actions. For example, Timmy's cookie quest enabled him to learn about gravity, to develop confidence in his climbing ability, and to experience that certain behaviors have consequences (even if he closes his eyes).

Children's *fine motor skills*, or small body movements, also improve during this period, but the changes are less pronounced. Nevertheless, children become increasingly able to build towers with wooden blocks, draw with thick pencils and crayons, and eat with spoons and forks.

Cognitive Development

As children grow physically, they also change mentally, and Piaget observed that a small miracle occurs in children's cognitive development when they approach two years of age. While the cognitive activity of infants in the *sensorimotor stage* centers on the reflexes and responses that were present at birth such as sucking, grasping, rooting, and the orienting response, major changes occur when childhood begins. As children move out of infancy, they no longer rely exclusively on sensory and motor schema such as reflexes or simple repetitive actions, but instead develop *mental schema*, or internal representations of actions. Children begin to use *symbols*—images, words, or actions that stand for something else—to represent their worlds. They can think about people and things that are no longer present, and can plan actions before actually engaging in them. Not only are they beginning to understand simple concepts and develop initial ideas about how the world works, they are also able to use words to describe to others what they are experiencing.

In spite of such tremendous gains, Piaget tended to focus on the logical errors that children make during the *preoperational stage*, which lasts from around ages 2 through 7. An *operation* refers to a mental representation of an action, and Piaget considered this period to be preoperational because of children's inability to grasp a number of logical principles. This stage was further divided into two substages based upon the way children reason, which he designated *preconceptual* (ages 2–4), and *intuitive* (ages 4–7).

With the emergence of symbolic thought, children develop the ability to form concepts about objects and events in their environment. Piaget labeled the first substage *preconceptual*, because the concepts of two- to four-year-old children are not complete like those of adults and are often fraught with logical errors. The second stage was referred to as *intuitive*, because, although four- to seven-year-olds' concepts are better developed, their reasoning is based more on intuition than logic and they frequently are overly dependent on single cues in their experiences (e.g., considering only length but not width when determining if something is bigger).

Although children sometimes arrive at the right answer by chance, they lack a clear, logical rationale. While the intuitive substage is slightly more refined than the preconceptual substage, there is much overlap between the two, and many of the following logical errors appear in both.

EGOCENTRISM

Children in the preoperational stage consider things entirely from their own perspective or own frame of reference. This characteristic, which Piaget (1954) called *egocentrism*, does not imply that young children are selfish, but rather that they are unaware that others' perceptions may differ from their own. It is this characteristic that enabled Timmy to believe that by closing his eyes he would make the world as invisible to his mom as it was to him.

Piaget's classic mountain experiment illustrates the difficulties children have in assuming the perspective of another individual. A child, seated at a table that holds models of three mountains, is asked how a doll would see the mountains from various positions around the table. Piaget found that preoperational children typically respond by selecting the picture that shows the mountain from their own angle, regardless of where the doll is placed. According to Piaget (1954), children can only be successful at this task when they can shift away from using themselves as the exclusive frame of reference.

ANIMISM

In addition to having difficulty assuming the perspective of others, Piaget found that young children often attributed their own human characteristics to inanimate objects. For example, children responded in the affirmative when Piaget (1929) asked questions such as "Are bicycles alive?" and "Can a bench feel anything if someone burns it?" *Animism*, which is akin to egocentricism, is the belief that inanimate objects are alive and have internal states and motivations. Because young children associate life with movement (Elkind, 1991), everything that moves is also thought to be alive, just as they are. Things that do not move are considered to be dead, yet may come alive again if movement resumes. Thus in the magical world of childhood—a leaf tumbling in the autumn breeze may be a playful companion that brings delight, while a shadow dancing on the bedroom wall may be an insidious and terrifying monster.

CLASSIFICATION

Another area of difficulty for children in this stage is that of *classification*. For example, although young children form concepts that allow them to successfully distinguish between members of different species (e.g., they know the difference between dogs and cats), they may not be able to differentiate between individuals within the same species. Piaget discovered this problem one day while taking his young son, Laurent, for a walk in the woods. As they strolled, little Laurent noticed a snail, which he excitedly brought to the attention of his father. After they had progressed further into the woods, Laurent found another snail, but jubilantly proclaimed that the snail was there again! Not realizing that two objects can belong to the same class while still being different objects (or that humans walk faster than snails), the child assumed that the second snail was the first.

After his walk with Laurent, Piaget began studying children's problems with classification by giving them picture cutouts of animals, people, and toys, and asking them to put together those that went together or were similar (Piaget & Inhelder, 1969). While two- and three-year-olds could rarely perform the task at all and simply made pictures with the cutouts, four-year-olds would systematically sort objects into groups, but did so on the basis of idiosyncratic and changing criteria. This *syncretic reasoning* is demonstrated when a child groups together cutouts of a yellow spoon and yellow fork because "you eat with them," but adds a yellow ball to the same group because "it's yellow too."

As he studied children's difficulties with classification, Piaget found that young children lack full understanding of the principle of *class inclusion*. This rule of logic refers to the fact that some classes are completely contained within other classes, just as ice cream cones and pizza are both contained within the larger class of food. In an experiment in which a five-and-a-half-year-old girl was given a set that contained a large number of primroses and a few other mixed flowers, Piaget and Inhelder (1969, p. 108) demonstrate the child's confusion regarding class inclusion:

> *Piaget:* "If I make a bouquet of all the primroses and you make one of all the flowers, which will be bigger?"
>
> *Child:* "Yours."
>
> *Piaget:* "If I gather all the primroses in a meadow, will any flowers remain?"
>
> *Child:* "Yes."

Although the child realized that the larger class of flowers contains more than primroses, she did not yet grasp that all primroses are a subset that is included within this larger class. Piaget and Inhelder (1969) found that although children can readily compare subsets with each other, they usually cannot compare one subset with the whole group until they are approximately seven years of age.

Why do children have so much trouble with class inclusion and classification? Piaget assumed that such difficulties were caused by children's inability to *decenter* their thinking, that is, to consider more than one dimension at a time. In the example above, Piaget's first question required the child to consider not only whether there are more primroses than other flowers, but also what falls under the broader rubric of flowers in general. His second question was easier, for it involved thinking only of what would be left if the primroses were gone.

When young children observe two events happening at about the same time, they are likely to assume that one causes the other. An example of such *transductive reasoning*, or *phenomenalistic causality*, was provided one afternoon when Piaget's daughter Lucienne, who was late in taking her daily nap, proclaimed, "I haven't had my nap so it isn't afternoon." Lucienne, assuming that her nap caused the afternoon, was reasoning from one particular event to another particular event, although the two events bore no causal connection to each other and were simply related in time.

LeFrancois (1993) elucidates the fallacy of transductive logic by comparing it with two valid types of logical reasoning. In *deductive reasoning*, one goes from a general premise to arrive at a particular conclusion (e.g., All dogs are mammals; Barky is a dog; therefore Barky is a mammal). *Inductive reasoning*, on the other hand, involves observing a number of particular instances to establish a general rule (e.g., after noticing that every person I watch for a long-enough time eventually has to eat, I might conclude that all humans have this need). *Transductive reasoning*, however, lacks the validity of the previous two logical processes because it involves making inferences from one unrelated particular to another. An example of transductive reasoning would be:

A swims; *B* swims; therefore *A* is *B*.

Although the statement may at first seem intuitively valid, and may even make some strange sense (e.g., if *A* is a fish and *B* is one too, then both may be swimming fish), consider how problematic it becomes if *A* is my husband and *B* is my dog. Yet it is this type of fallacious reasoning that allows young children to boldly claim that a long-haired man is a woman, or a cat is a squirrel.

CONSERVATION

Toward the end of the sensorimotor stage, children grasp the concept of object permanence and realize that objects continue to exist even when out of view. Objects, however, possess other qualities that also remain constant, or are *conserved*, that young children do not yet understand. Piaget used the term *conservation* to refer to the concept that the quantitative aspects of objects, such as weight or number, do not change simply because the objects change in appearance. In his classic beaker experiment, Piaget showed a child two tall beakers of equal size filled with a colored liquid. When asked if the beakers contained the same amount of liquid or if one had more, the child confirmed that they had the same amount. Piaget then poured the liquid from one of the tall beakers into a short, wide beaker and asked the child, "Is there more water in the wide glass than in the tall glass, or less, or just as much?" After observing Piaget pouring the liquid and seeing that none was lost in the transition, the child still responded that the tall beaker had more. The child's answer was thus based upon how the liquid appeared and indicated a lack of understanding regarding the constancy of the liquid's quantity.

SERIATION

Children in the preoperational stage also have difficulties with *seriation*, which refers to the ability to arrange objects according to some quantified dimension such as length or weight. For example, when young children are presented with six sticks of varying lengths, they can easily pick out the shortest and longest ones. They find the task of placing the sticks in order, from shortest to longest, to be much more problematic, however, because of their failure to grasp the concept of seriation.

PSYCHOSOCIAL THEORY

We often hear frustrated parents talk about "the terrible twos" when their young children seem to know only one word, and that word is "NO!" Why do preschoolers become so obstinate and insist on doing everything themselves, rather than letting more competent adults perform the tasks for them? Why should a harried mom let little Francesco make her late for work as he clumsily attempts to put on his boots and button his coat without any help?

Erikson's psychosocial theory elucidates why young children go through such a radical transformation of will as they move out of infancy. As we discussed in the previous chapter, infants begin life faced with the issue of determining whether or not the world is a safe place. If their needs are met satisfactorily and they are made to feel secure as they explore their new environments, they will develop a sense of trust. They then must achieve a sense of autonomy by developing control of their bodies and by learning that their intentions can be carried out. If they are not granted freedom or approval as they attempt to become autonomous, they will suffer shame and self-doubt, which will impair their ability to successfully resolve subsequent issues (Erikson, 1963).

If children do receive parental support as they demonstrate more autonomous behavior, they will move into Erikson's third stage, *initiative versus guilt*, which lasts from around ages 2 or 3 through 6. Children's development of initiative can be considered an extension of their struggle for autonomy, because they are attempting not only to do things, but also to understand how things work and to change their environments to meet their needs. Just as toddlers established autonomy by gaining bodily control via dressing and feeding themselves, using the toilet, and moving around, preschoolers establish initiative by asking questions and creatively engaging in activities to procure desired results. Thus parents can expect to answer an endless series of "why?" questions, and to discover that their young children are applying their newly acquired knowledge in a variety of unusual ways, such as when Keisha uses Mommy's bright-pink nail polish to paint pretty flowers on her new white suit.

It is easy to see how children's developing sense of initiative, coupled with incomplete conceptual understanding, can lead to mishaps, as in the example above. While, in Keisha's mind, the suit needed some shiny pink flowers to be "more pretty," Mommy probably preferred it in its un-adorned state and may be less than pleased with the child's beautification efforts. Although parents may wish their children had a bit less initiative at such times, it is important to avoid instilling excessive guilt when applying discipline. If Keisha is recognized and praised for her efforts, while at the same time taught that white suits need to stay white, she will retain her sense of mastery and competence. If, instead, she is criticized and blamed, she may grow up to be passive and dependent. Several stud-ies suggest that children who are not afforded opportunities to engage in independent activities fail to learn competence (White & Watts, 1973) and do not develop the confidence necessary to actively pursue learning. While young children require close supervision and much guidance as they show initiative, they also need freedom and approval from watchful guardians. The father who lets his four-year-old son put groceries into the shopping cart, while ensuring that the bottom orange is not taken from the display, is cultivating a sense of self-efficacy that will contribute to the child's success in later life. On the other hand, parents who are overly protective or critical may squelch their children's initiative and make them fearful to venture forth as adults.

Although Erikson warned of the psychological danger of producing children who are overwhelmed by guilt, it is equally dangerous to raise children without any sense of ethical accountability. Research suggests that *guilt*—defined by Izard (1977) as an emotion accompanying a sense of being responsible for an unacceptable thought, fantasy, or action—serves an adaptive function. Because guilt is usually accompanied by remorse and a desire to rectify the imagined wrong, it contributes to social harmony. Without guilt, aggression could go unchecked and anti-social acts could be viewed as expedient means to achieve personal gain. Studies show that normal levels of guilt are associated with high levels of empathy and prosocial behavior (Tangney, 1991). Yet the daily news abounds with such a sordid assortment of bombings, murders, rapes, and other atrocities that one wonders if the concept of guilt has become an anachronism in contemporary life.

Life Transitions

PLAY IN CHILDHOOD

Whether building forts from scattered twigs, taking tea with glitter-ing genies, or being chased by scary monsters, children engage in play with at least as much dedication and zeal as adults feel for work—and perhaps even more! In many ways, play *is* the "work" of children, for it serves a number of important purposes in their cognitive and social development and is their primary medium of expression. Of course, children don't engage in play to achieve critical developmental milestones—they do it simply because it is fun. Perhaps we should take lessons from two-year-olds.

TYPES OF PLAY

While all preschoolers spend long hours playing, not all of their play is the same. Play activities fall into distinct categories that are age-related and serve specific functions. By observing children at play, we can learn much about their developing cognitive abilities.

Sensorimotor or Practice Play. Infants and toddlers spend much of their play time performing repetitive actions focusing on their own bodies that are conducted for no apparent purpose other than experiencing movement and sensation. This type of play offers children opportunities to learn about the physical world and to explore the effects of their actions. Typical examples of sensorimotor play include shaking rattles, splashing water, putting objects in their mouths, running wildly, and jumping on beds that are bouncy.

As you will recall from chapter 4, Piaget (1962) believed that every act of intelligence was characterized by an equilibrium between the two opposing tendencies of assimilation and accommodation. In assimilation, we incorporate events, objects, or situations into our existing mental structures or ways of thinking; while in accommodation, we change our existing mental schemas to incorporate this new information from the external environment. While intelligence requires both assimilation and accommodation—namely, we must integrate new information with our prior understanding—Piaget considered play to be characterized primarily by assimilation. In other words, play involves assimilating objects and situations from the external world into our preexisting schemas to serve the needs of our egos. Piaget assumed that the primary benefit children derive from practice play is the pleasure that comes from mastering motor activities by exercising their existing mental structures.

Constructive Play. At around two years of age, sensorimotor play evolves into *constructive play* that involves using objects to create or build things. As children's cognitive schemas develop, they begin to move from performing purposeless repetitive actions to goal-directed behaviors. Thus children may no longer simply pound clay for the physical sensation of doing so, but instead attempt to form it into some desired shape. While sensorimotor play does not disappear, children spend less time involved in it and often combine elements of it with constructive endeavors such as building block towers, then knocking them down and rebuilding them.

Pretend Play. As children become able to form mental representations, they begin to engage in an important new type of activity—that of *pretend play* or *imaginative play* (Goldstein, 1994). Pretend play is defined as "a subcategory of play in which actions, objects, persons, places, or other aspects of the here and now are transformed or treated nonliterally" (Haight & Miller, 1993, p. 20). By pretending that objects and other people (as well as themselves) are other than what they are in reality, children exercise their developing cognitive abilities and cultivate creativity. Imaginative play takes many forms, which include pretending that inanimate objects are alive (e.g., Teddy Bear is hungry), enacting imaginary scripts (e.g., playing house), constructing fantasy objects (e.g., building a castle), giving new attributes to items (e.g., this big block is a bed), and having imaginary companions.

Pretend play usually emerges at around twelve months and reaches its peak during the preschool years, gradually being replaced by other forms of play as children reach school age. Piaget (1962) found pretend play to be infrequent and brief during the second year of life, but to increase in frequency during the next three or four years. One longitudinal study, in which nine children were observed daily between the hours of 8 A.M. and 5 P.M., confirmed Piaget's results and showed significant changes in the amount of time spent in pretend play as the children aged. At twelve months, approximately half the children engaged in pretend play, but only very briefly—on average 1.3 minutes each day. At age 2, the children spent an average of half an hour in pretend play each day, while at age 3, they spent more than an hour, and at age 4, approximately two hours. Both the number of episodes and the length of each episode of pretend play increased steadily during these years (Haight & Miller, 1993). Other studies have shown that all children except those who are autistic engage in some form of pretend play by the beginning of their third year (Goldstein, 1994).

Why do young children devote so much time to this interesting pursuit? Although there are differing theories regarding the contributions of pretend play, there is general agreement that it is essential to the developmental process. Extensive research shows that it impacts the child's cognitive, social, and emotional development.

According to Piaget (1962), pretend play enables children to go beyond simply deriving pleasure from manipulating objects in the physical world. By forming mental representations, they can symbolically assimilate the external world to the ego and transform it in any way desired. Thus pretend play provides opportunities to derive satisfaction from fantasy conflict resolution and wish fulfillment. It also provides practice in forming mental representations, which contributes to children's cognitive development. Piaget believed that this type of play declines as children become increasingly able to subordinate the ego to reality, or to accommodate.

While Piaget primarily emphasized the cognitive contributions of pretend play, Vygotsky held a more integrated view that stressed its social aspects. He believed that pretend play enables children to learn about different roles (e.g., Mommy, Daddy, police officer, teacher), and the rules of behavior associated with each role. As children create imaginary situations and become various characters in their play, they enact the behaviors that go with the role. If they choose inappropriate behaviors that are inconsistent with role expectations, other children quickly alert them to their errors (e.g., "Daddies don't wear dresses—mommies do!" or "When you're in school you have to raise your hand before you talk"). Although it may seem that imaginative play is completely spontaneous and free-wheeling, Vygotsky maintained that children create definite implicit rules associated with each role, thus learning about what is expected in social interactions. Although the rules may not be apparent to us as we observe children's make-believe scenes, they are quite evident and important to the children who are playing.

In addition to helping children gain awareness of rules and roles, Vygotsky credited pretend play with creating a *zone of proximal development* that facilitates learning. Regarding this point, Vygotsky (1978) wrote:

> Play also creates the zone of proximal development of the child. In play the child is always behaving beyond his age, above his everyday behavior; in play he is, as it were, a head above himself. Play contains in a concentrated form, as in the focus of a magnifying glass, all developmental tendencies; it is as if the child tries to jump above his usual level. The relationship of play to development should be compared to the relationship between instruction and development. . . . Play is a source of development and creates the zone of proximal development. (p. 74)

Because children often enact behaviors in play scenes that they have not yet mastered in real life, Vygotsky believed that by playing they are actually learning how to perform those actions successfully—that play is instructional. For example, consider the case of Alfonzo, who always cries at bedtime because he is afraid of the dark. In pretend play, he may assume the part of a child who is not afraid to go to bed and who has no trouble falling asleep, or he may pretend to be afraid but then talk himself out of his fears. In either case, he accomplishes a task that he has yet to achieve in reality. The play scene, which is much less threatening than real life, thus provides just enough challenge and support to prepare him for future action and give him confidence for achieving his goal.

Pretend play also enables children to separate thought from actions and objects, thus paving the way for abstract thinking. Regarding the separation of thoughts from objects, Vygotsky (1978) wrote: "The child sees one thing, but acts differently in relation to what he sees. Thus a condition is reached in which the child begins to act independently of what he sees" (p. 97). By pretending that things are other than what they are in reality, children learn the distinction between ideas and the tangible items or behaviors for which they stand. By substituting the idea of something for the object itself (e.g., "Let's pretend this stick is a magic wand"), children learn that the meaning of "magic wand" can exist independently of the reality of "stick." As they pretend, children acquire practice in mentally manipulating ideas, which frees them from the constraints of having to deal exclusively with external objects. The mental flexibility that is gained from this practice eventually culminates in the development of abstract thinking, which involves the manipulation of ideas without any reliance on concrete objects (Berk, 1994).

Finally, Vygotsky believed that pretend play enhances children's ability to regulate their own behavior by requiring them to conform to the rules specific to a given scenario (Bodrova & Leong, 1996). For example, when Alicia pretends to be the family dog, she must bark when someone comes to the door, but then stop upon Daddy's command. Although she may wish to continue barking, she must regulate her behavior in accordance with the rules of the role or face the reprimands of the other children. By barking and stopping at will, Alicia practices deliberate behavior and learns the fundamentals of self-control. (Wouldn't it be lovely if all of us had learned to control our barking in early childhood?)

Because of its critical role in children's cognitive and social development, much research has been conducted to investigate how pretend play evolves and the various factors that influence it. Some observational studies suggest that imaginative play, which is primarily social in nature (Haight & Miller, 1993), is facilitated and occurs earlier when caregivers talk to and laugh with their children while carrying out pretend games themselves (Fein, 1987). Other research suggests that caregivers can facilitate the development of children's imaginative play by telling and reading stories to them, initiating games of make-believe, and making space and toys available for their use (Garvey, 1990; Goldstein, 1994; Singer & Singer, 1990). In addition, studies show that it is essential for children to have key persons in their lives who create an encouraging climate and inspire them to play by delighting in their attempts (Singer & Singer, 1990). Because mothers are the primary play partners for children aged 1 through 3 (Haight & Miller, 1993), it can be especially beneficial to help them learn how to cultivate pretending in their children.

Games with Rules. As children begin elementary school, pretend play decreases and is replaced by more formal play involving games with rules. Although children sometimes develop rules as they engage in pretend play (e.g., "you be the mommy and I'll be the daddy"), the rules tend to arise spontaneously and to be specific to the immediate situation. During the late preschool years, the focus shifts to games with rules that endure over time such as hopscotch, softball, marbles, checkers, and jump rope.

Piaget (1962) considered children's emerging interest in games with rules to be significant, because it marks their transition into socialized play. Because rules involve the interaction of two or more individuals, and because rules serve to regulate the social group, such play signifies children's entry into the social order. When playing games with rules, children achieve a balance between assimilation, which characterizes all play, and social life. As they progress beyond the egocentricity of the pre-operational stage and enter into concrete operational thought, children use external rules to regulate and maintain social interactions, rather than the inner rules that had been employed previously in pretend play. To successfully play games with rules, children must not only assimilate their understanding of the game into preexisting mental structures, but also accommodate their mental schemas in order to abide by the rules and play the game more effectively. By doing so, they strike a balance between assimilation and accommodation, the two cognitive processes that Piaget considered critical to intellectual development. Thus play helps children move from the purely individual process of assimilation, that characterizes practice and pretend play, into the more balanced incorporation of both assimilation and accommodation that characterizes the collective symbolism of games with rules.

SOCIAL LEVELS OF PLAY

In addition to the typology just presented, play can be categorized into levels depending on how much social interaction it involves. Many years ago, Parten (1932) studied preschool children (aged 2 to 5) and presented a stage model showing how social interactions develop sequentially in play. The stages, which are based upon the type and amount of social interaction involved, form a developmental sequence, but also include much overlap between levels.

Unoccupied Play. At this level, the child is simply watching other children play. He or she wanders around and observes what others are doing, but does not engage in their play except very briefly. For example, a child sees children playing in the sand tray and picks up a toy, puts it down, meanders over to check out what some other children are painting, and then departs to the back of the room to watch several children playing with puppets.

Solitary Play. At this level, as the name implies, the child plays alone and has little awareness of other children who may be playing nearby. For example, a child sits alone and makes no attempt to involve other children as she places toys in a doll house.

Onlooker Play. Here, children actively observe others play, but do not become directly engaged in the activity themselves. This differs from unoccupied play in that children now exhibit a sustained interest in what others are doing, often making comments or asking questions about what is occurring. For example, a child, while watching another child paint, says, "You need to put a smiley face on that sun."

Parallel Play. At this level children play side by side, but without any interaction. Although they may be using similar toys, they rarely speak to one another, share their toys, or show any awareness of what the others are doing. They are cognizant of the others' presence, however, and sometimes watch, or stop playing if the others leave. For example, a child plays with a toy truck and seems to pay no attention to the children beside him who are playing with cars and boats, other than glancing at them occasionally to make sure they are still there.

Associative Play. At this point, children begin to interact while playing, but do so without shared rules or common goals. They sometimes play separately, yet talk to each other while doing so. At other times they engage in a shared activity, but without much organization. For example, several children make a group drawing; but because there is no planning or coordination regarding what should be in it, the picture has four suns and fish swimming around the moon.

Cooperative Play. Here, children deliberately play together and coordinate their actions to achieve common goals. At this highest level of social play, children cooperatively share their toys and converse about what they are trying to accomplish, often assigning roles and developing rules to govern their behavior. Regardless of whether children are engaging in pretend situations or are playing more formal games with rules, cooperative play involves joint effort. For example, four children decide to play house and, after much discussion, finally agree who will play mommy, daddy, brother, and sister and what each family member is like.

Because cooperative pretend play requires that children have the cognitive capacity to understand that nonliteral meaning can be shared (e.g., we can both pretend that this tree is a horse) and an awareness of social roles, it usually does not occur until about age 3 (Howes, Phillips, & Whitebook, 1992). Between the years of three and six, however, when pretend play reaches its peak, children can collaboratively construct elaborate fictitious scenarios that involve transformed props, sustained imaginary characters, and continuing play themes (McGurk, 1992).

Although Parten's model is useful for conceptualizing the development of social play, it should be noted that subsequent research has shown that children do not always follow the developmental sequence exactly as proposed. While the model assumes that unoccupied, onlooker, and solitary play decline with age, these are still the most frequent forms of activity for 3- to 4-year-olds and amount to as much as a third of the free play time of kindergartners (Berk, 1993).

As we watch children, it is often easy to spot clear differences in the *way* that they play, and these variations seem to be based upon whether we are observing males or females. In the next section, we will examine the issue of gender-role development in early childhood and consider what it means to say, "Girls will be girls and boys will be boys." Are there real differences between the sexes? And if so, how did they arise?

Gender Roles in Childhood

While most cultures have differing expectations for males and females, the expectations are not universal from one society to the next and may depend upon which gender has the greater potential to earn money and achieve power. Yet in each culture, children must at least partially conform to the societal expectations for their respective genders, or risk social ostracism. In order to do so, they must develop an understanding of *gender roles*—the behaviors and personality characteristics that are considered to be masculine or feminine (Bem, 1989; Maccoby, 1988). The process by which children learn appropriate gender behaviors is referred to as *gender typing*. How do children develop an understanding of gender? Are gender roles biologically based, socially conditioned, or a combination of both?

SEX DIFFERENCES IN PLAY

While infants are not concerned with whether their rattles are pink or blue, it does not take long before boys and girls choose different types of toys. Children in the United States show distinct preferences for gender-specific toys at around 2 years of age, with these differences emerging sometimes as early as 18 months (Caldera, Huston, & O'Brien, 1989; Fein, Johnson, Kosson, Stork, & Wasserman, 1985; Weintraub et al., 1984). Not only toys, but also games, tools, household goods, articles of clothing, and even colors become associated with one gender or the other in the minds of preschoolers (Huston, 1983; Picariello, Greenberg, & Pillemer, 1990). When given choices of playthings, girls tend to select dolls and household items, while boys more often choose trucks and soldiers. Although girls sometimes pick masculine toys, they do so with less frequency than boys (Almqvist, 1989; Eisenberg, Wolchik, Hernandez, & Pasternak, 1985). Moreover, gender differences in toy selection and play do not diminish but rather become more pronounced as children age (Moller, Hymel, & Rubin, 1992), with similar patterns being reported in other cultures such as in Europe and Asia (Suito & Reifel, 1992; Wegener-Spohring, 1989).

Boys and girls not only choose different types of toys, they also exhibit differences in the way they play. Boys engage in more noisy, rough-and-tumble outside play such as running, jumping, wrestling, and fighting, and enact fantasy games in which they are superheros, adventurers, spacemen, and television characters. Girls tend to participate in quieter, more nurturant activities indoors in which they draw, read, play with dolls, dress up in adult clothing, and enact family roles such as playing house (Eisenberg, Murray, & Hite, 1982; Garvey, 1990; Goldstein, 1994). By age 5, both boys and girls have developed *gender-role stereotypes*, or attitudes regarding what constitutes gender-appropriate play (Carvalho,

Smith, Hunter, & Costabile, 1990). Yet Singer and Singer (1990) suggest that such gender differences may be decreasing. Girls are

> moving closer to boys in their identification with heroic figures, adventur-
> ous achievement, and pretend aggression than previous data claimed. This
> appears to reflect changes in television action programs, where more female
> heroines now appear, as well as the increased willingness of parents to tol-
> erate adventure themes in girls' play. . . . We do not see a comparable trend
> among boys—that is, a move toward playing female games and using
> traditionally female toys. (p. 80)

Although gender roles in children's play are beginning to show some convergence, there are still marked distinctions. Let us now consider the factors that may cause such gender-typed behaviors and attitudes to arise.

COGNITIVE DEVELOPMENTAL THEORY OF GENDER

Kohlberg (1966) proposed that gender identity develops in stages, with the stages reflecting children's growing understanding of the meaning of gender. The developmental sequence, which occurs in early childhood, consists of the fundamental gender concepts that must be grasped, including gender labels, gender stability, and gender constancy.

Gender Labels. During infancy, children become aware that some people are designated as male, while others are female. They learn which label applies to them by imitating the comments of their caregivers such as "Good boy" or "Good girl."

Gender Stability. By around age 3, children correctly label others as being male or female and begin to look for gender differences in males and females. They also understand that gender remains permanent over time. Until this concept is grasped, a child may ask her father whether he was a boy or girl when he was little.

Gender Constancy. Between the ages of 4 and 7, children realize that gender has a genital basis and does not change with superficial changes in appearance or behavior. Thus if a man has hair down to his waist and wears a tunic, he is still a man. At this point, children have developed gender identities and begin to conform to gender-role expectations.

Kohlberg assumed that after developing an understanding of gender constancy, children imitate the gender-appropriate behaviors that they have observed in others of their sex. By conforming to the behavioral norms that they believe to exist for males or females, they achieve a sense of cognitive consistency.

SOCIAL LEARNING THEORY OF GENDER

While Kohlberg emphasized the cognitive aspects of gender development, others have placed primary importance on the vast influence of parents, peers, and the media in shaping children's gender identities.

Social learning theory maintains the view that gender-typing occurs as a function of socialization.

Family Influences. From the time children are born (and probably before), parents hold differing expectations for sons and daughters and promote gender-typic behavior in their children. While boys are encouraged to engage in activities such as playing with trucks or shoveling snow, girls are reinforced for playing with dolls and helping prepare meals (Lytton & Romney, 1991). Boys generally receive a more positive parental response than girls for active, assertive behaviors such as demanding attention or taking others' toys (Fagot & Hagan, 1991). On the other hand, girls are more likely to have parents discuss emotions with them, direct their play, and provide help, thereby eliciting emotional sensitivity and dependency (Dunn, Bretherton, & Munn, 1987; Lytton & Romney, 1991). Parents tend to purchase different types of toys for sons and daughters—especially parents with traditional gender-role attitudes (Eckerman & Stein, 1990; O'Brien & Huston, 1985). Parents also tend to express approval when children select toys that they consider appropriate to their gender (Garvey, 1991).

Peer Influences. Although segregation by sex increases during the elementary school years, children begin to prefer the company of same-sexed peers as early as age 3 or 4 (Maccoby, 1988, 1990). Indeed, age-related sex segregation may be a universal phenomenon (Whiting & Edwards, 1988). Cross-cultural research shows that children between the ages of 4 and 10 associate mainly with same-sexed peers in not only the United States, but also India, Okinawa, Mexico, Kenya, and the Philippines. Thus most children are surrounded by same-sex peers who model and reinforce gender-appropriate behavior.

Maccoby (1990) found that 3- and 4-year-old boys and girls differ greatly in their manner of exerting social influence. Boys are more likely to try to get their way by using physical force, threatening, or commanding (e.g., "Give me that toy!"); girls are more prone to ask politely or make requests. Interestingly, although girls respond positively to the methods of influence used by either sex, boys tend to comply best when aggressively confronted by other boys. When girls try to have their wishes met by verbal persuasion, they are usually ignored by boys. For this reason, girls may find play with same-sexed companions to be more rewarding, and simply decide to avoid the possibility of having negative encounters with boys.

Peers also exert influence regarding which toys are socially acceptable. Four- and 5-year-old children identified playthings as being either boys' toys or girls' toys based upon which sex had been observed using them (Shell & Eisenberg, 1990), and children approached same-sexed peers who played with what were considered to be gender-appropriate toys (Eisenberg, Tryon, & Cameron, 1984; Moller, Hymel, & Rubin, 1992). Apparently children can make such distinctions quite early and tend to avoid toys associated with the other sex (Ruble, Balaban, & Cooper, 1981). Thus children may select gender-typed toys to gain peer approval and to ensure that same-sexed companions will continue to play with them (Shell & Eisenberg, 1990).

Media Influences. In addition to being influenced by peers and parents, children receive messages about gender from the media. Television places males and females in extremely stereotypic roles, with men being portrayed as more active, independent, aggressive, and adept at problem-solving, while women are frequently shown as sex objects and as being more emotional, passive, and submissive (Huston & Alvarez, 1990). Even elementary school textbooks have been found to be guilty of gender stereotyping: an examination of reading books used in 1972 and 1989 revealed a preponderance of males and females shown in stereotypic gender roles (Purcell & Stewart, 1990).

BIOLOGICAL THEORY OF GENDER

Erikson (1977) proposed that gender differences in play arise from the anatomical differences between the sexes. While boys build vertical structures with active themes, girls construct enclosures with passive themes, thus reflecting the differences between male and female genitalia. Although few would support this theory, some believe that there are valid reasons to assert that gender has biological determinants.

Some of the most compelling support for the biological stance comes from research showing the effects of hormones on development. Children of both sexes who were exposed prenatally to the synthetic female hormone, progesterone, exhibited less rough-and-tumble play (Meyer-Bahlburg, Feldman, Cohen, & Ehrhardt, 1988). In addition, children who experienced high levels of prenatal and early postnatal exposure to the male hormone, androgen, showed a greater preference for male gender-typed toys between the ages of 3 and 8 (Berenbaum & Hines, 1992).

Finally, it has been suggested that because of their higher activity levels, boys prefer masculine toys that provide opportunities for more active play (Eaton & Enns, 1986). Similarly, Maccoby (1990) suggests that hormonal differences may account for children's preferences for same-sexed playmates. Just as boys are biologically predisposed to engage in rough and noisy play, girls are inclined to participate in quiet and gentle activity—so both sexes seek out compatible companions. Additional support for this view can be found in animal research, which shows that same-sex peer groups are characteristic of the young in many primate species (Nakamichi, 1989).

GENDER SCHEMA THEORY

Gender schema theory, which combines elements of both cognitive developmental and social learning theory, is a relatively new approach to understanding the formation of gender identity. It assumes that gender identity develops as a result of the interaction between children's cognitions and environmental influences, with children forming mental schema that serve as guiding forces in the collection of gender information (Bem, 1984; Martin & Halverson, 1981, 1983; Ruble, 1987). Regarding these schema, Martin & Halverson (1983) write: "The basic idea [is] that stereotypes are 'schemas,' or naive theories that are relevant to the self, and function to organize and structure experience by telling the perceiver the kinds of information to look for in the environment and how to interpret such information" (p. 563). By about age 2 or 3, children are aware of some basic differences between males and females, usually distinguish between the two, and know which gender label applies to them. This primitive understanding enables children to form gender schemas for organizing their experiences into categories of maleness and femaleness that are used to interpret their world. Because their thinking is still dichotomous, however, these categories are thought of in "either-or" terms, resulting in gender schemas that are quite rigid or stereotypic. Thus it is not uncommon for young children to assume that "trucks are for boys" or "girls can't be doctors." Because they apply these schemas to themselves, children develop gender-typed behavior—choosing same-sexed playmates and what they consider to be gender-appropriate toys (Martin, Wood, & Little, 1990).

While this approach may sound much like Kolhberg's theory, it differs in one major respect. While Kohlberg assumed that children must understand gender constancy before forming gender schemas, this theory holds that the converse is true (Bee, 1992). Gender schema theory maintains that gender schemas are formed much earlier than Kohlberg envisioned and that they provide the means by which children organize both their perceptions and behavior (Martin & Halverson, 1983). This explains why young children's conception of gender tends to be so stereotypic: due to their limited understanding, they are simply applying a rule too rigidly (as they frequently do in all areas of cognition). By attempting to assimilate all information into their existing schemas (e.g., distinct categories of "male" and "female" that have no overlap), they develop rigid views on masculinity and femininity. Later, they will learn to accommodate and change their schemas to fit new information and will realize that although many doctors are men, women can be doctors too.

CULTIVATING ANDROGYNY IN CHILDREN

Much research suggests that adherence to rigid gender stereotypes limits emotional and intellectual development in both sexes (Bem, 1984). Thus although it is quite normal for young children to develop stereotypic views on gender, many adults would prefer that they form schemas that allow for more role flexibility and less rigidity. They would ultimately like to help children become *androgynous*—that is, to develop a blend of both masculine and feminine personality characteristics (Bem,

1984). Both boys and girls would thereby possess traditionally masculine traits (e.g., ambition, assertion, and self-reliance) as well as traditionally feminine traits (e.g., sensitivity, gentleness, and devotion to others).

How can adults help children become more androgynous? Berk (1993) suggests a number of ways that adults can assist children to develop schemas that will be free of gender stereotypes. First, adults can model androgynous behavior for children. For example, mothers and fathers can take turns cooking, mowing the lawn, driving the car, and changing diapers. Furthermore, caregivers can ensure that children have access to both masculine and feminine toys such as dolls, trucks, and trains as well as pink and blue clothing. In addition, adults can teach children that sex is determined solely by anatomy, rather than by behavior. Because young children have often not fully grasped this concept, they may feel that they must demonstrate stereotypic behavior in order to continue being a boy or girl. Finally, as children become aware of gender stereotypes within our society, adults can bring their attention to exceptions. For example, it is helpful to allow children to meet men and women who have nontraditional careers such as male nurses and female pilots, while at the same time pointing out that interests and skills, rather than gender, determine a person's occupation. As a career-awareness activity in their guidance program, elementary school counselors can invite adults from the community to talk to children about their nontraditional careers.

Issues in Early Childhood

Because there is much overlap between early and middle childhood, we will address the family of origin, situational, and existential issues that children face in the following chapter. Because most counselors will not begin working directly with children until they are of school age, we will discuss the concerns of both preschoolers and elementary-school-age children in chapter 8 and present counseling applications for both groups in chapter 9.

EXERCISE 7

Overview of My Life

Objective: To get a quick overview of your unfolding life.

Materials: You will need a large sheet of newsprint 24" × 36", felt markers, crayons or colored pencils, a sheet of writing paper, and a writing instrument.

Procedure: Sit in front of a desk or table where you can draw and write. Close your eyes and try to imagine your life from the very earliest moment to the present. Visualize the path or course your life has taken with its crossroads, dead ends, and meandering routes. As you imagine your life, become aware of those points where events, situations, and people influenced its course. Imagine where changes occurred, where alternatives were available, and where outside events were influential but not controllable. When you are ready, open your eyes and draw the course of your life, placing symbols or other identifiers at the influential points.

Write four column headings at the top of the page: *Early Childhood, Childhood, Adolescence,* and *Early Adulthood.* If you are well into adulthood, make five column headings, with one for *Middle Adulthood.* Look at your life-line and the identifiers. Place each identifier under the appropriate heading. If others occur to you at this time, list those. Also list the people who were important in your life during the particular period.

Chapter Eight

Middle Childhood
Development and Theories

F OR MOST CHILDREN, the years of middle childhood are an active time of making new friends, acquiring personal competencies, and moving into a world that includes not only family, but also school and peers. In this chapter we will delve into the intriguing realm of middle childhood and examine the numerous transitions that occur as children grow and change on their journey toward adolescence.

Life Transitions

PHYSICAL AND MOTOR DEVELOPMENT

Middle childhood spans the approximate years from ages 6 to 11 and ends when adolescence—which commences with puberty—begins. Because puberty is occurring earlier in Western society than in the past, the last year of middle childhood may be included in early adolescence. During the middle childhood years, physical growth slows and is much less rapid than during the earlier stages. Because physical growth is occurring at a slower rate, children require fewer calories and therefore are at risk of obesity if they consume too many high-caloric foods and fail to get adequate exercise. With the contemporary trend of children eating large amounts of junk food and spending long hours playing video games, obesity is becoming a significant problem in the United States.

COGNITIVE DEVELOPMENT

At the end of early childhood, most children enter Piaget's period of concrete operations, which begins at age 6 or 7 and lasts until approximately age 11. During this stage, children develop what Piaget referred to as *logical operations*—logical thought processes (operations) that can be used to solve concrete problems. Children's thinking is no longer dominated by perception as in the preoperational period, but is now logical. The errors that children made in the conservation experiments due to the appearances of objects (e.g., water in a tall, narrow beaker reaches a higher level and looks like more than the same amount in a short, wide beaker), begin to be replaced by correct answers based upon logic. Children's thinking becomes *decentered*—that is, they are able to think about more than one dimension or characteristic at a time (e.g., one beaker may be taller, but the other is wider). They also understand *reversibility* and realize that operations can be reversed so that they will again be as they were initially (e.g., the water can be poured back into the short, wide beaker). Children can now correctly solve problems related to classification and seriation, which they were unable to do in the previous period. Concrete operational thought loses the egocentricity of the preoperational period, and children realize that others do not necessarily share the same perceptions of the world as themselves, so they will check out their views to see if others agree.

Although children make many gains in cognitive abilities during this period, they still have not reached the peak of their logical abilities because their thought is tied to concrete (real, observable) objects and events. They typically cannot solve problems that are hypothetical or purely verbal, but must instead have concrete examples to consider and manipulate. For example, it is not difficult to imagine the futility of teaching fractions to elementary school children without showing them a concrete example of how fractions relate to the real world, such as a cardboard pie cut into variously sized slices. Children will not develop the ability to grasp abstract, hypothetical concepts until they reach the final stage of formal operations.

PSYCHOSOCIAL DEVELOPMENT

In the middle childhood stage of industry versus inferiority, Erikson (1963) felt that children are preparing for their future lives by learning to win recognition through producing things. As children are provided instruction in school, they become literate and seek to achieve their goals through their own efforts. Play becomes more serious and oriented to winning over competitors through being skillful at using the tools of the trade—whether a basketball or a video game—and children seek to gain competence in pursuits valued by their peers. If children are not successful at achieving their goals or in gaining acceptance by peers, they may develop a sense of inferiority and inadequacy that will discourage their future efforts.

School counselors can help children achieve a sense of industry through encouragement and assisting each in recognizing his or her own uniqueness and special talents. While not all children are gifted academically or athletically, all have some characteristic that can be acknowledged and nurtured. By helping children to become aware of and appreciate their own strengths, such as persistence or congeniality, school counselors can facilitate the development of healthy self-esteem. Providing recognition for academic progress, rather than strictly for excellence, is another way that school counselors can promote children's sense of industry. For children who are not being fully accepted by peers, school counselors can offer friendship groups as a means of teaching social skills and enhancing their social inclusion

Family of Origin Issues

THE IMPACT OF CHILD REARING ON DEVELOPMENT

Much of our development is shaped by the interactions that we have with significant adults during the first years of our lives. Think of how different you might be if, from the moment of birth, you had been raised by different people in a family environment that was the polar opposite of what you experienced as a child. Perhaps you may be saying to yourself, "Yes, and how much better off I would be today if that had been the case!" Now consider how likely it is that you would be reading this text and taking this class if you had grown up in a radically different situation. How many of your present personality and behavioral characteristics, beliefs, goals, and values would be the same? For better or worse, family interactions during our early years can have a tremendous impact on our later lives.

PARENTING STYLES

While most parents love their children and want to raise them well, there is much variation in how—and whether—they convey nurturance and apply discipline. In several landmark longitudinal studies, Diana Baumrind (1967, 1975, 1980, 1991) collected information regarding how parents interacted with their preschoolers in various situations. Based upon her extensive observations, Baumrind identified two dimensions—demandingness and responsiveness—that could be used to form a typology of four parenting styles. The first dimension, *control/demandingness*, refers to whether or not parents set high standards and exert control to ensure that their children exhibit mature behavior. The second dimension, *warmth/responsiveness*, refers to whether or not parents convey warmth and acceptance in their communication and are responsive to their children's feelings and views. As table 8.1 shows, the two dimensions yield a typology of four basic parenting styles: *authoritative, authoritarian, permissive,* and *uninvolved*. Baumrind studied the first three of these types.

TABLE **8.1**

Parenting Styles

Warmth/Responsiveness		Control/Demandingness	
Little warmth/ Low responsiveness	*Much warmth/ High responsiveness*	*Little control/ Low demandingness*	*Much control/ High demandingness*
A	B	C	D

AUTHORITARIAN PARENTS

A + D ⟶ Conflicted/Irritable child behavior

PERMISSIVE PARENTS

B + C ⟶ Impulsive/Aggressive child behavior

UNINVOLVED PARENTS

A + C ⟶ Alienated/Irresponsible child behavior

AUTHORITATIVE PARENTS

B + D ⟶ Energetic/Friendly child behavior

Authoritative Parents. Of the four parenting styles, the authoritative approach produced the best results in children. Authoritative parents conveyed warmth and acceptance and maintained open communication with their children. Although they established high standards and set firm limits for behavior, these parents were democratic and enlisted their children's help in resolving problems. When children voiced reasonable objections to rules, authoritative parents responded in a caring manner and were flexible enough to make appropriate changes.

Baumrind found the children of authoritative parents to be the most well adjusted—exhibiting friendliness, happiness, confidence, self-control, and high achievement (Baumrind, 1967). Much subsequent research has confirmed these results, showing that children have the most positive outcomes when parents practice child-centered patterns of discipline, accompanied by clearly communicated demands, careful monitoring, and an atmosphere of acceptance (Baumrind, 1989; Maccoby, 1984; Maccoby & Martin, 1983).

Authoritarian Parents. While these parents also set high standards and exerted firm control, they did not interact warmly or respectfully with their children. Instead, authoritarian parents demanded unquestioning compliance and did not allow children to voice opinions regarding discipline. Children were expected to conform to parental expectations or face punishment for their transgressions.

The children of authoritarian parents were found to be relatively distrustful, unhappy, and socially anxious. In addition, they tended to be withdrawn and respond with hostility when they became frustrated with peers (Baumrind, 1967). Other studies have shown that authoritarian parenting produces children with low self-esteem who lack spontaneity and confidence (Coopersmith, 1967; Lamborn et al., 1991; Lempers, Clark-Lempers, & Simons, 1989). In adolescence, children from authoritarian homes are obedient, but lack competence (Steinberg, 1990).

Permissive Parents. Unlike the first two groups, these parents did not establish limits or impose restraints on children's behavior, but instead unconditionally accepted whatever their youngsters chose to do. Permissive parents conveyed considerable warmth and acceptance, but offered no structure and gave children more freedom than their maturity warranted.

The children of permissive parents demonstrated highly immature behavior and had difficulty controlling their impulses. Lacking confidence in themselves, they were excessively demanding and showed extreme dependence on adults. Although some were creative and outgoing, others were socially inept. They tended not to persist in nursery school tasks and were often rebellious or aggressive when others' needs conflicted with their own (Baumrind, 1967, 1971). Later research shows that in adolescence, children from permissive backgrounds are self-confident but have higher levels of substance abuse and school difficulties (Steinberg, 1990).

Uninvolved Parents. Although Baumrind did not study this group, Maccoby and Martin (1983) described uninvolved parents as being highly permissive but lacking in warmth. These parents demonstrate no concern for their children's welfare and are disengaged from parenting. Perhaps because of overwhelming stress in their own lives, uninvolved parents allow children to engage in unsupervised behavior without appearing to care what happens to them. Parental neglect and failure to monitor children's behavior have been found to be related to truancy, alcohol problems, precocious sexuality, and delinquency in adolescence and adulthood (Lamborn et al., 1991; Patterson, 1982; Pulkkinen, 1982).

Situational Conditions

THE CHANGING NATURE OF CONTEMPORARY FAMILIES

The stereotype of the typical American family—consisting of a mother, father, and several children—is, for many, more a nostalgic memory from the past than a present reality. In recent years, the family structure has changed dramatically; so much so that it is today difficult to articulate what constitutes a "typical" family. What we can say with certainty is that there are now many options and that families take many forms.

SINGLE-PARENT FAMILIES

During the last three decades, the proportion of children living in single-parent families has increased significantly around the world, but in developed countries, the United States now has the highest proportion (Burns, 1992; Hobbs & Lippman, 1990). From 1960 to 1990, the proportion of single-parent families in America increased from 9.1 to 24.7 percent (U.S. Bureau of the Census, 1992a). In some ethnic groups, the proportion is even higher, with almost 55 percent of African-American children living in one-parent homes. About one in three births are to unwed mothers, and one in sixty children sees their parents divorce in any year (Children's Defense Fund, 2001). Current statistics show that one in four children in the United States lives with only one parent, and half of all American children will live in a single-parent family at some point in their childhood (Children's Defense Fund, 2001).

These statistics are especially alarming because many studies have shown that when compared to their peers in two-parent homes, children from single-parent families have more behavioral and adjustment problems, lowered academic achievement, and bear children at earlier ages. For this reason, it is not uncommon to hear politicians citing the breakdown of the American family as the primary cause of our society's ills. A point that is often overlooked, however, is that one-parent families are not all the same. Because there is tremendous variation in the nature of these families, it can be assumed that their effects on children will be equally diverse (Weinraub & Gringlas, 1995). Consider the possibilities: single-parent families may result from divorce, death of a spouse, bearing children out of wedlock, or adopting children while unmarried. Single parents may be male or female, affluent or impoverished, or young or old. In addition, while some did not plan to raise children alone, others *chose* to be single parents for economic reasons, for lack of a suitable mate, or because the legal system precluded them from marrying a homosexual partner. Because this group is so heterogeneous, it is reasonable to expect that children will be impacted more by the circumstances specific to each home situation than by simply living in a one-parent family. Let us now consider some of the factors that create stress in one-parent families and thereby put children at risk.

STRESS IN SINGLE-PARENT FAMILIES

Poverty and Financial Strain. Although only 10 percent of two-parent families live in poverty, half of all families headed by a single mother do (McLanahan & Booth, 1989), and these families remain poor longer than any other group (Garfinkel & McLanahan, 1986). Such impoverished conditions often mean that children live in crowded, shoddy residences in dangerous neighborhoods, experience frequent moves, and receive poor nutrition and inadequate medical care (McLoyd & Wilson, 1991). Following a divorce, custodial mothers are much more likely than custodial fathers to experience a significant decrease in financial resources (Zill, 1991).

Task Overload. Because the demands of parenting are immense, single parents can feel overwhelmed. Having the combined responsibility of work and child-rearing is reported by both mothers and fathers to be one of the greatest stressors of single parenting (Greif, 1985; Kissman & Allen, 1993). Because child care often necessitates missing time from work, many single parents report having employment difficulties, and some suffer job loss as a result. It is not surprising that the struggle both to maintain adequate performance on the job and fulfill domestic responsibilities at home too often leaves single mothers and fathers with little physical and emotional energy left for their children.

Social Isolation. As they attempt to handle a formidable workload, single parents must cope with the added stress of social isolation. While divorced parents sometimes lose the social network they once had while married, single unwed mothers often never experience social support. In a series of studies comparing solo mothers (those who raised their children alone from birth) with married mothers, Gringlas and Weinraub (1995) found that the primary difference between the two groups was a lack of emotional and parenting support during the preschool years. This distinction was important, because maternal social support predicted parenting and child outcomes for both married mothers and solo mothers. The mothers who had greater support engaged in more positive interactions with their preschoolers. Furthermore, maternal support for solo mothers was found to predict the quality of children's academic performance during the preadolescent years.

Emotional Vulnerability. In addition, social isolation may make single parents especially susceptible to stress. In the same study, Gringlas and Weinraub (1995) found that when stressful life events occurred, the solo mothers showed less nurturance toward their preschoolers and demonstrated less effective communication and parenting skills. The children of these mothers were found to be moodier, to have lower scores on measures of intelligence and learning readiness, and to have more behavior problems when they reached preadolescence.

Interestingly, no significant differences were found between the children from solo- and two-parent families that had *not* encountered significant stress. For this reason, it may well be that stress, rather than family structure, is the better predictor of children being at risk. Thus, while it may not matter whether children grow up in solo- or two-parent families in low-stress situations (e.g., when single parents have financial security, assistance with child care, and supportive family members or friends), there may be a clear advantage to living in a two-parent home when life is less kind.

DIVORCE AND ITS EFFECTS ON CHILDREN

As we have seen, parental stress affects children; and few life events are more stressful to parents than divorce. Thus when a divorce occurs, children feel the impact in a variety of ways and are likely to experience its effects for years to come. Because divorce has become almost a normative event, with approximately 48 percent of first marriages ending in divorce (U.S. Bureau of the Census, 1992b) and an additional 17 percent of couples separating without getting a divorce (Castro-Martin & Bumpass, 1989), many children will witness the demise of their parents' relationship and be subjected to the accompanying pain. In this section we will consider the various factors that influence how children respond to the troubling, albeit common, phenomenon of divorce.

Age-Related Effects of Divorce. Numerous studies have suggested that children's responses to divorce vary according to age and developmental level (Amato & Keith, 1991; Cantell, 1986; Goldman & King, 1985; Kalter, 1990; Wallerstein, 1984, 1989; Wallerstein & Kelly, 1974, 1975, 1976, 1980). Children may be especially vulnerable to the stress of divorce if it occurs as they are adapting to other major life transitions, such as the onset of adolescence (Hetherington & Stanley-Hagan, 1995).

Preschoolers typically exhibit more overt distress when parents divorce, such as bewilderment, fearfulness, listlessness, nightmares, and prolonged crying. In addition, they sometimes regress to former infantile behaviors such as bed-wetting, stuttering, using "me" instead of "I" in sentences, clinging to parents, and restricting food intake to a few types of food or using a bottle (Kalter, 1990). Due to their limited understanding of adult relationships, children often blame themselves for the separation and assume that their bad behavior caused the parents to split. Yet, in spite of their greater display of emotional turmoil at the time of the divorce, Wallerstein and Kelly's longitudinal research showed that preschoolers had the best long-term adjustment.

Because they have a more accurate understanding of what is occurring, children of elementary school age may initially be better able to cope with divorce. While cognizant that divorce is caused by difficulties in adult relationships, these children may still feel intensely sad, abandoned, and sometimes angry at one or both parents for causing the marital dissolution. Because they have developed a conception of the family as a unit, they experience a profound sense of loss. Older elementary school children often manifest their distress by fighting with peers or siblings, arguing with parents, withdrawing from social interactions, and developing somatic complaints such as headaches or stomachaches (Kalter, 1990).

Adolescents usually have a much deeper understanding of their parents' difficulties and are more objective regarding the reasons why the divorce occurred (Springer & Wallerstein, 1983). Because they have a more realistic idea of what went wrong in their parents' relationship, they are less likely to experience guilt or extreme anger toward one or both parents. Due to the intensity and volatility of emotions during puberty, however, adolescents are at greater risk of engaging in highly self-destructive behaviors such as substance abuse, promiscuous sexual behavior, fighting, truancy, and running away from home. Their distress may also result in diminished academic performance, somatic complaints, depression, and, in some severe cases, self-injuring behavior and suicidal ideation (Dornbusch et al., 1985; Kalter, 1990). On the other hand, some adolescents respond to parental divorce by developing more mature behavior such as performing domestic tasks, caring for younger siblings, and providing emotional support to a depressed parent. If burdened with too many adult responsibilities, however, adolescents are likely to eventually become resentful and distance themselves from the family, sometimes resorting to the self-destructive behaviors mentioned previously (Hetherington, Stanley-Hagan, & Anderson, 1989; Wallerstein & Kelly, 1980).

Sex-Related Effects of Divorce. Although studies suggest only minimal differences in how boys and girls respond to parental divorce (Amato & Keith, 1991), some patterns have emerged. Custodial mothers tend to have more coercive interactions with sons than daughters and are less likely to monitor their behavior, which sometimes leads to mutual mother–son distancing in adolescence (Hetherington, 1993; Hetherington, Law, & O'Connor, 1992). In addition, boys experience more problems in school adjustment and academic achievement and are more likely to drop out (Hetherington & Parke, 1993). Unlike boys, preadolescent girls often develop very close, harmonious relationships with custodial mothers (Hetherington, 1991). Such congenial relationships can deteriorate in adolescence, however, when mothers try to assume tighter control of their daughters' behaviors, especially if the girls are involved in sexual or antisocial activities (Hetherington, 1993).

Because mothers retain custody of the children in 69 percent of divorce cases while fathers have custody in only 9 percent (U.S. Bureau of the Census, 1997), little is known about children's relationships with custodial fathers. However, custodial fathers report more difficulty in dealing with adolescent daughters than sons, and studies suggest that girls who live with their divorced fathers have more adjustment problems than their peers in mother-custody homes (Camara & Resnick, 1988; Lee, Burkam, Zimilies, & Ladewski, 1994; Maccoby et al., 1993; Peterson & Zill, 1986). Custodial fathers seem to have more success with sons, at least during the school years. Studies show these boys to be more socially competent, to have higher self-esteem, and to exhibit fewer behavior problems than boys living with divorced mothers (Hetherington & Stanley-Hagan, 1995). This difference may be explained by the fact that custodial fathers rarely engage in coercive relationships with their sons. Because they are less efficient than custodial mothers at monitoring their children's activities, however, custodial fathers are more likely to have both sons and daughters exhibit delinquent behavior during adolescence (Buchanan, Maccoby, & Dornbusch, 1992; Maccoby & Mnookin, 1992). Thus while both sexes need careful supervision in single-parent homes, some slight evidence suggests that children may adjust better when living with the parent of the same sex.

Situational Effects of Divorce. When a divorce occurs, children's adaptation may be more greatly influenced by situational factors than by their ages or sex. As we have seen, when single parents experience financial strain, lack of social support, and stress, children are adversely affected. In addition, children of divorce may be negatively impacted if noncustodial parents cease to maintain contact with them. While custodial parents play the more salient role in children's development, noncustodial parents also make important contributions. If former spouses cooperate in child-rearing, sustain amicable attitudes toward each other, and refrain from conflict, frequent visitation by an emotionally stable noncustodial parent is associated with more positive adjustment and self-control in children (Hetherington & Parke, 1993). Boys may particularly benefit from having such continuing contact with their noncustodial fathers. However, if the former spouses maintain a conflictual relationship—especially if children are caught in the middle—frequent visitation by the noncustodial parent may be associated with disruptions in children's behavior (Buchanan, Maccoby, & Dornbusch, 1991; Camara & Resnick, 1988). Children's adjustment is more adversely affected by parental conflict than by losing contact with a noncustodial parent (Hetherington, 1991).

STEPFAMILIES

While divorce constitutes a major transition in children's lives, remarriage comprises another. Yet most divorced parents remarry, so children of divorce can expect to spend part of their childhood with a stepparent and perhaps stepsiblings. Approximately half of all marriages that occur today are remarriages (U.S. Bureau of the Census, 1992b), which have a 50 percent higher probability of ending within five years than first marriages (Pill, 1990). If there are stepchildren, remarriages are especially likely to fail—particularly if the stepchildren are over nine years of age (Visher & Visher, 1988). Thus many children will see their family composition change a number of times before they reach adulthood.

Because 82 percent of blended families are headed by a custodial mother and a stepfather (U.S. Bureau of the Census, 1992b), a remarriage usually brings financial relief to the household. Although improved economic circumstances and parenting support eradicate some of the stress that custodial mothers often experience following a divorce, tension arises as a new person must be integrated into the family system (Hetherington & Stanley-Hagan, 1995). This stress is further exacerbated when stepsiblings are present.

Because the addition of one or more new members into the family system brings changes in both daily routines and parent–child relationships, most children require a period of time to adjust. During the period immediately following remarriage, custodial mothers often focus on incorporating the stepfather into the family and temporarily decrease their monitoring and control of children's behavior. For sons, who have had primarily coercive interactions with their custodial mothers, the addition of a benevolent stepfather can result in more harmonious family relationships. Daughters, on the other hand, are more likely to view a stepfather as an intruder who impairs the close, confiding relationship that developed with the custodial mother following the divorce. This resentment that daughters experience as a result of their changed status may lead to increased conflict with both the mother and stepfather (Hetherington & Stanley-Hagan, 1995). For these reasons, preadolescent boys seem to suffer more adverse effects from parental divorce, while preadolescent girls seem to be more negatively impacted by parental remarriage (Hetherington, 1989; Hetherington & Parke, 1993). While such sex differences typically are not found in adolescence, early adolescence seems to be an especially difficult time for both girls and boys to adjust to parental remarriage (Hetherington, 1991; Hetherington & Clingempeel, 1992).

One of the major sources of stress in blended families arises from a lack of clarity in role expectations for stepparents. Due to uncertainty regarding how to discipline and show affection to stepchildren, both stepmothers and stepfathers assume a less active role in parenting than do biological parents (Bray, 1988; Hetherington, 1991; Hetherington & Clingempeel, 1992; Hetherington & Parke, 1993; Santrock & Siterle, 1987). Because stepparents often receive mixed messages from their spouses and encounter resistance from children if they attempt to exert authority in the family, disengagement is common. While approximately half of nondivorced fathers become actively involved in parenting, only about one-third of stepfathers do (Hetherington, 1993). In contrast, stepmothers are typically forced to assume a more active role in child care and discipline and are thereby more likely to have conflictual relationships with stepchildren, especially stepdaughters. This may explain why children have been found to exhibit more resistance and to have poorer adjustment in stepmother families (Brand, Clingempeel, & Bowen-Woodward, 1988; Furstenberg, 1988; Santrock & Siterle, 1987).

Children's adjustment to stepparents may also be affected by their ages at the time of the remarriage. Younger children are more likely to accept a stepparent in a parental role, but older adolescents and young adults sometimes experience relief at the improved economic conditions and emotional security that a remarriage offers to custodial mothers. Children in early adolescence often have greater difficulty as they must deal with their own emerging sexuality and autonomy needs while concurrently adjusting to significant changes in the family (Hetherington,

1991, 1993). It should be noted, however, that most children eventually adjust to their parents' marital transitions, with only about 25 percent showing long-term deleterious effects (Hetherington & Parke, 1993). The outcomes for children are most positive when stepparents gradually engage in authoritative parenting in conjunction with their spouses. This process should not occur too quickly, however, as studies show that the marital satisfaction of both partners remains higher if stepfathers build a warm relationship with stepchildren before becoming directly involved in discipline (Bray & Berger, 1993). When stepfathers have not assumed an active role in authoritative parenting, but have established warm relationships with stepchildren and supported mothers' attempts to discipline, children have also adjusted well (Bray & Berger, 1993; Hetherington, 1988; Hetherington & Stanley-Hagan, 1995).

HELPING CHILDREN AND PARENTS COPE WITH DIVORCE AND REMARRIAGE

When a marriage ends, all members of the family go through a grieving process. Yet it is easy for spouses to either overlook or be unaware of how to address children's grief as they struggle with their own pain associated with the marital dissolution. It is important for parents to realize that children mourn just as adults do, but often without the ability to clearly articulate their feelings and fears. For this reason, it is helpful to teach parents how to talk to children about divorce and how to help children express their emotions (Parker, 1994). Because children often blame themselves for the separation, or fear that the remaining parent will leave them also, parents should attempt to correct such misconceptions. Most public libraries have a variety of children's books about divorce that parents can read to children as a means of letting them know that the emotions they are experiencing are very normal and that they will eventually adjust and feel better.

As parents remarry, they should be advised not to expect instant love between their children and new partners. It is not unusual for children to resent the stepparent, who may be viewed as an intruder, and to do everything within their power to ensure that the new marriage fails. Understandably, stepparents may often find it difficult to feel genuine affection for stepchildren who are hostile or unresponsive to their attempts at establishing a relationship or providing discipline. The stepparent's role is further complicated by having to become integrated in a preexisting family system with previously established norms and expectations. If the ex-spouse, grandparents, and other extended family members maintain extensive involvement with the children, it can prove especially challenging to establish appropriate boundaries in the remarriage family. Family counseling can help develop semipermeable boundaries that allow for consistent structure and rules within the new family system while permitting reasonable input from members of the extended family (Martin & Martin, 1992). A useful method of ensuring that children receive consistent discipline is to develop a parenting alliance in which custodial and noncustodial parents and their partners agree on some rules and jointly participate in making decisions regarding the welfare of the children. If children spend significant time with other family members such as grandparents, it may be necessary to also include them in the parenting alliance; however, parents should be the ultimate decision-makers. The Stepfamily Association of America (SAA, 1989) offers an eight-step program and a variety of other resources that can help remarriage families successfully adjust to life as a blended family.

In addition to providing educational and therapeutic interventions to parents and families, counselors in school settings can help children adjust to changes in the family by offering individual or small-group counseling. By using stories, games, and play media, counselors can help children express their feelings and learn to cope with family issues. Small-group counseling can be especially beneficial in helping children understand that their parents' divorce or remarriage does not make them different from other children, and can enable them to discover how their peers have adjusted. When conducting small groups with preschoolers, however, it is important to include only children who are mature enough to engage in cooperative play (Hoffman, 1991).

CHILD ABUSE AND NEGLECT

Unfortunately, sometimes the very adults who are supposed to provide safety, love, and protection to children are the ones who harm them the most. Child abuse, which constitutes a severe breakdown in the family, involves not only maltreatment, but also a serious breech of trust between caregivers and children. The resulting traumatizing effects can last a lifetime. Nevertheless, child abuse is prevalent in our society and everyone who provides services to children is likely to confront it. In this section, we will consider the nature of child abuse, factors that place children at risk, and interventions for protecting children and decreasing the likelihood that abuse will occur.

NATURE OF CHILD ABUSE AND NEGLECT

Using records of investigations conducted by Child Protective Services, Barnett, Manly, and Cicchetti (1993) developed the following classification system to categorize the various forms of child maltreatment.

Physical Abuse. This form of maltreatment involves inflicting injury on a child's body by other than accidental means. Examples of physical abuse include extensive bruises, burns, lacerations, welts, abrasions, bone fractures, and other injuries that may result in hospitalization or death.

Sexual Abuse. This refers to any sexual contact between a child and responsible adult for the purpose of the adult's gratification or financial gain. Sexual abuse includes genital or tactile penetration, sodomy, prostitution, and exposure to inappropriate sexual stimuli. Sexual abuse does not necessarily entail physical contact, but may also consist of behaviors such as exhibitionism and sexual propositioning.

Physical Neglect. This type of maltreatment is comprised of the two subcategories of *failure to provide* and *lack of supervision.* Failure to provide refers to the adult's failure to meet the minimum requirements of care for the child's physical needs, such as food, shelter, clothing, medical attention, and personal cleanliness. For example, children are being neglected if they come to school in winter without a coat or receive no medical care when they are ill. Lack of supervision entails negligence in providing age-appropriate care and monitoring to ensure the child's safety. For example, while ten-year-olds can sometimes safely remain alone at home for several daytime hours, three-year-olds should never be left unsupervised.

Emotional Abuse. This refers to a form of mental cruelty in which there is a persistent or extreme disregard of the child's emotional needs for safety, security, self-esteem, and love. Emotional abuse includes behaviors such as constant denigrating, ridiculing, or threatening a child, abandoning a child with no indication that the adult will return, or locking a child in a small, enclosed space for long periods of time.

Moral–Legal–Educational Maltreatment. This category refers to a failure to ensure that the child is exposed to appropriate activities for acquiring the moral standards of society. This form of maltreatment might include behaviors such as failing to ensure the child's regular school attendance or allowing the child to watch adults engaging in sexual activity or illegal drug use.

FACTORS ASSOCIATED WITH CHILD ABUSE

Child abuse is not limited to individuals of any particular race, religion, educational level, or socioeconomic status. The fact that children live in a middle-class home headed by college-educated parents offers no guarantee that they will be free from the ravages of abuse. Although child abuse can strike anywhere, researchers have identified various factors that place children at greater risk. While it is unlikely that abuse will occur when only one factor is present, children's chances of abuse increase as more risk factors interact, especially in the absence of other protective variables that serve to ameliorate the risks, such as a satisfying marital relationship and supportive community resources (Cicchetti & Rizley, 1981). The factors indicated below interact to increase the risk of abuse.

Parental History of Maltreatment. Parents who as children were abused themselves are estimated to have about a 30 percent chance of abusing their own children, which makes them six times more likely than others in the general population to do so (Kaufman & Zigler, 1989). Even more significant is the extremely high percentage of known child abusers that have a history of being abused themselves. One study showed that approximately 70 percent of young, lower-socioeconomic-status mothers who abused their children had been abused in their own youth (Pianta,

Egeland, & Erickson, 1989). Thus although a relatively small percentage of those who suffered abuse as children will grow up to be perpetrators, a high percentage of those who do become abusers will have been abused themselves. The intergenerational cycle of abuse is less likely to continue when women who were abused as children have an emotionally supportive spouse, and had some prior contact with a warm, caring adult and therapy (Egeland, Jacobvitz, & Sroufe, 1988).

Emotional Disturbance. Maternal depression, with its accompanying low self-esteem, has also been linked to parental dysfunction (Cicchetti & Aber, 1986; Field, 1994; Zahn-Waxler & Kochanska, 1990; Zuravin, 1989). Depressed mothers are more likely to be hostile, rejecting, and emotionally detached toward their children and to feel hopeless about their ability to be effective parents. A study of impoverished women showed twice the rate of depression in mothers who abused their children as in those who did not (Gilbreath & Cicchetti as cited in Rogosch, Cicchetti, Shields, & Toth, 1995), and emotional instability (which includes depression) has been identified as the best predictor of maltreatment in low-income mothers (Pianta et al., 1989).

Unsatisfying Marital Relationships. A stressful, conflictual marital relationship that drains partners of energy for parenting increases the risk that parents will respond inappropriately and engage in negative interactions with children (Wilson & Gottman, 1995). Parents who are angry, frustrated, and impatient with their spouses are unlikely to have the emotional resources necessary to cope with children. Studies have shown that families that abuse children are characterized by unstable, conflictual intimate relationships of short duration that sometimes involve a series of temporary partners (Cicchetti & Manly, 1990; Howes & Cicchetti, 1993). Furthermore, families that mistreat children have a high incidence of spousal abuse (Cicchetti & Howes, 1991; Howes & Cicchetti, 1993).

Lack of a Social-Support Network. Abusive families are often socially isolated and have no friends or family members to provide companionship, emotional support, parenting information, or assistance with childcare (Trickett & Susman, 1988). Because they have no one to give them feedback or offer advice on parenting strategies, they may resort to harsh methods of discipline that are injurious to children.

Financial Strain. Economic hardship creates tremendous stress in families and can lead to depression, marital conflict, and family dysfunction. Abusive parents are primarily of lower socioeconomic status (Huston, McLoyd, & Coll, 1994) and are more likely to be unemployed or receiving public assistance (Trickett, Aber, Carlson, & Cicchetti, 1991).

Unrealistic Parental Cognitions. Abusive parents often have unrealistically high expectations that children will demonstrate mature behavior and exhibit self-control and independence before they are developmentally ready (Trickett et al., 1991). In addition, they tend to believe that children should meet the needs of parents (Dean, Malik, & Richards, 1986).

They are often unable to assume the child's perspective regarding parental demands (Pianta et al., 1989).

Difficult Children. Some children are quite challenging to parents and are at greater risk of being maltreated. Children with difficult temperaments (e.g., irritability, hyperactivity, withdrawal) evoke negative emotions in parents and are less likely to receive responsive caregiving (Crockenberg, 1986; Crockenberg & Acredolo, 1983). While children are never responsible for their own abuse, difficult children may produce the additional stress that pushes already-overwhelmed parents over the edge into abusive encounters.

PREVENTING CHILD ABUSE AND NEGLECT

State statutes designate counselors and other professionals who work with children as mandated reporters of child abuse and neglect. While culpable for not alerting Child Protective Services when child abuse or neglect is suspected, counselors are guaranteed immunity from civil and criminal liability when reporting suspected cases in good faith. It is important to note, however, that counselors are not expected to perform investigations to determine if children have been abused or neglected, but only to report their suspicions to the appropriate authorities in the local Department of Social Services, who will then determine whether the claim is valid.

Due to their extensive daily contact with children, school counselors play an especially key role in the prevention of child abuse and neglect. According to the American School Counselor Association (1988, 1999), school counselors should engage in the activities indicated below to help ensure children's safety.

Coordination. School counselors can coordinate team efforts involving the principal, school nurse, teacher, protective-services worker, and the child. After the initial report has been filed, school counselors can facilitate contact between the social worker and the child, while helping to relieve the child's anxiety about the investigative process. Many children fear that investigations necessarily result in their being removed from the home and placed in foster care.

Counseling. After the initial crisis has passed, school counselors should continue to counsel the child—and perhaps the family—or make a referral to an appropriate community agency. It is important to maintain contact with the child and attempt to rebuild his or her trust in the counseling relationship.

Education. School counselors can present workshops for teachers and administrators to help them understand the dynamics of abuse so that they will respond nonjudgmentally when faced with crisis situations in families. In addition, counselors can provide programs to help children develop coping skills to ensure their own safety, such as learning to recognize their parents' stress and becoming aware of cues that suggest that abuse is likely to occur if their behavior does not change. Finally, school counselors can present developmental workshops and organize support groups for parents that emphasize authoritative parenting, effective discipline, and strategies for handling anger and frustration.

SUBSTANCE ABUSE

Substance abuse is a significant problem in the United States, and the children of alcoholics and substance abusers have their own special issues that can follow them into adulthood. The children of substance abusers (COSAs), a group that includes those with alcoholic parents, are at risk of physical and emotional abuse and neglect, instability in the home, greater likelihood of becoming substance abusers themselves, impaired academic performance, possible loss of a parent to incarceration, exposure to HIV and AIDS, social stigma associated with parental participation in illegal activities, and poverty (Austin & Prendergast, 1991; Gross & McCaul, 1991). These children's needs often go unmet, and they are likely to experience emotional distress that can continue to plague them as adults, including low self-esteem, guilt, a sense of failure, and difficulty in asking for help.

Because of the family "code of silence" in substance-abusing homes, COSAs often go unrecognized and fail to receive the help they need. Because many of these children compensate for their unhappiness at home by excelling in school, they may be viewed as star students or simply go unnoticed because they try so hard to be perfect. Ackerman (1983) suggests that possible indicators of parental substance abuse include child-behavioral patterns of absenteeism, fluctuating academic performance, problems controlling mood and behavior, neglected physical appearance, fatigue and lack of energy, people-pleasing behaviors, conflict avoidance, difficulty paying attention, social isolation, physical complaints such as headaches and stomachaches, and psychological problems such as anxiety, sadness, or fearfulness. Other indicators of familial substance abuse include parental failure to keep appointments with school personnel, attend school functions, or sign their children's report cards.

When attempting to identify and work with COSAs, school counselors must be careful to avoid further stigmatizing these children. Knight (1994) recommends that school counselors use extreme discretion when sharing their suspicions with others about parental substance abuse and avoid publicly labeling children as "COSAs." Counselors should strive to create a safe school and classroom environment in which children will feel free to either self-identify or remain anonymous if they choose. To assist and support COSAs, school counselors can provide education regarding the issues associated with familial substance abuse and collaborate with teachers, parents, and community members to bring about greater awareness and understanding of the needs of these children. Small-group counseling can be an effective intervention to help identified COSAs understand that they are not alone or "different" and to develop coping behaviors to deal with family stress.

Serious Physical and Emotional Conditions

ATTENTION-DEFICIT/HYPERACTIVITY DISORDER *(ADHD)*

As we discussed earlier, middle childhood is a time in which children are expected to engage in industrious behavior to achieve a sense of accomplishment. School performance, one of the chief arenas in which children seek to achieve success, requires concentration and paying attention. Unfortunately, for children with attention-deficit/hyperactivity disorder (ADHD) the ability to pay attention for long periods of time is a feat that is not easily achieved so that their academic performance is compromised. ADHD is estimated to affect 5 to 10 percent of children in U.S. schools (Hosie & Erk, 1993) and may be the most common childhood disorder in our society (Barkley, 1995).

The *Diagnostic and Statistical Manual of Mental Disorders*, 4th edition *(DSM-IV)* (American Psychiatric Association, 1994) lists the following symptoms for ADHD. To be diagnosed with ADHD, either A1 *or* A2 must be present, as well as B, C, and D:

(A1) *Inattention:* At least six of the following symptoms of inattention must have persisted for a minimum of six months to a degree that is maladaptive and inconsistent with the developmental level:

 (1) Often fails to give close attention to details or makes careless mistakes in schoolwork, work, or other activities.

 (2) Often has difficulty sustaining attention in tasks or play activities.

 (3) Often does not seem to listen when spoken to directly.

 (4) Often does not follow through on instructions and fails to finish schoolwork, chores, or duties in the workplace (not due to oppositional behavior or failure to understand instructions).

 (5) Often has difficulty organizing tasks and activities.

 (6) Often avoids, dislikes, or is reluctant to engage in tasks that require sustained mental effort (such as schoolwork or homework).

 (7) Often loses things necessary for tasks or activities (e.g., school assignments, pencils, books, tools, or toys).

 (8) Is easily distracted by extraneous stimuli.

 (9) Is often forgetful in daily activities.

(A2) *Hyperactivity-Impulsivity:* At least six of the following symptoms of hyperactivity-impulsivity must have persisted for a minimum of six months to a degree that is maladaptive and inconsistent with the developmental level:

(1) Often fidgets with hands or feet or squirms in seat.

(2) Often leaves seat in classroom or in other situations in which remaining seated is expected.

(3) Often runs about or climbs excessively in situations in which it is inappropriate.

(4) Often has difficulty playing or engaging in leisure activities quietly.

(5) Is often "on the go" or acts as if "driven by a motor."

(6) Often talks excessively.

(7) Often blurts out answers before questions have been completed.

(8) Often has difficulty awaiting one's turn.

(9) Often interrupts or intrudes on others (e.g., butts into conversations or games).

(B) Some hyperactive-impulsive or inattentive symptoms that caused impairment were present before age seven years.

(C) Some impairment from the symptoms is present in two or more settings (e.g., at school and at home).

(D) There must be clear evidence of clinically significant impairment in social, academic, or occupational functioning.

(E) Exclude the diagnosis if it occurs exclusively during the course of a pervasive developmental disorder, schizophrenia or other psychotic disorder, and is not better accounted for by another mental disorder (e.g., a mood disorder, anxiety disorder, dissociative disorder, or a personality disorder).

ADHD is further categorized into three subtypes (Power & DuPaul, 1996):

♦ ADHD-I: This refers to predominately inattention (i.e., attention deficit without hyperactivity)

♦ ADHD-C: This combined type includes both inattention and hyperactivity

♦ ADHD-HI: This new type refers to predominately hyperactivity and impulsivity, and is found mainly in preschoolers who may be at risk of developing ADHD-C in the future.

ADHD is believed to result from an imbalance of the neurochemicals that act as triggers, transmitters, and receptors within the brain. Because it occurs more frequently in family members of individuals with the disorder, ADHD may be linked to heredity. Although environmental factors—such as poor parenting, inadequate discipline, or junk food—do not cause ADHD, they may exacerbate the symptoms (Barkley, 1990, 1996).

The accurate assessment of ADHD requires gathering information from multiple sources in various settings and using a variety of assessment methods (McBurnett, Lahey, & Pfiffner, 1993). These methods include clinical interviews with the child, his or her parents, and teachers; behavior-rating scales; behavioral observation of the child in the classroom and social settings; and psychological and/or psychoeducational tests. No single objective measure can effectively diagnose ADHD, however, so it is important to collect as much information as possible. The child's history and behavioral observations are critical in diagnosing ADHD.

The treatment of ADHD also requires a variety of methods and interventions (Brown, 2000). Parent education and training can be used to teach parents how to more effectively manage their children's behaviors and decrease negative interactions between parent and child. Client education can help children understand the disorder and learn how to compensate for the areas in which they are weak. Social-skills training is another intervention that can help children develop strategies for controlling their impulsivity when relating to others. Individual and group counseling can provide a safe environment in which children can feel accepted and supported as they attempt to deal with the problems associated with ADHD. School personnel can make accommodations to meet the special learning needs of students with ADHD, such as providing the child with individualized attention and altering the educational environment to minimize distractions. Finally, a stimulant medication such as Ritalin, Dexedrine, or Cylert can be prescribed to increase children's attentiveness and decrease their impulsivity and overactivity. Much controversy surrounds the use of medication, however, because some suspect that it is prescribed too quickly and without adequate assessment of ADHD; that it is accompanied by adverse side effects such as retarded growth and the development of tics; and that it may lead to substance abuse.

The American School Counselor Association (2000) suggests that school counselors play a key role in assisting children with ADHD. To implement services to these children, school counselors' professional activities may include: 1) serving on a multidisciplinary team to provide multifaceted interventions to children with ADHD; 2) serving as consultants to parents, teachers, and other school personnel regarding the characteristics and problems of students with ADHD; 3) providing regular feedback regarding students' social and academic performances to members of the interdisciplinary team; 4) helping staff design appropriate programs for students with ADHD that include training in social skills and self-management; 5) providing activities to increase the self-esteem of students with ADHD and encouraging them to practice the skills learned in counseling sessions; 6) promoting ADHD workshops for staff and support groups for parents and families of children with ADHD; and 7) serving as advocates in the community for students with ADHD.

Existential Issues

Life is full of suffering, and children are not immune to the pain of loss. Whether it is the loss of a pet, the death of a grandparent, parental divorce, separation from siblings, or a geographic move, children have numerous reasons to grieve. But because they lack the conceptual understanding and life experience of adults, children require special assistance when confronted with significant grief.

Grief, defined as the "emotional suffering caused by a death or bereavement" (Wolfelt, 1983, p. 26), is a process that each individual must work through in his or her own unique way. According to Worden (1991), this process involves accepting the reality of the loss, experiencing the emotions associated with the loss, adjusting to the absence of the significant person or the changed environment, and withdrawing the energy from the loss and reinvesting it in new relationships and life events.

If the loss is due to death, children's grief will be influenced by their chronological age and developmental level. Most children under age 6, who are in the preoperational stage, will believe that death is reversible and assume that the person will return. Although young children may cry at a funeral and appear to greatly miss a deceased relative, they may soon resort to pestering their grieving parents with questions such as, "When is Grandma coming back?"

Elementary school children, in the stage of concrete operations, grasp the finality of death but struggle with understanding why it occurs. Thus they may believe that death is something that happens only to old people, and have tremendous difficulty accepting the death of a younger person. Because they are also in the stage of preconventional moral reasoning, elementary school children may believe that death is punishment for misdeeds. Thus when loved ones die, children may think that the death was due to their own misbehavior or disobedience. Regardless of age, death is frightening and confusing to children and they may need extra comfort at a time when their bereaved family members are caught up in their own grief.

McGlauflin (1998) suggests the following ways in which counselors can help children grieve at school:

♦ Use "teachable moments" to help children learn that grieving is a valuable life skill (e.g., using historic occasions such as Veteran's Day to discuss death)

♦ Learn to recognize opportunities to acknowledge grief, such as when children mention deceased loved ones or on holidays and anniversaries. Respond with compassion for the child's grief (e.g., "You miss your dad a lot at this time of the year")

♦ Respect the altered state of consciousness that accompanies grief. Show understanding and support when children express overwhelming emotions, random thoughts, or disorientation

♦ Honor every possible departure in the school and create rituals to prepare for transitions (e.g., acknowledging sadness when families leave the community, having a special ceremony for the highest grade leaving, or having a memorial service when a death occurs)

♦ Speak to children about a death or loss rather than remaining silent (e.g., "I was sad to hear about the death of your uncle")

♦ Be as honest as possible when discussing a death. State what is known, what is not known, and what cannot be discussed

♦ Relate to grieving children with compassion rather than pity. Show respect for them and treat them as equals as they face the pain of loss

♦ Do not be afraid to show emotion. Sharing emotions can be a meaningful way of modeling successful grieving

♦ Offer children outlets for grieving such as journal writing, drawing, or going to a "feeling area" room to have quiet time

♦ Continue with routines, discipline, and high expectations. Do not treat children differently after a loss, other than realizing that they may be temporarily confused or inefficient

♦ Honor losses, even after years have passed. Validate the loss by remembering anniversaries and allowing children to talk (e.g., "This may be a sad time of year for you")

♦ Support one another. Encourage school personnel to support each other, as they support children when losses occur.

By allowing children to work through the grieving process at their own pace, counselors can provide a strong foundation for facing later losses. The gentle support that children receive from caring adults may enable them to find the strength within themselves that will get them through times of sorrow and achieve a sense of renewed hope for the future.

EXERCISE **8**

"My Childhood Events"

Materials: Paper and a writing instrument.

Directions: Return to the list of events that you drew for exercise 7 and select two to three events from your childhood to explore. Write each event at the top of a separate page. Explore each event by writing about the following:

- ♦ It was a time when . . .
- ♦ Relationships that were important for me were . . .
- ♦ I remember feeling . . .
- ♦ I really like doing . . .
- ♦ I did not like . . .

Try to be descriptive in finishing each of the statements, and write as much as you can about each. Conclude with a description of the feelings aroused in you as you were writing these.

Chapter Nine

Counseling Children
Applications

I N THIS CHAPTER we will consider ways to help children face the changes and negotiate the challenges inherent in growing up. Because children are dependent upon and often at the mercy of the significant adults in their lives, we will begin our explorations by discussing how counselors can assist parents in facilitating children's development. We will then discuss more direct interventions for child clients, such as individual and group counseling, play therapy, affective education, and peer-helper programs.

Effective Parenting

As we saw in the previous chapter, authoritative parenting is associated with the best outcomes in children. It is therefore helpful to consider the factors that make this approach so efficacious. First, parents model respectful behavior, flexibility, and empathy by explaining the rationale for rules, as well as by listening and responding in a sensitive manner when children express concerns. In addition, by establishing high standards and setting limits, parents let children know what constitutes acceptable behavior and convey a belief in their ability to act responsibly, thereby engendering high self-esteem. Because discipline is applied consistently and fairly, children feel secure. Finally, this approach teaches problem-solving strategies, because parents democratically encourage children to help find solutions to problematic issues.

Drawing from these concepts, Nelson, Lott, and Glenn (1993) developed a model of positive discipline that can be used for optimal child-rearing. Here are a few of their tips for caregivers:

1. Conduct weekly family meetings in which everyone has an opportunity to brainstorm solutions to family problems. Let everyone bring up issues for discussion, and make sure that all family members reach a consensus before problems are deemed resolved.

2. Be both kind and firm in interactions with children.

3. Whenever possible, allow children to choose between at least two acceptable alternatives. With very young children, the choices will need to be limited; for example, "You may come to dinner when you are called, or you may wait until breakfast tomorrow to eat."

4. Use logical consequences rather than punishment. Logical consequences are actions that caregivers apply that logically follow from the child's behavior, but that are not arbitrarily punitive. To be effective, logical consequences must be directly *related* to the child's behavior, *respectful* of the child, and *reasonable* to both child and caregiver. For example, if a child does not put his dirty laundry into the hamper, it does not get washed.

5. Focus more on finding solutions than on applying consequences. Have children help brainstorm ideas for solving problems.

6. Have children assist in planning consequences in advance— before actual behaviors occur. By doing so, children will be less likely to feel punished when consequences are applied. For example, a topic of discussion at a family meeting might be, "What should be a logical consequence for leaving cookie crumbs on the carpet?"

7. Follow through on enforcing rules by taking kind, firm action— rather than by nagging or punishing. For example, if a preschooler refuses to go to bed, simply say "Bedtime" and take him or her by the hand to the bedroom. If the child resists, give him or her a limited choice such as "So do you want to pick out your bedtime story, or do you want me to? We have until 8:00 to read your story."

8. Establish routines in which all family members participate in doing chores. Plan the routines at a family meeting, and use visual aids to remind everyone of their responsibilities. For example, the family sets up a house-cleaning routine in which each person is in charge of specific tasks such as dusting, vacuuming, cleaning sinks, and polishing windows. At a designated time each week, the whole family performs the tasks together.

9. Use "time-out" when children misbehave. Explain that the purpose of time-out is to give children an opportunity to calm down,

and that they can return after they have sorted out their feelings and are more in control of their behavior.

10. Finally, make sure that the message of love is conveyed to children. Let them know that they are valued and important so that they will develop high self-esteem. Give children some special time alone with each parent every week.

Counseling Children

As we have seen, helping parents develop optimal parenting skills is one of the best ways to have a positive impact on the lives of children. Because children are almost totally dependent on adult caregivers and have only limited autonomy, it is expedient to provide consultation and training to parents or guardians to maximize children's chances for healthy growth and development. Counselors can teach parents how to discipline and communicate with their children effectively and can offer instruction regarding normal developmental concerns most children face. Parents are frequently relieved to learn that they are not alone in their struggle with child-rearing issues, and they are reassured to discover that the developmental stages their children are moving through are normal and will pass. In addition to offering consultation and training to caregivers, counselors can work with the family system to elicit change, which is often necessary when more severe dysfunction is present. Family counseling can be especially beneficial when caregivers are experiencing extreme stress, when problematic interactions have escalated into violent outbursts.

While counselors provide indirect services to children by assisting caregivers in becoming more adept at child-rearing and in addressing children's issues, they can also counsel children directly. Because children are socially embedded and very dependent on the adults in their lives, however, individual counseling may be most effective when combined with consultation to support and reinforce the child's progress.

Individual Counseling with Children

When conducting individual sessions with children, Vernon (1999) states that the counseling process typically moves through the following stages:

♦ Intake
♦ Meeting for the first session
♦ Establishing a relationship and developing a focus
♦ Working together toward change
♦ Closure.

INTAKE

When working with child clients, intake information usually includes the age and grade of the child, the reason for referral, the child's birth date and place in the family constellation, the names and ages of siblings and parents, the parents' employment, the child's birth and medical history, and any medications the child takes. The counselor may also procure information about the child's developmental history, including strengths and weaknesses, relationships with others, and school performance. Other family-background information that might relate to the reason for the child's referral can also be explored (e.g., deaths, births, divorce, remarriage, incarceration, job changes, or geographic moves). Such information may be obtained via a telephone interview with a parent, a face-to-face interview with the child and one or more family members, or with just the child alone. Although school counselors may not conduct formal intake interviews, they may derive relevant information from the child, from his or her teacher(s), or from a careful review of the child's school records.

As part of the intake process, it is important to allay any misconceptions that may be held by the child or the adults in the child's life. Because many believe that counseling is for those who are "bad," "crazy," or "sick," the counselor should emphasize that counseling is designed to address normal developmental issues and other problems of living that can be challenging to everyone. Rather than being "advice-givers," counselors should be presented as helpers who will work collaboratively with the child to address the child's worries and concerns.

Confidentiality issues must also be clarified during the intake process. Minor children present special concerns regarding confidentiality, because parents have a legal right to access their children's information. Although absolute confidentiality for minors cannot be guaranteed, counselors should emphasize to children and parents that most of the specific content of their counseling sessions will not be disclosed to parents. Counselors may instead reveal to parents their children's general feelings or concerns or may encourage the children themselves to discuss such issues with their parents. If children are in severe danger, however, counselors must contact parents or appropriate child-protective-service workers.

In the intake phase, it is also essential to consider the system of which the child client is a part. Understanding the child's family, school, ethnic group, neighborhood, and social peers can shed light on his or her issues and can assist the counselor in determining how to maximize success.

MEETING FOR THE FIRST SESSION

The first session is critically important for creating an inviting environment, building the counseling relationship, and establishing trust. If the client is not self-referred, the counselor can begin the process by clarifying to the client why he or she is there (e.g., teacher request, parent referral, course planning, etc.). The client may have concerns that will need to be addressed at this point such as whether he or she is "in trouble," who will have access to his or her information, and what will happen in the session. As the counselor focuses on building the relationship by listening well and showing empathy, he or she should also assess the client's situation and needs. Both informal and formal assessment measures can be employed such as unfinished sentences, board games, play media, and psychological tests and behavioral-rating scales.

ESTABLISHING A RELATIONSHIP AND DEVELOPING A FOCUS

In order to establish a relationship with child clients, counselors need to provide an ample supply of play media such as puppets, sand trays, crayons, paint, and other creative materials. Play media provide a means by which young children can express ideas and emotions that they cannot adequately verbalize, and allow older children to feel comforted as they manipulate objects while discussing painful feelings. We will discuss play media and the process of play therapy in greater detail in the next section.

As the child plays, the counselor's role is to show unconditional positive regard and provide feedback to the child that accentuates his or her strengths and past successes. Through such affirmation and encouragement, the counselor increases the child's self-esteem and empowerment to work through his or her problems. While carefully listening to and observing the child's actions, the counselor and child can together develop a focus for addressing any issues that may begin to emerge.

If the counselor suspects that the child has concerns that need to be explored, counseling process questions and the use of immediacy can elicit further client disclosures. The following are some examples:

"How are you feeling right now?"

"What's it like for you to have me ask questions about your family?"

"What feelings do you have as you remember that time with your dog?"

"You've just gotten very quiet, and I'm wondering what you're thinking."

WORKING TOGETHER TOWARD CHANGE

After the relationship has been established and a focus defined, the counselor can begin working with the client to bring about desired change. Although the client's presenting problem may be only superficial and a symptom of deeper issues, it offers a starting point from which to begin work. The counselor may later need to assist the client with additional issues that emerge as the child develops trust and more openly confides.

Appropriate interventions for child clients are numerous and include play therapy, role playing, bibliotherapy, problem solving, brief counseling, contracting, homework, and structured exercises. As part of this process, the counselor may help the child explore alternatives and present ideas as possibilities that he or she had not previously considered. On the other hand, advice-giving is not highly facilitative, because it can create dependency and cause the child to rely on an adult to make decisions. Older children and adolescents may find advice-giving to be particularly offensive and may rebel against any well-meaning adults who attempt to "help" them. Instead, counselors can more effectively assist children by affirming their resilience, which may be derived from factors such as personal strengths, support from others, faith, motivation, and the desire to change.

CLOSURE

As the child achieves his or her goals, closure time draws near. Because the child may feel very attached to the counselor, it is critical to provide sufficient preparation before termination occurs. The counselor can help the child deal with his or her separation anxiety by processing feelings of abandonment, pain, or fear, creating a closing ritual to mark the end of counseling, scheduling a "check-up" session, and offering reassurance that he or she still cares about the child and will be available in the future. If the child requires additional services, the counselor may make a referral to another professional or agency.

Play Therapy

As more agencies and public schools develop preschool programs for three- and four-year-olds, it is likely that many agency workers and elementary school counselors will regularly provide developmental counseling and affective educational activities for very young children as well as for older youngsters (Hoffman, 1991; Hohenshil & Hohenshil, 1989). For this reason, it is critical that counselors understand children's early developmental needs in order to plan and implement appropriate programs. Because counseling young children is not essentially different from counseling older individuals, it is important to create a safe environment that facilitates the free expression of thoughts and feelings. The therapeutic arena most conducive to creating such an environment for young children is the world of play. Sigmund Freud (1953) described play as being a valuable means of understanding children's emotions:

> We ought to look in the child for the first traces of imaginative activity. The child's best loved and most absorbing occupation is play. Perhaps we may say that every child at play behaves like an imaginative writer, in that he creates a world of his own, or more truly, he arranges the things of his world and orders it in a new way that pleases him better. It would be incorrect to say that he does not take his world seriously; on the contrary, he takes his play very seriously and expends a great deal of emotion on it. (pp. 173–174)

The technique of *play therapy*, which utilizes play media as a therapeutic tool, was initially developed by Hermine Hug-Helmuth (1921), Melanie Klein (1955), and Anna Freud (1946, 1965) as an alternative psychoanalytic strategy for working with young children whose limited verbal skills precluded the use of free association. Drawing from a different orientation, Virginia Axline (1947a, b) developed a nondirective play-therapy model as an adaptation of Carl Rogers's client-centered approach for providing therapy to children. Play therapy was later modified for use in the schools and referred to as *play counseling*. Although the terms are often used synonymously and the techniques are similar, play counseling is short-term, typically involves little or no interpretation, and is used extensively by school counselors to assist children who are experiencing normal developmental concerns (Hoffman, 1991; Muro & Dinkmeyer, 1977).

Using Play Media in Counseling

THE PLAY AREA

The first step in counseling children involves setting up a play area with appropriate play media. As children's play tends to be noisy, play sessions should be held in a soundproof location that affords privacy and is free of interruptions. The counselor's office, although often quite small, is usually a better choice than a teacher's workroom or a vacant classroom that is larger but more likely to have traffic or offer distractions. The room should be bright, cheerful, and inviting, and should be large enough to accommodate a small group of five or six children. Low, open shelves that are easily accessible by young children provide a convenient way of displaying and storing play media. Because it is generally preferable to sit on the floor during the sessions, the room should have a rug and bean-bag chairs or large pillows for comfortable seating.

TYPES OF PLAY MEDIA

A variety of play materials should be provided that allow children to express themselves creatively and vent their emotions. While the therapeutic relationship that is established between the counselor and child is more important than the specific toys that are available, certain types of play media tend to facilitate various forms of emotional expression. Landreth (1991) recommends that counselors provide three broad categories of play materials, including: 1) real-life toys; 2) acting-out, aggressive-release toys; and 3) toys for creative expression and emotional release.

Real-Life Toys. These toys enable children to enact scenes from their everyday lives and include items such as doll houses with furniture, bendable doll families, puppets, toy cars, trucks, and boats, a nursing bottle, cooking utensils, a medical kit, and a cash register with play money.

Acting-Out, Aggressive-Release Toys. Acting-out toys provide a means of releasing pent-up feelings for young children, who often lack the appropriate labels for intense negative emotions such as anger or hostility. Such toys include bop bags, toy soldiers and army equipment, cowboys and Indians, alligator and other wild animal puppets, toy guns, suction throwing darts, Nerf balls, handcuffs, rubber knives, and a pounding bench and hammer.

Toys for Creative Expression and Emotional Release. In addition to the other play materials, the playroom should include a variety of unstructured media that children can creatively transform to release emotions. These include hats, masks, and dress-up clothes; building blocks, Tinker toys, and Legos; art materials such as pencils, finger paints, felt-tip markers, crayons, blunt scissors, colored construction paper, and large sheets of newsprint; Play-Doh or clay; chalkboard and colored chalk; and simple musical instruments such as cymbals, drums, or a xylophone. Two of the best materials in this category are sand and water, which although sometimes messy, lend themselves especially well to children's creative expression. A simple and inexpensive sand tray can be constructed from a plastic sweater box that is filled with sand purchased from a building supply store. If a clear plastic box with a blue lid is used, the lid can be placed under the box when in use to simulate the depths of the ocean, which can be particularly therapeutic. A variety of small plastic figures representing people of all ages and genders, action figures, scary creatures, soldiers, cowboys and Indians, farm animals, vehicles, trees, and buildings should also be provided so that children can enact scenes in the sand tray. A small jug of water can be poured into the sand tray if children desire.

LIMITS IN PLAY COUNSELING

Although play sessions should enable children to experience complete safety and acceptance as they freely explore their worlds, limits must be placed on behaviors that could potentially harm the client, the counselor, or the playroom and its contents. While it is natural for children to push the limits in play sessions, it is important for counselors to respond consistently and firmly while validating the client's feelings and desire to perform the inappropriate behavior. Because children should not initially be saddled with excessive rules, it is better to wait until a limit is about to be broken before admonishing the child. Landreth (1991) recommends that play sessions should include the following limits: 1) children are not to attack the counselor, other children, or harm themselves; 2) toys and the playroom itself are not to be randomly destroyed; 3) play materials must remain in the playroom at all times; 4) sessions end on time; 5) children are not to undress or urinate in the playroom; 6) children are not to play with the counselor's personal items, such as eyeglasses; 7) only limited amounts of water can be poured into the sand tray (e.g., two jugs full); and 8) children are expected to stay in the playroom for the entire session (with the exception of the occasional bathroom emergency).

When it appears that a child is about to go beyond a limit, Landreth (1991) suggests following a three-step process that conveys acceptance of the child's feelings, makes a clear statement of the limit, and suggests an alternative course of action that the child can pursue. For example, let us suppose that four-year-old Horatio announces angrily that he is going to hit the counselor and make her cry. In this process, the first step consists of acknowledging the child's motives and feelings. By fully accepting the child's feelings or motivations such as anger or the desire to hurt someone, the counselor validates the child and shows empathy. In this example, the counselor might say, "Horatio, you are angry and would like to hurt me." The second step consists of clearly and firmly communicating the limit, leaving no doubt as to what is expected. Here, the counselor might continue by saying, "But I am not for hitting." Finally, the third step consists of targeting acceptable alternatives that the child can use to express his or her feelings. In this case, the counselor might offer an alternative by saying, "You may hit the Bobo doll or the bean-bag chair." If Horatio ignores the limit and hits the counselor anyway, a fourth step will need to be employed in which he is given a final choice. The counselor, while remaining calm, might state, "If you choose to hit me again, you choose to leave the playroom." It is important for children to learn that the behaviors that they choose have consequences, and that sanctions are not imposed arbitrarily but are a direct result of their choices. If counselors patiently adhere to the three-step process, however, the fourth step should rarely be necessary.

PLAY-COUNSELING TECHNIQUES

Just as in counseling adults, the establishment of a warm, trusting, therapeutic relationship is the most essential aspect of the counseling process when working with young children. Although play media serve as a valuable tool for enabling children to express feelings, the relationship between the counselor and client is of greater importance than the toys. In her nondirective approach, Axline (1947a) recommends that the counselor establish a sense of permissiveness in the relationship so that children feel completely free to express their emotions in total safety. In this relationship, children are to be accepted just as they are and shown unconditional positive regard. The counselor shows empathy and helps children gain insight into their behaviors by reflecting the feelings, thoughts, and actions conveyed through their play. Sessions proceed at the children's own pace, rather than being hurried or directed by the counselor. In play counseling the counselor serves as a facilitator while the child leads. By being given the freedom to control the sessions, children gain confidence and feel fully accepted.

Because a central assumption of play therapy is that children have the ability to solve their own problems when given the opportunity, child clients should be allowed the freedom to make choices in the sessions (Axline, 1947a). To foster a sense of self-direction, children should be told from the beginning that they may play with any of the toys in the play-room. To enhance children's belief in their own abilities, counselors should refrain from giving advice or doing things for the children that they can do for themselves (Hoffman, 1991). Thus if a child asks the counselor to draw a tree for her because she doesn't do them well, the counselor might respond, "You would like me to draw it for you because you are afraid yours won't be good enough, but I believe that you can do it. You may draw the tree any way you want."

As the child plays, the counselor reflects the feelings and actions that arise without interrupting the flow of the play. Landreth (1991) recommends that the therapist's responses be short and interactive, and that they should accurately mirror the child's feelings. It is better to para-phrase, clarify, and summarize than to interpret, since the counselor's interpretation of the child's meaning may be quite wrong. It is also preferable to use reflection rather than questioning techniques, because young children generally lack the ability to verbally communicate cognitive insights. (If they were proficient in verbal communication, there would be no need for play counseling.) In addition, questioning can interfere with the child's play and deny the child the opportunity to lead in the session. Finally, evaluative remarks such as "Good job!" should be avoided, because they imply that the child's performance is being judged. If children feel that they are being judged in the playroom, they may experience anxiety and attempt to please the counselor rather than engage in spontaneous play.

The following dialogue illustrates the play-counseling process:

CHILD (placing a circle of soldiers around a big fish in the sand tray) *Now he won't get away!*

COUNSELOR *The soldiers will keep the fish from getting out.*

CHILD *He's a bad fish and he'll bite somebody if they let him get away.*

COUNSELOR *The bad fish will hurt people if the soldiers let him escape.*

CHILD (enacting a battle in which the fish attacks the soldiers, and the soldiers scream) *Ouch! Ouch!*

COUNSELOR *The fish is biting the soldiers and they are hurting.*

CHILD (making the soldiers fight back) *Now we'll kill you for all the mean things you did, you bad fish!*

COUNSELOR *The soldiers are angry and are going to destroy the fish for being so bad.*

CHILD (burying the fish in the sand) *Goodbye, evil fish!*

COUNSELOR *The bad fish is dead.*

As this dialogue shows, play counseling gently and nonintrusively facilitates the child's expression of feelings as he or she enacts pretend situations. Although the counselor may surmise that the evil fish represents the child's abusive father, it is neither necessary nor appropriate to share this interpretation with the child. It is enough instead to offer the child empathy and full acceptance as he or she releases and works through intense emotions in the safety of the therapeutic environment.

ETHICAL CONSIDERATIONS IN COUNSELING CHILDREN

Although parents and other adults in children's lives may inquire about what transpired in the counseling sessions, only general information should be provided. Although children are minors and cannot give legal consent for the release of information, they have a right to expect that what they do in the playroom will remain confidential. Just as adult clients expect their disclosures to remain private, child clients need to feel that the specific details of their play will not be revealed (Landreth, 1991). Thus parents or teachers should be told in advance that they will be kept apprised of the child's progress, but that they should not expect to be informed of specific occurrences in the sessions. Obviously, if the child appears to be suicidal or in clear or imminent danger, confidentiality would have to be broken. If the counselor feels that there is a compelling reason for a parent or teacher to be made aware of something that the child said or did in the session, it is helpful to ask the child if this information may be revealed (Hoffman, 1991). Most children eagerly agree and are pleased to have the counselor speak to the adults who so greatly impact their lives.

Affective Education in the Classroom

In addition to providing direct counseling services, counselors in school settings can play an important role in preventing the occurrence of many problems in childhood through *affective education,* or classroom guidance. Classroom-guidance activities, which should be provided to all students in the school, enable children to acquire necessary personal and social skills that are essential for mastering age-appropriate developmental tasks such as developing high self-esteem and getting along well with others. Because children are often reticent about talking to adults who are unfamiliar to them, classroom guidance also serves the function of introducing the counselor as a friendly person in whom they can confide. As children interact with the counselor in enjoyable classroom activities, they become aware that the counselor is approachable, listens well, and can help when they have problems or just need to talk to someone. They also learn that the counselor has a playroom full of fun toys, which tends to ease any fears they may have about visiting the counselor's office.

Affective education should be an integral component of a proactive, comprehensive developmental-guidance program, beginning as early as during preschool and continuing through the secondary-school years (Myrick, 1993). School counselors and teachers at each grade level should work together to plan and implement a curriculum that helps children achieve sequential outcomes based upon their developmental needs. During the preschool years, classroom guidance can be particularly valuable for helping children develop prosocial behavior (Morganett, 1994; Paisley & Hubbard, 1994). Topics of special relevance to prekindergarten children include taking turns and sharing, cooperating in play, following directions, seeking attention in appropriate ways, discovering feelings and how they are expressed, making choices, initiating friendships, and coping with frustrations (Hoffman, 1991). In order to make the lessons comprehensible and captivating to young children, the counselor may use puppets, art, stories, music and songs, movement and dance, cooperative games, role plays, creative dramatics, relaxation, and discussion. In addition to activities and materials that the counselor develops, there are a variety of commercially prepared kits that can be effectively employed in guidance lessons.

Small-Group Counseling

Although much of the affective curriculum can be conveyed through large-group guidance, some children have special needs or concerns that require additional attention. Small groups provide an excellent means of assisting children with issues such as study skills, parental divorce, social skills, and bereavement. In the safe environment of the small group, children can practice new skills, gain support from others who have similar concerns, and receive feedback regarding their own thoughts and behaviors. They can take comfort in discovering that they are not alone as they struggle with challenging issues or work through intense pain.

GROUP SIZE

When working with children, the size of the group should be based upon the participants' age and developmental level. Counselors must also consider their ability to effectively manage the interactions that occur in the group. Vernon (1999) recommends that groups with primary-grade youngsters should be limited to three or four members, while groups for older children and adolescents usually have from six to eight members. Counselors who plan to conduct larger groups (e.g., ten older children or adolescents) may wish to consider having a co-leader.

GROUP RULES

All groups must have rules, and they should be clearly defined when the group meets initially so that all members understand what is to be expected. It is important, however, to not overburden children with too many rules, so their number should be kept to a minimum. Other rules can be added later if the need arises. Typical group rules might include:

♦ Members are to maintain confidentiality regarding what is discussed in the group

♦ Only one person may speak at a time

♦ Everyone gets a turn to speak, but a person may choose to skip his or her turn

♦ Members are to treat others respectfully (i.e., no "put-downs" are allowed)

♦ Members are to keep their hands to themselves (i.e., no pushing, shoving, or hitting others).

GROUP PROCESS

Groups move through stages, and effective group leadership requires understanding group process and using appropriate skills at each stage (Vernon, 1999). The four stages are

♦ Initial stage

♦ Transition stage

♦ Working stage

♦ Termination.

In the *initial stage*, group members are getting to know one another, and the counselor's task is to help them develop a sense of trust and co-hesion. Ice-breaker activities can enable the group to get off to a positive start by helping members feel comfortable and at ease. During this stage, the purpose of the group is explained, rules are discussed, and group members' expectations are explored.

The *transition stage* is a time of change in which members confront the reluctance of the group to proceed. During this stage, anxiety surfaces and members often show resistance, which may manifest as avoidance behaviors such as lateness to group sessions, superficial chatting, or refusal to self-disclose. Resistance can also appear as hostility and challenges directed at other group members and/or the group leader. The counselor must carefully respond to the members' concerns and attempt to build trust so that the group can negotiate the turmoil of this stage.

After the group moves through the transition stage, members start to focus on their real concerns and the *working stage* begins. Members have sufficient trust to give and receive authentic feedback, to try out new behaviors, and to work through their issues. The counselor may use role playing and modeling to help members acquire new skills.

The final stage of the group process is *termination*. Members evaluate their own progress in achieving their goals, give feedback to others, and make plans to continue working independently on their issues after the group has concluded. The counselor prepares members for the ending of the group by attempting to bring about closure in the last several sessions. At termination, an evaluation of the group is conducted and a follow-up group session may be planned for a future date.

ETHICAL ISSUES IN GROUP WORK WITH MINORS

As in individual counseling, children have a right to expect confidentiality regarding what is discussed in group-counseling sessions. Although counselors cannot guarantee that every group member will keep all information absolutely confidential, they can set the norm of confidentiality and let group members know that they are expected to keep disclosures private. Because children are minors, parents have a legal right to know of matters that impact the well-being of their children. As in individual counseling, however, counselors should attempt to respect the confidentiality of children as much as possible, and speak to parents in general terms regarding their children's progress in group sessions. The specific content of a child's disclosures should generally not be revealed to parents unless the counselor has an ethical duty to warn them in cases of clear and imminent danger to the child or others. To ensure that parents understand and accept the purpose and nature of group work, school counselors can send written consent forms home to parents before the group begins informing them that their children have been selected to participate in a group. The consent forms would give a brief description of the group's purpose, rules, number of sessions, expectations regarding confidentiality, and process. If the group sessions are to be videotaped or audiotaped, parents must give specific written consent allowing their children to be taped. Parents always have the option of choosing not to allow their children to participate in a group or to be taped.

Counselors have the primary responsibility of ensuring the safety of group members and protecting them from physical and psychological harm. To accomplish this mandate, counselors should screen potential group members to assess their suitability for group work. Pregroup interviews with possible participants can allow counselors to identify children that might pose a threat to others or who might be better served in individual counseling. Even with careful screening, however, children may sometimes engage in hurtful behaviors toward others. When such behaviors occur in a group, counselors must quickly and skillfully intervene to protect the welfare of each child and to ensure that the group provides a positive learning experience for all participants.

Peer Helping

In addition to group counseling, school counselors can expand services to assist children and adolescents by setting up peer helping programs. According to the American School Counselor Association (ASCA, 1999), peer helping involves a variety of interpersonal helping behaviors assumed by nonprofessionals who undertake a helping role with others of approximately the same age who share related values, experiences, and lifestyles. Peer-helping programs provide the following services to students:

♦ *One-to-one assistance:* Talking with peers about personal or school concerns, providing information about career options, or making referrals to community resources.

♦ *Group helping:* Serving as group leaders, peer-helping trainers, communication-skills teachers, and counseling-group assistants.

♦ *Educational assistance:* Providing tutoring in academic areas, serving as readers for nonreaders, assisting special-education professionals in working with learning and behaviorally disabled students.

♦ *Hospitality:* Welcoming and guiding new students and their parents around the school.

♦ *Outreach:* Helping increase peers' use of counseling services, serving as listeners for students who feel uncomfortable talking with counselors, alerting counselors to problems of a serious nature so as to prevent crisis situations.

♦ *Growth:* Increasing peer helpers' own personal growth and learning by assisting others, training peer helpers to become more effective adults, and preparing them for future careers in the helping professions.

In order to plan and implement effective peer-helping programs, the American School Counselor Association (1999) recommends that school counselors first determine the needs of the population served and then select appropriate peer helpers to address the identified concerns. Training, supervision, and support must be provided to peer helpers on a regular basis, so school counselors should schedule time each week to meet with and monitor these students. Because program evaluation is essential, school counselors should also conduct follow-up studies of the effectiveness of the program and report the results to the population served and to other interested individuals (e.g., school boards).

By providing parental support, offering individual and group counseling, teaching affective education, and developing peer-helping programs, counselors can help to ensure children's successful passage into adolescence. Childhood—that magical time of both wonder and bewilderment—can thus have a happy ending.

EXERCISE **9**

"Life Aspirations"

Choose to do one of the following: write a poem *or* draw a symbolic picture.

Materials: Paper and pen for the poem. Paper 9" × 12" or larger newsprint, crayons or felt markers in a variety of colors.

Directions: Sit in silence. You may close your eyes if you wish. Reflect on the dreams, wishes, and aspirations you have for your life. Allow images, impressions, and feelings to emerge. When you are ready, open your eyes and either write a poem or draw a picture of your "life aspirations."

Reflection Questions:

1. Did you discard or change any images that emerged? If you did, go back and recapture these and list them, or re-do the exercise.
2. Where are you in terms of achieving your aspirations?
3. Have your aspirations changed from those you had as a child, an adolescent, or adult?
4. How satisfied are you with your aspirations?

Chapter Ten

Adolescents
Development and Theories

A TEEN, BRENDON, DESCRIBED HIMSELF in the following way: "I'm the kind of person who does the minimum. I don't want to put out the effort because I have better things to do, like just hanging out and watching TV" (Hersch, 1999, p. 79). As you reflect on your own adolescence, what were you like? What adjectives would you use to describe yourself in your teen years? As one of the authors thinks back to the days of her youth, the popular saying comes to mind, "If you can remember the '60s, you weren't really there." While there may be much that I don't remember from those wild times, I will certainly never forget the emotions that I felt—sometimes the heights of bliss . . . other times the depths of despair—but always, always intense.

In this chapter we will delve into the often topsy-turvy world of adolescence and consider the factors that combine to make the teen years so dramatic. Perhaps at this point, we should congratulate you on surviving your own adolescence . . . because, if you were like many of us, the teen years were not without peril and the road to adulthood was risky indeed.

Physical Changes of Adolescence

PHASES OF ADOLESCENCE

The physical changes of adolescence commence with the adolescent growth spurt that produces rapid increases in height and weight. It is not uncommon for individuals to grow three to four inches within a single year during this period, which usually begins for girls at around age 11 or 12, and for boys at 13 to 14. Puberty, which immediately follows the growth spurt, marks the beginning of adolescence, which is beginning almost two years earlier than it did a century ago.

In the United States, adolescence lasts for a number of years and can be divided into three phases: 1) early adolescence, which extends from approximately ages 10 through 14; 2) middle adolescence, which lasts from ages 15 through 17; and 3) late adolescence, for those who delay entry into adulthood due to educational or social factors, which can extend from 18 into the twenties (Carnegie Council on Adolescent Development, 1995).

PRIMARY SEX CHARACTERISTICS

Puberty constitutes the beginning of reproductive life and is accompanied by major changes in the primary sex characteristics that make reproduction possible. For girls, these include changes in the ovaries, fallopian tubes, uterus, and vagina that lead to *menarche*—the beginning of the menstrual periods. For boys, these changes include the development of the penis, scrotum, testes, prostate gland, and seminal vesicles to produce enough sperm to make reproduction possible.

SECONDARY SEX CHARACTERISTICS

In addition to the changes in primary sex characteristics, puberty brings new developments in secondary sex characteristics for both boys and girls. Female breasts and hips enlarge, and male faces grow hair. Both sexes experience the growth of pubic and underarm hair, deepening of voices, and increases in hormone levels. Increased estrogen production in girls stimulates greater subcutaneous fat deposits that create the curvaceous female body shape, while increased testosterone in boys leads to the more lean and muscular male physique. Because our society places so much emphasis on physical appearance, adolescents whose secondary sex characteristics develop earlier or later than their peers often experience much anxiety about being different.

Cognitive Characteristics of Adolescence

FORMAL OPERATIONS

The cognitive shifts that occur in adolescence are no less significant than the physical changes that occur. Piaget found that at around age 11 or 12, children move from the stage of concrete operational thought into that of formal operations (Inhelder & Piaget, 1958). The transition into formal operations is marked by the ability to think hypothetically and abstractly. No longer are cognitions limited to reasoning about actual objects that exist, but now thinking can encompass abstract concepts and ideas. Formal operational thought is *propositional*, in that it is characterized by the ability to use logical propositions to draw specific conclusions (e.g., all dogs are mammals. Fido is a dog. Therefore Fido is a mammal). In addition, formal operational thought is *combinatorial*, in that adolescents can consider numerous possible combinations of variables as they attempt to solve logical problems. The ability to engage in formal operational thought broadens adolescents' horizons because they become able to imagine possibilities that they have never experienced and to dream of what could be, rather than just accepting what is. For this reason, adolescence can be a time of intense idealism, but also extreme frustration when teens' visions of a more perfect world do not immediately turn into reality.

ADOLESCENT EGOCENTRISM

For adolescents, the ability to use formal operational thought is tantamount to acquiring a new skill. It is therefore not difficult to understand that, like with any new skill, they will attempt to practice it. What can be more difficult to understand, however, are the adolescents themselves as they practice their newly acquired cognitive abilities and seem to place extraordinary emphasis on the power of their own thoughts and logic. Adolescents' belief in the omnipotence of their own ideas, their preoccupation with themselves, and their relative inability to assume that others' perspectives are as legitimate as their own is known to as *adolescent egocentrism*.

In studying adolescents, Elkind (1967) noted that adolescent egocentrism is especially evident in what he termed the *imaginary audience* and the *personal fable*. The imaginary audience refers to all the individuals that might be concerned about the adolescent's appearance and behavior. The imaginary audience is typically the "they" that adolescents refer to so frequently in their conversations; for example, when 13-year-old Julie disgustedly says to her mom who is taking her to school, "Just drop me off at the corner before we get to school—what would *they* say if they saw me in the car with *you*?" Because the imaginary audience is so pervasive and important during the teen years, adolescents are often self-conscious and worry excessively about how they are being perceived. Fortunately, the older we get, the smaller and less important our imaginary audiences become. Thus although we may still feel uncomfortable around certain people when we're having a "bad hair day," we usually don't stay home because of it as we are likely to have done when we were teens.

The personal fable refers to the adolescents' fantasies of being special and not subject to the circumstances that befall other humans. The sense of invulnerability present in the personal fable, in which the hero is the adolescent, explains the risk-taking that is so prevalent during the teen years. An adolescent can believe wholeheartedly, "No one has ever felt the way I feel," "I can do drugs, but I won't get addicted," or "Even though I may speed, I'm a safe driver and I won't have an accident." As we mature, we still believe in our own personal fables, but never with as much conviction as when we were young. Even though we may still speed up to get through the yellow light just as it turns red, we usually have a lurking suspicion that someday—but of course, not today!—we may receive the ticket that we know we richly deserve. Adolescents' personal fables, however, free them from the fear of consequences and provide them with the illusion that just about any risky behavior will be acceptable, because negative outcomes cannot happen to them.

Issues, Tasks, and Concerns of Adolescents

LIFE TRANSITIONS

As adolescents traverse the rocky road from childhood to adulthood, they are faced with developmental tasks that can have a lasting impact on their future lives. According to Havighurst (1972), these include

♦ preparing for a career
♦ developing more mature relationships with peers
♦ achieving socially responsible behavior
♦ gaining greater independence.

Career preparation gains prominence in the adolescent years, and most adolescents realize that after the elementary school years are over, academic performance becomes increasingly important. Many adolescents need an extra nudge from concerned adults, however, to ensure that they enroll in courses and focus on studies that will provide them options for attending college and other institutions of higher education. Recently, much attention has focused on the "digital divide" that precludes poor and minority students from having the same opportunities that students in more technologically advanced schools enjoy. In this information age, it is critically important that all students have access to, and are encouraged to enroll in, educational programs that will prepare them for the jobs of the future in which technology will prevail.

During the teen years, adolescents are expected to assume more mature relationships with peers. The teasing and bullying that can be prevalent in childhood and early adolescence are supposed to diminish and be replaced with greater empathy and tolerance for others. Socialization in early adolescence typically occurs with boys and girls congregating in same-sex groups, while later adolescence finds more teens dating and associating with their peers in pairs. Friendships deepen as teens mature, and the superficial conversations of earlier years become more serious, showing a heightened awareness of the needs of others.

The achievement of socially appropriate behavior can be challenging for many teens. Armed with the sense of invulnerability that adolescent egocentrism presents, many teenagers take risks that can be both personally damaging and socially inappropriate. Opportunities abound for adolescents to make choices that have potentially negative outcomes—for example, sexual experimentation, drug use, and weapons possession.

Pressing needs for peer acceptance in adolescence can also lead to behaviors that teens know to be inappropriate, but engage in for fear of social ostracism. It is therefore essential that adults not only help adolescents acquire factual information about real risks, such as sexually transmitted diseases and drug addiction, but also assist them in developing the courage and skills to assertively enact their convictions.

The struggle for increased independence may be the task on which teenagers focus the majority of their attention. Adolescents tend to assume that they are ready for more freedom than their parents may believe their maturity warrants. Formal operational thought, which allows teens to imagine all kinds of hypothetical possibilities, can accentuate adolescents' frustration at having to deal with parental rules that they consider juvenile. Yet in spite of their demands for autonomy, adolescents require structure in their lives and their behavior needs to be monitored.

FAMILY OF ORIGIN ISSUES

According to Erikson (1963), the primary psychosocial issue of adolescence is *identity versus role confusion*. Adolescents struggle to define who they are and attempt to achieve an identity that is uniquely their own. This process involves questioning, and sometimes blatantly challenging, the authority of parents and other adults that have power over them. Because a certain amount of rebellion is normal and healthy, parents usually should not be unduly alarmed at the unusual changes they see in their teens' clothes, hairstyles, and behavior. Erikson suggested that even trying on negative identities, such as engaging in delinquent behavior, was not unusual in adolescence.

In their studies with women, Gilligan (1982) and Miller (1976) questioned the emphasis Erikson placed on the role of autonomy in identity formation. While autonomy may be an integral part of male identity development, they suggested that the process may differ for females. While boys may strive to become more independent and separate from others, girls' identities may be shaped through their affiliation and interdependence with others. Gilligan (1982) stated: "Although independent assertion in judgment and action is considered to be the hallmark of adulthood, it is rather in their care and concern for others that women have both judged themselves and been judged" (p. 70). It is therefore necessary for helping professionals to respect the importance of relationship, connection, mutuality, and empathy in female identity development, rather than placing exclusive emphasis on autonomy.

As they attempt to define themselves, teens of both sexes try on various identities and evaluate how their peers react to their new behaviors and ways of being. A typical telephone conversation between adolescents illustrates the value that is placed on peer feedback as a form of self-exploration:

What are you wearing tomorrow? I'm probably going to wear my new jeans, what do you think? You're wearing a dress? Maybe I should do that too, but I don't know. I'm just not into that whole feminine thing. But then if you do, and I don't, they may think I'm making some kind of statement or something. Do you think they'd think I was weird? Now I don't know what to do.

Teens often spend long hours engaged in animated discussions about topics that seem trivial to adults, but which contribute to their understanding of themselves. Such experimentation, whether through words or action, provides a foundation for self-discovery and is a natural part of growing up. Problems can arise when adolescents are not allowed to assert their own preferences, but are instead expected to adhere to the rigid expectations of adults. Adults must provide a careful balance between exerting too much control over teens and not providing enough.

Situational Conditions

A GENERATION AT RISK

In late 1995, the Carnegie Council on Adolescent Development published a ground-breaking study, *Great Transitions: Preparing Adolescents for a New Century*, which included a vast compilation of current research findings regarding adolescent behavior and issues. The council found early adolescence (ages 10–14) to be a time of both tremendous opportunity and great risk for teens because of the extensive demands and expectations placed upon them. The risks and threats that face teenagers are far more serious than they were in the past, and yet millions of adolescents receive little guidance or support from adults. Without adequate monitoring and supervision, teens are left alone to cope with social pressure from peers involving drugs, sex, and antisocial activity. The report cited the following alarming statistics:

- The firearm homicide rate for 10–14 year olds more than doubled between 1985 and 1992 (from 0.8 to 1.9 per 100,000). For Black males, the rate increased from 3.0 to 8.4 per 100,000 during the same period.
- Injuries are the leading cause of death for young adolescents, and the major injuries experienced by young adolescents involve motor-vehicle crashes.
- In a national representative sample of adolescents 10–16 years old, one-fourth of the respondents reported having experienced an assault or abuse during the previous year. Approximately 20 percent of the documented child abuse and neglect cases in 1992 involved young adolescents between the ages of 10 and 13.
- Although it is illegal to sell alcohol to individuals under 21 years

of age, two-thirds of eighth-graders report that they have already tried alcohol, and a quarter say that they are current drinkers. Twenty-eight percent of eighth-graders say that they have been drunk at least once.

♦ Marijuana use among eighth-graders more than doubled between 1991 and 1994, from 6.2 to 13 percent.

The situational conditions that face adolescents might be challenging to individuals of any age, but can be especially troublesome to young teens who have limited maturity, a sense of their own invulnerability, a spirit of rebelliousness, and an almost desperate need to be accepted by peers. The early adolescent years therefore present a critical time for prevention and interventions to occur. The Carnegie Council cited the following trends within our society as posing significant risks to adolescents:

♦ Changes in the family structure that have led to diminished parental nurturance and guidance

♦ The shifting nature of work that has resulted in more dead-end jobs for those without college degrees

♦ The gap between adolescents' early reproductive capacity and adult roles

♦ The dominance of the media as an influence in adolescents' lives

♦ Diversity in the population in which there are large numbers of disadvantaged minorities.

CHANGES IN THE FAMILY STRUCTURE

Research shows that today, slightly more than half of all American children and adolescents will spend part of their youth in a single-parent home. With the rising divorce rate and more parents in the workforce, teens are spending more time alone or in the company of peers, rather than with caring adults. In our transient society, the neighborhood networks and extended family that used to be available to monitor children's behavior also seem to have vanished.

Although teens demand freedom, a growing concern is that due to adult absence, teens have far too much autonomy and lack of structure in their lives. "Latchkey kids," who spend their after-school hours unsupervised while their parents work or engage in other activities, operate in isolation from the adult world. According to Patricia Hersch (1999), these teens constitute a "tribe apart" and are at extreme risk. In her three-year longitudinal study of suburban teens, Hersch's findings supported the trends found by the Carnegie Council and showed cause for concern:

> In the vacuum where traditional behavioral expectations for young people used to exist, in the silence of empty houses and neighborhoods, young people have built their own community. The adolescent community is a

creation by default, an amorphous grouping of young people that constitutes the world in which adolescents spend their time. Their dependence on
each other fulfills the universal human longing for community, and inadver-
tently cements the notion of a tribe apart. More than a group of peers, it
becomes in isolation a society with its own values, ethics, rules, worldview,
rites of passage, worries, joys, and momentum. It becomes teacher, adviser,
entertainer, challenger, nurturer, inspirer, and sometimes destroyer. (p. 21)

In the absence of a strong and nurturing adult presence, some teens
join gangs to achieve a sense of family and inclusion. Gangs provide a
sense of identity, offer respect, and recognize the competence of adolescents who conform to their strict norms. The acceptance that comes from
gang membership is procured at a high price, however, as gangs tend to
expect members to participate in dangerous and/or antisocial activities.

THE SHIFTING NATURE OF WORK

In the past, a high school education was sufficient to enter the workforce and eventually earn enough to comfortably support a family. This
is no longer the case, and thousands of high school graduates are finding
themselves locked into low-paying, dead-end jobs with no hope of
advancement. The growing emphasis on technology and the globaliza-
tion of the marketplace has left fewer high-paying, secure jobs available
to those who lack a college education. Staying in school is now the single
most-important action adolescents can take to improve their future economic prospects. In 1992, high school graduates earned almost $6,000
more per year than high school dropouts; however, high school graduates earned a mean annual income of only $18,737 compared to the
$32,629 earned by college graduates (U.S. Department of Commerce,
1994). Yet one in eight youths in the United States never graduates from
high school, and two in five never completes a single year of college
(Children's Defense Fund, 2001). For teens from poor families who lack
the financial resources to attend college, the future can appear bleak. It is
not surprising that some teens turn to alternative means of acquiring
money (e.g., drug dealing and prostitution) that promise high incomes,
albeit at great cost.

THE GAP BETWEEN EARLY ADOLESCENTS' REPRODUCTIVE CAPACITY AND ADULT ROLES

Puberty is truly a turning point, because before puberty individuals *are*
children, while after puberty, they *can have* children. With puberty occurring approximately two years earlier than in the last century, the rate of
"children having children" is on the rise. Recent statistics show one in
eight U.S. children being born to a teenage mother (Children's Defense
Fund, 2001), with the greatest rate of increase in teen births in girls aged
15 and under (Carnegie Council on Adolescent Development, 1995).

Teen pregnancy poses a variety of significant risks for both parent and child. Women who give birth as teens are more likely to live in poverty longer than those who have children later in life, to have diminished educational opportunities, and to experience difficulties in identity development (Kuziel-Perri & Snarey, 1991). In addition, there are much higher health risks for both mother and child in teen deliveries, and the children of teen mothers are more likely to be raised in poverty, suffer maltreatment, achieve less academically, develop problem behaviors, and become teen parents themselves (Donnelly & Voydanoff, 1991). Most teen pregnancies are unplanned, but not all are unwanted. Some girls believe that a baby will provide the love they long for and help them feel needed, while some boys think that fathering children is a sign of virility and manhood.

THE DOMINANCE OF THE MEDIA

By the time children reach adolescence, they will have spent more hours watching television than with teachers (Carnegie Council on Adolescent Development, 1995). Teens spend enormous amounts of time— often without adult supervision—playing video games, listening to music, surfing the Internet, and watching television. The influence of the media on naturally impressionable adolescents is pervasive, but not always positive. Themes of violence, hatred, hopelessness, and death permeate the messages that teens imbibe and hence have had some devastating aftermaths.

Consider the case of John McCollum, a teen who committed suicide while lying on his bed with his headphones on, listening to the music of Ozzy Osbourne. John spent the last day of his life in his own room listening to songs by Osbourne such as "Suicide Solution." The song argues that suicide is the only way to escape the evils of existence—and that in the face of death's inevitability, it is a rational and even enviable choice. The recording included words that were sung at one-and-a-half times the normal rate of speech and repeated for approximately ten seconds, urging the listener to get a gun, give up struggling with life, and use it on oneself.

Apparently John McCollum got the message and acted on it. His family filed suit against both Osbourne and CBS records for negligence, product liability, and intentional misconduct, alleging that the song contained lyrics that were not immediately intelligible and that its strong, pounding rhythm utilized a hemisync process of sound waves that impact the listener's mental state (*McCollum v. CBS*, 1988). The influence of the media is increasingly being implicated when teens commit desperate acts of violence against themselves and others, yet without adult supervision, adolescents will undoubtedly continue to partake of all that the media offers regardless of its content.

DIVERSITY IN THE POPULATION

While the United States has always been a nation comprised of individuals from many racial and ethnic groups, diversity is increasing at a rapid rate. Today, one-third of our teens are of non-European descent, and by the year 2050 approximately half of our entire population is expected to be African American, American Indian, Latino/Hispanic, and Asian/Pacific Islander (Carnegie Council on Adolescent Development, 1995). Many urban schools now have large numbers of disadvantaged minority students whose needs must be addressed, and the numbers are growing. It will become more and more important to ensure that all students receive an education that qualifies them for the jobs of the future, and that all students learn to respect others who are different from themselves.

VIOLENCE

In addition to the major trends, there are other important situational conditions that affect adolescents in contemporary society. Perhaps one of the most disturbing is that of violence. While some question the significance of the media's influence, few can deny that violence presents a tremendous risk to adolescents in the United States. One in 1,056 children in the country will be killed by guns before age 20 (Children's Defense Fund, 2001). The number of teens affected by violence is staggering but, perhaps even more disturbing, is that it is happening to adolescents at younger and younger ages. Nearly a million adolescents between ages 12 through 19 are victims of violent crimes each year, and young adolescents are victims of assault more than any other group (Carnegie Council on Adolescent Development, 1995).

Teens are not only the victims of violence, however, but are also often the perpetrators of it. Shock waves resounded through our nation when we watched two teens from affluent backgrounds slaughter their peers in the library of Columbine High School and then take their own lives. Many wondered how such a crime could have been committed by such intelligent and supposedly normal adolescents, whom few would have suspected of presenting a serious threat to society. Could this tragedy have been predicted and, with appropriate interventions, been avoided? Although the reasons why the murders and suicides occurred may never be known, the predictors that are often mentioned are that the boys appeared to be isolated and different, that they surfed the Internet to find instructions for making bombs, and that they spent much time without their parents' awareness that they were building weapons and collecting firearms.

SUBSTANCE USE AND ABUSE

Teens are also becoming involved with alcohol and drugs at younger ages. One-third of eighth-graders reported the use of illicit drugs, including inhalants; 15 percent of eighth-graders claimed that they drank more than five alcoholic beverages in a row during the past two weeks; and marijuana use more than doubled between 1991 and 1994 (Carnegie Council on Adolescent Development, 1995). Because alcohol, marijuana, and inhalants are considered gateway drugs that often lead to more dangerous substance use, such early adolescent involvement is even more problematic.

ACQUAINTANCE RAPE

Associated with substance abuse is acquaintance rape, which is also sometimes referred to as "date rape." More sexual assault occurs among individuals who know each other than is perpetrated on victims by total strangers. For teens, this often consists of forced sexual contact imposed on them by other teens. In some cases, the perpetrator simply overpowers the victim and ignores any protestations that might occur. Frequently, however, such rapes occur while adolescents are under the influence of alcohol or drugs. Though the contact may be unwanted, the teen may be too intoxicated to wage enough resistance to keep the act from happening. As one teen stated, "When you're drunk, you'll have sex with people you wouldn't even have lunch with when you're sober." The effects of acquaintance rape can be both devastating and long lasting, and may include posttraumatic stress disorder, sexually transmitted diseases, sexual dysfunction, and unwanted pregnancies.

PREVENTIVE INTERVENTIONS

Because the teen years are a time of transition, preventive interventions can play an essential role in ensuring a safe passage into adulthood. The Carnegie Council on Adolescent Development (1995) recommends that the following interventions begin in the early adolescent years:

♦ Sustain parental involvement in middle schools

♦ Create parent peer support groups

♦ Provide prospective guidance to parents on adolescent transitions

♦ Assess public and private policies and practices.

Sustaining Parental Involvement. Parental involvement in the schools typically diminishes after the elementary years, yet there is a critical need for parents to stay in close contact with school personnel and to participate in school activities. Parents should be encouraged to volunteer in the schools and to serve on school governance committees. In low-income neighborhoods, it can be especially beneficial to have schools serve the role of family-resource centers and offer educational-support services for parents, such as employment counseling, computer literacy, English-as-a-second-language, health promotion, and citizenship. Schools can also teach parents about the normal transitions of adolescence and how to assist their children with homework.

Creating Parent Peer Support Groups. Because so many parents find dealing with adolescents to be challenging, parent peer support groups can provide opportunities for mutual support and encouragement. Participants can share information, learn from each others' experiences, discover how to set and enforce limits, develop enhanced communication skills, and find out about community resources. Parents can also form networks to help one another gain access to health care, adult education, job placement and training, and literacy.

Providing Guidance on Adolescent Transitions. The American Medical Association (1997) has recommended that parents be given their *Guidelines for Adolescent Preventive Services* as part of adolescents' annual health examinations. Schools might also provide parents with information regarding the normal developmental changes of adolescence, including physical, sexual, and social development, symptoms of physical diseases and emotional distress, and ways to promote healthy development and prevent future problems (e.g., monitoring adolescents' activities, restricting use of tobacco and sexual behavior, helping teens drive safely).

Assessing Public and Private Policies. Because many policies have not kept pace with the needs of families in today's world, it is recommended that certain changes be made. Professionals who work with adolescents (e.g., counselors, teachers, nurses, physicians) must also be prepared to work with their families. Employers should give parents options that would allow them greater involvement with their adolescent children, such as flex-time, job-sharing, telecommuting, and part-time work with benefits. Congress should extend the child-care tax credit from its present ceiling of age 10 to age 14 to allow parents to procure child-care for their young adolescents in the afternoon and early evening hours while they work.

The Carnegie Council on Adolescent Development believes that if such preventive measures are implemented, adolescents will be at much less risk than they presently are. Because early adolescence is such a critical time in the lives of teens, these recommendations may help to prevent the development of later problems.

Major Physical and/or Emotional Disorders and Conditions

EATING DISORDERS

Our society places a premium on physical appearance, yet few real people conform to the ideal image that the media presents. The "waif look" that is so popular today depicts females with bodies so lean and without curves that they appear boyish and prepubescent. While models often starve themselves or undergo surgery to achieve this look, adolescent girls sometimes mistakenly assume that it is the norm that they must achieve. Many teens have body-image concerns and worry about being overweight when they are not; however, some adolescents develop major eating disorders such as anorexia and bulimia that can be life threatening.

Anorexia nervosa is an eating disorder characterized by a dramatic loss of weight caused by self-starvation, rather than by a medical condition. The *Diagnostic and Statistical Manual of Mental Disorders*, 4th edition (*DSM-IV*) (American Psychiatric Association, 1994) criteria for this disorder include the following:

♦ Refusal to maintain body weight at or above a minimally normal weight for age and height (e.g., weight loss leading to maintenance of body weight less than 85 percent of that expected weight gain during the period of growth, leading to body weight less than 85 percent of that expected)

♦ Intense fear of gaining weight even though being underweight

♦ Disturbance in the way in which one's body weight or shape is experienced, undue influence of body weight or shape on self-evaluation, or denial of the seriousness of the current low body weight.

Anorexics may be further specified by type:

• *Restricting type:* During the current episode of anorexia nervosa, the person has not regularly engaged in binge-eating or purging behavior (i.e., self-induced vomiting or the misuse of laxatives, diuretics, or enemas)

• *Binge-eating/purging type:* During the current episode of anorexia nervosa, the person has regularly engaged in binge-eating or purging behavior.

Bulimia nervosa is a related eating disorder in which an individual engages in recurrent episodes of binge-eating in which he or she feels out of control. The *DSM-IV* (American Psychiatric Association, 1994) lists the following characteristics for bulimia:

♦ Recurrent episodes of binge-eating, characterized by both of the following:

• Eating, in a discrete period of time (e.g., within any two-hour period), an amount of food that is definitely larger than most people would eat during a similar period of time and under similar circumstances

• A sense of lack of control over eating during the episode (e.g., a feeling that one cannot stop eating or control what or how much one is eating)

♦ Recurrent inappropriate compensatory behavior in order to prevent weight gain, such as self-induced vomiting, misuse of laxa-

tives, diuretics, enemas, or other medications, fasting, or excessive exercise

♦ The binge-eating and inappropriate compensatory behaviors
  both occur, on average, at least twice a week for three months

♦ Self-evaluation is unduly influenced by body shape and weight

♦ The disturbance does not occur exclusively during episodes of
  anorexia nervosa.

Bulimics may also be further specified by type:

• *Purging type:* During the current episode of bulimia nervosa,
  the person has regularly engaged in self-induced vomiting or
  the misuse of laxatives, diuretics, or enemas

• *Nonpurging type:* During the current episode of bulimia nervosa,
  the person has used other inappropriate compensatory behaviors
  such as fasting or excessive exercise, but has not regularly engaged in self-induced vomiting or the misuse of laxatives,
  diuretics, or enemas.

Although the behaviors of anorexia and bulimia differ, both disorders
involve a preoccupation with food and a persistent determination to be
thin. Both disorders are also frequently accompanied by other associated
symptoms such as depression, anxiety, and perfectionistic thinking.

Because anorexics are at risk of death, treatment often involves inpatient hospitalization to refeed the client until a healthy target weight is
achieved. In addition, behavioral interventions that include nonpunitive
reinforcers (e.g., empathic praise, exercise-related limits and rewards, bed
rest, and privileges related to achieving weight goals) can be employed
(American Psychiatric Association, 2001).

The primary goal of treatment for bulimia is to reduce binge-eating
and purging. Because bulimics are often of normal body weight, it is not
usually necessary to have weight restoration as a goal. Instead, the goals
of interventions would include improving the client's attitudes about the
eating disorder, increasing the variety of foods eaten, minimizing food
restriction, encouraging healthy exercise patterns, and addressing underlying themes related to eating disorders. These may include developmental issues, body-image concerns, self-esteem, sexual and aggressive
difficulties, gender-role expectations, coping styles, problem-solving, and
family dysfunction. Cognitive behavioral therapy has been found to be
the most efficacious treatment for bulimia (American Psychiatric Association, 2001).

In treating bulimia, Browers and Wiggum (1993) observed perfectionism to be evident in their clients' unrealistic expectations of themselves
and in their dichotomous thinking. Bulimics hold unrealistic expectations
of themselves that involve thinking in terms of *shoulds* and *musts* (e.g., "I

must eat 'good' foods all the time," "I should be in control all the time," "I shouldn't get angry"). Dichotomous, or all-or-nothing, thinking refers to the perfectionistic tendency to think in terms of a continuum that has only two extremes, and no middle ground. With dichotomous thinking, there is only complete success or total failure (e.g., "If I don't lose twenty pounds, I've failed," or "If I'm not thin, I'm fat").

To control such perfectionistic thinking, Browers and Wiggum (1993) recommend a treatment approach that consists of the following steps:

(1) Help the client understand perfectionism. Use a cognitive approach to teach the client about unrealistic expectations and dichotomous thinking

(2) Identify and express fears. Address the client's concerns that letting go of perfectionism will plunge him or her into the opposite extreme (e.g., "If I give up trying to be thin, I'll just get fat," or "If I'm not slim, people won't like me")

(3) Develop courage. Teach coping techniques for dealing with fear such as cognitive restructuring, relaxation training, and visualization. Encourage the client to participate in a group for support and interaction.

DEPRESSION

Adolescence is a time of intense emotions—both positive and negative. While it is not uncommon for adolescents to be moody, sad, and irritable at times, some teens suffer from major depression and have the potential to become suicidal. A study sponsored by the National Institute of Mental Health suggested that the prevalence of depression in 9 to 17 year olds is more than 6 percent in a six-month period, with 4.9 percent having major depression (Shaffer, Fisher, & Dulkan, 1996). It is estimated that up to 2.5 percent of children and 8.3 percent of adolescents in the United States suffer from depression (Birmaher, Ryan, & Williamson, 1996). These statistics are especially troubling, because a recent longitudinal study found that depression in adolescents is associated with substance abuse and suicidal behavior, often recurs and continues into adulthood, and may predict more serious illness in adulthood (Weissman, Wolk, & Goldstein, 1999).

Although the symptoms and diagnostic criteria for depression are the same for children and adolescents as for adults, the disorder is often unrecognized in youth. The symptoms of depression are expressed differently at various developmental stages, and children and adolescents sometimes lack the ability or willingness to verbally describe their internal emotional states. Rather than stating how bad they feel, they may simply appear irritable or act out their feelings through misbehavior or disobedience. The *DSM-IV* (American Psychiatric Association, 1994) lists the following symptoms of major depressive disorder for children, adolescents, and adults:

- Persistent sad or irritable mood
- Loss of interest or pleasure in activities once enjoyed
- Significant change in appetite or body weight
- Difficulty sleeping or oversleeping
- Psychomotor agitation or retardation
- Loss of energy, fatigue
- Feelings of worthlessness or inappropriate guilt
- Difficulty concentrating
- Recurrent thoughts of death or suicide.

An individual must have five or more of these symptoms for two or more weeks before a diagnosis of major depression can be made. A less serious but usually more chronic form of depression is Dysthymic Disorder. Children and adolescents are diagnosed with Dysthymic Disorder when they show a depressed mood that persists for at least a year that is accompanied by at least two other symptoms of major depression.

Although depression is sometimes difficult to recognize in children and adolescents, the following indicators may suggest its presence:

- Frequent absences from school or poor school performance
- Frequent vague, nonspecific physical complaints such as headaches, stomach aches, muscle aches, or fatigue
- Outbursts of crying, shouting, complaining, or unexplained irritability
- Talk of or attempts to run away from home
- Withdrawal from friends and activities once enjoyed
- Boredom and lack of enthusiasm
- Alcohol or substance abuse
- Reckless behavior
- Difficulty with relationships
- Social isolation and poor communication
- Extreme sensitivity to rejection or failure
- Increased irritability, hostility, or agitation
- Recurring thoughts of death or suicide.

If a child or adolescent exhibits symptoms of depression, there are several inventories that can be used for screening. For children ages 7 to 17, screening can be done with the Children's Depression Inventory (Kovacs, 1992), while for adolescents, the Beck Depression Inventory (Beck,

1967) and the Center for Epidemiologic Studies Depression Scale (CES-D) are available. If the screening indicates depression, a thorough evaluation should be done by mental health professionals that includes interviews with the youth and his or her parents. If possible and appropriate, others who know the child or adolescent well, such as friends or a teacher, may also be consulted.

Treatment for child and adolescent depression may include short-term psychotherapy; interventions involving the home or school environment; and, in some severe cases, medication. Cognitive-behavioral therapy is a short-term approach that has been shown to be highly effective in treating depression in children and teens. This therapy involves helping clients learn to identify and challenge their cognitive distortions that produce a sense of hopelessness about themselves, the world, and the future (e.g., "I'm just a loser," "Everyone hates me," "I'll never be happy").

Home and school interventions may involve working with parents or school personnel to help them understand the symptoms of depression and find ways to support the child or teen. These interventions may also include providing family therapy and conflict-resolution sessions, teaching parenting and communication skills; and offering group counseling with other adolescents on issues such as anger control, coping with depression, and substance abuse.

In very severe cases, antidepressant medication such as serotonin reuptake inhibitors (e.g., Prozac and Paxil) may be given on a short-term basis. Because the use of antidepressant medication with youth is controversial, however, drug treatments are generally only recommended for those who are unable or unwilling to undergo therapy, have not responded after eight to twelve counseling sessions, have bipolar, atypical, or severe depression, or who have chronic or recurring depression (Renaud, Axelson, & Birmaher, 1999).

SUICIDE

Children and teens who are depressed may view suicide as the only viable solution to their problems. While adolescents have probably always had occasional thoughts of suicide, more teens are successfully completing the act. From 1980 to 1997, the rate of suicide among 15 to 19 year olds increased by 11 percent, and among 10 to 14 year olds by 109 percent (Centers for Disease Control and Prevention, 2000). This makes suicide responsible for more deaths than any disease in 15 to 19 year olds. Easy access to firearms and other weapons may ensure a higher success rate for those who attempt suicide, and the compelling influence of the media may provoke more suicide attempts.

Not all teens who listen to songs with disturbing lyrics contemplate suicide, but it is important for helping professionals to be aware of risk factors and assessment procedures for children and adolescents who appear to be potentially suicidal. Research shows that more than 90 percent of children and adolescents who commit suicide have a mental disorder (Shaffer & Craft, 1999), with the most common diagnosis being a mood disorder with or without a substance abuse disorder and/or anxiety disorder (Shaffer, Gould, Fisher, Trautment, Moreau, Kleinman, & Florey, 1996). Other risk factors include family dysfunction, feelings of hopelessness, school problems, interpersonal issues, homosexuality, and exposure to the suicidal behavior of others (Cotton & Range, 1996; McLaughlin, Miller, & Warwick, 1996; Wannan & Fombonne, 1998).

Stoelb and Chiriboga (1998) suggest a four-stage process model for determining teens' risk for suicide that includes the assessment of:

STAGE 1
- *Primary risk factors*—presence of affective disorders, previous suicide attempts, and hopelessness. Affective disorders can be assessed by comparing information gained from clinical interviews, observations, and third-party reports with the diagnostic criteria for depression in the *DSM-IV*. Previous suicide attempts and hopelessness can be determined by questioning the adolescent. The presence of any one of these factors can place the teen at severe risk.

STAGE 2
- *Suicidal ideation, intent, and plan*—direct questioning of the adolescent can reveal the nature of the ideation, intensity of the intent, and specificity of the plan (e.g., "Have you ever thought of harming yourself?" "Do you think you would kill yourself?" "How would you do it?" "Do you have a gun, pills, etc.?"). The more specific the plan and the greater availability of the means, the more serious the risk. If there is suicidal ideation, intent, and plan, teens deemed to be at severe risk in stage 1 should still be considered to be at great risk. Without these, teens may be judged to be at moderate or low risk.

STAGE 3
- *Secondary risk factors*—presence of substance abuse and personality disorders. If either of these factors is present, the teen is at greater risk because of the likelihood of impulsive behavior. If they are absent, the teen's risk remains unchanged.

STAGE 4
- *Situational factors*—family dysfunction, unhappy interpersonal relationships, lack of social supports, exposure to suicide, homosexuality, and life stressors. If any of these are present, the diagnosis would include the specifier "with situational factors."

In addition to the above factors, Stanard (2000) suggests assessing the adolescent's reasons for living. Teens who have positive expectations about the future and who believe in their own self-efficacy to cope with stress are less likely to attempt suicide; while those who lack optimism, doubt their own ability to cope, and place a lower value on life are at greater risk. The Reasons for Living Inventory for Adolescents (RFL-A) has been shown to be a valid and reliable instrument for assessing these cognitive factors (Osman, Downs, Kopper, Barrios, Baker, Osman, Besett, & Linehan, 1998).

Treatment for suicidal teens must be based upon the degree of risk they present. Greater protective action is required for those who are at severe risk; with treatment ranging from hospitalization for those who are in clear and imminent danger, to intensive outpatient therapy for those who are at less risk. Adolescents who are at lower risk may be treated similarly to other teens who suffer from depression.

Existential Issues

With the acquisition of formal operational thought often comes an intense idealism and disatisfaction with the world as it is. Many teens struggle to find a sense of purpose and question the meaning of life. Alienation and isolation can lead some to despair, while others experience adolescence as a time of tremendous spiritual growth and personal fulfillment. In looking back, adults sometimes remember feeling more totally alive and exhileratingly aware during these years than they ever have since then, and they long for the exuberance that has passed.

This struggle to make sense of life is beautifully described by psychologist William Sheldon of Columbia University (as cited in Smith, 2001): "Continued observations in clinical practice lead almost inevitably to the conclusion that deeper and more fundamental than sexuality, deeper than the craving for social power, deeper even than the desire for possessions, there is a still more generalized and universal craving in the human makeup. It is the craving for knowledge of the right direction— for orientation" (p. 26). Teens strive to achieve this insight in a relativistic society that offers little guidance regarding what the "right direction" actually is, so they are left to orient themselves via peers, the media, and popular culture.

Jonathan, a teen interviewed by Hersch (1999), spoke of his experiences during the years between seventh and twelfth grades: "I go through huge struggles and I come to realizations. Then I go through huge struggles and realizations and it's kind of like I'm climbing these mountains. One of my biggest fears is that there's so much behind me. I've had so many wonderful times behind me that it's kind of scary. I don't want to spend my whole life thinking about what's behind" (p. 367).

Like Jonathan, many adolescents ponder what lies ahead for them. Fowler (1981) discussed adolescence as the time when stage 3, synthetic-conventional faith, emerged. This stage of faith development involves adolescents composing myths of their personal pasts as well as their possible futures. They define themselves in relation to an authority that is external to the self and are therefore in danger of being dominated by the "tyranny of the *they*" (p. 154). Thus adolescents are easily influenced by the expectations of others in leadership roles and may not question their teachings, but rather accept them wholeheartedly as a source of identity and meaning.

Coupled with the attributes of synthetic-conventional faith is the monumental amount of change that encompasses the teen years. Because individuals are extremely vulnerable when going through periods of tremendous transition, Robinson and Bradley (1998) suggest that teens may be especially susceptible to cult recruitment and cult involvement. A cult is characterized by having: a) a self-proclaimed leader who claims to be led by a higher power, b) members' acceptance of the leader's right to establish rules and lead, c) one set of rules for members and another set for nonmembers, and d) complete allegiance to the leader by the members (Singer, 1978). Cults serve as a support system that provides a sense of purpose and inclusiveness to adolescents as they separate from their families. They offer a source of identity, feelings of security, and hope for the future to teens who dedicate their lives to the cult.

To decrease adolescents' susceptibility to cults, Robinson and Bradley (1998) recommend that counselors help teens learn to cope with transitions. Preventive interventions might include reframing transitions as positive opportunities for growth rather than just negative life events, providing assistance as teens grieve about losses they encounter with transitions, offering encouragement to teens who are struggling, and helping teens prepare in advance for transitions that are coming in the future.

If teens are already involved in cults, treatment should include the client's family in the early stages of the counseling process. Interventions for former cult members should emphasize the identification of maladaptive patterns of responding to transitions and setting goals for establishing a new lifestyle. To decrease feelings of powerlessness, counselors can assist former cult members in identifying their personal strengths and in learning how to use these strengths in daily life. In addition, counselors can help former cult members identify individuals who can serve as a support system, reestablish relationships with family members, relearn decision-making skills, and develop stress-management strategies. Finally, counselors may need to use cognitive restructuring to help rid former cult members of irrational messages they may have accepted without question during their cult membership.

In conclusion, it is necessary to note that although adolescence can be a time of great risk and challenge, most teens negotiate the changes fairly gracefully and reach adulthood without too many lasting scars. As counselors, we can take proactive measures to help ensure that adolescents are prepared for the transitions that await them and are given the assiduous attention they require from caring adults. In the next chapter we will discuss specific counseling interventions that can be used to assist teens in their journey to adulthood.

EXERCISE **10**

"Achievements and Disappointments"

Materials: Six 5" × 8" cards, crayons or felt markers, paper, and a writing instrument.

Directions: Sit in silence with your eyes closed. Reflect on your adolescent years from ages 13 to 17. Allow images and memories to emerge in no particular order or sequence. Sit for as long as you wish. When you are ready, open your eyes and draw a symbol or symbols on separate cards to represent your greatest disappointments. Use one card per disappointment. Do the same for your greatest achievements during your adolescent years. When you are finished, spread all the cards out on a table and look at what you drew. Give each card a title.

Reflection Questions:

1. Did you have more achievements than disappointments? Or, was it more disappointments than achievements? An equal number of each?
2. As you remember the achievements and disappointments, write the feelings you remember for each on the back of the card. Make a list of feelings aroused as you review the cards today.
3. Write a brief description of how the events portrayed on the cards shaped you as you are today.

Chapter Eleven

Counseling Adolescents
Applications

A DOLESCENCE ITSELF CAN BE A TRYING TIME for teens as they struggle with forming a distinct self-identify, developing plans for the future, trying to fit in and be part of a group, starting the last stages of separation and individuation, coping with physical and hormonal changes, and many other developmental and societal tasks that will have a significant impact on the course of their lives. Counseling can range from selecting appropriate coursework and preparing for a career, to working through more serious problems such as substance abuse and clinical depression. Even seemingly simple concerns for the adolescent, such as school absenteeism, can mask more complex problems. The *presenting* problem is often not the *real* problem, but is merely a symptom.

This chapter presents an overview of factors to consider when working with adolescents. Discussed are risk factors, protective or coping factors that prevent difficulties and problems, expected presenting concerns of teens, problems that adolescents face, common adolescent concerns, needed counselor characteristics and knowledge, and guidelines for counseling.

Risk factors are those that are present in the adolescent's environment and/or a part of the person that contribute to difficulties in completing expected development. Many of the factors are not within the person's control, but are imposed on him or her and exert considerable influence on responses and subsequent growth and development. These are factors such as abusive parents, unsafe living environments, physical and emotional conditions, and the instability of the family.

Attention is also given to protective factors. These are the characteristics and environmental forces that can play a major role in prevention of major problems; foster healthy emotional, social, psychological, spiritual, and physical development; and help guide adolescents in completing expected stage transitions. These factors emphasize strengths that can be built on to help guide the adolescent. Malekoff (1997) describes three categories of protective strategies: individual characteristics, bonding, and healthy beliefs and clear standards. Examples of protective factors include resiliency, caring and empathic adults in the adolescent's world, and positive social-group involvement.

The stage of adolescence brings its own set of unique problems and concerns that are exacerbated when other risk factors are present. There are common concerns and problems that all adolescents face such as developing a self-identity, choosing a career, becoming independent, and learning to achieve meaningful intimate relationships, and these are presented along with some more unique problems and concerns. Examples of presenting problems that counselors can expect are discussed. These problems are also common in the sense that they are not unusual. They are not common in the sense that they are a commonality for most, or all, adolescents.

Because of the unique needs of adolescents, counselors and other mental health professionals who work with them must have certain personal characteristics, attitudes, and behaviors. Those that contribute the most to success with adolescents are identified and described.

Success for Adolescents

Although the focus of this chapter is on guiding adolescents through the many and varied developmental tasks, working to resolve issues and concerns, and building inner resources, it is helpful to begin with a picture of what constitutes success for this group. It is all too easy to get caught up in their struggles and emotional intensity where the emphasis is on solving problems and thereby to forget to highlight successes and strengths. The following keys to success highlight strengths that some adolescents possess. These keys can provide a guide for helping adolescents grow, develop and achieve, and serve as benchmarks for success. Keys to success for adolescents include:

- the extent to which they are able to be empathic
- the ability to form and maintain lasting and meaningful relationships with both genders
- the ability to tolerate diversity of opinion and values
- a system of ethics and moral guidelines for behavior
- the capacity to be both independent and work collaboratively

- success in academic endeavors
- the ability to be assertive and to resist peer pressure
- relationships with important adults
- social and emotional skills appropriate to the age group
- the ability to express a wide range of emotions
- understanding how to reach out to others in meaningful ways
- creativity and a sense of humor
- beginning acceptance of personal responsibility
- planning for the future.

The final topic focuses on guidelines for counseling and therapy—counseling in the sense of addressing life-transition concerns, and therapy in the sense of addressing more severe problems. These guidelines are general and appropriate for all sorts of conditions and concerns.

Risk Factors

Malekoff (1997) categorized risk factors for adolescents as community, family, school, and individual. *Community factors* include safety (e.g., availability of drugs, presence of firearms, and social norms about antisocial behavior). *Family factors* are those that describe the nurturing, or lack of nurturing, behavior of the parents, how conflict is managed, and the quality of support available to the adolescent. *School factors* are focused on learning problems (e.g., learning disabilities and academic failure). The *individual risk factors* are categorized as alienation and rebelliousness, and as constitutional factors such as physiological and neurological conditions. Thompson (1998) reviews risk factors and categorizes them as

- a disruptive home environment
- low self-esteem
- learning disabilities
- developmental delays
- emotional difficulties
- interpersonal problems
- lack of social support.

These categories seem to parallel those of Malekoff and include individual, family, and community factors. Although school is a community factor, it is so important in the adolescent's life that it merits a separate category.

Individual characteristics such as intelligence and developmental disabilities can play a major role in the vulnerability and resiliency of adolescents. It is hard to document the specific impact of individual characteristics on responses, but studies support the notion that there is a relationship among personal characteristics, risk factors, and individual responses (Dryfoos, 1990; Garmenzy, 1981; Garmenzy & Rutter, 1983; Werner, 1992; Werner & Smith, 1992).

Protective Factors

Hawkins, Catalano, and Miller (1992) consider protective factors as buffers that reduce the impact of the risk or change the way a person responds to a risk. Protective factors can be individual, such as having a resilient temperament, or may include bonding with parents and other important adults, having social-group involvement, receiving recognition and reinforcement, and having healthy beliefs and clear standards (Hawkins et al., 1992).

Katz (1990) emphasizes the bonding category as being crucial when treating adolescents. He proposes that adolescents want a relationship with an adult who is

- ♦ emotionally available
- ♦ accepting and approving
- ♦ nonjudgmental
- ♦ recognizes the adolescent's potential.

Thus it can be important to assess the extent to which the adolescent has support and encouragement from adults in his or her world as a part of gauging the protective factors available.

Polarities

Scheidlinger (1985) proposes five polarities for adolescence:

- ♦ rebellion against adult control versus need for direction
- ♦ a wish for closeness versus a fear of intimacy
- ♦ acting to push and test limits versus perceiving limits as evidence of caring
- ♦ thoughts of the future versus an orientation to the present
- ♦ being sexually mature versus being cognitively not ready to experience sexuality.

These polarities illustrate the formidable counseling task of working with adolescents—what they need and desire are the very things they push away, devalue, or even rebel against. The counselor has to remain aware that the resistance encountered may be masking a deep need, yearning, or fear.

Common Presenting Problems

Capuzzi and Gross (1995) categorize adolescents' common concerns and problems as

- physical size and appearance
- academic concerns
- social relations
- search for identity
- sexuality.

These categories are illustrated in some typical presenting problems such as

- career and educational choices and plans
- body image (e.g., eating disorders)
- difficulty with acceptance (e.g., joining a gang)
- substance use and abuse
- depression.

In addition to personal and interpersonal problems for the individual, there are also the wider contextual problems such as the family, racial/ethnic conflict, and the unique problems of immigrants from other cultures. Poverty is a major factor in many problems encountered by teens, as noted by Dryfoos (1990). He points out that school failure and dropout, depression and suicide, substance abuse and violence, running away, premature pregnancy, and sexually transmitted diseases correlate with socioeconomic and cultural factors.

Further complications for expected problems in adolescence are some conditions that are no longer unusual. For example, conditions such as the following are found in urban, suburban, and rural communities among adolescents of all social and racial/ethnic groups. These conditions include

- teen pregnancy
- runaways
- homelessness
- sexual abuse
- sexual activity
- sexually transmitted disease
- substance abuse
- suicide
- violent crimes

- ◆ abuse and neglect
- ◆ poverty
- ◆ gangs.

It is not unusual for one or more of these conditions to be part of a presenting problem.

The Counselor

MacLennan and Dies (1992) consider working with adolescents to be difficult and demanding. To be successful, counselors and therapists must have considerable self-understanding and to have worked through their own personal adolescent issues. This self-knowledge is critical to all counseling and therapy but may be even more so when working with adolescents, because their behavior and attitudes can easily trigger unresolved issues. Characteristics, attitudes, and behaviors that are desirable for counselors and therapists include

- ◆ respect for adolescents and their concerns
- ◆ a real enjoyment of working with this age group
- ◆ sensitivity to their moods and meaning of behaviors
- ◆ clarity about personal standards
- ◆ willingness to consider differing viewpoints
- ◆ considerable energy and vitality
- ◆ a sense of humor
- ◆ ability to accept a problem-solving attitude toward life
- ◆ willingness to admit errors
- ◆ genuineness and honesty
- ◆ a nondefensive stance.

These characteristics can be categorized as knowledge, self-understanding, and attitudes. While these are important when working with all clients, they can be especially important when working with adolescents because teens are

- ◆ actively seeking ways to be included
- ◆ trying to develop meaningful intimate relationships
- ◆ seeking to understand who they are
- ◆ preparing to be self-supporting in the future
- ◆ taking significant steps toward separation and individuation.

Coping with dimly understood physical changes, engaging in risky behaviors, and rebelling against parental control and values can accompany many of the usual adolescent tasks and concerns. The counselor has to remain acutely aware of all these factors at all times, and this is not easily accomplished.

Knowledge is crucial. It is important to know and understand

♦ the expected developmental tasks throughout the lifespan

♦ the course of expected physical development and what deviations can occur

♦ the impact of family of origin issues and how these are manifested in the adolescent's behavior

♦ the typical behavior and attitudes for the age group and in the prevailing adolescent culture

♦ how to assess and interpret measures of cognitive ability, achievement, aptitude, and personality

♦ specific information to provide adolescents about such diverse topics as sexually transmitted disease, substance abuse, "normal" growth and development, and career education and choice.

Understanding *developmental tasks* can be important for identifying areas in which adolescents are experiencing possible delays in achieving developmental milestones. Some presenting problems and observed behavior can be understood from the knowledge that certain expected developmental tasks have not been completed or are in progress. This knowledge can help you meet adolescents where they are, rather than trying to work with them on the false assumption that age equals completion of certain developmental tasks.

Physical development and possible deviations are important, because body image and physical changes are of paramount concern to adolescents. Early and late growth spurts and the onset of puberty can produce considerable emotional distress for some adolescents as they compare themselves with others of the same age group. For example, the girl who develops secondary sex characteristics early can be the target for unwanted attention from boys and men who remain unaware of her chronological age. Because of her young age and immaturity, however, the girl may not know how to handle this attention. Boys also can experience similar attention when their physical characteristics do not match expectations for their chronological age, whether their physical development occurs early or late.

The impact of *family of origin issues* cannot be underestimated because adolescents will be dealing with these at the same time they are trying to achieve the expected developmental tasks. Relationships with parents can become strained as adolescents try to achieve more separation and individuation, while their parents simultaneously attempt to keep them safe. Further, adolescents may be trying to determine their personal values, and these may be very different from those held by the family of origin, thus producing considerable tension and distress. At the very least, there may be unresolved family of origin issues that are influential and to which the adolescent remains unaware.

Counselors must know *typical behaviors and attitudes* for adolescents in their community, as well as on the national level, and must also understand developmental expectations for teens in the contemporary world. It is a fatal mistake to approach adolescents today with the assumption that they are as you were during the same period, even if you are not that long out of your teens. Societal changes are occurring rapidly and have significant direct and indirect impacts on individuals, families, and institutions such as schools. Pay attention to the prevailing adolescent culture for a better understanding of your adolescent client.

Your knowledge of *assessment* is vital, as many developmental tasks for adolescents involve gathering information to make choices and decisions. Informed decisions on things such as career choice, academic preparation, and college versus other postsecondary educational options, are examples of decisions that can be enhanced with the use of assessment data. Getting the adolescent the services he or she needs requires first the correct identification of the need. For example, suspected learning disabilities can be identified initially through a battery of tests. There are assessment instruments to help identify and verify a variety of conditions such as depression, sexual trauma, substance abuse, emotional disturbance, and personality disorders. Your job as a counselor demands that you know and use a variety of assessment instruments, as well as knowing when to refer for more in-depth assessment.

The last category of knowledge is the most comprehensive, in that you should have *specific information* on a variety of topics and that you cannot always anticipate what knowledge is needed. For example, consider what you might tell an adolescent client who had concerns about any of the following:

- diabetes
- a mother diagnosed with cancer
- a sexually transmitted disease
- ovarian cysts
- a brother with muscular dystrophy
- a grandfather who is paranoid-schizoid
- catching AIDS
- an incarcerated sibling
- incestuous experiences
- the possibility that he or she is alcoholic.

You are not expected to know everything, but you are expected to have some information, to research the needed topic, and be ready to give your clients factual information.

Self-understanding is also critical as noted by MacLennan and Dies (1992), Fromm-Reichmann (1950), and Sullivan (1953), who considered therapy to be mutual. Katz (1990) emphasizes the importance of engaging the adolescent in his or her treatment, and Carrell (1993) highlights the importance of cooperation and collaboration. In short, you are not "fixing" or doing something to the adolescent, but are instead working with him or her through guiding, encouraging, empowering, and demonstrating your faith and confidence in his or her efficacy. Your self-reflection and self-understanding significantly impact your ability to accomplish these, and the perception the adolescent client has of you will be critical. Who you are will come through more clearly than what you say. Your self-understanding of your values, morals, ethics, ability to accept and tolerate diversity and differing viewpoints, ability to be genuine and honest, ability to empathize, and sensitivity to adolescents' concerns will emerge from your personal work on issues. You can better understand the adolescent if you have a good understanding of your own developmental issues, family of origin issues and concerns, unfinished business, lingering aspects of underdeveloped narcissism, and values, attitudes, and beliefs.

ATTITUDES

Your attitudes toward adolescents and their concerns will be the other critical component. You have to genuinely like and care for them. This does not mean that you have to approve of behaviors that are self-defeating and destructive. It does mean that you must be able to separate the person from the deed. The polarities noted by Scheidlinger (1985) point to the need to undergo an examination of your attitudes, because where adolescents are can be opposite from where they need to be, and you have to be able to handle both. For example, the polarity of rebellion against adult control versus the need for direction calls for your understanding of both, being able to "be" with their desire for rebellion. Your adult understanding of the need, comfort, and safety of limits does not carry nearly as much impact and importance as will your attitude and understanding of the need to rebel.

Katz (1990), a psychiatrist working with adolescents, points out that therapists have to be able to offer understanding, knowledge, empathy, and warm and positive regard. These are the core conditions espoused by counseling and are even more essential when working with adolescents.

Guidelines for Counseling

PLANNING

Planning counseling for adolescents involves consideration of several important factors such as family involvement, site, and mode for treatment. These factors are parts of the pretreatment process and are considered to be critical whether the counseling deals with academic concerns, career development, problem behaviors, or serious conditions such as depression.

Family involvement at its most basic level requires the notification of parents and securing their signed approval for the proposed treatment. In addition, Wilkes, Belsher, and Rush (1994) consider the family as a source of emotional support for the adolescent during treatment that can provide checks for validation of the adolescent's expectations and reality. Further, families can assist with treatment when they are educated regarding information, behaviors, and attitudes that would be of assistance.

The *site of treatment* refers to whether counseling takes place in a school-setting, an agency, or in a private practice. Each site has different expectations, requirements, and constraints. Counselors have the responsibility to know what mandatory procedures are required for the setting, reporting guidelines, and the extent to which confidentiality can be maintained. For example, the school-setting may mandate reporting adolescent drug use to authorities and/or parents, while the counselor in private practice can exercise professional judgment on the necessity for reporting such behavior.

The *mode for treatment* can be complex but, at its basic level, requires choosing among individual, group, or family counseling. However, it is wise to do some literature review on the presenting problem prior to beginning treatment, because there is new information appearing every day that can make a considerable difference in the decision on treatment. The example that follows illustrates the need for understanding research findings rather than using what appears to be logical reasoning.

If we were to take a poll of the readers of this book, the authors' hunch is that the majority would agree that optimum treatment for high-risk male adolescents (e.g., those with substance abuse, problem behaviors in school, and delinquency) would involve groups of peers with similar problems. This treatment might include providing wholesome activities such as the Boy Scouts and YMCA or, given sufficient funding, summer camps that offer sports, games, crafts, and opportunities for learning new social skills. Some brief findings from such programs follow.

The Cambridge–Somerville Youth Study Evaluation. This study evaluated a comprehensive program for high-risk male adolescents that included activities (e.g., summer camps, activities focusing on academic, personal, and family problems) such as those described above (McCord, 1978,

1981). The study used control groups for comparison. The findings revealed that the males who received the most attention over time (i.e., participated in the most treatment activities), were more likely to turn out worse than control groups—worse in the sense of delinquency, substance abuse, and other problem behaviors.

The Adolescent Transition Program. Dishion, Reid, and Patterson (1988) tested parent and peer influences on adolescent development for 119 high-risk adolescents, with an additional 38 adolescents used as a quasi-control group. The 119 male and female adolescents were randomly assigned to one of four conditions:

♦ parent-skills training for the teens' parents

♦ peer group with a focus on self-regulation, prosocial goals, peer reinforcement

♦ both parent and teen focus

♦ a self-directed change group that used videotapes and written material on a volunteer basis.

Results were analyzed for both short- and long-term (one year) effects. Findings for the short-term effects showed positive results for the combined teen and parent group. Positive results included a reduction in observed negative family interactions and a reduction in family tensions and conflict. However, the long-term analyses revealed negative effects for the peer group (i.e., increase in the use of tobacco, teacher reports of problem behavior), and the combined group that had positive short-term effects had negative effects in the long term (e.g., did not reduce risk for substance abuse and delinquency). The three-year follow-up showed that tobacco use and delinquency persisted in the peer group.

Other Literature Support. There are other meta-analyses and studies that support the notion that it is counterproductive to have groups of teen peers with similar problems. For example, several studies have shown that early adolescents who had moderate levels of delinquency and friends who were also deviant tended to be those who engaged in more serious forms of antisocial behavior later (Coie, Miller-Johnson, Terry, Maumary-Gremaud, & Lochman, 1996; Vitaro, Tremblay, Kerr, Pagani, & Bukowski, 1997). Lipsey (1992) found that 29 percent of the studies on interventions with adolescents showed negative effects. Patterson, Dishion, and Yoerger (1999) found that 35 percent of the variance for young adults' maladjustment five years later was related to their association during the teen years with peers that provided "deviancy training." There seems to be evidence that some relationships during adolescence are not conducive to healthy development (Hartup, 1996).

The bottom line is that it is risky to make assumptions about effective treatment. You need to be guided by empirical findings from the literature. There is no substitute.

The need for self-knowledge and having worked through personal adolescent issues can be seen in the contrasting emotions that the adolescent and counselor bring to treatment. Both have fears and both can experience anger. The adolescent fears

♦ loss of control over his or her personal destiny
♦ punishment
♦ failure to receive needed help.

The counselor fears

♦ loss of control over the case
♦ helplessness to effect needed changes
♦ legal action for not fulfilling requirements of the case
♦ the inability to enlist the adolescent's cooperation.

The counselor and the adolescent enter treatment with numerous fears, some of which may be realized. For example, because of family and/or community demands, the counselor is helpless to effect needed changes, or the adolescent fails to get needed help.

Anger can emerge at any moment when working with adolescents and it is helpful if the counselor understands how to manage and contain personal anger as well as the adolescent's. The adolescent can experience anger by the risk of humiliation and over the loss of privacy. The counselor always runs the risk of humiliation and that can engender anger.

GENERAL GUIDELINES AND STRATEGIES

The guidelines presented here relate to knowledge, the therapeutic relationship, the setting, and basic client characteristics. The guidelines may serve as strategies for working with adolescents. Because adolescents can differ from one another in significant ways, MacLennan and Dies (1992) recommend that therapists become familiar with the client's subculture and cliques, typical behavior and attitudes, habits, values, style, and language. For example, adolescents can have a language or words that are used in unique ways, and the therapist needs to know what that language or usage is to understand just what the client means. Adolescents use language to keep others out, especially adults, to show uniqueness, and to convey exclusiveness. The therapist will want to know the language, but not use it in conversing with adolescents, because an adult's usage can be a turn-off.

The Therapeutic Relationship. Katz (1990) recommends that considerable attention be given to preparing for therapy by knowing and understanding what emotions you and the client will experience, the goals for therapy, and developing an assortment of responses. He emphasizes that the first few moments of meeting with the client set the pattern and tone for therapy, and may even be the deciding factor for success or failure.

As foundations for success, Carrell (1993) highlights the connections made (e.g., the therapeutic alliance), the therapist's authenticity and positive regard, the client's positive perception of the therapist, and an understanding of adolescent culture. This model echoes Katz (1990) in accentuating the therapeutic relationship and the adolescent's perception of the counselor as crucial components. Your "Being" seems to be more important than your "Doing" and should be a significant part of your preparation as a counselor. MacLennan and Dies (1992) also agree in noting that your issues, especially those around your own adolescence, should be worked through prior to trying to do therapy with adolescents.

The Setting. The setting in which counseling takes place has to be considered as a significant factor, since it can guide or specify what is to be done, as well as how it will be done. The setting refers to a school, an agency, a hospital or other treatment facility, or a private practice. For example, school systems have very specific guidelines for strategies that are acceptable and unacceptable, parental notification, and the services that can be provided (e.g., classroom guidance must be provided). The setting may also influence the conditions, disorders, and other client needs that will be prevalent.

SOME BASIC ADOLESCENT CHARACTERISTICS

Although each adolescent is a unique individual, there are some commonalties that can be expected (Hanna, Hanna, and Keys, 1999), such as

- ♦ an insistence on immediate results or relief
- ♦ a desire for clarity of limits and boundaries
- ♦ ready access to intense feelings (e.g., anger, hostility, shame, and guilt)
- ♦ attempts to startle, surprise, and shock adults
- ♦ awareness of sexual power and sexuality.

These also will play an important role in successfully working with adolescents, because your responses and handling of these factors will be crucial in achieving positive outcomes. Each one is briefly described.

Immediate Relief. Adolescents can be very much like toddlers in their insistence on getting what they want and demanding it "Now!" They respond to what is quick, brief, and effective at getting and maintaining their attention and interest, and at fulfilling their perceived needs. This calls for considerable understanding of possible needs and other preparation before meeting with adolescent clients, as well as having a repertoire of techniques to foster quick engagement and interest. A deeper relationship needs time to unfold, but the counselor should be prepared to deal with the immediate as the longer term relationship unfolds.

In addition to good preparation and personal work, counselors can emphasize the importance of the adolescent's need for immediate relief and solutions by ascertaining what the client considers to be his or her most pressing concern at the moment. A focus on the client's needs and a candid discussion of the counselor's limits, or of the possibility of meeting these needs, can do much to engage the adolescent. Limits refer to unrealistic expectations of what can be accomplished (e.g., changing another person such as a teacher or parent to do what the adolescent wants). Possibilities refer to realistic expectations of what can be accomplished, the time needed to work towards those goals, strategies that can be used, and an appraisal of what the client can contribute.

Limits and Boundaries. Adolescents may fear that their personal control will be lost, that the counselor is out to change them against their will, or that they are fatally flawed or weird. In order to develop safety and trust, such fears may be significant factors that need to be addressed at the very beginning of counseling or therapy. Some basic factors that define limits and boundaries, and contribute to developing safety and trust include

- ◆ collaborative goal setting
- ◆ explaining what you intend to do and why
- ◆ describing how the client can contribute to treatment or education
- ◆ explaining the basic rules and expectations for behavior
- ◆ defining the parameters for confidentiality.

For example, if the school or agency mandates that you report suspected alcohol or drug use, this would be explained to the client prior to working with him or her. Another example is the legal and professional standards for mandated reporting of suspected physical or sexual abuse. In many school districts, school counselors can be fired for not reporting abuse. The client needs to know these responsibilities before counseling begins. Adolescents want to know that the counselor cares, but it may be more important for them to understand the limits and boundaries.

Intense Feelings. Adolescents seem to have ready access to their feelings, especially their more intense ones. Some intense moods may have a physiological component such as hormones, but not all moods and their intensity can be explained by the adolescent's physical state. Counselors have to stay aware that intense feelings can be triggered immediately and be prepared for these explosive outbursts.

Some clients will try to suppress their feelings because they are fearful that, if expressed, all control will be lost and that they will be overwhelmed. Others may have grown up in homes where feelings were not expressed and therefore have not learned appropriate ways to express them, nor perceive that expression of feelings is expected in counseling. Still others may suppress feelings for fear that when they do express them, they will be considered "weird." None of these examples means that the adolescents are not experiencing intense feelings. The examples simply indicate that the teens are keeping a tight lid on them.

Shocking Adults. The search for a unique personal identity can lead adolescents to do and say things designed to startle, surprise, and shock adults. Your unresolved issues can be easily triggered, your values mocked, and your caring and nurturing manipulated when working with adolescents. Their desires to separate and individuate, to be special, to feel competent and capable while, at the same time, feeling that society is set up to prevent this from happening, contribute to their attitudes. Rebelling against convention seems to be expected at this stage and can take many forms:

♦ Are you shocked or surprised at outrageous dress, hairstyles, and makeup?

♦ How do you feel about tattoos and body piercing? (These are current undertakings by many adolescents)

♦ Does profanity offend you?

♦ What's your reaction to talk of death by adolescents?

♦ Do you have objections to current fads?

Even if you come to terms with current fads and fashions, they will not last and something new will take their place. Whatever it is will be designed to shock adults, and that is its value. You must continually examine your reactions to the acts, behaviors, and attitudes to which adolescents gravitate in their search for uniqueness.

Sexuality and Sexual Power. Adolescence is the stage in which the awareness of sexuality can be especially acute. Heterosexual, homosexual, and bisexual males and females are in the process of discovering their sexual identity. They receive a constant flow of attention to sex from the media, are made aware of the personal impact of sexual feelings on their bodies, and can receive considerable attention from adults that is sexual in nature. They can be flooded with sexual feelings triggered by inner and external influences.

Brenner (1984) describes the long-term effects of sexual abuse. Many of these will be encountered by therapists who work with adolescents, although the presenting problem may be something else. Some effects are

♦ an inability to trust others

♦ depression

♦ poor self-concept

♦ believing self to be ugly and/or impure

♦ belief that one is unworthy of love or self-respect

♦ hostility

- self-destructiveness
- suicidal feelings
- poor social skills
- use of seductiveness to initiate friendships
- inability to get along with parents or siblings
- promiscuity or prostitution
- belief that sex is the only aspect of self that is valued by others.

The effects of this abuse can be severe and long-lasting. Many will attempt to displace or project onto others what was done to them, and this can easily happen in therapy where intimacy is encouraged. A counselor may find himself or herself to have unwittingly aroused these feelings that have their roots in sexual abuse. It is important for therapists to stay in touch with both what the client is doing and saying, as well as with their own feelings. What you may consider to be friendly may be considered by the adolescent to be provocative, a come-on, or an invitation to have sex. This is not what you want to have happen.

It is important that you not underestimate the importance of the impact of your attitudes and responses about sex and sexuality to adolescents. All are struggling to come to terms with the physical, psychological, and emotional changes they are experiencing, the ambiguity present in the larger world about sex and sexuality, and adults' inability to discuss sexual matters with adolescents. Thus you will have to become comfortable with discussing sex without erotic overtones.

AN EXAMPLE OF A LITTLE-UNDERSTOOD PROBLEM

A frequently overlooked source of distress for many adolescents is peer sexual harassment. This situation is pervasive throughout all settings and can have long-lasting effects on both the victim and the harasser (Wetzel & Brown, 2000). Peer sexual harassment tends to fall into the hostile-environment category in which the victim is the target of physical and/or verbal sexual attention that can be mild to severe. Mild physical sexual harassment may include acts such as leering, while severe physical harassment may involve groping body parts. Mild verbal sexual harassment is seen in whistles or catcalls, while severe is expressed by acts such as in spreading sexual rumors. As defined by the American Association of University Women Educational Foundation (AAUW) (1993) and Brandenburg (1997), sexual harassment consists of unwanted and unwelcome sexual behavior that interferes with one's well-being.

There have been numerous studies of peer sexual harassment (Corbett, Gentry, & Pearson, 1993; Lee, Croninger, Linn, & Chen, 1996; Stein, 1995), but the most scientific and comprehensive was commissioned by the AAUW in 1993. This was a national survey of a stratified random sampling of 1,632 students in grades 8 through 11 from 79 schools across the United States. This survey found that 81 percent reported that they felt sexually harassed by their peers at some point during their school experience. Eighty-seven percent of white girls, 84 percent of African-American girls, 75 percent of white boys, and 81 percent of African-American boys reported being sexually harassed. Of considerable interest was the finding that the 66 percent of boys and 52 percent of girls reporting being sexually harassed, became sexual harassers themselves. It is difficult to separate victims and harassers.

Confirming the importance of understanding the impact of peer sexual harassment are the findings by Eitel (1996), who reported the following effects:

◆ *Psychoemotional problems*—such as increased self-consciousness, decreased self-confidence, fear of intimacy, and anger

◆ *Psychosocial and behavioral consequences*—such as transferring to a new school, and lowered motivation to complete school and/or schoolwork

◆ *Academic problems*—such as declining grades, increased absenteeism, and tardiness

◆ *Physical concerns*—such as headaches and the development of stress-related disorders such as colitis.

Because of the prevalence of peer sexual harassment, especially in school-settings, counselors should become familiar with these symptoms listed and begin to address the cause rather than exclusively focusing on the outcome (e.g., increased absenteeism and other academic problems). Further, counselors can help all students by becoming an advocate for the complete elimination of peer sexual harassment.

Wetzel and Brown (2000) describe specific actions that can be taken to reduce or eliminate peer sexual harassment. Actions range from district-wide to individual interventions and include

◆ school-district-wide policies for zero tolerance for peer sexual harassment

◆ removal of sexual graffiti

◆ taking reports of peer sexual harassment seriously

◆ intervening to stop observed harassment such as whistling and name calling

◆ educating students about sexual harassment and its effects

◆ having guest speakers who can talk about the legal and employment consequences of sexual harassment on the job

◆ investigating accusations of peer sexual harassment

◆ initiating a school-level commitment to address peer sexual harassment in all forms.

EXERCISE **11**
"Photo Collage"

Materials: One sheet of memory-book paper or other stiff paper, photos, glue or double-sided tape.

Directions: Collect 8 to 10 photographs of yourself from an early age to the present. If you have access to a scanner and printer, you may wish to scan and print the pictures so that you are not using your valuable photographs. You could also copy them using a color copier.

♦ Once you have the photos you want to use, place them in chronological order.
♦ Arrange the photos on the paper to form a collage. You will need to crop some photos to make them all fit on the page. Once you have a satisfactory arrangement, glue or tape your pictures to the paper.
♦ Write a one-page reaction to seeing how you have changed, developed, and so on.

Reflection Questions:
1. Were you unable to find pictures from a particular period in your life?
2. Were you dissatisfied with pictures from a particular period? If so, reflect on that period and write a brief summary about what was happening with you, your life in general, and your family during that period.
3. What relationships are depicted in the pictures?
4. What feelings are aroused as you look at your collage? Make a list of these feelings, or write a brief description of them.

Chapter Twelve

The Early and Middle Adult Years

Development and Theories

Adult Development Theories

THE THEORIES PRESENTED IN CHAPTERS 12 and 13 emphasize issues and tasks for the early and middle adult years. These theories show various perspectives regarding the problems, tasks, issues, and other concerns faced by adults in this era. Readers need to remember that the world is dynamic and ever-changing, so there will be new discoveries emerging every day that have major impacts on our lives and development. New and better processes are developed for almost everything, and there continues to be an uncovering of knowledge and understanding of people, their needs, and their environments. The dynamic nature of our lives and our development makes it difficult for any one theory to account for the totality of adult development. Thus many theories focus on a single developmental aspect (e.g., moral development) and study it in depth. Other theories are broader but still omit major portions of individuals' lives, such as the physical and spiritual aspects. There is a major dearth of studies and theories about the effects of culture and cultural differences on adult development, although there is increasing attention being given to gender differences.

The major thrust for this book is on counseling across the lifespan, and theories provide some structure for understanding how problems faced by adults are manifested, assessed, and resolved. Theories are general and global about normal adult development, but do not provide much information about individual development. The exceptions are the theories categorized here as "psychodynamic." They too are general in their perspectives, but have some focus on individual development.

The value of these theories is that they can increase your understanding for the particular client you encounter in counseling. You do not have to select a particular theory to explain everything; but instead you can understand each theory well enough to use all or part of its perspectives. This chapter presents an overview of some adult development theories and explains two, Erikson's and Kohut's, in more detail. Chapter 13, "Counseling Adults: Applications," discusses three additional theories as they can be applied in counseling. The theories presented here are not all-inclusive of available theories; readers are encouraged to search out and read other theories, and to study in more depth the ones presented here.

Categories for Adult Development Theories

Table 12.1 presents a scheme for categorizing some major developmental theories. The categories were selected to describe the primary emphases and foci for the various theories. It was difficult to categorize some theories because they cover topics that define more than one category (e.g., Erikson's theory of psychosocial development). The categories are *psychodynamic, developmental, focused topics, life events,* and *stage/age.*

PSYCHODYNAMIC ADULT DEVELOPMENT THEORIES

The *psychodynamic* category contains theories that address psychological growth and development. These theories emphasize the continuous nature of development from birth to death. Also emphasized are early childhood events and conflicts with parents that get reactivated and reen-

TABLE **12.1**

Adult Development Theories in Categories

Psychodynamic	*Developmental*	*Focused Topics*
Freud (1905)	Havighurst (1972)	Kohlberg (1969)
Kohut (1977)	Reigel (1975)	Gilligan (1982)
Erikson (1963)	Neugarten (1979)	Perry (1970)
Gould (1978)	Golan (1981)	Loevinger (1976)
		Valliant (1977)

Life Events	*Stage/Age*
Lowenthal et al. (1975)	Levinson et al. (1978)
Brim and Ryff (1980)	Erikson (1963)
Baltes and Goulet (1970)	Valliant (1977)
	Gould (1978)
	Schlossberg (1984)

acted as continuing influences on behavior, thoughts, feelings, and attitudes. Rutan (1993, p. 141) describes five principles of psychodynamic theory: "There is psychological determination, there are unconscious processes, human behavior is dynamic and goal directed, human behavior is epigentic, and functions of the mind are at work at any given point in time." These theories are discussed in chapters 5 and 12.

DEVELOPMENTAL THEORIES

Developmental theories propose sequences for growth and development that are thought to be universal. The sequence has stages in which specific tasks are to be completed before moving to the next stage in the sequence. The next stage builds on previous tasks' accomplishments and stages cannot be skipped.

The theories included in this category can also be included in the *stage/age* category. What differentiates developmental theories from others in that category are their focus on universal tasks (Havighurst, 1972), levels (Riegel, 1975) and issues (Neugarten, 1979). Developmental theories do not factor in individual differences, environmental or cultural determinants, or life events. However, there does seem be adequate evidence of their applicability for understanding the course of human growth and development.

FOCUSED TOPICS

This collection of theories has different specific topics as their primary focus: Kohlberg (1969)—moral development; Gilligan (1982)—gender differences in development; Perry (1970)—adult cognitive development; Loevinger (1976)—ego control; and Valliant (1977)—ego defenses. Some are concerned only with adults and do not present information for development across the lifespan.

Some of these theories also use stages of development (e.g., Kohlberg and Loevinger) to account for growth and individual differences. Others (e.g., Valliant and Perry) seem more interested in intrapsychic processes to explain differences and changes. This category has no underlying unifying thread or theme, hence the title of *focused topics*.

LIFE EVENTS AS ADULT DEVELOPMENT THEORIES

The theories in this category propose that critical events throughout life shape individual development, and there are not specific stages or phases of human growth and development that are universal. These theorists minimize or reject the influence of early experiences on subsequent adult development.

Brim and Ryff (1980) propose three dimensions for life events: the objective reality, individual perceptions, and the effects of perceptions on behavior. This approach is similar to that proposed by Baltes and Goulet (1970) for a multicultural perspective that accounts for both external events and the internal processing of these events. Lowenthal, Chiriboga, and Thurnber (1975) introduce gender differences in perceptions and reactions to life events that provide an added dimension.

STAGE/AGE ADULT DEVELOPMENT THEORIES

The final category for adult development theories is termed *stage/age* because these theorists tried to provide age ranges for the various stages, or described expectations for a particular age range. For example, Schlossberg (1984) proposes that there is a universality of experiences around age, and Gould (1978, p. 352) says that "people change with age because new priorities in the life cycle require new attitudes and new behavior."

Productive Phases

The early and middle adult years could be termed the *productive phases*, in which all the psychological, physical, academic, educational, and social preparation begins to exert its influence on individuals':

+ career choice and development
+ work productivity
+ creative endeavors
+ significant relationships (e.g., marriage)
+ ability to delay gratification
+ assumption of responsible behavior
+ decisions about having children
+ parenting.

It is during this period that all the life experiences, environmental influences, and personal characteristics interact to promote growth and adaptation, or failure to grow and adapt. While both personal and professional or work productivity is at its peak, there are other conditions that can influence individual differences in responses to life challenges. One such condition involves the expectations of the culture regarding individuals in their young and middle adult years.

In the United States, the expectation is that adults will

+ achieve financial independence
+ contribute to the functioning of society
+ care for the next generation, and in some cases also care for the previous generation
+ develop satisfying intimate relationships
+ have meaning and purpose in life
+ develop a social network

- make wise decisions
- participate in civic responsibilities
- continue the journey toward self-actualization.

While stress is present in every stage of life, it is more prevalent for adults in the productive phases. These adults are dealing with personal expectations, parental expectations, and societal expectations. The extent to which the "self" is developed and fortified contributes to the extent to which stress is tolerated and expectations are met.

This chapter presents the major tasks for adults in the early and middle stages as described by Erikson (1959), healthy adult narcissism as defined by Kohut (1977), common and/or major conditions using the lifespan model that can be addressed in counseling, and examples of common presenting problems. Although this phase covers approximately forty years, there are concerns and issues that continue throughout the phases, and even beyond in some instances. Chapter 13 presents the adult development theories for Golan (1981), Schlossberg (1984), and Gould (1978).

ERIKSON'S ADULT DEVELOPMENT PHASES

Erikson (1963) divides this phase into two stages: *intimacy versus isolation* for ages 20 through 40; and *generativity versus stagnation* for ages 40 through 60.

The major task for young adults, *intimacy versus isolation*, revolves around establishing meaningful and lasting relationships such as marriage and a family. Associated with these tasks are numerous other concerns such as

- education and training
- financial independence
- choosing a career
- desire for children
- parenting skills
- willingness to commit to a relationship
- physical, psychological, and emotional health.

When intimacy is not achieved, isolation is the outcome. Isolation is not simply being alone, because you can feel alone in a family setting or other similar settings in which others are present. It is instead an internal state in which personally meaningful connections with other people are absent. Some of the concerns associated with this stage contribute to isolation. For example, the college student who is taking a full load of classes and working a full-time job, or almost a full-time job, is in a situation that contributes to feeling isolated. This person may very well not have time to make friends or maintain existing relationships, since he or she is either busy in class, preparing for class, or at work.

Another example is seen in the person who has a job that necessitates considerable travel and/or relocation. Promotions at work that entail additional responsibilities can also interfere with the completion of this stage's major task. The saddest examples are those who do not achieve intimacy because they did not successfully complete the tasks at earlier stages.

Generativity versus Stagnation. The task for middle adults, ages 40 through 60, is *generativity versus stagnation* (Erikson, 1959). The assumption is that you have to successfully complete the previous stage in order to progress to this one. It would appear that, given the divorce rate, changes in careers, and life circumstances, individuals in this stage could be at any age between 20 and 60. For example, the person who does not marry or establish a lasting meaningful relationship until reaching his or her forties would enter the middle adult stage much later than the person who attained intimacy in his or her twenties or thirties. Just as there can be late adolescence, there can also be delayed adulthood, and some people may never achieve this stage or phase.

Generativity refers to producing, creating, and bringing into existence (Erikson, 1980). The ability to be productive, creative, and original can be especially fruitful during this period if the tasks for the previous stage, *intimacy versus isolation*, were successfully completed. Adults in this stage, aged 40 through 60, are assumed to

- ♦ have completed the education and training needed for establishing a career
- ♦ be gainfully employed and financially secure
- ♦ have established an intimate or marital relationship
- ♦ be likely to have one or more children
- ♦ now be in a position in which they can begin to become generative.

Regardless of status, job, or economic position, these adults are expected to have the time and resources to enable them to use their education, training, life experiences, wisdom, and other talents to

- ♦ further personal goals
- ♦ address community needs
- ♦ propose and carry out societal goals
- ♦ invent and/or create new products and processes
- ♦ refine existing products and processes.

This phase is less clear-cut, however, because it can be attained earlier than age 40 or never be attained, regardless of age.

HEALTHY ADULT NARCISSISM

The early and middle adult years can see the emergence of healthy adult narcissism as defined by Kohut (1977), which has empathy, creativity, and a sense of humor. When psychological separation and individuation are on-track, the cohesive self has turned from self-absorption and is able to clearly understand where self ends and others begin. It can relate to others as separate unique individuals and not as extensions of self. Many relationship problems have lingering aspects of underdeveloped narcissism at the core for one or both persons.

Age-appropriate healthy adult narcissism, as described in chapter 5, contributes significantly to accomplishing Erikson's task for this stage (i.e., achieving intimacy). *Intimacy* is defined here as a meaningful, deep, and reciprocal relationship. Adult intimacy does not involve exploitation, manipulation, and satisfying one's needs at the expense of the other person, but consists of a mutual respect and caring for the significant other. This kind of intimacy can only be attained when the person's psychological development is sufficient that

- lowering his or her boundaries to be empathic does not also involve enmeshment, manipulation, or becoming overwhelmed
- there is an observing ego that keeps the person anchored in reality
- attention and admiration needs do not involve jealousy and envy, and can be shared or deferred
- the person has a wide and deep range of emotions felt and expressed
- the need for outside approval and recognition is contained, managed, and is moderate
- others' emotions can be felt
- other people can be recognized and appreciated as being worthwhile, unique individuals
- there is a realistic appraisal and acceptance of "self."

Healthy adult narcissism is also a contributor to one's self-esteem, self-efficacy, and self-confidence. Care is taken that self-confidence is based on reality and not on grandiosity. These states, in turn, play a considerable role in establishing meaningful and satisfying relationships, and in achievements in other areas (e.g., school and careers).

The middle adult years can be the period in which lingering aspects of underdeveloped narcissism become acute and troubling to the person, and the basic concerns or problems center around the "self." Many adults will voluntarily seek counseling or therapy for

♦ dissatisfaction with current relationships

♦ chronic feelings of emptiness

♦ lack of meaning and purpose in life

♦ an inability to form and maintain an intimate relationship

♦ other concerns that are not the result of physical or emotional conditions such as depression, or situational concerns such as employment.

Assessment of Developmental Level

Tables 12.2 and 12.3 present some behaviors and attitudes that can serve as guides when assessing the extent to which an individual has successfully completed tasks for the previous stage, and whether the person's issues are from early adulthood or middle adulthood. These assessments are subjective and do not take the place of more formal assessment and diagnoses for presenting problems. They are suggestions that are intended as guides for expected adult attitudes and behaviors.

TABLE **12.2**

Lifespan Model and Examples for Young Adults

Life Transitions

Engaging successfully in education and/or training
Preparing for a career of personal interest
Has a social-support network
Has established one or more meaningful relationships
Is, or has a plan to become, financially independent

Family of Origin Issues

Can form lasting relationships
Extent of emotional expressivity
Ability to be empathic
Awareness of personal needs and extent to which they are met
Level of completion for separation and individuation

Situational Concerns

Reaction to loss and grief
Tolerance for stress, and how stress is managed
Self-competence questions

Serious Physical and/or Emotional Conditions and Disorders

Substance abuse and/or treatment needs
Borderline disorders
Depression

ASSESSMENT OF YOUNG ADULTS

The young adult may be in the process of completing those tasks that will prepare him or her to be successful in the life transitions that characterize this phase (e.g., completing college and other training). This situation may also contribute to the young adult's lack of financial independence, just as the economy and job market contribute to the availability of employment, which in turn determines if there is even an opportunity to become financially independent. The tasks of forming social and intimate relationships may also be in progress.

The extent to which significant *family of origin issues* are resolved, or compensated for, plays a major role in the young adult's ability to successfully complete life-transition tasks, resolve situational concerns, cope with serious physical and/or mental conditions and disorders, and confront life's existential issues. Family of origin issues together with the person's personality combine to exert considerable influence on choices, decisions, coping ability, resilience, and outlook.

It is not possible to list all *situational concerns* that can appear at this stage, since many are dependent on outside sources such as the economy. Indeed, there are some that can surface throughout the entire lifespan, being not unique to any particular period. The coping processes used by young adults when challenged with situational concerns are also dependent on personality characteristics and family of origin issues, both resolved and unresolved.

Major *physical and/or emotional disorders and conditions* can have a major impact on young adult development. Substance abuse, while declining, can become especially acute and troubling, because it negatively impacts some of the most important tasks these young adults are expected to accomplish. Their relationships can be impaired, resulting in isolation and alienation. At the very least, their relationships can be less than satisfying if substance abuse or addiction is present. Career choices and career development are also impacted, as are financial resources. Other emotional and psychological disorders can emerge during this period that significantly impact the young adult's ability to function and accomplish developmental tasks. If these are accompanied by substance abuse, eating disorders, or other conditions, the impact is compounded. Young adulthood is also the period in which major physical illnesses and conditions can emerge. Hypertension, arthritis, diabetes, and other such conditions are not uncommon. Young adults may also face cardiac conditions, cancer, multiple sclerosis, and other chronic illnesses that seriously impact their lives.

Existential concerns can become especially acute during this phase, because young adults begin to become more consciously aware of

- ♦ the search for meaning and purpose in their lives
- ♦ the inevitability of death

♦ the unfairness and indifference of the universe
♦ the interrelatedness of freedom and responsibility
♦ the need for intimacy to reduce feelings of isolation and alienation.

Life transitions, family of origin issues, situational concerns, and serious physical and/or emotional disorders or conditions—whether personal or those of a significant other—can serve to foster the emergence of existential concerns.

DEVELOPMENTAL TASKS FOR MIDDLE ADULTS

Many of the same tasks, issues, and concerns that were discussed for young adults also apply to middle adulthood (ages 40–60). However, it is

TABLE **12.3**
Lifespan Model and Examples for Middle Adults

Life Transitions

Satisfying marital relationship
Satisfaction as a parent
Established in a meaningful career or job
Achievement of financial independence

Family of Origin Issues

Tend to re-emerge as unfinished business

Situational Concerns

Declining physical condition
Caring for aging parents
Divorce
Remarriage
Death
Loss of job
Empty nest
Menopause (women)

Serious Physical and/or Emotional Conditions and Disorders

Heart attacks, strokes, and other vascular diseases
Complications from diabetes
Psychiatric disorders as described in the *DSM-IV*
Substance abuse
Cancer
Complicated mourning

Existential Issues

Meaning and purpose in life
Death

---

expected that, because many of the major tasks of the young adult phase are successfully completed, middle adults will have a firmer foundation from which to address the tasks for this phase. For example, it is expected that mid-life adults

♦ have achieved financial independence

♦ are established in a career

♦ are fully functioning members of society

♦ are in a lasting intimate relationship

♦ are nurturing and rearing the next generation

♦ are secure enough in their personal development to have healthy adult narcissism characterized by empathy, creativity, humor, and wisdom (Kohut, 1977).

If the tasks were completed or mostly completed, the individual has the energy and resources to begin work on the task for middle adulthood, *generativity versus stagnation*. This is the period of life in which the person's knowledge, education, training, talents, and experiences can combine and interact to produce new ideas, products and processes. At first, it may seem that only those very talented people can be generative. Nothing could be farther from the truth! There are considerable opportunities to be generative at home, in the community, on the job, and in one's personal life. Generativity is possible in every aspect of one's everyday life and may include

♦ raising a family

♦ producing nutritious meals

♦ maintaining a home

♦ streamlining needed forms

♦ finding new ways to accomplish tasks

♦ doing repair work

♦ sewing clothes

♦ making crafts

♦ developing a process to help a child learn to read or accomplish other academic tasks

♦ awareness of how to prevent potential injuries

♦ numerous other creative or altruistic activities.

Middle adulthood is also the phase in which physical decline begins to be increasingly noticed and the passing years felt more keenly, and dissatisfaction with personal accomplishments can arise. Hence there is much discussion about the "mid-life crisis." People can become more acutely aware that they have not done some things that are personally important, have failed to reach their potentials, have made unwise decisions, or that, in spite of their best efforts, life circumstances have resulted in the loss of opportunity to become what they wanted. This angst at mid-life can result in stagnation. Thus the middle adult years offer either a chance to be more generative or to be weighted down to stagnate. Making a mid-life change or correction can be helpful or devastating. Some changes result in more life satisfaction and generativity, while others result in less life satisfaction and stagnation. This can be especially true if the change is a regression to an earlier period (e.g., adolescence or young adulthood), or if the tasks of the previous stages were not successfully completed.

PRIMARY CONCERNS FOR MIDDLE ADULTS

The categories that assume the most prominence for middle adults are situational concerns, physical and/or emotional conditions and disorders, and existential issues. All of these are impacted and influenced by the individual's successful completion of previous developmental tasks, family of origin issues that remain as unfinished business, and the person's personality.

Situational concerns can become especially important, since this is the period when

♦ children begin to move out of the house

♦ parents need more care as old age sets in

♦ personal health concerns arise (e.g., the need for diet and exercise)

♦ divorce and remarriage can occur because of mid-life crises.

Of course, each person reacts differently. But old, unresolved *family of origin issues* can reemerge and contribute to even more difficulties in trying to cope with situational concerns. Chronic *physical and/or emotional conditions and disorders* can become worse as the body is less able to tolerate the stress of the condition or disorder. New health problems can compound already existing ones. Sometimes due to family history and genetics, the fear of what can happen becomes a concern. *Existential issues* emerge in many ways during middle adulthood. Of particular concern is death, as individuals can be constantly confronted with the deaths of family, friends, colleagues, and other personal acquaintances. It becomes difficult for mid-life adults to escape awareness of their own finiteness and mortality.

The discussion to this point has focused on the individual himself or herself. Of almost equal concern because of their impact on completing developmental tasks are the same issues for significant others such as one's spouse, children, and parents. For example, the chronic or transitory illness of a child impacts the entire family, as does the death of a parent or grandparent. Having significant others who have situational concerns, who have failed to successfully complete life-transition tasks, or who have serious physical and/or emotional conditions and disorders can impact the mastery of developmental tasks for adults in this phase almost as much as can their own inner resources.

Presenting Problems for Young and Middle Adults

YOUNG ADULTS

Capuzzi and Gross (1995) list the following as being typical presenting problems and issues for young adults (aged 20–40):

♦ achieving independence
♦ finding a marital partner
♦ parenting concerns
♦ divorce
♦ work demands
♦ forced relocation
♦ career choices and other career issues
♦ the need to reduce stress.

These are developmental problems and issues akin to what we term *life transitions*. However, these presenting problems will almost always have underlying concerns that feature one or more of the other categories, such as family of origin issues. While the presenting problem may appear less complex when first described, it would be unusual if there were not more complex underlying problems.

MIDDLE ADULTS

Presenting problems for many middle adults (aged 40–60) tend to center around the following concerns and issues (Capuzzi & Gross, 1995):

♦ physical decline
♦ career dissatisfaction
♦ death of a spouse or parent
♦ interpersonal conflicts
♦ the "empty nest"
♦ retirement planning
♦ altered sexual capacity
♦ worries about becoming elderly.

Middle adulthood is the stage in which the person is most likely to have responsibilities that encompass three generations, as well as having to cope with personal concerns about health, aging, and marital and/or other relationship problems. In addition, underlying existential concerns and unresolved family of origin issues may further exacerbate the individual's difficulties. All these combine to make this phase especially stressful.

Mid-life adults are most likely to be voluntary clients who seek out counseling because they recognize that professional assistance may be helpful. Thus they are likely to be highly motivated and at a point where they are willing to work on painful issues and problems.

Stressors for Young and Middle Adults

Hafen, Karren, Frandsen, and Smith (1996) list the following stressors for young adults:

♦ academic concerns
♦ career decisions
♦ self-doubts
♦ changing roles in the family
♦ intimate relationships with sexual partners.

Both young and middle adults experience stress related to

♦ changes in expectations of family roles
♦ marriage
♦ divorce
♦ remarriage
♦ parenthood (including single and stepparenting)
♦ financial problems
♦ dual-career families
♦ gender roles (e.g., sexual harassment).

The role that stress plays in physical and mental health continues to be researched. The Holmes-Rahe Scale, which assigned numerical values for life-event stressors, was an early indicator of the impact of stress. The researchers assigned values ranging from a low of 11 for "minor law violations" and 12 for "Christmas," to a high of 100 for "death of a spouse" and 73 for "divorce." Their theory was that the more life events that occurred for someone within a short period, the more likely that person was to become physically ill. Most life events in their list were negative, such as "being fired" (47) and "jail term" (63), but some would be considered positive, such as "marriage" (50) and "pregnancy" (40). Fifty percent of the listed life events that produce stress are "changes"—that is, the change could be positive or negative, but the effect on the person would be the same. Thus it would be important to know what changes the client had experienced in a short time, what his or her reactions were to the changes, and what were the effects on his or her health.

Following are two exercises to expand your awareness and understanding of your personal development as a young adult and your hopes and visions for your middle adult years.

EXERCISE **12.1**

My Early Adult Years

Materials:

♦ *collage*—a sheet of memory-book paper, glue stick, magazines, catalogs, and scissors.

♦ *poem*—a sheet of paper and a writing instrument.

♦ *drawing*—felt markers, crayons, or oil pastels; newsprint 18" × 24" or larger.

♦ *writing*—4 to 5 sheets of paper and a writing instrument.

♦ *photocollage*—photographs (copies), a glue stick, and a sheet of memory-book paper.

Procedure: Select *one* of the projects listed above, such as the poem. Secure the needed materials for that project. You may want to consider completing more than one project. Directions for each follow.

Collage: Cut out pictures that are symbols for your young adult years, defined roughly as ages 18 through 29. Use symbols for activities, people, achievements, decisions, and any other significant events in your life during these years. Glue the pictures on the paper and title your collage. Write a paragraph summarizing your symbols for this time in your life.

Poem: Sit in silence at a table and reflect on the course of your young adult years. Allow images, thoughts, and feelings to emerge. Do not change or edit them, just allow them to come to you. Using these images, write a poem that captures the essence of your feelings about this period in your life.

Drawing: Use the same process as that described for creating a poem, but instead make a drawing. The drawing can be realistic, symbolic, or abstract. Title your drawing and write a summary about it.

Writing: Sit in silence at a table. Using the points you produced for exercises 1 and 2 for this period in your life, begin writing about each. Or you can list the significant events, people, activities, decisions, disappointments, and achievements and write about each of those on your list. Start each with, "It was (is) a time that I felt _____," and describe each point in as much detail as possible. Conclude with a summary statement or paragraph that expresses your feelings about this period.

Photocollage: Gather photographs of important people, events, accomplishments, and other artifacts from your young adult years. Be sure to have some pictures of yourself. Copy these so that the originals remain intact. Construct your photocollage and title it using the procedure described for a collage. Write a brief summary about your collage and the feelings that arise as you review it.

EXERCISE **12.2**

My Middle Adult Years

Materials: List of expectations for productive adults taken from this chapter, three sheets of paper, and a writing instrument.

Procedure: On the first sheet of paper, list the expectations for productive adults, leaving space for two columns at the top of the page. Label the columns "Accomplished" and "Not Yet Accomplished." Place a check mark in the correct column for each item on the list.

On the second sheet of paper, describe your achievements and your feelings about them. On the third sheet, describe your plans and vision for your future productivity and achievements.

Chapter Thirteen

Counseling Adults
Applications

THE ADULT PHASE IS WHEN all of the basic tasks and problems described in the lifespan model (chapter 1) will be encountered, and it may be difficult for the counselor to separate out and work with only one task. For example, in middle adulthood existential concerns about the meaning and purpose of life can be intertwined with situational conditions (e.g., empty nest) that have some of their basis in family of origin issues and that arise together with a serious health problem. This interrelatedness adds to the complexity of treatment because it may be almost impossible to deal with the presenting problem in isolation from all of the other concerns and relevant issues. The challenge will be for the counselor to stay aware of the complexity without feeling overwhelmed, and to not try to oversimplify by attempting to deal with the presenting problem in isolation.

This chapter presents three approaches to applying adult development theories: Golan (1981), Schlossberg (1984), and Gould (1978). Golan focuses on transitions for the adult phase and uses a social-skills model and theoretical applications perspective. Schlossberg presents a content-process model that emphasizes both the knowledge-base and helping skills of the counselor. Gould uses his experience as a psychodynamic clinician to describe a developmental applications model with a sequence of developmental processes for client change. These are but three of the many models of adult development and the reader is encouraged to read others in more depth, such as those described in the previous chapter, to better understand the complexity of counseling adults.

Golan

Focusing on expected and unexpected transitions during the adult years, Golan (1981) points out the inevitability of facing change and its disruptiveness. It is almost as though we will not be allowed to become complacent or comfortable, but must constantly expect that events and situations will emerge to force us to alter our course in some way. The significant transitions during this time period are

♦ work and career choice

♦ marriage and becoming a couple

♦ parenthood

♦ geographic moves and migrations

♦ past parenthood

♦ separation, divorce, and remarriage

♦ widowhood, grief, and bereavement

♦ preretirement and retirement.

Golan does not include physical illnesses and disorders as a significant transition, nor are existential concerns discussed. However, Golan does emphasize the situational concerns and life transitions similar to those in the lifespan model used in this book. These are important issues and should not be minimized.

Golan also considers the effects of class, ethnicity, and other such variables on transitions, and how these variables may dictate what sources of help are available. Considerable attention is given to sources of help that are divided into three categories: psychosocial, nonprofessional, and professional.

Psychosocial sources that should be considered when working with adults who have transition concerns are the "self," family, and friends. Even today, with people separated from many psychosocial sources of help, the sources on this list should not be neglected as part of treatment. Attention to the "self" may mean that family of origin factors need to be explored to better understand what resources are available and what is unavailable. The necessity of determining the client's current support system can be very important as a valuable supplement to counseling. These psychosocial sources can increase support and encouragement, reduce isolation, and promote connectedness, all of which can assist the client in successfully navigating the transitions facing him or her.

According to Golan, *nonprofessional sources* that can also be of assistance include voluntary service, community caregivers, and paraprofessionals. The use of these resources will depend on what the particular transition is. For example, the community caregivers may provide services for the client and/or the family, while voluntary service may be a suggestion for the client to take up. The use of nonprofessional sources may not be as widespread as the use of psychosocial and professional sources, but it can be beneficial for some circumstances.

Professional resources refer to types of counseling services such as family counseling, group counseling, individual counseling, couples counseling, and education. Understanding what resources are available and knowing how to access these resources is mandatory for the counselor. You also need to understand the benefits and possible negative aspects for external resources (e.g., couples counseling) that may also have ethnic and cultural implications.

This model can be applied to all issues and concerns that adults face, but seems particularly suited to address the life transitions in the lifespan model, and many of the situational concerns from the model. Golan's model does not provide specific guidelines, but is more of a framework for conceptualizing assessment and treatment planning.

Schlossberg

Schlossberg (1984) provides guidelines for counseling adults that incorporates four elements to consider:

♦ the event or movement

♦ relationships

♦ coping resources

♦ a new or different perspective.

These can be reframed as questions for which answers are sought in the interview as part of problem-formulation and -treatment planning. Such questions might include:

♦ Is the presenting problem a transition concern that is expected during this period?

♦ Was there a precipitating event that brought the client to counseling?

♦ What is the quality of the client's current relationships? Are there noticeable gaps in his or her social-support system?

♦ What are the quantity and quality of coping resources available by and for the client?

♦ Does resolution require the client to develop a new or different perspective? What are the possibilities for developing new or different attitudes or perspectives?

These questions are an adjunct to formal assessment and diagnosis, but the answers can provide valuable information to guide assessment and planning for interventions.

Schlossberg (1984) calls this a "content-process model" (1984) in which the client is guided to explore, understand and cope, and the counselor's knowledge-base and helping skills are critical in reaching the goals. Schlossberg categorizes all adult problems, issues, and concerns as *transitions*—that is, any events or nonevents that cause change.

The first step in the content-process model is to explore the transition and determine the type of transition, the content, and its impact on the client. Both the client and counselor then move to understand the ramifications by appraising the coping resources, which are defined as a balance of assets and liabilities. Phases of assimilation and changing reactions over time are the primary components for the third step (i.e., coping). Schlossberg (1984) defines the needed counselors' skills as

♦ listening and responding
♦ attending and focusing
♦ interpretation
♦ identification of themes
♦ confrontation
♦ giving information
♦ problem solving
♦ teaching coping skills
♦ structuring support
♦ individual and/or group counseling.

Central to Schlossberg's model is an understanding of adult development theory and the transitions adults face.

Gould

Gould (1978) proposes a psychodynamic clinical model for working with adults that is an outgrowth of his clinical work and training in psychodynamics. He considers this model to be both developmental and existential. It is developmental in the sense that there are stages of growth and development in which tasks and events at each stage hold importance both for the present and the future. The model is existential in the sense that there are continuing human existence concerns that persist throughout life and emerge in differing forms at different periods. Gould's model takes into account both internal and external factors, influences, and realities. Gould proposes the following sequence of developmental processes:

♦ a challenge emerges
♦ individualistic responding occurs
♦ internal conflict results

- ◆ resolution of conflict occurs
- ◆ self-identity changes and successful adaptation are achieved.

The developmental challenge occurs when the person faces the necessity for new skills, attitudes, and/or new self-regulating responses. These challenges can be life transitions, situational conditions, serious physical and/or emotional disorders, or existential concerns described in the lifespan model. Whatever is causing the person to need to adapt, alter, or change in some way is the precipitating incident that causes the challenge to emerge.

The individualistic response is termed *developmental tension* by Gould (1978). This is the difference between where the individual is psychologically and emotionally, and where he or she needs to be. Even when the individual may appear, on the surface, to have accepted and responded to the challenge, the person may not be psychologically, nor emotionally, adapting. This tension may be what brings him or her to counseling.

The third component of the sequence is the developmental conflict that focuses on internal conflict, such as certainty versus ambiguity, success versus failure, the desire to change versus the desire to remain the same, and self-efficacy versus self-doubt. The conflicts go hand-in-hand with anxieties about real and imagined negative consequences. *Not doing* is as anxiety-producing as *doing*, and the consequences for both are unknown and threatening. Many internal conflicts are the result of unresolved family of origin issues and other unfinished business. Adults can be more keenly aware of the complexities of such problems and the possible choices and solutions.

The next part of the sequence is the resolution of the developmental conflict, which can free the adult to perform self-regulatory or adaptative-structure formation, leading to mastery, internalization, and integration. The person's self-perception changes, which liberates him or her to make choices, reach decisions, and solve problems. This does not mean that all previous issues and unfinished business are resolved; it just means that there is sufficient change so that the person can move on. This may mean not doing anything, as not doing is also a decision. If the individual can work through this sequence, he or she can emerge with a significant change in his or her self-representation and overall sense of identity. The outcomes have implications for both the internal and external states of the client.

Gould (1978) describes the components of the model as existential, contextual/developmental, recovery of a function, and successful adaptation. He considers the existential frame of reference to be how current decisions affect the future. The existential themes of awareness of being and nonbeing, freedom and will, the inherent unfairness of the universe, and uncertainty and ambiguity are all part of the human condition. These issues may hold special poignancy for adults, however, because their experiences make them more keenly aware of possibilities and outcomes.

The contextual/developmental frame of reference refers to the conflict between parts of the self and the demands of life situations. The "self" is in conflict with its parts (internal) and with external events. Because these issues can be extremely difficult to sort out, the expertise of the counselor is critical.

The psychodynamic frame assumes that the recovery of some previously sacrificed function is needed in order to make a successful adaptation. It also assumes that the sacrificed function was a response to a previous adaptation, which was not eliminated. These functions are hidden or not accessible to the individual because of defenses, resistance, transference, and projections. Gould (1978) illustrates the importance of this frame of reference by recalling that the recovery of function has been the goal of psychoanalysis since Freud helped rid patients of the symptoms that interfered with the function. Other ways of describing this concept and process include:

♦ addressing the dichotomy between conflictual and conflict-free zones of ego-function (Hartman, 1958)

♦ transmuting internalization of self-object functions (Kohut, 1977)

♦ healing the split of the self (Gould, 1978)

♦ reintegration of the self (Rogers, 1951)

♦ recovery of fragmented parts of self (Perls, 1969).

The recovery of function and successful adaptation are the desired outcomes. A major role is played in this recovery and adaptation by what Gould terms "volitional conflict"—a conflict existing between the realities of the external world and the intrapsychic world. The will (i.e., volition) is not sufficient in and of itself to effect change. There is also the need to understand what internal psychic forces may be acting to prevent change.

The AIR Model

Table 13.1 presents a conceptual model—AIR—for applying adult development theories to counseling adults that is intended to cover the full range of problems, issues, and concerns presented in the lifespan model. The AIR model has three categories for tasks that provide information for treatment planning: *assess*, *identify*, and *rule in/rule out*. The tasks listed under each category are not all-inclusive, but are the minimum. Each piece of information gathered may indicate the need for additional information. Furthermore, these tasks are in addition to more formal assessment.

ASSESS

Assess in the model refers to using your clinical judgment to gather information and evaluate the client's current status and functioning, his

TABLE **13.1**

The AIR Model

Assess	Identify	Rule In/Rule Out
Current status and functioning	Coping resources	Emotional distress
"Self" factors or inner-resources available	Basic problem or concern	Physical illness
Psychological developmental level	Social-support system	Uncontrollable external factors (e.g., unemployment)
Cognitive resources	Relationships strengths/deficits	Addictions or substance abuse; trauma

FORMAL ASSESSMENT

Case Conceptualization	Treatment-Planning Possibilities
Physical well-being	Physical examination
Cognitive acuity	Psychological assessment
Emotional stability	Psychoeducational groups
Social relationships	Support groups
Spiritual resources	Individual counseling
Lifestyle habits	Group counseling/therapy/psychotherapy
	Family counseling
	Couples counseling
	Special conditions treatment (e.g., substance-abuse treatment)

or her inner resources that would be available for assistance (i.e., "self" factors), his or her psychological developmental level, and his or her cognitive resources. This information is gathered from observing and talking with the client and constitutes an unfolding process that continues throughout treatment. However, even the initial interview can provide sufficient information to begin forming judgments.

Understanding the client's current status and functioning are essential, because they tell you if the client is in an acute crisis situation (e.g., suicidal ideation requiring immediate intervention), if the situation is chronic, and if the client is maintaining an acceptable level of functioning.

"Self" factors are personality characteristics, psychological traits, and other strengths that can be mobilized to effect positive outcomes for counseling. Initially focusing on the client's strengths and inner resources is one of the most useful things a counselor can do to instill hope and assist with counseling. Such strengths and inner resources—which are often unrecognized, underdeveloped, or not used—may be of great assistance as you and the client become aware that they exist. Examples of "self" factors include: personality characteristics such as determination and perseverance; traits such as reaching out to others and openness; strengths such as an observing ego and realistic self-appraisal; and inner resources such as the will to effect changes. Because adults typically have many strengths built up over a lifetime of experiences, there may be numerous other factors to consider in the assessment process.

You will need to get more information and practice in order to assess the client's psychological development level. This assessment is more subjective and qualitative than some of the others (e.g., personality assessment), and much of the information has to be inferred from your observations, from what the client tells you, and from a review of his or her life experiences. For example, you will have to use your judgment about the extent of impulse control the client has based on what he or she tells you about his or her life experiences. Among other factors, psychological development incorporates:

♦ the level of impulse control
♦ the areas of stable or healthy narcissism
♦ the emergence of an observing ego
♦ the degree of separation and individuation.

These internal states are not directly observable, although there are assessment instruments available that could aid in judging psychological development.

Understanding the level of psychological development is important for treatment planning, because it provides clues to which developmental tasks have been successfully completed and which have not. For example, it is unrealistic to expect self-regulating behavior from the client who has yet to develop an observing ego. In this case, therapy would need to be geared to an earlier developmental stage to reduce frustration for both the counselor and client and to increase the effectiveness of treatment.

Cognitive resources may refer to both intellectual ability and Perry's cognitive development scheme. Intellectual ability incorporates the facility to

♦ acquire new information
♦ understand and integrate new information
♦ use analytical skills
♦ transfer training and make applications
♦ synthesize various kinds of information
♦ learn new ways of perceiving the world.

Intelligence tests provide some information, as does the client's educational level. However, tests are insufficient sources of information about intellectual levels and should not be used as the definitive indicator of cognitive resources. Access to cognitive resources is another issue, because it is possible to have adequate or even considerable intellectual abilities but to lack the access that makes them viable and useful. Here, the cognitive resources exist but are not being used.

Assessment of cognitive resources should include a review of previous test results and educational achievement, current intelligence-tests results, and your subjective judgment from information and impressions gained from the interview. Care must be taken to avoid jumping to conclusions based on only one source of information.

IDENTIFY

The second AIR component is to *identify* the client's

♦ coping resources
♦ fundamental problem or concern
♦ social-support system
♦ relationship strengths and deficits.

There should be an preliminary identification of these factors based on the initial interview, and continual identification and changes as new information emerges throughout treatment. The models by Golan (1981), Schlossberg (1984), and Gould (1978) all make direct or indirect mention of these factors.

Coping resources refer to the client's willingness to confront needed changes, the ability to be somewhat objective and realistic about personal qualities and abilities, his or her outlook on life, and a realistic appraisal of his or her self-competency, self-efficacy, and self-adequacy. One of the best indicators of a client's coping resources is his or her past reactions to adverse situations, even when past experiences or situations are very different from the current one. Individuals tend to be consistent in their reactions, even when the reactions are counterproductive. For example, if a client's reaction based on past experiences is to self-medicate and withdraw, then that is the reaction that is to be expected for the current situation. If the reaction is to pray and attend church, then that also is to be expected.

Identification of coping resources, however, should also be focused on the strengths the client has. These are the inner resources that the counselor will want to identify and effectively use. All too often, clients who are either in crisis or unable to perceive what solutions or possibilities exist, stay focused on what is not working, their perceived personal weaknesses, or blaming others. The counselor's task is to help the client realize underused strengths and to capitalize on them, as well as working with the identified problem, issue, or concern.

Clients come to counseling with an identified problem. In many instances, the presenting problem is only a reflection of the *fundamental problem or concern*. That is, the presenting problem has many layers, and the underlying problems may not be evident at first. However, if you are not open to the possibility that the presenting problem is a surface manifestation of more and deeper problems or issues, you may find that you spent a lot of time and effort going in the wrong direction. For example, a child's underachievement in school could be caused by unresolved grief over a loss. Working on the underachievement or the depression underlying the lack of school progress will not be as productive as recognizing and working with the unresolved grief. This is an important reason for trying to identify the fundamental problem or issue.

Identifying and working with the fundamental problem and issue does not necessarily mean long-term psychotherapy. In this era of managed care, many clients will not have the resources for that. There are other ways to identify some fundamental problems and issues, and each counseling theoretical perspective has its own unique way. For example, cognitive therapy uses automatic thoughts and RET uses irrational beliefs. While the best prognosis for deep and lasting change seems to be longer-term dynamic- or psychotherapy, basic problems can be identified for shorter-term counseling and therapy.

The primary purpose for having this component in the model is to heighten the awareness that the presenting problem may mask a deeper, more significant concern or issue. The client may not be aware of its existence or may not realize its impact, so counselors need to stay open to the possibility and learn how to read clues to its identity. Your expertise and knowledge about various conditions, underlying causes, and other antecedents provide the information needed to begin exploration of fundamental issues and concerns.

The identification of the client's *social-support system* is important. Considerable evidence exists that supports the idea that the quality of relationships plays an important role in individuals' physical, psychological, spiritual, and emotional well-being. These external supports interact with the individual's internal resources to

♦ promote hope
♦ encourage optimism
♦ give additional meaning and purpose to life
♦ reduce feelings of isolation and alienation
♦ provide comfort and support
♦ open-up avenues for altruism.

These effects are positive and can do much to assist clients in therapy.

The social-support system, or connections with others, also aids in counseling by giving the client other outlets for emotional expression and sources of external support. Counselors cannot expect to provide clients everything they need or want while they are participating in counseling or therapy. It is important that the counselor determines what additional relationships are available—not to do therapy, but just to listen when needed and provide encouragement. The people in these relationships do not have to know that the person is in counseling nor anything about the problem. In fact, others in the support system provide connections in other areas of the person's life. These other connections can

- ◆ halt the erosion of self-confidence and self-efficacy
- ◆ boost self-esteem by showing competence in other areas
- ◆ allow the person to give as well as to receive
- ◆ give reassurance of being valued
- ◆ keep the individual from becoming mired in misery.

Thus it is very important to obtain information about the client's social-support system and to identify additional and unrealized or underused sources. Each source may be different and perform a different function. For example, current friends and relatives perform different functions than do past friends, distant relatives with whom there has been no recent contact, or others in the person's world such as acquaintances from the workplace.

The client should be encouraged to *identify possible relationships* that he or she can strengthen and use as additional support. These relationships are not intended to provide direct support for the problem that brought the client to counseling, as that is the counselor's responsibility; the support in other areas provides additional assistance as the client attempts to explore the various facets of his or her life in counseling.

There will be clients who have very meager support systems or none at all. These clients have two primary options: they may either begin to develop a new support system, or reconnect to individuals from previous times and/or support systems. Developing new connections takes time but can begin at any point. Reconnecting can also take time and effort, but may take much less time because there may still be vestiges remaining of the previous relationships. Encourage and obtain a commitment from the client to call, write, e-mail, or talk with someone from his or her past with whom he or she had a positive relationship. This person may be a relative, childhood friend, college roommate, pastor from a church or temple previously attended, neighbor, elementary or high school teacher, coach, counselor, teammate, and so on—there is a long list of possibilities. Some clients may need to be taught communication and relating skills to help ensure a positive encounter, but reconnecting is the first step.

Another identification that can be helpful is to determine what the client perceives to be his or her relationship strengths and weaknesses. Presenting problems rarely occur in isolation from relationship difficulties. The client's relating, social, and communication skills are an additional area for identification. These can be considered to be a subset of relationship strengths and weaknesses, because these skills play an important role in forming and maintaining satisfactory relationships. Deficits in these skills can point to the need for specific instruction, such as a psychoeducational group that teaches social skills. There is considerable literature on the value of social-, relating-, and communication-skills development on optimum personal well-being and relationship strength.

The quality of the client's relationships can play a part in his or her self-esteem, self-confidence, and self-efficacy, because these are in part derived from the interactions and reactions of others. While internal factors also play an important role, the relationships others have with the client are significant influences. How the client feels about himself or herself is related to how he or she thinks others feel about him or her.

The first interview can provide many clues to help identify relationship strengths and weaknesses. Examine how the client relates to you, the appropriateness of his or her relating, and the communication and social skills that are present or absent. Also, ask about the extent and quality of his or her relationships. Do not confine your examination of the client's relationships to the immediate family, although these may be the most important ones. Determine the client's satisfaction, or lack of satisfaction, with work relationships, social relationships, extended family relationships, and other significant past relationships. Look for patterns in relating, nonrelating, unfinished business, termination of relationships, and longing for reconnections. These are all sources for examination during counseling and can serve as sources for strengthening and extending the client's social-support system.

Some clients who have no or few satisfying relationships may have deficits in relating, communication, and social skills. Others may be existentially isolated and alienated from others, with the result that they also have few or no satisfying relationships. Still others may be experiencing grief or depression because they are unable to connect with others. There are many reasons why clients have or do not have satisfying relationships, and it can be important for therapy outcomes to identify relationship strengths and deficits.

RULE IN/RULE OUT

Diagnosis is a process of assessing, identifying, and sorting through numerous variables to arrive at an understanding of the most important ones as a prelude to treatment planning. While what is described in the AIR model is not formal assessment leading to a diagnosis, it does provide guidance for planning the mode of treatment.

"Sorting through" means evaluating the relative importance of information and deciding what should be kept in making judgments, and what is not as important or relevant and should be eliminated from the judging and decision-making process. It also includes ruling in certain options, and ruling out other options. What to keep, what to discard, what to consider, and what not to consider are subjective based on the counselor's knowledge, expertise, and experience.

The major categories for considering what to *rule in* and what to *rule out* are emotional distress, physical illness, and uncontrollable external factors. Each is briefly described, as conceptualized for the AIR model.

Emotional Distress. The degree of emotional distress present for the client is an important consideration. This is not the formal assessment that uses the *Diagnostic and Statistical Manual of Mental Disorders*, 4th edition (*DSM-IV*) (American Psychiatric Association, 1994) criteria for diagnosis, which is important and a part of the intake process. What is referred to here is more immediate and informal and is focused on gauging the intensity, extent, and direction of the client's emotional state.

Always of primary concern are the client's potentials for either harm to self and/or harm to others. This is a vital and critical piece of information to gather in the initial interview of some clients. There are some presenting problems or concerns in which the threat is low or nonexistent, such as career choice and decisions. However, the potential for harm to self and/or others can be a concern for children, adolescents, and adults and should be considered and ruled in or ruled out. The threat may emerge during the course of counseling and dealt with at that time, but the client's potential to do harm should also be considered in the initial review. Needless to say, any time the threat of harm is clear and imminent, immediate action is needed on the part of the counselor.

Counselors will want to estimate the degree of emotional distress for the client whether or not the client visibly displays the distress or verbally acknowledges it. Indeed, many adults will down play their distress for fear of being perceived as weak or incompetent. Do not dismiss anything the client says as being superficial or of little importance. Through experience you will learn that there is a great deal of emotion concealed in the most off-hand remark, and that you can easily miss emotional distress because it does not appear to be overt or intense.

The extent of emotional distress goes beyond a crisis (e.g., a possible suicide or homicide). You will want to evaluate if the distress is acute or chronic. How long has the client felt this way? Did it begin gradually or did the onset occur very quickly? What is the impact on the client's functioning, self-perception, and relationships? What has the client done to address the emotional distress? Exploring the manifestations and conditions of the distress can be a way of accessing the underlying problems or concern.

Emotions have been shown to significantly impact physical health. Some connections documented by research are reported in Hafen, Karren, Frandsen, and Smith (1996). These include

♦ repressed anger and high blood pressure
♦ hostility and heart disease

♦ depression and addictions
♦ repressed anger and rheumatoid arthritis
♦ repressed depression and cancer
♦ anxiety and irritable bowel syndrome.

These examples highlight the need for counselors to pay close attention to the level of emotional distress in clients, and to have considerable information about the effects of emotions on physical functioning and vice versa.

Physical Illness. The importance of counselors for learning about the effects of physical illnesses on psychological and emotional functioning cannot be overestimated. The mind–body connection is a strong one, with the influence of each being felt on the other. You do not have to engage in extensive medical studies, but you do have to know more than the average person, especially about the effects of unrecognized or undiagnosed physical illnesses or functioning.

Following are some items relating to physical illnesses that have psychological and/or emotional effects. Answer each "true" or "false":

1. It is not unexpected for a heart-attack victim to become depressed.
2. Alzheimer's disease only strikes people over sixty years old.
3. Significant changes in a person's personality (e.g., bursts of anger) can signal a brain tumor.
4. Uncontrolled high blood pressure makes a person cry or become angry for no discernable reason.
5. Chronic fatigue syndrome has no physical basis.*

Also, there are medications that produce attitudinal and emotional side effects. These include not only prescription drugs, but also over-the-counter ones. The client's current drug use may therefore provide some clues regarding his or her functioning. Determining the date of the client's last physical examination and the current state of his or her health are also highly beneficial. The counselor can take an important step to recommend physical examinations in those instances in which physical health may be an important factor in the person's ability to constructively resolve his or her problems.

Uncontrollable External Events. Adults are subject to numerous uncontrollable external factors, and understanding which, if any, are present for the client can assist in treatment planning. Possible uncontrollable external factors that can have a significant impact on the person's well-being and functioning include

---

*Answers: True; False; True; False; and False.

- ◆ loss of job
- ◆ illness or death of one or more parents
- ◆ automobile accidents that result in injuries and/or extensive damage
- ◆ weather-related problems such as floods or hurricanes
- ◆ war
- ◆ relative or friend's death
- ◆ assault, rape, or other violent acts on client or family
- ◆ accidental death
- ◆ racism.

The presenting problem may be a reaction to a factor, or the factor may be the real issue that underlies the presenting problem. Uncontrollable external factors constantly happen to everyone and can be frustrating and anxiety-provoking. They can arouse considerable negative feelings (e.g., inadequacy, helplessness, and despair) that, in turn, can negatively impact the physical, psychological, and emotional functioning. It is very important to determine what, if any, external events are present in the client's life, and the extent to which these are impacting his or her functioning and/or the presenting problem. Ultimately, the impact will depend on the client's internal responses to the events, but just knowing what the events are provides clues for addressing the presenting problem.

Counselors will have to be emotionally prepared to help clients realize that their reactions may be contributing to the presenting problems, and that there is nothing, or very little that can be done to change the circumstances or situations. This may be especially difficult to accept for clients who are action oriented, who have been successful through previous adversity, or who expect miracles. But sometimes the situation is as bad as it appears and there is nothing anyone can do about it. The only possibility is to address the client's reactions and attitudes. That does not change the situation, but it can bolster feelings of self-confidence and self-efficacy and reduce feelings of helplessness, despair, inadequacy, and other self-defeating attitudes.

Other Considerations for Rule In/Rule Out. It would not be uncommon to find that some adult clients have one or more addictions or that there is substance abuse. Addictions and substance abuse impact functioning, relationships, physical health, and psychological and emotional well-being. The impact is felt by others (e.g., family, friends, and work relationships). Thus it becomes critical to rule in or rule out the possibility of addictions or substance abuse. Other considerations are trauma and its effects. Since trauma can have both immediate and long-term effects on the person, a history is essential as is your exploration to rule in/rule out trauma for that client.

Counselors need to know the physical, psychological, and relational indications of possible addiction or substance abuse, as well as understanding treatment options. Clients may go to considerable effort to hide their addictions and abuse of substances, and it may be well into the counseling process before the issues surface. However, there are some overt signs of the possibility that the knowledgeable and experienced counselor can detect. These warning signs and implications are too extensive to review here, so the reader is encouraged to seek additional information and learn more about addictions and substance abuse.

Some addictions may be overlooked or minimized. Drug use such as alcohol, cocaine, heroin, and amphetamines can be the first thought when considering the possibility of addiction or substance abuse. However, this is a very limiting view of addictions and substance abuse. Some other addictions include gambling, shopping, sex, food (over- or under-consumption), and the acquisition of money. Other substances that can be abused are inhalants, food, prescription medication, nicotine, and caffeine.

It is not necessary to make a decision initially whether there is an addiction or substance abuse. Both diagnoses require more formal assessment, and until that is done, noting the possibility is enough. If there is strong evidence, then the counselor would need to take immediate steps to obtain the needed assessment so that treatment could begin as soon as possible. Strong evidence that there may be substance abuse or addiction is indicated by any and all of the following:

♦ a skeletal body

♦ arriving at the session drunk or high

♦ openly seductive behavior

♦ frank admission of compulsion

♦ acknowledgment of helplessness to control behavior such as shopping.

All counselors must learn the warning signs of addiction and substance abuse if they are to be effective, because these conditions greatly affect other aspects of clients' lives and must be addressed first if treatment is to be effective.

To a certain extent, trauma has been addressed in the section on uncontrollable external events. The previous section, however, only included societal conditions and trauma to others (e.g., family). This section focuses on the trauma to the individual himself or herself that does not have to be current—that is, the trauma, which may have occurred many years ago, is still unaddressed and having implications for the individual's life and treatment in the present. Trauma, as used in this discussion, is anything that causes a wounding of the person's physical and/or psychological self and produces lasting effects. Wounding includes acts such as

♦ narcissistic wounding

♦ emotional abuse

♦ physical abuse

- sexual abuse
- neglect in childhood
- rape and other sexual assault
- severe deprivation
- racism
- physical attacks such as beating and being shot
- accidents that produce paralysis or disabilities.

It is not uncommon for many people who experience some of these acts to suffer from post-traumatic stress disorder (PTSD), which does not just occur to those who have been in active combat; it can also result from traumatic life events.

Psychological effects can arise from physical traumas, and research is showing that these effects often linger longer than do the physical ones. Thus current problems and concerns may very well be related to prior trauma and not necessarily to the current situation. Persistent effects of trauma can lead to both physical and psychological symptoms, which in turn lead to relational difficulties. Physical symptoms include:

- sleeplessness
- overeating
- substance abuse
- gastrointestinal disorders and distress
- aches and pain
- high blood pressure.

Psychological effects can be more difficult to detect, because these can be more easily masked or denied. However, these can be very powerful and affect every part of an individual's life. A few of the psychological effects include:

- hypersensitivity
- inability to trust others
- inability to form and maintain meaningful and satisfying relationships
- sadism
- masochism
- a deflated and impoverished self
- fear of intimacy.

There are numerous other psychological effects, so it is important to remember that the aftermath of past trauma cannot be underestimated or overlooked.

Case Conceptualization

Even without formal assessment you now have considerable informa- tion to begin planning for treatment options. Table 13.1 presented some basic categories to be explored when conceptualizing cases. These cate- gories may not be needed for all clients, but can be helpful when planning treatment for serious physical and/or emotional conditions. For example, people in crisis need immediate attention, and those seeking guidance for career choice do not need an in-depth case conceptualization.

This step provides a summary for information, observations, and im- pressions gathered from both informal and formal assessment. The cate- gories for the case-conceptualization model are intended to be a holistic approach for identifying clients' needs, strengths, weaknesses, and re- sources for all aspects of their lives. The focus is not just on the present- ing problem, although that remains the primary concern and highest pri- ority. The steps outlined in treatment planning emphasize the importance of retaining this focus. Humans, however, are complex, and considerable research documents the effects of relationships, social-support systems, physical states, emotional states, and spiritual resources on overall func- tioning and the sense of well-being. Whatever the presenting problem may be, it can be better addressed when the whole person is considered, even if all aspects are not put into the treatment plan. The categories of physical well-being, cognitive acuity, emotional stability, social-support systems, and relationships were presented in previous sections. Spiritual resources and lifestyle habits have not been discussed thus far. Brief dis- cussions for these two important areas follow.

SPIRITUALITY

This is a difficult concept to describe or define because definitions and descriptions use words, and much of what spirituality is or means cannot be expressed in words. The spiritual side of one's life (Hafen et al., 1996) is that part that

♦ emphasizes a quality of existence

♦ has connections to self, to others, and to the universe

♦ gives a sense of meaning and purpose to life

♦ recognizes powers and forces that are beyond the natural and rational.

Viktor Frankel (1963, p. xxiv) states: "The spirituality of man is a thing- in-itself: It cannot be explained by something not spiritual: It is irre- ducible. It may be conditioned by something without being caused by it." Frankel developed a psychotherapy called *logotherapy*, which is not reli- gious or faith-based, that recognizes the existence and importance of the *logos* (soul) or *spirit*. Indeed, Frankel (1986) felt that logotherapy was applicable to "each and every patient including the irreligious and that it is usable in the hands of each and every psychiatrist, including the agnostic" (1963, p. xii). Religion, if conceptualized as an expression of the search for ultimate meaning, is an important part of human lives.

Spirituality can be conceptualized as a journey and emerging process. To appreciate the many manifestations and ways it can be expressed, you have to begin with accessing and understanding your own spirituality. It is important to recognize spirituality's separateness from religion, even though religion can be a part of spirituality, and to arrive at a conceptualization of it that words cannot adequately express. To understand what spiritual resources your clients may have, you need to understand the resources that may be available to you and others.

LIFESTYLE HABITS

Lifestyle habits refer to both self-destructive and self-care actions that clients have as part of their regular lives. Counselors need to have some ideas of how clients take care of themselves, ideas such as proper nutrition, regular dental and physical checkups, exercise, recreational pursuits, hobbies, and outreach activities such as volunteering. These kind of activities can be a source of strength and can provide additional resources for instilling hope, optimism, and feelings of self-efficacy and competence.

On the other hand, destructive lifestyle habits are certainly not helpful and can undermine any treatment provided. Life is not without risk and danger, but we do not have to engage in behaviors that decrease the likelihood of being safe. Some risky and/or self-destructive lifestyle behaviors include

- ◆ having multiple sex partners on a continuing basis
- ◆ having unprotected sexual encounters
- ◆ failing to get proper nutrition
- ◆ hiding the need for medical assistance
- ◆ refusal to follow medical advice
- ◆ engaging in illegal activities.

Most of all, destructive lifestyle habits are those that are contrary to constructive habits. Failing to include constructive habits is the biggest culprit, especially since many positive and constructive lifestyles are generally known.

Treatment Possibilities

The last component in the AIR model is treatment possibilities. The list in table 13.1 does not provide all possible treatment options. The intent of this list is to make it apparent that there are not just two or three treatment options; instead, there are many, and some cases may warrant two or more forms of treatment. Use the holistic approach described in the case-conceptualization section when planning treatment. Try to incorporate all six areas, even if there is scant attention given to some. For example, it can be recommended that the client receive a physical examination to check on the possibility of a medical problem as part of his or her distress. Treatment planning generally involves the following components:

♦ problem selection
♦ problem definition
♦ goal development
♦ objective construction
♦ intervention creation
♦ diagnosis determination.

Wiley and Jossey-Bass publish a series of treatment planners for targeted age groups and special conditions such as adults, adolescents, chemical dependence, and traumatic events. Beginning counselors may find this resource to be of assistance, because specific treatment plans are described for a variety of conditions.

Treatment planning is complex and individualistic. The personal resources of the client, availability of treatment and other services in the community, managed-care guidelines and restrictions, and the counselor's knowledge and awareness of treatment possibilities all combine to become a part of treatment planning. Because of the complexity, this discussion presents only a brief introduction, because it is expected that your preparation will include formal instruction and practice in planning treatment for a variety of conditions.

EXERCISE **13**

"A Picture of Me"

Materials: One or two sheets of memory-book paper, glue, scissors, and a variety of magazines and catalogs. Paper and a writing instrument are needed for processing reflection questions.

Directions:

1. Draw a shape large enough to nearly fill the page. Examples of shapes are a circle, oval, rectangle, heart, star, or square.
2. Select pictures that are symbolic of your achievements, values, likes, dislikes, accomplishments, disappointments, and life satisfaction.
3. Cut out the pictures and glue them in the shape to form a collage.
4. Write an explanation of your collage.

Reflection Questions: Write a brief response to each of the following questions:

1. What aspect of you (e.g., achievements) was the focus for your collage? For example, what aspect has the most symbols?
2. Did you focus primarily on positives when selecting symbols? Why was this important for you?
3. Did you focus primarily on negatives (e.g., disappointments) when selecting symbols? Why was this important for you? Did you ignore negatives?
4. Now assume that you are in your late middle adult years. How might your collage change? What additional accomplishments and achievements do you hope to have in your life? What disappointments might appear? How do your think your values, likes, dislikes, and life satisfaction will compare to how they are today?

Chapter Fourteen

The Late Adult Years

Development and Applications

L ATE ADULTHOOD, WHICH SPANS the approximate years of age 60 and beyond, represents the final developmental stage and is the culmination of a lifetime of growth and change. For most people, these years offer opportunities for continued learning and achievement, as well as reflection on the accomplishments of earlier days. With increased longevity and a massive population of aging "baby boomers," the "graying of America" is quickly becoming a major factor in our society. In November 2000, the estimated number of U.S. citizens aged 65 and over was 34.9 million, comprising about one in every eight individuals, representing a 12 percent increase over 1990. The 2000 census figures also showed an estimated 68,000 U.S. centenarians, representing double the total in 1990; but by 2050, centenarians are expected to number 1.1 million (Administration on Aging, 2001). Many estimates suggest that elders 85 years and older comprise the fastest-growing age group in the United States (American Association for Geriatric Psychiatry, 2001). With such an expanding population of elderly individuals, there will be a growing need for *gerontological counselors*—mental health professionals who work with older adults—to address the needs of elders and their families.

Life Transitions

RETIREMENT

Although some of us optimistically envision retirement as offering opportunities for exquisite leisure, journeys to exotic places, and unlimited pleasure, the reality may be somewhat different. For many, a lack of adequate retirement financial planning in young adulthood may necessitate postponing retirement, starting another career after retirement, accepting part-time employment to supplement retirement benefits, or simply living inexpensively during the later years. Although most older adults do not have to exist on a daily diet of dog food, many will find money to be tight, especially if social security benefits are cut. In 1999, the median household income for adults aged 65 and older was $22,812, compared to a median income of $40,816 for all householders in the United States (Administration on Aging, 2001).

Perhaps even more than financial concerns, however, retirement brings about changes in roles and prestige. For those individuals who derived a major source of identity from their careers, retirement may present a loss of status. Consider the case of Sam:

> Sam had eagerly looked forward to retiring from his career as a naval officer. After "walking the plank" and receiving a gold watch at a wonderful ceremony honoring his accomplishments, Sam was ready to hit the golf course. Although he initially delighted in having more freedom to spend time with his friends, boredom eventually engulfed Sam. To combat a growing sense of purposelessness, Sam decided to surprise his wife by "taking charge of the house" and rearranging all of their furniture while she was away at work. Unfortunately, Sam's industrious activity did not produce the anticipated result and, rather than praise, his wife offered a strong reprimand and admonition for Sam to find something else to do with himself. At that point, Sam enrolled in graduate school to prepare for a second career as a counselor.

PHYSICAL AND MENTAL CHANGES ASSOCIATED WITH AGING

In our youth-oriented culture, it can be difficult to accept the physical signs of aging. Wrinkles, gray hair, baldness, sagging skin, extra pounds, and cellulite may make some individuals feel unattractive and unlovable. Although these physical changes can be troubling, there are more serious concerns associated with aging. Due to the loss of estrogen that occurs after menopause, women are at a higher risk of osteoporosis, high blood pressure, and heart attacks. There is also some reason to suspect that decreased estrogen increases women's risk of Alzheimer's disease. Other physical changes that can occur in the elderly of both sexes include impaired vision, hearing loss, diminished postural control, sexual difficulties, and urinary incontinence (Miller, Zylstra, & Standridge, 2000).

Although the mind ages along with the body, it is a myth to assume that mental functions diminish with advanced years. Although *fluid intelligence*—the ability to take in new information, process it, and learn new tasks—declines with age, *crystallized intelligence*—the ability to draw from accumulated experiences—continues to grow. Declines in fluid abilities are compensated for by increases in crystallized intelligence, so that aging does not produce an overall diminishment in cognitive skills. Elderly individuals may thus do less well on timed tests that require quick thinking, but may ultimately make more reasoned, and perhaps better, decisions than those who are younger.

Situational Concerns

LIVING ARRANGEMENTS

Although it was once assumed that most elderly people lived in nursing homes or with their children, the reality is that most older adults continue to live independent and full lives into advanced age. In fact, 81 percent of U.S. householders aged 65 and over owned the homes in which they lived in 2000 (Administration on Aging, 2001). Many older adults, however, do make changes to ease the burden of house and yard maintenance, such as moving from a large home to a smaller one, going from a house to an apartment or condo, or opting for a place in a retirement community. Retirement communities can be an attractive possibility for some adults because they often offer a variety of services and options, such as various levels of assisted living, meal plans, nursing-home care for those who may need it, educational and recreational activities, exercise facilities, transportation to shopping malls and areas of interest, and hosting community events.

If older adults can no longer function independently, however, adult children may be faced with the difficult decision of whether to admit their parents to a nursing home or have them move in with them. Admitting parents to a nursing home may leave family members with overwhelming feelings of guilt, while having them move into their homes can create tremendous strains on the entire family. Having skilled nurses or respite workers available to relieve family members of some of the responsibilities of elder care can make the situation more manageable for all concerned. The case of Charlotte illustrates this point:

> Until they were in their seventies, Charlotte's mother and father lived in their own home in the town of their birth. When Charlotte's father was in the latter stages of Parkinson's disease and her mother's health began to fail, however, Charlotte became worried about her parents' welfare. Because Charlotte and her husband lived in a different state, she knew she would be unable to get there quickly enough to help her parents deal with emergencies. After much agonizing and heated discussion, Charlotte convinced her parents to sell their home and move into an apartment in a retirement community in the state where Charlotte and her husband resided. The new living arrangements worked out very well for a while; Charlotte's dad received excellent care and her mom was able to make new friends and play bridge without fearing for her husband's safety. When Charlotte's father needed to be placed in the attached nursing home, her mom could walk down the hallway from her apartment and visit him any time she wanted. The problems arose when Charlotte's father died and her mother became physically frail and clinically depressed. When her mother begged to move

into their home, Charlotte and her husband decided to try it. Unfortunately, Charlotte quickly found that her mother's needs were so great that she no longer had time for herself. For example, she frequently went more than a month without leaving the house except to take her mother to doctors' appointments or to dash to the grocery store. Charlotte's marriage was undergoing strain and she was finding herself becoming more and more stressed. Charlotte eventually realized that she needed to find a sitter for her mother to allow her some time each week to care for her own needs and to ensure that she and her husband could again have a life as a couple.

COPING WITH THE DEATH OF A PARTNER

The death of a spouse is believed to be the most stressful of all life events (Holmes & Rahe, 1967). For older adults this loss can be particularly difficult, because it may signify the end of a very long relationship, the loss of a shared history of significant life events (e.g., parenting), the end of a satisfying sexual relationship, and the loss of a best friend and trusted companion. The death of a life partner may also mean that the remaining spouse will have to assume household responsibilities that he or she never performed before, such as balancing the budget or doing yard work. When the death of a spouse is accompanied by other losses, such as the deaths of other relatives or close friends, the impact can be devastating and lead to feelings of loneliness, hopelessness, and purposelessness. Without adequate social support, the loss of a spouse may propel an older adult from normal bereavement into clinical depression.

Major Physical and/or Emotional Disorders and Conditions

DEPRESSION

Although it is normal for older adults to experience depression following major losses, some individuals move from normal grief to clinical depression. Wolfelt (1988) distinguishes between *normal bereavement* and *clinical depression* by the following:

- Bereaved individuals typically respond to comfort and support from others, while clinically depressed individuals do not.
- Bereaved individuals often openly express anger and attribute their depressed feelings to the loss they have suffered, while those with clinical depression often complain and appear irritable but do not relate their feelings to a given life event or express their anger directly.
- Bereaved individuals may experience temporary physical complaints and transient loss of self-esteem, but these symptoms persist in those who suffer from clinical depression.

Although the prevalence of major depression declines with age, depressive symptoms increase, and it is estimated that in a given year 6 percent of U.S. citizens aged 65 and older—about two million individuals—have a diagnosable depressive illness (American Association for Geriatric Psychiatry, 2001). The prevalence of depressive illness in the elderly is alarming, because the rate of suicide is highest among older adults compared to any other age group, and the suicide rate for individuals 85 years and older is the highest of all—twice the overall national rate (American Association for Geriatric Psychiatry, 2001). Even more disturbing is that depression often goes undiagnosed and undertreated in older adults, with many individuals receiving no treatment at all. If depressive illness is suspected, *The Geriatric Depression Scale* (Sheikh & Yesavage, 1986) may be a useful screening tool for older adults.

ALZHEIMER'S DISEASE

Unlike the minor cognitive changes associated with normal aging, Alzheimer's disease (AD) is a pathological condition that produces major deficits in mental functioning. With symptoms usually appearing after age 60, Alzheimer's disease is an age-related and irreversible brain disorder that occurs gradually and results in memory loss, behavior and personality changes, and a decline in thinking abilities (Progress Report on Alzheimer's Disease, 2000). Caused by amyloid plagues and neurofibrillary tangles in the brain, AD produces a breakdown of the connections between neural cells and the eventual deaths of many of these cells.

Alzheimer's disease, which begins with simple forgetfulness, advances to a totally debilitating condition in which the individual no longer recognizes family members, knows his or her own name, nor is able to control his or her own bodily functions. Individuals in the advanced stage of Alzheimer's disease are incapable of independent living and must have constant care and supervision to ensure their safety. They will eventually become bedridden and most likely develop other illnesses and infections, usually dying of pneumonia. Although there is presently no cure for AD, medications can slow down the onset of symptoms so that a person can retain the ability to function for a longer period of time. The Food and Drug Administration has approved three medications—Cognex, Aricept, and Exelon—for the treatment of mild-to-moderate symptoms of AD.

Diagnosing Alzheimer's disease in its early stages is important, because the medications are more likely to be helpful and the patient may still possess the cognitive ability to be involved in planning his or her future care. It is not, however, always easy to diagnose this devastating disease. Because Alzheimer's disease is a diagnosis of exclusion, other conditions have to be ruled out before it is given. If Alzheimer's disease is suspected, an individual will be given a thorough physical examination as well as extensive neurological testing such as MRIs, PET scans, and neuropsychological testing. After all other causes have been eliminated, the diagnosis of Alzheimer's is made. The only truly definitive way to diagnose Alzheimer's disease, however, is in a postmortem examination of an individual's brain for the presence of plagues and tangles.

Most individuals with AD live an average of eight to ten years after they are diagnosed; however, the disease can last up to twenty years (Progress Report on Alzheimer's Disease, 2000). Researchers estimate that up to four million people in the United States currently have AD, and that the prevalence of the disease doubles every five years beyond age 65. With the elderly population increasing at such a rapid rate, AD is expected to put a tremendous strain on individuals, families, the health-care system, and society as a whole.

As the disease progresses, caring for an individual with AD can become exceedingly challenging and draining. To make the task a little easier, the National Institute on Aging (2001) lists the following tips for caregivers, which can also be useful for counselors:

- Try to establish eye contact and call the person by name, thereby ensuring that you have his or her attention before speaking
- Use simple words, short sentences, and a gentle, calm tone of voice
- Avoid talking to the person with AD as though he or she were a child, or acting as though he or she were not there
- Minimize distractions and noise (e.g., television, radio) to help the person focus on what you are saying
- Allow ample time for a response, and do not interrupt
- If the person with AD is struggling to find a word or communicate a thought, gently attempt to suggest a word to him or her
- Try to frame questions and instructions in a positive way
- Allow the person with AD as much independence as possible, even if it means that some things will be done imperfectly
- Encourage exercise and physical activities (e.g., walking, gardening)
- Make sure the person carries some kind of identification or wears a medical bracelet to alert others to his or her identity and medical condition, in case he or she wanders
- Avoid arguing with the person about any delusions or hallucinations he or she may experience. Instead, show empathy for the person's feelings and provide reassurance
- Make sure the person is safe and that he or she does not have access to anything that could harm anyone.

Chronic Health Conditions and Illnesses

In the later years, many chronic illnesses may occur that require ongoing attention. Arthritis, hypertension, cardiac problems, and diabetes may require lifestyle changes and medication. Cataract surgery is common for elders, bone fractures can easily occur, and many older adults face treatment for more serious conditions such as cancer. It is imperative that elders receive regular medical evaluations to diagnose medical conditions in the early stages and to ensure that medications are working effectively. Medications must be monitored very carefully in the elderly to avoid adverse drug-interaction effects that can be potentially life-threatening.

Existential Issues

Pain is inherent in life and, in the later years, individuals often confront especially painful losses. When faced with significant life changes, such as the deaths of loved ones or the diminution of their own abilities, some individuals question the meaning of their lives and wonder whether their lives have a purpose. The ultimate existential issue arises when individuals must come to grips with their own mortality and accept that life on earth is finite and time-limited.

EGO INTEGRITY VERSUS DESPAIR

According to Erikson (1963), the last psychosocial life stage—*ego integrity versus despair*—occurs in late adulthood as individuals reflect on their lives and attempt to make sense of the vast multitude of experiences acquired over the years. He described integrity as "acceptance of one's one-and-only lifecycle as something that had to be and that, by necessity, permitted no substitutions" (1963, p. 268). Integrity implies that when one looks back upon his or her life, the individual is able to derive a sense of satisfaction and closure even though mistakes have been made and some goals have been left unachieved. This sense of closure might be expressed as, "I made some mistakes in my life and I wasn't perfect, but I did the best I could with what I had." Integrity arises from the successful resolution of the previous psychosocial issues and leads to wisdom.

On the other hand, Erikson (1963) described despair as a state that "is signified by fear of death . . . (and) expresses the feeling that the time is now short, too short for the attempt to start another life and to try out alternate roads to integrity" (p. 269). Individuals sometimes manifest this despair as bitterness about life itself and display an attitude of disgust. To mask their own feelings of failure, these individuals may project their negativity outside of themselves by showing contempt for others and blaming others for their mistakes. They exhibit the characteristics of earlier unresolved stages such as mistrust, shame, guilt, inferiority, identity confusion, isolation, and stagnation. With despair, individuals may be fearful of facing their own disappointments and thus avoid doing the necessary reflection that could enable them to work through issues and make greater sense of the totality of their lives.

Counseling Older Adults

LIFE REVIEW

Because individuals achieve a sense of ego integrity by reflecting upon their past experiences, Butler (1963) developed *life review* as a therapeutic technique to help older adults work through unresolved issues and find meaning in their lives. Life review is described as "a naturally occurring, universal mental process characterized by the progressive return to consciousness of past experiences, and, particularly, the resurgence of unresolved conflicts" (Butler, 1963, p. 66). As death draws near, individuals tend to examine their lives and deal with existential questions such as "How did I live my life?" "What did I accomplish?" "Did my life have meaning?" "How do I feel about my life overall?" Older adults often engage in reminiscence as part of their daily lives, and these acts of remembering transpire on various levels (LoGerfo, 1980):

♦ *Informative reminiscence*—superficial remembering of past events that frequently occurs throughout life

♦ *Evaluative reminiscence*—deeper level of remembering in which life experiences are reviewed and evaluated to achieve greater meaning

♦ *Obsessive reminiscence*—intrusive remembering of unresolved conflicts from the past.

Using life review as part of the therapeutic process can help elders engage in evaluative reminiscence and to work through issues about which they obsessively reminisce. Life review can be especially useful for assisting older adults who experience distress due to unfinished business from the past, such as personal deeds that cannot be undone or disputes with others who are now deceased. Obsessive reminiscence about earlier events can contribute to feelings of despair in older adults who cannot change what came before and have only limited access to the future. Aging individuals who may have lost their earlier sources of support, such as relatives and friends, can easily feel powerless in setting new goals or hoping for a better tomorrow. Butler (1975, p. 412) described the value of life review in helping older individuals work through such painful issues:

A major goal of a life review is to deal with the resurgence of unresolved conflicts which can now be surveyed and reintegrated. The old are not only taking stock of themselves as they review their lives, they are trying to think and feel through what they will do with the time that is left and with whatever emotional and material legacies they have to give others.

Counselors can conduct life reviews with both individuals and groups, and can use a variety of media to facilitate clients' reminiscing. Edinberg (as cited in Waters, 1990) suggests the following triggers to stimulate clients' life reviews in either individual or group settings:

- *Music*—old records or live sing-alongs
- *Scents*—spices, perfumes, flowers, foods, candles
- *Imaging based on affect or social interactions*—asking clients to remember particular times that were happy, sad, or frightening; and having them recall holidays or specific historical events
- *Memorabilia*—old photographs, postcards, school yearbooks, election buttons, greeting cards, newspapers, magazines, old household items, or favorite knickknacks.

Group life reviews offer the added advantage of allowing elders to have a shared experience with others in their cohort and to possibly realize that they are not alone in having certain feelings. Waters (1990) used guided imagery together with a sharing of recollections as a form of life review in a small-group setting. Clients were told that they would have an opportunity to think back on their lives and the people who were significant to them. Group members were then invited to get comfortable, close their eyes, and to pictures themselves as children. The group leader asked questions such as "Where are you?" "Is anyone with you?" "What sights and smells are you aware of?" "What are you thinking about?" "How are you feeling?" The group leader next asked members to imagine themselves as young adults, and similar questions were asked for that and subsequent life stages up to the present. At the conclusion of the guided imagery exercise, the group leader asked individuals to share their recollections and then led a discussion of each one's memories. This activity is reported to have produced both pride in the individual participants and closeness among group members.

For elders who engage in obsessive reminiscing, gestalt techniques can be combined with life review to address unfinished business. Crose (1990) suggests the following strategies to facilitate a client's resolution of unresolved issues from the past:

- Have the client reenact stories from the past by expressing them in present-tense language and vivid detail (e.g., change "I fell off my horse when I was twenty," to "It's a bright, summer day in my twentieth year and all around me the tall meadow grass is blowing in the breeze. I'm galloping on my big, golden stallion and feeling like I'm on top of the world. Suddenly everything changes when the horse races up to a huge, fallen tree and takes a jump that I'm not expecting. Now I'm on the ground bleeding, hurting, and terrified that I may never walk again." This change in language allows the client to relive and process the experience, thereby gaining insight and hopefully closure.

◆ Use the empty chair to allow the client to work through unre-solved issues with individuals who are no longer present. For example, if the client feels guilty for not expressing enough love to a relative who is now deceased, the empty chair affords an opportunity to express the sentiments that were never articulated. Similarly, conflicts with others that were never resolved can be addressed with this method.

◆ Focus on incongruencies between the client's words and affect (e.g., "I notice that as you talk about that scary situation of being chased by the neighborhood bullys, you are smiling"). Bringing such incongruencies to the client's awareness can prompt the client to be in the here-and-now and promote the exploration of his or her present feelings.

Although life review can be a powerful tool, there are caveats that counselors must heed to avoid harming clients. While many clients are helped by remembering the past, some clients can be hurt by dwelling too long or deeply upon excruciatingly painful memories. When disturb-ing reminiscences emerge, the counselor will need to decide whether to comfort the client, encourage further exploration of the distressing feel-ings, or move the client away from the subject (Waters, 1990). The deci-sion will be based upon various factors such as the client's resiliency, the degree of trust between the therapist and client, the client's support sys-tem, and how much time the counselor has to work through the client's issues.

HELPING OLDER CLIENTS COPE WITH LOSS

Later adulthood can be a time of numerous losses, such as deaths of spouses, friends, and relatives, reduced status or income, changed living arrangements, geographic relocation, physical limitations, impaired mo-bility, chronic health problems, and diminished independence. Morgan (1994) recommends the following interventions to help older clients cope with loss:

◆ Provide mutual social support with other bereaved individuals who have been confronted with significant losses themselves. Such support may be offered through a support group or by a trained peer-helper who has coped with a similar loss. Senior peer helping programs have been established by mental health agencies in numerous locations throughout the United States to provide training to older adults who are willing to serve as peer counselors for bereaved adults in the community. The peer counselors, who have successfully coped with the same life issues as their clients, make home visits, listen to their clients' concerns, provide free support and guidance, and refer clients for professional counseling when necessary.

♦ Provide counseling for seniors who are suffering from clinical depression. Focus on helping the client accept the loss, deal with feelings and problems associated with the loss, explore both positive and negative memories related to the loss (e.g., happy and sad times with a deceased spouse), and help the client reinvest in life again.

♦ Address unfinished business associated with the loss and help the client understand the grieving process.

♦ Encourage the client to become involved in meaningful activities and to strengthen ties with others who would be supportive.

♦ Explore the possibility of referring the client for prescription medication, such as antianxiety or antidepressant drugs, if needed.

WORKING WITH A TEAM OF HEALTH CARE PROFESSIONALS

Gerontological counselors who work with older adults with physical or mental impairments often function as members of an interdisciplinary-treatment team that includes physicians, social workers, physical therapists, occupational therapists, nurses, and home-care providers (Myers & Schwiebert, 1996). Typical roles for members of the treatment team include the following:

♦ *Physician*—leads the team and oversees all aspects of the client's treatment; including medical treatment, prescriptions for medications, prescriptions for physical and occupational therapy, consultation with other medical specialists, and referrals for mental health counseling.

♦ *Social worker*—assists the client in obtaining necessary social services, home health care services, and durable medical equipment such as wheelchairs, in-home hospital beds, and walkers; helps families make decisions about in-home care or nursing home placements; and provides family counseling.

♦ *Physical therapist*—helps the client regain physical strength and stamina; provides exercises to enable the client to walk, enhance upper-body strength, or improve cardiovascular endurance.

♦ *Occupational therapist*—helps the client perform activities of daily living, such as feeding oneself, bathing, and dressing.

♦ *Nurse*—provides skilled nursing care such as for administering medications, changing dressings on wounds, and changing catheters.

♦ *Home care provider*—may be a nurse's aide or homemaker. Nurse's aides provide services such as bathing, shaving, and dressing the client; homemakers assist the client with household tasks such as doing laundry, washing dishes, vacuuming, and mopping.

♦ *Gerontological counselor*—works with the other team members to meet the client's mental health needs; provides emotional support, information (e.g., strategies for assisting individuals with Alzheimer's disease), and skills-development training (e.g., stress management) to the client and his or her family.

It is essential for each member of the team to be apprised of the client's treatment plan so that all will be working together to achieve unified goals. Counselors should be prepared to advocate for the client if it appears that aspects of his or treatment are being overlooked or are not serving his or her best interests.

WORKING WITH FAMILY MEMBERS

It is not unusual for older adults to be referred for counseling by concerned family members who fear that an aging parent is in need of mental health assistance for issues such as depression or anxiety. Sometimes following a major loss or life transition, family members may notice a change in their loved one and worry that the elder is giving up on life or wonder whether he or she has physical or cognitive impairments that would preclude independent living.

As adult children move into caregiving roles with their aging parents, unresolved childhood issues may emerge (Myers, 1989). To effectively work with this population, counselors need to consider previous relationships between parents and adult children, past patterns of family dynamics, and the ability and motivation of adult children to provide care. The case of Martha illustrates this point:

> Martha's mother, Hortense, was an alcoholic for most of Martha's childhood through her early adult years. Although Martha remembers Hortense as being a loving mother when sober, Hortense's intoxicated behavior was quite different. Martha recalls her mother as "getting fairly drunk almost every evening, being extremely verbally abusive, and then having no memory of it the next day." When Hortense developed Alzheimer's disease and needed extensive caregiving, Martha wanted to provide it but felt resentful that she had not received such loving care from her mother. As a result of her conflicted emotions, Martha found herself frequently becoming impatient and snapping at her mother and then feeling guilty and selfish for "being such a bad daughter."

Legal and Ethical Issues Associated with Counseling Older Adults

ELDER ABUSE

Just as children are considered to be vulnerable and in need of protection from various forms of abuse and neglect, so are older adults who may be unable to adequately protect themselves. Elder abuse has been defined as "any act of commission or omission that results in harm or threatened harm to the health and welfare of an elderly person" (American Medical Association Council on Scientific Affairs, 1987, p. 966). Elder abuse or maltreatment can occur in institutions or in private homes, and it assumes five major forms (Welfel, Danzinger, & Santoro, 2000):

♦ *Neglect*—the most common form of elder abuse, consisting of failure to provide essential physical or mental care for an older adult. Physical neglect includes failing to give adequate food or water, withholding proper hygiene, or not offering physical aids or safety precautions. Neglect is not necessarily intentional, but can instead arise anytime an older person is receiving insufficient care. Some older adults fail to adequately care for themselves, resulting in self-neglect (e.g., failing to take required medications, skipping meals, not bathing).

♦ *Physical violence*—acts of violence that can result in pain, injury, disease, or impairment (e.g., slapping, pushing, striking, force-feeding, over-medicating, sexual assault).

♦ *Psychological abuse*—any action that causes fear, confusion, isolation, or disorientation in an elder (e.g., verbal berating, intimidation, harassment, threats of punishment, humiliation, or deprivation).

♦ *Financial exploitation*—misuse of an elder's income or resources for the personal gain of another (e.g., stealing money or possessions, coercing an older person into signing contracts, denying things to which an elder is entitled). This form of abuse is often committed by a caretaker, such as an adult child.

♦ *Violation of rights*—deprivation of any inalienable or legal right (e.g., voting, free speech, privacy, liberty, assembly, personal property).

All fifty states have passed legislation to reduce the incidence of elder maltreatment, and forty-five states (with the exceptions of Colorado, North Dakota, Pennsylvania, South Dakota, and Wisconsin) require mandated reporting by designated professionals who suspect elder abuse (Welfel, Danzinger, & Santoro, 2000). Mental health professionals are mandated reporters in many states and are subject to civil or criminal penalties for failing to report suspected cases to adult protective-services authorities. Older adults may refuse protective services, however, unless deemed by a judge to be mentally incompetent to make that decision.

Assessing and reporting elder maltreatment can prove challenging for counselors, because it is often difficult to detect and sometimes deliberately concealed by elderly victims. Signs of physical abuse can be covered by clothing or dismissed as being due to aging skin that bruises easily. Emotional abuse, financial exploitation, and neglect often present no obvious symptoms and may go unmentioned by older adults who wish to protect the family members who are perpetrating the maltreatment. Even when directly questioned, some older adults will deny abuse and neglect for fear of making their living situations even worse by causing their caretakers to retaliate against them. It is therefore essential for counselors to be aware of the vulnerabilities of older adults, as well as the possibility of maltreatment, and to proceed carefully if abuse or neglect is suspected.

Welfel, Danzinger, and Santoro (2000) offer the following guidelines to assist counselors in reporting suspected cases of elder maltreatment:

- ◆ Routinely consider the possibility of maltreatment in all older adults who are dependent on others for care, but do not assume that all elders are victims.
- ◆ Provide an empathic and supportive environment in which to discuss the elder's concerns. Develop a trusting relationship with the client and ask only nonconfrontative and nonjudgmental questions (e.g., not "Does your daughter ever try to hurt you?" but instead "How safe do you feel in your daughter's home?").
- ◆ Collect information related to the risk factors for elder abuse (e.g., poor health, impaired cognitive abilities, social isolation, substance abuse or unresolved psychological disorders in caretakers, financial dependence of caretakers on elders, history of violence in the family).
- ◆ Interview family members separately so that embarrassing information will not be uncovered in the presence of others (e.g., issues of personal hygiene, feelings of anger or fear).
- ◆ Educate clients and family members about services available to assist them (e.g., support groups, housing, home-care and respite services, financial advice).

COMPETENCY ISSUES

When working with older adults, issues of competency can arise regarding the elder's ability to make reasoned decisions regarding his or her own welfare (e.g., living arrangements, medical treatments, financial matters). Concerned family members may believe that they know what is best for an aging parent, while the older adult staunchly disagrees. Consider the following cases:

Franklin is a very generous man who has always donated money to his church and charitable organizations. Now that he is in his eighties, it seems that he is giving even more than ever. His phone rings constantly with callers soliciting money from him for a variety of questionable causes and his daughter worries that he is a victim of scams. In spite of his daughter's concerns, Franklin continues to agree to give money to everyone who calls because he claims "it's hard to say no to worthy causes when I have so many blessings myself."

Rose Marie is frail and has become increasingly forgetful since the death of her husband a year ago. Recently, while her son was visiting, Rose Marie left the stove on several times after the meal was cooked and once got lost on the walk home from a local park where she has been many times. Although her son wants her to move into a nursing home, Rose Marie adamantly refuses, stating, "I'll never give up my home to be put in a place like that. Why don't you just kill me instead?"

In both of these cases, the autonomy of the elder seems to be in conflict with the need for others to protect the older adult's welfare or safety. The question of competency then becomes pertinent because if the elder is mentally competent to make decisions for himself or herself, autonomy should generally prevail. However, if the older adult is not mentally competent, protection must be provided while protecting the older adult's autonomy as much as possible. When gerontological counselors are caught up in such power struggles between aging parents and adult children, they may need to consider, "Who is the client?" and "What are the real issues?"

In the case of Franklin, the daughter may have legitimate concerns that her father may be a victim of telephone scams. If so, Franklin's daughter may need to obtain the power of attorney and become involved in Franklin's financial contributions. On the other hand, Franklin may be spending his money as he desires and, although his daughter disagrees, should have the right to continue to do so. A possible solution to this problem might involve Franklin's using an answering machine to take messages for all incoming calls, and then returning those from friends and family members. Because telephone solicitors usually do not leave messages, Franklin would be spared of having to refuse their requests.

In the case of Rose Marie, factors such as stress, depression, or drug interactions may make the older adult appear to be suffering from dementia and less able to care for herself than she actually is. Rose Marie's son's wish to move his mother into a nursing home may be primarily to relieve his own anxiety rather than because the move is actually warranted. The possibility also exists, however, that Rose Marie is no longer able to function independently and needs assistance to ensure her safety. A careful examination of Rose Marie's mental status, physical condition, and living situation would need to be conducted to determine the best course of action to take, as well as Rose Marie's competency to decide for herself. One solution might be to explore the possibility of hiring someone to live with Rose Marie and assist with household tasks.

Although all counselors have an ethical responsibility to protect the welfare and rights of their clients, gerontological counselors may need to play a special role in serving as advocates for the elderly. Because of bias against the elderly and ignorance regarding normal aging in our youth-oriented society, counselors who work with older adults must take active steps to ensure the preservation of autonomy and dignity for their clients. Except in cases of potential danger to themselves or others, all adults should maintain the right of self-determination and the ability to freely choose their own destinies throughout life.

Successful Aging

Although everyone ages, some individuals are far more successful at aging well than others. Havighurst (1961) coined the term *successful aging* to denote "adding life to the years" rather than just years to the life, and "getting satisfaction from life" in later adulthood. Successful aging has been defined as "reaching one's potential and arriving at a level of physical, social, and psychological well-being in old age that is pleasing to both self and others" (Gibson, 1995, p. 279). According to Palmore (1995), a comprehensive definition of successful aging "would combine survival (longevity), health (lack of disability), and life satisfaction (happiness)" (p. 914). The factors that most strongly contribute to successful aging include: 1) a high level of engagement with life, 2) a low risk of disease, and 3) high levels of physical and cognitive functioning (Seeman, 2000).

A landmark research project, the MacArthur Studies of Successful Aging, examined factors that influence physical and cognitive functioning in a cohort group of highly functional male and female volunteers between the ages of 70 and 79 (Seeman, 2000; Seeman, Lusignolo, Albert, & Berkman, 2001). Subjects were selected for the study from a pool of 4,030 potential participants based upon specific physical and cognitive criteria to identify those functioning at the top third of the entire group. The group that was selected for participation initially consisted of 1,189 subjects who were to be studied for a 7.5 year period; however, 273 (23 percent) died before the study concluded in 1996. Of the surviving 916 participants, 722 (79 percent) completed face-to-face interviews, 107 (11.7 percent) had proxy-partial interviews, 44 (4.8 percent) refused, and 43 (4.7 percent) were unable to be contacted. Throughout the study, participants were periodically interviewed, including detailed assessments of their physical and cognitive abilities, overall health status, and social, psychological, and lifestyle characteristics. This ground-breaking longitudinal study revealed surprising results that hold important implications for successful aging.

First, the participants with optimal levels of lung function were less likely to show physical decline in older age. Those who engaged in regular physical activity, either moderate or strenuous, were only half as likely to show physical decline as those who were inactive. Because physical activity increases lung capacity and functioning, these two factors may be linked.

Second, subjects who participated in social activities or groups (e.g., work, volunteering, socializing with friends) experienced the same protective factors against physical decline as those who exercised. Interestingly, even those who had chronic conditions when they began the study experienced the protective benefits of exercise and socialization, showing that it is never too late to adopt healthy habits.

Third, cognitive ability was found to be similarly influenced by exercise and social involvement. Participants who engaged in any physical activity, whether moderate or strenuous, were less likely to experience cognitive decline than their inactive counterparts. Likewise, subjects who had three regularly scheduled social activities on their calendars were less likely to lose mental acuity than those who had no regular activities. The participants who had greater levels of emotional support, derived from a network of social relationships, tended to have higher cognitive functioning.

Finally, a positive mental attitude was found to relate to better physical and cognitive functioning. Because exercise, social involvement, and a positive attitude predicted better outcomes, perhaps the best way to increase the likelihood of successful aging is therefore to combine the three by keeping an upbeat outlook on life while regularly engaging in enjoyable physical and social activities with friends.

Other longitudinal research found additional variables to be associated with successful aging. The Normative Aging Study investigated individual differences in physical and psychological health trajectories in 1,515 men, aged 28 to 80 (mean age = 47.15 years), for an average of 18 years (Aldwin, Spiro, Levenson, & Cupertino, 2001). The study supported the widely held assumption that individual differences increase with age; thus some healthy people showed little age-related impairment in health until very late in life, while others started declining rapidly at mid-life. The differences in individuals' health trajectories became even more pronounced with age. Men who smoked, were overweight, and had higher levels of hostility and anxiety were found to have health trajectories characterized by more numerous and serious physical and psychological symptoms. On the other hand, men who were emotionally stable, thin, educated, and did not smoke were found to have health trajectories characterized by few symptoms. Overlap was found between physical and psychological symptoms, with over 85 percent of the men showing a pattern of low levels of physical-health symptoms associated with a stable pattern of few psychological-health symptoms.

The Normative Aging Study also found mortality rates to be related to various personality traits, health habits, and socioeconomic factors. The subjects who were in the lowest socioeconomic cluster had the highest mortality rate. Anxiety, however, appeared to be a risk factor that increased men's vulnerability for health problems in relation to various environmental and genetic factors. In addition, the men who had the lowest mortality rates tended to be more emotionally stable and less hostile, suggesting that positive personality characteristics played a protective role regarding at least some health problems. Furthermore, the healthiest cluster consisted of men who tended to have the best health behaviors. The findings from this multifaceted study showed that successful aging may result from a complex combination of health-behavior habits, personality characteristics, and socioeconomic variables, as well as a probable multitude of other genetic and environmental factors.

Based upon the results of longitudinal research, the implications for successful aging are clear. In order to age well, one must exercise, get proper nutrition, abstain from smoking, stay socially involved, keep a positive mental attitude, and acquire strategies for managing anger and reducing anxiety. The following cases offer glimpses of aging at its best:

> Until age 93, Marguerite has lived alone and enjoyed cooking all of her own meals. To celebrate holidays, she has festively decorated her apartment and entertained friends with elaborate parties, gourmet food, and ornately wrapped gifts. Marguerite still has impeccable taste, a razor-sharp mind, and a genuine zest for living.
>
> Due to her recently failing health, however, Marguerite has planned her funeral, picked out stylish clothes in which to be buried, purchased her casket, selected her favorite music, bought flowers for the service, and hired a bugler to play "Taps." She has meticulously attended to each detail so that no family members or friends will be burdened with making funeral arrangements, and so that the service will be as elegant and unique as her life.
>
> A widow for over 40 years, Marguerite says, "I've had a full and interesting life, and I'm ready to go." Although Marguerite may be ready, her extensive network of friends and family members are not quite ready for her to leave. In a recent hospital stay, Marguerite had a steady stream of visitors coming from different states to see her and bring exotic gifts.

> Marguerite's brother-in-law, Payne, is another example of successful aging. At 86, Payne walks seven miles a day, attends church every Sunday, goes dancing once a week, and spends his days helping others. As a friendly gesture, he grows flowers and distributes their blossoms to acquaintances all over town. Payne always carries his deceased wife's picture in his pocket and brings it out to share with her moments of special beauty, such as a summer sunset on the water. Payne knows the habits of all the aquatic creatures that congregate in the river behind his house, and he waves vigorously at every boat full of potential friends that pass by his pier. Payne's motto is, and has always been, "Things are looking up, up, up!"

Counseling can undoubtedly help individuals achieve optimal levels of wellness throughout the lifespan, promising a harvest of memories in the later years of lives lived to the fullest and with dreams realized. Successful aging does not begin in the later years, but commences with the decisions made in each stage of life. May your own optimal aging begin now!

EXERCISE **14**

"In Memory of Me"

Materials: Paper and a writing instrument, your favorite music for a memorial service, and an audio cassette or compact-disk player.

Procedure: Imagine that you can travel through time into the future, and that you are able to be present at your own memorial service. You may wish to play the music you have selected as you write answers to the following questions:

1. Who is present? Are there many people or only a few close family members and friends? Will there be people present who are not in your life at the present moment (e.g., a partner you haven't yet met, unborn children, family members with whom you've lost contact)?
2. What music is playing? Do the songs have words or are they instrumentals? Is the music religious or secular?
3. Who speaks at the memorial service? What was your relationship to these individuals? What does each say about you? Which of your personal attributes or qualities do they mention? What achievements do they describe? Is there a common theme running through many of their reminiscences, or does each person know you in a very different way? How well do these individuals know you? Which things make them laugh as they remember you, and which make them cry? What are some of their fondest memories of you?
4. Where do they say you've gone? Are they right?
5. As the service concludes and you reflect on the words and feelings that were expressed, how do you feel about your life?

Appendix: ACA Code of Ethics

ACA Code of Ethics Preamble

The American Counseling Association is an educational, scientific, and professional organization whose members are dedicated to the enhancement of human development throughout the life-span. Association members recognize diversity in our society and embrace a cross-cultural approach in support of the worth, dignity, potential, and uniqueness of each individual.

The specification of a code of ethics enables the association to clarify to current and future members, and to those served by members, the nature of the ethical responsibilities held in common by its members. As the code of ethics of the association, this document establishes principles that define the ethical behavior of association members. All members of the American Counseling Association are required to adhere to the Code of Ethics and the Standards of Practice. The Code of Ethics will serve as the basis for processing ethical complaints initiated against members of the association.

ACA Code of Ethics

Section A: The Counseling Relationship
Section B: Confidentiality
Section C: Professional Responsibility
Section D: Relationships With Other Professionals
Section E: Evaluation, Assessment, and Interpretation
Section F: Teaching, Training, and Supervision

Section G: Research and Publication

Section H: Resolving Ethical Issues

SECTION A: *THE COUNSELING RELATIONSHIP*

A.1. Client Welfare

a. *Primary Responsibility.* The primary responsibility of counselors is to respect the dignity and to promote the welfare of clients.

b. *Positive Growth and Development.* Counselors encourage client growth and development in ways that foster the clients' interest and welfare; counselors avoid fostering dependent counseling relationships.

c. *Counseling Plans.* Counselors and their clients work jointly in devising integrated, individual counseling plans that offer reasonable promise of success and are consistent with abilities and circumstances of clients. Counselors and clients regularly review counseling plans to ensure their continued viability and effectiveness, respecting clients' freedom of choice. (*See* A.3.b.)

d. *Family Involvement.* Counselors recognize that families are usually important in clients' lives and strive to enlist family understanding and involvement as a positive resource, when appropriate.

e. *Career and Employment Needs.* Counselors work with their clients in considering employment in jobs and circumstances that are consistent with the clients' overall abilities, vocational limitations, physical restrictions, general temperament, interest and aptitude patterns, social skills, education, general qualifications, and other relevant characteristics and needs. Counselors neither place nor participate in placing clients in positions that will result in damaging the interest and the welfare of clients, employers, or the public.

A.2. Respecting Diversity

a. *Nondiscrimination.* Counselors do not condone or engage in discrimination based on age, color, culture, disability, ethnic group, gender, race, religion, sexual orientation, marital status, or socioeconomic status. (*See* C.5.a, C.5.b, and D.1.i.)

b. *Respecting Differences.* Counselors will actively attempt to understand the diverse cultural backgrounds of the clients with whom they work. This includes, but is not limited to, learning how the counselor's own cultural/ethnic/racial identity impacts her or his values and beliefs about the counseling process. (*See* E.8 and F.2.i.)

A.3. Client Rights

a. *Disclosure to Clients.* When counseling is initiated, and throughout the counseling process as necessary, counselors inform clients of the purposes, goals, techniques, procedures, limitations, potential risks, and benefits of services to be performed, and other pertinent information. Counselors take steps to ensure that clients understand the implications of diagnosis, the intended use of tests and reports, fees, and billing arrangements. Clients have the right to expect confidentiality and to be provided with an explanation of its limitations, including supervision and/or treatment team professionals; to obtain clear information about their case records; to participate in the ongoing counseling plans; and to refuse any recommended services and be advised of the consequences of such refusal. (*See* E.5.a and G.2.)

b. *Freedom of Choice.* Counselors offer clients the freedom to choose whether to enter into a counseling relationship and to determine which professional(s) will provide counseling. Restrictions that limit choices of clients are fully explained. (*See* A.1.c.)

c. *Inability to Give Consent.* When counseling minors or persons unable to give voluntary informed consent, counselors act in these clients' best interests. (*See* B.3.)

A.4. Clients Served by Others

If a client is receiving services from another mental health professional, counselors, with client consent, inform the professional persons already involved and develop clear agreements to avoid confusion and conflict for the client. (*See* C.6.c.)

A.5. Personal Needs and Values

a. *Personal Needs.* In the counseling relationship, counselors are aware of the intimacy and responsibilities inherent in the counseling relationship, maintain respect for clients, and avoid actions that seek to meet their personal needs at the expense of clients.

b. *Personal Values.* Counselors are aware of their own values, attitudes, beliefs, and behaviors and how these apply in a diverse society, and avoid imposing their values on clients. (*See* C.5.a.)

A.6. Dual Relationships

a. *Avoid When Possible.* Counselors are aware of their influential positions with respect to clients, and they avoid exploiting the trust and dependency of clients. Counselors make every effort to avoid dual relationships with clients that could impair professional judgment or increase the risk of harm to clients. (Examples of such relationships include, but are not limited to, familial, social, financial, business, or close personal relationships with clients.) When a dual relationship cannot be avoided, counselors take appropriate professional precautions such as informed consent, consultation, supervision, and documentation to ensure that judgment is not impaired and no exploitation occurs. (*See* F.1.b.)

b. *Superior/Subordinate Relationships.* Counselors do not accept as clients superiors or subordinates with whom they have administrative, supervisory, or evaluative relationships.

A.7. Sexual Intimacies with Clients

a. *Current Clients.* Counselors do not have any type of sexual intimacies with clients and do not counsel persons with whom they have had a sexual relationship.

b. *Former Clients.* Counselors do not engage in sexual intimacies with former clients within a minimum of 2 years after terminating the counseling relationship. Counselors who engage in such relationship after 2 years following termination have the responsibility to examine and document thoroughly that such relations did not have an exploitative nature, based on factors such as duration of counseling, amount of time since counseling, termination circumstances, client's personal history and mental status, adverse impact on the client, and actions by the counselor suggesting a plan to initiate a sexual relationship with the client after termination.

A.8. Multiple Clients

When counselors agree to provide counseling services to two or more persons who have a relationship (such as husband and wife, or parents and children), counselors clarify at the outset which person or persons are clients and the nature of the relationships they will have with each involved person. If it becomes apparent that counselors may be called upon to perform potentially conflicting roles, they clarify, adjust, or withdraw from roles appropriately. (*See* B.2 and B.4.d.)

A.9. Group Work

a. *Screening.* Counselors screen prospective group counseling/therapy participants. To the extent possible, counselors select members whose needs and goals are compatible with goals of the group, who will not impede the group process, and whose well-being will not be jeopardized by the group experience.

b. *Protecting Clients.* In a group setting, counselors take reasonable precautions to protect clients from physical or psychological trauma.

A.10. Fees and Bartering (See D.3.a. and D.3.b.)

a. *Advance Understanding.* Counselors clearly explain to clients, prior to entering the counseling relationship, all financial arrangements related to professional services including the use of collection agencies or legal measures for nonpayment. (*See* A.11.c.)

b. *Establishing Fees.* In establishing fees for professional counseling services, counselors consider the financial status of clients and locality. In the event that the established fee structure is inappropriate for a client, assistance is provided in attempting to find comparable services of acceptable cost. (*See* A.10.d, D.3.a, and D.3.b.)

c. *Bartering Discouraged.* Counselors ordinarily refrain from accepting goods or services from clients in return for counseling services because such arrangements create inherent potential for conflicts, exploitation, and distortion of the professional relationship. Counselors may participate in bartering only if the relationship is not exploitative, if the client requests it, if a clear written contract is established, and if such arrangements are an accepted practice among professionals in the community. (*See* A.6.a.)

d. *Pro Bono Service.* Counselors contribute to society by devoting a portion of their professional activity to services for which there is little or no financial return (pro bono).

A.11. Termination and Referral

a. *Abandonment Prohibited.* Counselors do not abandon or neglect clients in counseling. Counselors assist in making appropriate arrangements for the continuation of treatment, when necessary, during interruptions such as vacations, and following termination.

b. *Inability to Assist Clients.* If counselors determine an inability to be of professional assistance to clients, they avoid entering or immediately terminate a counseling relationship. Counselors are knowledgeable about referral resources and suggest appropriate alternatives. If clients decline the suggested referral, counselors should discontinue the relationship.

c. *Appropriate Termination.* Counselors terminate a counseling relationship, securing client agreement when possible, when it is reasonably clear that the client is no longer benefiting, when services are no longer required, when counseling no longer serves the client's needs or interests, when clients do not pay fees charged, or when agency or institution limits do not allow provision of further counseling services. (*See* A.10.b and C.2.g.)

A.12. Computer Technology

a. *Use of Computers.* When computer applications are used in counseling services, counselors ensure that (1) the client is intellectually, emotionally, and physically capable of using the computer application; (2) the computer application is appropriate for the needs of the client; (3) the client understands the purpose and operation of the computer applications; and (4) a follow-up of client use of a computer application is provided to correct possible misconceptions, discover inappropriate use, and assess subsequent needs.

b. *Explanation of Limitations.* Counselors ensure that clients are provided information as a part of the counseling relationship that adequately explains the limitations of computer technology.

c. *Access to Computer Applications.* Counselors provide for equal access to computer applications in counseling services. (*See* A.2.a.)

SECTION B: *CONFIDENTIALITY*

B.1. Right to Privacy

a. *Respect for Privacy.* Counselors respect their clients right to privacy and avoid illegal and unwarranted disclosures of confidential information. (*See* A.3.a and B.6.a.)

b. *Client Waiver.* The right to privacy may be waived by the client or his or her legally recognized representative.

c. *Exceptions.* The general requirement that counselors keep information confidential does not apply when disclosure is required to prevent clear and imminent danger to the client or others or when legal requirements demand that confidential information be revealed. Counselors consult with other professionals when in doubt as to the validity of an exception.

d. *Contagious, Fatal Diseases.* A counselor who receives information confirming that a client has a disease commonly known to be both communicable and fatal is justified in disclosing information to an identifiable third party, who by his or her relationship with the client is at a high risk of contracting the disease. Prior to making a disclosure the counselor should ascertain that the client has not already informed the third party about his or her disease and that the client is not intending to inform the third party in the immediate future. (*See* B.1.c and B.1.f.)

e. *Court-Ordered Disclosure.* When court ordered to release confidential information without a client's permission, counselors request to the court that the disclosure not be required due to potential harm to the client or counseling relationship. (*See* B.1.c.)

f. *Minimal Disclosure.* When circumstances require the disclosure of confidential information, only essential information is revealed. To the extent possible, clients are informed before confidential information is disclosed.

g. *Explanation of Limitations.* When counseling is initiated and throughout the counseling process as necessary, counselors inform clients of the limitations of confidentiality and identify foreseeable situations in which confidentiality must be breached. (*See* G.2.a.)

h. *Subordinates.* Counselors make every effort to ensure that privacy and confidentiality of clients are maintained by subordinates including employees, supervisees, clerical assistants, and volunteers. (*See* B.1.a.)

i. *Treatment Teams.* If client treatment will involve a continued review by a treatment team, the client will be informed of the team's existence and composition.

B.2. Groups and Families

a. *Group Work.* In group work, counselors clearly define confidentiality and the parameters for the specific group being entered, explain its importance, and discuss the difficulties related to confidentiality involved in group work. The fact that confidentiality cannot be guaranteed is clearly communicated to group members.

b. *Family Counseling.* In family counseling, information about one family member cannot be disclosed to another member without permission. Counselors protect the privacy rights of each family member. (*See* A.8, B.3, and B.4.d.)

B.3. Minor or Incompetent Clients

When counseling clients who are minors or individuals who are unable to give voluntary, informed consent, parents or guardians may be included in the counseling process as appropriate. Counselors act in the best interests of clients and take measures to safeguard confidentiality. (*See* A.3.c.)

B.4. Records

a. *Requirement of Records.* Counselors maintain records necessary for rendering professional services to their clients and as required by laws, regulations, or agency or institution procedures.

b. *Confidentiality of Records.* Counselors are responsible for securing the safety and confidentiality of any counseling records they create, maintain, transfer, or destroy whether the records are written, taped, computerized, or stored in any other medium. (*See* B.1.a.)

c. *Permission to Record or Observe.* Counselors obtain permission from clients prior to electronically recording or observing sessions. (*See* A.3.a.)

d. *Client Access.* Counselors recognize that counseling records are kept for the benefit of clients, and therefore provide access to records and copies of records when requested by competent clients, unless the records contain information that may be misleading and detrimental to the client. In situations involving multiple clients, access to records is limited to those parts of records that do not include confidential information related to another client. (*See* A.8, B.1.a, and B.2.b.)

e. *Disclosure or Transfer.* Counselors obtain written permission from clients to disclose or transfer records to legitimate third parties unless exceptions to confidentiality exist as listed in Section B.1. Steps are taken to ensure that receivers of counseling records are sensitive to their confidential nature.

B.5. Research and Training

a. *Data Disguise Required.* Use of data derived from counseling relationships for purposes of training, research, or publication is confined to content that is disguised to ensure the anonymity of the individuals involved. (*See* B.1.g and G.3.d.)

b. *Agreement for Identification.* Identification of a client in a presentation or publication is permissible only when the client has reviewed the material and has agreed to its presentation or publication. (*See* G.3.d.)

B.6. Consultation

a. *Respect for Privacy.* Information obtained in a consulting relationship is discussed for professional purposes only with persons clearly concerned with the case. Written and oral reports present data germane to the purposes of the consultation, and every effort is made to protect client identity and avoid undue invasion of privacy.

b. *Cooperating Agencies.* Before sharing information, counselors make efforts to ensure that there are defined policies in other agencies serving the counselor's clients that effectively protect the confidentiality of information.

SECTION C: PROFESSIONAL RESPONSIBILITY

C.1. Standards Knowledge

Counselors have a responsibility to read, understand, and follow the Code of Ethics and the Standards of Practice.

C.2. Professional Competence

a. *Boundaries of Competence.* Counselors practice only within the boundaries of their competence, based on their education, training, supervised experience, state and national professional credentials, and appropriate professional experience. Counselors will demonstrate a commitment to gain knowledge, personal awareness, sensitivity, and skills pertinent to working with a diverse client population.

b. *New Specialty Areas of Practice.* Counselors practice in specialty areas new to them only after appropriate education, training, and supervised experience. While developing skills in new specialty areas, counselors take steps to ensure the competence of their work and to protect others from possible harm.

c. *Qualified for Employment.* Counselors accept employment only for positions for which they are qualified by education, training, supervised experience, state and national professional credentials, and appropriate professional experience. Counselors hire for professional counseling positions only individuals who are qualified and competent.

d. *Monitor Effectiveness.* Counselors continually monitor their effectiveness as professionals and take steps to improve when necessary. Counselors in private practice take reasonable steps to seek out peer supervision to evaluate their efficacy as counselors.

e. *Ethical Issues Consultation.* Counselors take reasonable steps to consult with other counselors or related professionals when they have questions regarding their ethical obligations or professional practice. (*See* H.1.)

f. *Continuing Education.* Counselors recognize the need for continuing education to maintain a reasonable level of awareness of current scientific and professional information in their fields of activity. They take steps to maintain competence in the skills they use, are open to new procedures, and keep current with the diverse and/or special populations with whom they work.

g. *Impairment.* Counselors refrain from offering or accepting professional services when their physical, mental, or emotional problems are likely to harm a client or others. They are alert to the signs of impairment, seek assistance for problems, and, if necessary, limit, suspend, or terminate their professional responsibilities. (*See* A.11.c.)

C.3. Advertising and Soliciting Clients

a. *Accurate Advertising.* There are no restrictions on advertising by counselors except those that can be specifically justified to protect the public from deceptive practices. Counselors advertise or represent their services to the public by identifying their credentials in an accurate manner that is not false, misleading, deceptive, or fraudulent. Counselors may only advertise the highest degree earned which is in counseling or a closely related field from a college or university that was accredited when the degree was awarded by one of the regional accrediting bodies recognized by the Council on Postsecondary Accreditation.

b. *Testimonials.* Counselors who use testimonials do not solicit them from clients or other persons who, because of their particular circumstances, may be vulnerable to undue influence.

c. *Statements by Others.* Counselors make reasonable efforts to ensure that statements made by others about them or the profession of counseling are accurate.

d. *Recruiting Through Employment.* Counselors do not use their places of employment or institutional affiliation to recruit or gain clients, supervisees, or consultees for their private practices. (*See* C.5.e.)

e. *Products and Training Advertisements.* Counselors who develop products related to their profession or conduct workshops or training events ensure that the advertisements concerning these products or events are accurate and disclose adequate information for consumers to make informed choices.

f. *Promoting to Those Served.* Counselors do not use counseling, teaching, training, or supervisory relationships to promote their products or training events in a manner that is deceptive or would exert undue influence on individuals who may be vulnerable. Counselors may adopt textbooks they have authored for instruction purposes.

g. *Professional Association Involvement.* Counselors actively participate in local, state, and national associations that foster the development and improvement of counseling.

C.4. Credentials

a. *Credentials Claimed.* Counselors claim or imply only professional credentials possessed and are responsible for correcting any known misrepresentations of their credentials by others. Professional credentials include graduate degrees in counseling or closely related mental health fields, accreditation of graduate programs, national voluntary certifications, government-issued certifications or licenses, ACA professional membership, or any other credential that might indicate to the public specialized knowledge or expertise in counseling.

b. *ACA Professional Membership.* ACA professional members may announce to the public their membership status. Regular members may not announce their ACA membership in a manner that might imply they are credentialed counselors.

c. *Credential Guidelines.* Counselors follow the guidelines for use of credentials that have been established by the entities that issue the credentials.

d. *Misrepresentation of Credentials.* Counselors do not attribute more to their credentials than the credentials represent, and do not imply that other counselors are not qualified because they do not possess certain credentials.

e. *Doctoral Degrees From Other Fields.* Counselors who hold a master's degree in counseling or a closely related mental health field, but hold a doctoral degree from other than counseling or a closely related field, do not use the title "Dr." in their practices and do not announce to the public in relation to their practice or status as a counselor that they hold a doctorate.

C.5. Public Responsibility

a. *Nondiscrimination.* Counselors do not discriminate against clients, students, or supervisees in a manner that has a negative impact based on their age, color, culture, disability, ethnic group, gender, race, religion, sexual orientation, or socioeconomic status, or for any other reason. (*See* A.2.a.)

b. *Sexual Harassment.* Counselors do not engage in sexual harassment. Sexual harassment is defined as sexual solicitation, physical advances, or verbal or nonverbal conduct that is sexual in nature, that occurs in connection with professional activities or roles, and that either (1) is unwelcome, is offensive, or creates a hostile workplace environment, and counselors know or are told this; or (2) is sufficiently severe or intense to be perceived as harassment to a reasonable person in the context. Sexual harassment can consist of a single intense or severe act or multiple persistent or pervasive acts.

c. *Reports to Third Parties.* Counselors are accurate, honest, and unbiased in reporting their professional activities and judgments to appropriate third parties including courts, health insurance companies, those who are the recipients of evaluation reports, and others. (*See* B.1.g.)

d. *Media Presentations.* When counselors provide advice or comment by means of public lectures, demonstrations, radio or television programs, prerecorded tapes, printed articles, mailed material, or other media, they take reasonable precautions to ensure that (1) the statements are based on appropriate professional counseling literature and practice; (2) the statements are otherwise consistent with the Code of Ethics and the Standards of Practice; and (3) the recipients of the information are not encouraged to infer that a professional counseling relationship has been established. (*See* C.6.b.)

e. *Unjustified Gains.* Counselors do not use their professional positions to seek or receive unjustified personal gains, sexual favors, unfair advantage, or unearned goods or services. (*See* C.3.d.)

C.6. Responsibility to Other Professionals

a. *Different Approaches.* Counselors are respectful of approaches to professional counseling that differ from their own. Counselors know and take into account the traditions and practices of other professional groups with which they work.

b. *Personal Public Statements.* When making personal statements in a public context, counselors clarify that they are speaking from their personal perspectives and that they are not speaking on behalf of all counselors or the profession. (See C.5.d.)

c. *Clients Served by Others.* When counselors learn that their clients are in a professional relationship with another mental health professional, they request release from clients to inform the other professionals and strive to establish positive and collaborative professional relationships. (*See* A.4.)

SECTION D: RELATIONSHIPS WITH OTHER PROFESSIONALS

D.1. Relationships with Employers and Employees

a. *Role Definition.* Counselors define and describe for their employers and employees the parameters and levels of their professional roles.

b. *Agreements.* Counselors establish working agreements with supervisors, colleagues, and subordinates regarding counseling or clinical relationships, confidentiality, adherence to professional standards, distinction between public and private material, maintenance and dissemination of recorded information, work load, and accountability. Working agreements in each instance are specified and made known to those concerned.

c. *Negative Conditions.* Counselors alert their employers to conditions that may be potentially disruptive or damaging to the counselor's professional responsibilities or that may limit their effectiveness.

d. *Evaluation.* Counselors submit regularly to professional review and evaluation by their supervisor or the appropriate representative of the employer.

e. *In-Service.* Counselors are responsible for in-service development of self and staff.

f. *Goals.* Counselors inform their staff of goals and programs.

g. *Practices.* Counselors provide personnel and agency practices that respect and enhance the rights and welfare of each employee and recipient of agency services. Counselors strive to maintain the highest levels of professional services.

h. *Personnel Selection and Assignment.* Counselors select competent staff and assign responsibilities compatible with their skills and experiences.

i. *Discrimination.* Counselors, as either employers or employees, do not engage in or condone practices that are inhumane, illegal, or unjustifiable (such as considerations based on age, color, culture, disability, ethnic group, gender, race, religion, sexual orientation, or socioeconomic status) in hiring, promotion, or training. (*See* A.2.a and C.5.b.)

j. *Professional Conduct.* Counselors have a responsibility both to clients and to the agency or institution within which services are performed to maintain high standards of professional conduct.

k. *Exploitative Relationships.* Counselors do not engage in exploitative relationships with individuals over whom they have supervisory, evaluative, or instructional control or authority.

l. *Employer Policies.* The acceptance of employment in an agency or institution implies that counselors are in agreement with its general policies and principles. Counselors strive to reach agreement with employers as to acceptable standards of conduct that allow for changes in institutional policy conducive to the growth and development of clients.

D.2. Consultation (See B.6.)

a. *Consultation as an Option.* Counselors may choose to consult with any other professionally competent persons about their clients. In choosing consultants, counselors avoid placing the consultant in a conflict of interest situation that would preclude the consultant being a proper party to the counselor's efforts to help the client. Should counselors be engaged in a work setting that compromises this consultation standard, they consult with other professionals whenever possible to consider justifiable alternatives.

b. *Consultant Competency.* Counselors are reasonably certain that they have or the organization represented has the necessary competencies and resources for giving the kind of consulting services needed and that appropriate referral resources are available.

c. *Understanding With Clients.* When providing consultation, counselors attempt to develop with their clients a clear understanding of problem definition, goals for change, and predicted consequences of interventions selected.

d. *Consultant Goals.* The consulting relationship is one in which client adaptability and growth toward self-direction are consistently encouraged and cultivated. (*See* A.1.b.)

D.3. Fees for Referral

a. *Accepting Fees from Agency Clients.* Counselors refuse a private fee or other remuneration for rendering services to persons who are entitled to such services through the counselor's employing agency or institution. The policies of a particular agency may make explicit provisions for agency clients to receive counseling services from members of its staff in private practice. In such instances, the clients must be informed of other options open to them should they seek private counseling services. (*See* A.10.a, A.11.b, and C.3.d.)

b. *Referral Fees.* Counselors do not accept a referral fee from other professionals.

D.4. Subcontractor Arrangements

When counselors work as subcontractors for counseling services for a third party, they have a duty to inform clients of the limitations of confidentiality that the organization may place on counselors in providing counseling services to clients. The limits of such confidentiality ordinarily are discussed as part of the intake session. (*See* B.1.e and B.1.f.)

SECTION E: EVALUATION, ASSESSMENT, AND INTERPRETATION

E.1. General

a. *Appraisal Techniques.* The primary purpose of educational and psychological assessment is to provide measures that are objective and interpretable in either comparative or absolute terms. Counselors recognize the need to interpret the statements in this section as applying to the whole range of appraisal techniques, including test and nontest data.

b. *Client Welfare.* Counselors promote the welfare and best interests of the client in the development, publication, and utilization of educational and psychological assessment techniques. They do not misuse assessment results and interpretations and take reasonable steps to prevent others from misusing the information these techniques provide. They respect the client's right to know the results, the interpretations made, and the bases for their conclusions and recommendations.

E.2. Competence to Use and Interpret Tests

a. *Limits of Competence.* Counselors recognize the limits of their competence and perform only those testing and assessment services for which they have been trained. They are familiar with reliability, validity, related standardization, error of measurement, and proper application of any technique utilized. Counselors using computer-based test interpretations are trained in the construct being measured and the specific instrument being used prior to using this type of computer application. Counselors take reasonable measures to ensure the proper use of psychological assessment techniques by persons under their supervision.

b. *Appropriate Use.* Counselors are responsible for the appropriate application, scoring, interpretation, and use of assessment instruments, whether they score and interpret such tests themselves or use computerized or other services.

c. *Decisions Based on Results.* Counselors responsible for decisions involving individuals or policies that are based on assessment results have a thorough understanding of educational and psychological measurement, including validation criteria, test research, and guidelines for test development and use.

d. *Accurate Information.* Counselors provide accurate information and avoid false claims or misconceptions when making statements about assessment instruments or techniques. Special efforts are made to avoid unwarranted connotations of such terms as IQ and grade equivalent scores. (*See* C.5.c.)

E.3. Informed Consent

a. *Explanation to Clients.* Prior to assessment, counselors explain the nature and purposes of assessment and the specific use of results in language the client (or other legally authorized person on behalf of the client) can understand, unless an explicit exception to this right has been agreed upon in advance. Regardless of whether scoring and interpretation are completed by counselors, by assistants, or by computer or other outside services, counselors take reasonable steps to ensure that appropriate explanations are given to the client.

b. *Recipients of Results.* The examinee's welfare, explicit understanding, and prior agreement determine the recipients of test results. Counselors include accurate and appropriate interpretations with any release of individual or group test results. (*See* B.1.a and C.5.c.)

E.4. Release of Information to Competent Professionals

a. *Misuse of Results.* Counselors do not misuse assessment results, including test results, and interpretations, and take reasonable steps to prevent the misuse of such by others. (*See* C.5.c.)

b. *Release of Raw Data.* Counselors ordinarily release data (e.g., protocols, counseling or interview notes, or questionnaires) in which the client is identified only with the consent of the client or the client's legal representative. Such data are usually released only to persons recognized by counselors as competent to interpret the data. (*See* B.1.a.)

E.5. Proper Diagnosis of Mental Disorders

a. *Proper Diagnosis.* Counselors take special care to provide proper diagnosis of mental disorders. Assessment techniques (including personal interview) used to determine client care (e.g., locus of treatment, type of treatment, or recommended follow-up) are carefully selected and appropriately used. (*See* A.3.a and C.5.c.)

b. *Cultural Sensitivity.* Counselors recognize that culture affects the manner in which clients' problems are defined. Clients' socioeconomic and cultural experience is considered when diagnosing mental disorders.

E.6. Test Selection

a. *Appropriateness of Instruments.* Counselors carefully consider the validity, reliability, psychometric limitations, and appropriateness of instruments when selecting tests for use in a given situation or with a particular client.

b. *Culturally Diverse Populations.* Counselors are cautious when selecting tests for culturally diverse populations to avoid inappropriateness of testing that may be outside of socialized behavioral or cognitive patterns.

E.7. Conditions of Test Administration

a. *Administration Conditions.* Counselors administer tests under the same conditions that were established in their standardization. When tests are not administered under standard conditions or when unusual behavior or irregularities occur during the testing session, those conditions are noted in interpretation, and the results may be designated as invalid or of questionable validity.

b. *Computer Administration.* Counselors are responsible for ensuring that administration programs function properly to provide clients with accurate results when a computer or other electronic methods are used for test administration. (*See* A.12.b.)

c. *Unsupervised Test Taking.* Counselors do not permit unsupervised or inadequately supervised use of tests or assessments unless the tests or assessments are designed, intended, and validated for self-administration and/or scoring.

d. *Disclosure of Favorable Conditions.* Prior to test administration, conditions that produce most favorable test results are made known to the examinee.

E.8. Diversity in Testing

Counselors are cautious in using assessment techniques, making evaluations, and interpreting the performance of populations not represented in the norm group on which an instrument was standardized. They recognize the effects of age, color, culture, disability, ethnic group, gender, race, religion, sexual orientation, and socioeconomic status on test administration and interpretation and place test results in proper perspective with other relevant factors. (*See* A.2.a.)

E.9. Test Scoring and Interpretation

a. *Reporting Reservations.* In reporting assessment results, counselors indicate any reservations that exist regarding validity or reliability because of the circumstances of the assessment or the inappropriateness of the norms for the person tested.

b. *Research Instruments.* Counselors exercise caution when interpreting the results of research instruments possessing insufficient technical data to support respondent results. The specific purposes for the use of such instruments are stated explicitly to the examinee.

c. *Testing Services.* Counselors who provide test scoring and test interpretation services to support the assessment process confirm the validity of such interpretations. They accurately describe the purpose, norms, validity, reliability, and applications of the procedures and any special qualifications applicable to their use. The public offering of an automated test interpretations service is considered a professional-to-professional consultation. The formal responsibility of the consultant is to the consultee, but the ultimate and overriding responsibility is to the client.

E.10. Test Security

Counselors maintain the integrity and security of tests and other assessment techniques consistent with legal and contractual obligations. Counselors do not appropriate, reproduce, or modify published tests or parts thereof without acknowledgment and permission from the publisher.

E.11. Obsolete Tests and Outdated Test Results

Counselors do not use data or test results that are obsolete or outdated for the current purpose. Counselors make every effort to prevent the misuse of obsolete measures and test data by others.

E.12. Test Construction

Counselors use established scientific procedures, relevant standards, and current professional knowledge for test design in the development, publication, and utilization of educational and psychological assessment techniques.

SECTION F: *TEACHING, TRAINING, AND SUPERVISION*

F.1. Counselor Educators and Trainers

a. *Educators as Teachers and Practitioners.* Counselors who are responsible for developing, implementing, and supervising educational programs are skilled as teachers and practitioners. They are knowledgeable regarding the ethical, legal, and regulatory aspects of the profession, are skilled in applying that knowledge, and make students and supervisees aware of their responsibilities. Counselors conduct counselor education and training programs in an ethical manner and serve as role models for professional behavior. Counselor educators should make an effort to infuse material related to human diversity into all courses and/or workshops that are designed to promote the development of professional counselors.

b. *Relationship Boundaries With Students and Supervisees.* Counselors clearly define and maintain ethical, professional, and social relationship boundaries with their students and supervisees. They are aware of the differential in power that exists and the student's or supervisee's possible incomprehension of that power differential. Counselors explain to students and supervisees the potential for the relationship to become exploitive.

c. *Sexual Relationships.* Counselors do not engage in sexual relationships with students or supervisees and do not subject them to sexual harassment. (*See* A.6 and C.5.b)

d. *Contributions to Research.* Counselors give credit to students or supervisees for their contributions to research and scholarly projects. Credit is given through coauthorship, acknowledgment, footnote statement, or other appropriate means, in accordance with such contributions. (*See* G.4.b and G.4.c.)

e. *Close Relatives.* Counselors do not accept close relatives as students or supervisees.

f. *Supervision Preparation.* Counselors who offer clinical supervision services are adequately prepared in supervision methods and techniques. Counselors who are doctoral students serving as practicum or internship supervisors to master's level students are adequately prepared and supervised by the training program.

g. *Responsibility for Services to Clients.* Counselors who supervise the counseling services of others take reasonable measures to ensure that counseling services provided to clients are professional.

h. *Endorsement.* Counselors do not endorse students or supervisees for certification, licensure, employment, or completion of an academic or training program if they believe students or supervisees are not qualified for the endorsement. Counselors take reasonable steps to assist students or supervisees who are not qualified for endorsement to become qualified.

F.2. Counselor Education and Training Programs

a. *Orientation.* Prior to admission, counselors orient prospective students to the counselor education or training program's expectations, including but not limited to the following: (1) the type and level of skill acquisition required for successful completion of the training, (2) subject matter to be covered, (3) basis for evaluation, (4) training components that encourage self-growth or self-disclosure as part of the training process, (5) the type of supervision settings and requirements of the sites for required clinical field experiences, (6) student and supervisee evaluation and dismissal policies and procedures, and (7) up-to-date employment prospects for graduates.

b. *Integration of Study and Practice.* Counselors establish counselor education and training programs that integrate academic study and supervised practice.

c. *Evaluation.* Counselors clearly state to students and supervisees, in advance of training, the levels of competency expected, appraisal methods, and timing of evaluations for both didactic and experiential components. Counselors provide students and supervisees with periodic performance appraisal and evaluation feedback throughout the training program.

d. *Teaching Ethics.* Counselors make students and supervisees aware of the ethical responsibilities and standards of the profession and the students' and supervisees' ethical responsibilities to the profession. (*See* C.1 and F.3.e.)

e. *Peer Relationships.* When students or supervisees are assigned to lead counseling groups or provide clinical supervision for their peers, counselors take steps to ensure that students and supervisees placed in these roles do not have personal or adverse relationships with peers and that they understand they have the same ethical obligations as counselor educators, trainers, and supervisors. Counselors make every effort to ensure that the rights of peers are not compromised when students or supervisees are assigned to lead counseling groups or provide clinical supervision.

f. *Varied Theoretical Positions.* Counselors present varied theoretical positions so that students and supervisees may make comparisons and have opportunities to develop their own positions. Counselors provide information concerning the scientific bases of professional practice. (*See* C.6.a.)

g. *Field Placements.* Counselors develop clear policies within their training program regarding field placement and other clinical experiences. Counselors provide clearly stated roles and responsibilities for the student or supervisee, the site supervisor, and the program supervisor. They confirm that site supervisors are qualified to provide supervision and are informed of their professional and ethical responsibilities in this role.

h. *Dual Relationships as Supervisors.* Counselors avoid dual relationships such as performing the role of site supervisor and training program supervisor in the student's or supervisee's training program. Counselors do not accept any form of professional services, fees, commissions, reimbursement, or remuneration from a site for student or supervisee placement.

i. *Diversity in Programs.* Counselors are responsive to their institution's and program's recruitment and retention needs for training program administrators, faculty, and students with diverse backgrounds and special needs. (*See* A.2.a.)

F.3. Students and Supervisees

a. *Limitations.* Counselors, through ongoing evaluation and appraisal, are aware of the academic and personal limitations of students and supervisees that might impede performance. Counselors assist students and supervisees in securing remedial assistance when needed, and dismiss from the training program supervisees who are unable to provide competent service due to academic or personal limitations. Counselors seek professional consultation and document their decision to dismiss or refer students or supervisees for assistance. Counselors ensure that students and supervisees have recourse to address decisions made to require them to seek assistance or to dismiss them.

b. *Self-Growth Experiences.* Counselors use professional judgment when designing training experiences conducted by the counselors themselves that require student and supervisee self-growth or self-disclosure. Safeguards are provided so that students and supervisees are aware of the ramifications their self-disclosure may have on counselors whose primary role as teacher, trainer, or supervisor requires acting on ethical obligations to the profession. Evaluative components of experiential training experiences explicitly delineate predetermined academic standards that are separate and do not depend on the student's level of self-disclosure. (*See* A.6.)

c. *Counseling for Students and Supervisees.* If students or supervisees request counseling, supervisors or counselor educators provide them with acceptable referrals. Supervisors or counselor educators do not serve as counselor to students or supervisees over whom they hold administrative, teaching, or evaluative roles unless this is a brief role associated with a training experience. (*See* A.6.b.)

d. *Clients of Students and Supervisees.* Counselors make every effort to ensure that the clients at field placements are aware of the services rendered and the qualifications of the students and supervisees rendering those services. Clients receive professional disclosure information and are informed of the limits of confidentiality. Client permission is obtained in order for the students and supervisees to use any information concerning the counseling relationship in the training process. (*See* B.1.e.)

e. *Standards for Students and Supervisees.* Students and supervisees preparing to become counselors adhere to the Code of Ethics and the Standards of Practice. Students and supervisees have the same obligations to clients as those required of counselors. (*See* H.1.)

SECTION G: RESEARCH AND PUBLICATION

G.1. Research Responsibilities

a. *Use of Human Subjects.* Counselors plan, design, conduct, and report research in a manner consistent with pertinent ethical principles, federal and state laws, host institutional regulations, and scientific standards governing research with human subjects. Counselors design and conduct research that reflects cultural sensitivity appropriateness.

b. *Deviation From Standard Practices.* Counselors seek consultation and observe stringent safeguards to protect the rights of research participants when a research problem suggests a deviation from standard acceptable practices. (*See* B.6.)

c. *Precautions to Avoid Injury.* Counselors who conduct research with human subjects are responsible for the subjects' welfare throughout the experiment and take reasonable precautions to avoid causing injurious psychological, physical, or social effects to their subjects.

d. *Principal Researcher Responsibility.* The ultimate responsibility for ethical research practice lies with the principal researcher. All others involved in the research activities share ethical obligations and full responsibility for their own actions.

e. *Minimal Interference.* Counselors take reasonable precautions to avoid causing disruptions in subjects' lives due to participation in research.

f. *Diversity.* Counselors are sensitive to diversity and research issues with special populations. They seek consultation when appropriate. (*See* A.2.a and B.6.)

G.2. Informed Consent

a. *Topics Disclosed.* In obtaining informed consent for research, counselors use language that is understandable to research participants and that (1) accurately explains the purpose and procedures to be followed; (2) identifies any procedures that are experimental or relatively untried; (3) describes the attendant discomforts and risks; (4) describes the benefits or changes in individuals or organizations that might be reasonably expected; (5) discloses appropriate alternative procedures that would be advantageous for subjects; (6) offers to answer any inquiries concerning the procedures; (7) describes any limitations on confidentiality; and (8) instructs that subjects are free to withdraw their consent and to discontinue participation in the project at any time. (*See* B.1.f.)

b. *Deception.* Counselors do not conduct research involving deception unless alternative procedures are not feasible and the prospective value of the research justifies the deception. When the methodological requirements of a study necessitate concealment or deception, the investigator is required to explain clearly the reasons for this action as soon as possible.

c. *Voluntary Participation.* Participation in research is typically voluntary and without any penalty for refusal to participate. Involuntary participation is appropriate only when it can be demonstrated that participation will have no harmful effects on subjects and is essential to the investigation.

d. *Confidentiality of Information.* Information obtained about research participants during the course of an investigation is confidential. When the possibility exists that others may obtain access to such information, ethical research practice requires that the possibility, together with the plans for protecting confidentiality, be explained to participants as a part of the procedure for obtaining informed consent. (*See* B.1.e.)

e. *Persons Incapable of Giving Informed Consent.* When a person is incapable of giving informed consent, counselors provide an appropriate explanation, obtain agreement for participation, and obtain appropriate consent from a legally authorized person.

f. *Commitments to Participants.* Counselors take reasonable measures to honor all commitments to research participants.

g. *Explanations after Data Collection.* After data are collected, counselors provide participants with full clarification of the nature of the study to remove any misconceptions. Where scientific or human values justify delaying or withholding information, counselors take reasonable measures to avoid causing harm.

h. *Agreements to Cooperate.* Counselors who agree to cooperate with another individual in research or publication incur an obligation to cooperate as promised in terms of punctuality of performance and with regard to the completeness and accuracy of the information required.

i. *Informed Consent for Sponsors.* In the pursuit of research, counselors give sponsors, institutions, and publication channels the same respect and opportunity for giving informed consent that they accord to individual research participants. Counselors are aware of their obligation to future research workers and ensure that host institutions are given feedback information and proper acknowledgment.

G.3. Reporting Results

a. *Information Affecting Outcome.* When reporting research results, counselors explicitly mention all variables and conditions known to the investigator that may have affected the outcome of a study or the interpretation of data.

b. *Accurate Results.* Counselors plan, conduct, and report research accurately and in a manner that minimizes the possibility that results will be misleading. They provide thorough discussions of the limitations of their data and alternative hypotheses. Counselors do not engage in fraudulent research, distort data, misrepresent data, or deliberately bias their results.

c. *Obligation to Report Unfavorable Results.* Counselors communicate to other counselors the results of any research judged to be of professional value. Results that reflect unfavorably on institutions, programs, services, prevailing opinions, or vested interests are not withheld.

d. *Identity of Subjects.* Counselors who supply data, aid in the research of another person, report research results, or make original data available take due care to disguise the identity of respective subjects in the absence of specific authorization from the subjects to do otherwise. (*See* B.1.g and B.5.a.)

e. *Replication Studies.* Counselors are obligated to make available sufficient original research data to qualified professionals who may wish to replicate the study.

G.4. Publication

a. *Recognition of Others.* When conducting and reporting research, counselors are familiar with and give recognition to previous work on the topic, observe copyright laws, and give full credit to those to whom credit is due. (*See* F.1.d and G.4.c.)

b. *Contributors.* Counselors give credit through joint authorship, acknowledgment, footnote statements, or other appropriate means to those who have contributed significantly to research or concept development in accordance with such contributions. The principal contributor is listed first and minor technical or professional contributions are acknowledged in notes or introductory statements.

c. *Student Research.* For an article that is substantially based on a student's dissertation or thesis, the student is listed as the principal author. (*See* F.1.d and G.4.a.)

d. *Duplicate Submission.* Counselors submit manuscripts for consideration to only one journal at a time. Manuscripts that are published in whole or in substantial part in another journal or published work are not submitted for publication without acknowledgment and permission from the previous publication.

e. *Professional Review.* Counselors who review material submitted for publication, research, or other scholarly purposes respect the confidentiality and proprietary rights of those who submitted it.

SECTION H: RESOLVING ETHICAL ISSUES

H.1. Knowledge of Standards

Counselors are familiar with the Code of Ethics and the Standards of Practice and other applicable ethics codes from other professional organizations of which they are member, or from certification and licensure bodies. Lack of knowledge or misunderstanding of an ethical responsibility is not a defense against a charge of unethical conduct. (*See* F.3.e.)

H.2. Suspected Violations

a. *Ethical Behavior Expected.* Counselors expect professional associates to adhere to the Code of Ethics. When counselors possess reasonable cause that raises doubts as to whether a counselor is acting in an ethical manner, they take appropriate action. (*See* H.2.d and H.2.e.)

b. *Consultation.* When uncertain as to whether a particular situation or course of action may be in violation of the Code of Ethics, counselors consult with other counselors who are knowledgeable about ethics, with colleagues, or with appropriate authorities.

c. *Organization Conflicts.* If the demands of an organization with which counselors are affiliated pose a conflict with the Code of Ethics, counselors specify the nature of such conflicts and express to their supervisors or other responsible officials their commitment to the Code of Ethics. When possible, counselors work toward change within the organization to allow full adherence to the Code of Ethics.

d. *Informal Resolution.* When counselors have reasonable cause to believe that another counselor is violating an ethical standard, they attempt to first resolve the issue informally with the other counselor if feasible, providing that such action does not violate confidentiality rights that may be involved.

e. *Reporting Suspected Violations.* When an informal resolution is not appropriate or feasible, counselors, upon reasonable cause, take action such as reporting the suspected ethical violation to state or national ethics committees, unless this action conflicts with confidentiality rights that cannot be resolved.

f. *Unwarranted Complaints.* Counselors do not initiate, participate in, or encourage the filing of ethics complaints that are unwarranted or intend to harm a counselor rather than to protect clients or the public.

H.3. Cooperation with Ethics Committees

Counselors assist in the process of enforcing the Code of Ethics. Counselors cooperate with investigations, proceedings, and requirements of the ACA Ethics Committee or ethics committees of other duly constituted associations or boards having jurisdiction over those charged with a violation. Counselors are familiar with the ACA Policies and Procedures and use it as a reference in assisting the enforcement of the Code of Ethics.

References

Ackerman, R. J. (1983). *Children of alcoholics: A guidebook for educators, therapists, and parents* (2nd ed.). Holmes Beach, FL: Learning Publications.

Acuff, F. (1993). *How to negotiate anything with anyone anywhere around the world.* New York: American Management Association.

Adler, A. (1958). *What life should mean to you.* New York: Capricorn. (Original work published 1931.)

Administration on Aging. (2001). Fact for features from the Census Bureau. Retrieved November 1, 2001 from <http://www.aoa.dhhs.gov/aoa/STATS/2001pop/factsforfeatures2001.html>.

Ahlburg, D. A., & DeVita, C. J. (1992). New realities of the American family. In *Population Bulletin* (Vol. 47, No. 2). Washington, DC: Population Reference Bureau.

Aldwin, C. M., Spiro, A., III, Levenson, M. R., & Cupertino, A. P. (2001). Longitudinal findings from the Normative Aging Study: III. Personality, individual health trajectories, and mortality. *Psychology and Aging, 16,* 450–465.

Allison, P. D., & Furstenberg, F. F. (1989). How marital dissolution affects children: Variations by age and sex. *Developmental Psychology, 25,* 540–549.

Almqvist, B. (1989). Age and gender differences in children's Christmas requests. *Play and Culture, 2,* 2–19.

Amato, P. R., & Keith, B. (1991). Parental divorce and the well-being of children: A meta-analysis. *Psychological Bulletin, 110,* 26–46.

American Association for Geriatric Psychiatry. (2001). Geriatrics and mental health: The facts. Retrieved November 1, 2001 from <http://www.aagpgpa.org/prof/facts_mh.asp>.

American Association of University Women Educational Foundation. (1993). *Hostile Hallways: The AAUW survey on sexual harassment in America's schools* (pp. 4–25). Washington, DC: Author.

American Counseling Association. (1995). *Code of ethics and standards of practice.* Alexandria, VA: Author.

American Group Psychotherapy Association. (1991). *AGPA guidelines for ethics.* New York: Author.

American Medical Association. (1997). *Guidelines for adolescent preventive services.* Retrieved April 11, 2002 from <http://www.ama-assn.org/ama/upload/mm/39/gapsmono.pdf>.

American Medical Association Council on Scientific Affairs. (1987). Elder abuse and neglect. *Journal of the American Medical Association, 257,* 966–971.

American Psychiatric Association. (1994). *Diagnostic and statistical manual of mental disorders* (4th ed.). Washington, DC: Author.

American Psychiatric Association. (2001). Disease definition, epidemiology, and natural history. Retrieved January 26, 2001 from <http://www.psych.org/clin_res/guide.bk–4.cfm>.

American Psychological Association. (1993). Guidelines for providers of psychological services to ethnic, linguistic and culturally diverse populations. *American Psychologist, 48,* 45–48.

American School Counselor Association. (1988). *Ethical standards for school counselors.* Alexandria, VA: Author.

American School Counselor Association. (1999). Position statement: The professional school counselor and child abuse and neglect prevention. Retrieved November 15, 2001 from <http://www.schoolcounselor.org/content.cfm?L1=1000&L2=8>.

American School Counselor Association. (1999). Position statement: The professional school counselor and peer helping. Retrieved November 15, 2001 from <http://www.schoolcounselor.org/content.cfm?L1=1000&L2=28>.

American School Counselor Association. (2000). Position statement: The professional school counselor and attention deficit/hyperactivity disorder. Retrieved November 15, 2001 from <http://www.schoolcounselor.org/content.cfm?L1=1000&L2=4>.

Atkinson, D., Morten, G., & Sue, D. (1993). *Counseling American minorities: A cross-cultural perspective.* Dubuque, IA: William C. Brown.

Atkinson, R. C., & Shiffren, R. M. (1968). Human memory: A proposed system and its control processes. In K. W. Spence & J. T. Spence (Eds.), *Advances in the psychology of learning and motivation research and theory,* Vol. 2. New York: Academic Press.

Austin, G., & Prendergast, M. (1991). Young children of substance abusers. In *Prevention Research Update,* No. 8. Louisville, KY: Southeast Regional Center for Drug-Free Schools and Communities.

Axline, V. M. (1947a). Nondirective play therapy for poor readers. *Journal of Consulting Psychology, 11,* 61–69.

Axline, V. M. (1947b). *Play therapy.* New York: Ballantine.

Baltes, P., & Goulet, L. (1970). Status and issues of a life-span developmental psychology. In L. Goulet & P. Baltes (Eds.), *Life-span developmental psychology: Research and theory.* New York: Academic Press.

Bank, L., Patterson, G. R., & Reid, J. B. (1987). Delinquency prevention through training parents in family management. *The Behavior Analyst, 10,* 75–82.

Barkley, R. A. (1990). *Attention-deficit hyperactivity disorder: A handbook for diagnosis and treatment.* New York: Guilford.

Barkley, R. A. (1995). *Taking charge of ADHD: The complete, authoritative guide for parents.* New York: Guilford.

Barkley, R. A. (1996). Attention-deficit hyperactivity disorder. In E. J. Mash & R. A. Barkley (Eds.), *Child psychopathology* (pp. 63–112). New York: Guilford.

Barnett, D., Manly, J. T., & Cicchetti, D. (1993). Defining child maltreatment: The interface between policy and research. In D. Cicchetti & S. L. Toth (Eds.), *Child abuse, child development, and social policy* (pp. 7–73). Norwood, NJ: Ablex.

Baruth, L., & Manning, L. (1991). *Multicultural counseling and psychotherapy: A life-span perspective.* New York: Macmillan.

Bates, E., O'Connell, B., & Shore, C. (1987). Language and communication. In J. D. Osofsky (Ed.), *Handbook of infant development.* New York: Wiley.

Bates, J. E., Maslin, C. A., & Frankel, K. A. (1985). Attachment security, mother–child interaction, and temperament as predictors of behavior-problem ratings at age three years. In I. Bretherton & E. Waters (Eds.), *Growing points in attachment theory and research. Monographs of the Society for Research in Child Development, 50* (Serial No. 209), 167–193.

Baumrind, D. (1967). Child care practices anteceding three patterns of preschool behavior. *Genetic Psychology Monographs, 75,* 43–88.

Baumrind, D. (1971). Current patterns of parental authority. *Developmental Psychology Monograph, 4,* 1–103.

Baumrind, D. (1975). Early socialization and adolescent competence. In S. E. Dragastin & G. H. Elder, Jr. (Eds.), *Adolescence in the life cycle: Psychological change and social context.* New York: Wiley.

Baumrind, D. (1980). New directions in socialization research. *American Psychologist, 35,* 639–652.

Baumrind, D. (1989). Rearing competent children. In W. Damon (Ed.), *Child development today and tomorrow.* San Francisco: Jossey-Bass.

Baumrind, D. (1991). The influence of parenting style on adolescent competence and substance use. *Journal of Early Adolescence, 11,* 56–95.

Beck, A. T. (1967). *Depression: Clinical, experimental, and theoretical aspects.* New York: Harper & Row. (Republished as *Depression: Causes and treatment.* Philadelphia: University of Pennsylvania Press, 1972.)

Beck, J. (1995). *Cognitive therapy: Basics and beyond.* New York: Guilford.

Bee, H. (1992). *The developing child* (6th ed). New York: HarperCollins.

Behancourt H., & Lopez, S. (1993). The study of culture, ethnicity and race in American psychology. *American Psychologist, 48,* 45–48.

Belsky, J., & Kelly, J. (1994). *The transition to parenthood: How a first child changes a marriage. Why some couples grow closer and others apart.* New York: Dell.

Bem, S. L. (1984). Androgyny and gender schema theory: A conceptual and empirical integration. In R. A. Dienstbier & T. B. Sondregger (Eds.), *Nebraska symposium on motivation* (Vol. 34, pp. 179–226). Lincoln: University of Nebraska Press.

Bem, S. L. (1985). Androgyny and gender schema theory. In T. B. Sondregger (Ed.), *Nebraska symposium on motivation: Psychology and gender* (Vol. 32). Lincoln: University of Nebraska Press.

Bem, S. L. (1989). Genital knowledge and gender constancy in preschool children. *Child Development, 60,* 649–662.

Berenbaum, S. A., & Hines, M. (1992). Early androgens are related to childhood sex-typed toy preferences. *Psychological Science, 3,* 203–206.

Berk, L. E. (1993). *Infants, children, and adolescents.* Boston: Allyn & Bacon.

Berk, L. E. (1994). *Child development* (3rd. ed.). Boston: Allyn & Bacon.

Best, C. T., McRoberts, G. W., & Sithole, N. M. (1988). Examination of perceptual reorganization for nonnative speech contrasts: Zulu click discrimination by English-speaking adults and infants. *Journal of Experimental Psychology: Human Perception and Performance, 14*, 345–360.

Birmaher, B., Ryan, N. D., & Williamson, D. E. (1996). Childhood and adolescent depression: A review of the past 10 years. Part 1. *Journal of the American Academy of Child and Adolescent Psychiatry, 35*(11), 1427–1439.

Bjorklund, D. F., & Arce, S. (1987, April). Acquiring a mneumonic: Age and category knowledge effects. Paper presented at the biennial meetings of the Society for Research in Child Development, Baltimore.

Bjorklund, D. F., & Muir, J. E. (1988). Remembering on their own: Children's development of free recall memory. In R. Vasta (Ed.), *Annals of child development* (Vol. 5, pp. 79–124). Greenwich, CT: JAI Press.

Bodrova, D., & Leong, E. (1996). *Tools of the mind: The Vygotskian approach to early childhood education.* Englewood Cliffs, NJ: Merrill.

Bowlby, J. (1979). *The making and breaking of affectional bonds.* London: Tavistock.

Bowlby, J. (1988). *A secure base.* New York: Basic Books.

Brand, E., Clingempeel, W. G., & Bowen-Woodward, K. (1988). Family relationships and children's psychosocial adjustment in stepmother and stepfather families. In E. M. Hetherington & J. D. Arasteh (Eds.), *Impact of divorce, single-parenting, and stepparenting on children* (pp. 299–324). Hillsdale, NJ: Erlbaum.

Brandenburg, J. (1997). *Confronting sexual harassment: What schools and colleges can do.* New York: Teachers College Press.

Bray, J. H. (1988). Children's development in early remarriage. In E. M. Hetherington & J. D. Arasteh (Eds.), *Impact of divorce, single-parenting, and stepparenting on children* (pp. 279–288). Hillsdale, NJ: Erlbaum.

Bray, J. H., & Berger, S. H. (1993). Developmental issues in stepfamilies research project: Family relationships and parent–child interactions. *Journal of Family Psychology, 7*, 1–17.

Brehm, S. S. (1981). Oppositional behavior in children: A reactance theory approach. In S. S. Brehm, S. M. Kassin, & F. X. Gibbons (Eds.), *Developmental social psychology: Theory and research* (pp. 96–121). New York: Oxford University Press.

Brenner, A. (1984). *Helping children cope with stress.* Lexington, MA: Lexington Books.

Brim, O., & Ryff, C. (1980). On the properties of life events. In P. Baltes & O. J. Brim (Eds.), *Life-span development and behavior* (Vol. 3). New York: Academic Press.

Brody, G. H., & Schaffer, D. R. (1982). Contributions of parents and peers to children's moral socialization. *Developmental Review, 2*, 31–75.

Browers, M., & Wiggum, C. (1993). Bulimia and perfectionism: Developing the courage to be imperfect. *Journal of Mental Health Counseling, 15*, 141–149.

Brown, K., Covell, K., & Abramovitch, R. (1991). Time course and control of emotion: Age differences in understanding and recognition. *Merrill-Palmer Quarterly, 37*, 273–287.

Brown, M. B. (2000). Diagnosis and treatment of children and adolescents with attention-deficit/hyperactivity disorder. *Journal of Counseling and Development, 78*, 195–203.

Brown, N. (1996). *Expressive processes in group counseling.* Westport, CT: Praeger.

Brown, N. (1998). *The destructive narcissistic pattern.* Westport, CT: Praeger.

Brown, N. (2001). *Children of the self-absorbed*. Oakland, CA: New Harbinger.

Bryant, B., & Crockenburg, S. (1980). Correlates and discussion of prosocial behavior: A study of female siblings with their mothers. *Child Development, 51,* 529–544.

Buchanan, C. M., Maccoby, E. E., & Dornbusch, S. M. (1991). Caught between parents: Adolescents' experience in divorced homes. *Child Development, 62,* 1008–1029.

Buchanan, C. M., Maccoby, E. E., & Dornbusch, S. M. (1992). Adolescents and their families after divorce: Three residential arrangements compared. *Journal of Research on Adolescence, 2,* 261–291.

Burleson, B. R., & Fennelly, D. A. (1981). The effects of persuasive appeal form and cognitive complexity on children's sharing behavior. *Child Study Journal, 11,* 75–90.

Burns, A. (1992). Mother-headed families: An international perspective and the case of Australia. *Social Policy Report, 6,* 8–17.

Butler, R. N. (1963). The life review: An interpretation of reminiscence in the aged. *Psychiatry, 26,* 65–76.

Butler, R. N. (1975). *Why survive? Being old in America*. New York: Harper & Row.

Cairns, R. B., Cairns, B. D., Neckerman, H., Fergusen, L. L., & Gariepy, J. L. (1989). Growth and aggression: Childhood to early adolescence. *Developmental Psychology, 25,* 320–330.

Caldera, Y. M., Huston, A. C., & O'Brien, M. (1989). Social interactions and play patterns of parents and toddlers with feminine, masculine, and neutral toys. *Child Development, 60,* 70–76.

Camara, K. A., & Resnick, G. (1988). Interparental conflict and cooperation: Factors moderating children's post-divorce adjustment. In E. M. Hetherington & J. D. Arasteh (Eds.), *Impact of divorce, single-parenting, and stepparenting on children* (pp. 169–195). Hillsdale, NJ: Erlbaum.

Cantrell, R. G. (1986). Adjustment to divorce: Three components to assist children. *Elementary School Guidance & Counseling, 20,* 163–173.

Capuzzi, D., & Gross, D. (1995). *Counseling & psychotherapy*. Englewood Cliffs, NJ: Merrill.

Carkhuff, R., & Berenson, B. (1967). *Beyond counseling and psychotherapy*. New York: Holt, Rinehart & Winston.

Carnegie Council on Adolescent Development. (1995). *Great transitions: Preparing adolescents for a new century*. Retrieved January 20, 2001 from <http://www.carnegie.org/sub/pubs/reports/great_transitions>.

Carr, M., & Schneider, W. (1991). Long-term maintenance of organizational strategies in kindergarten children. *Contemporary Educational Psychology, 16,* 61–75.

Carrell, S. (1993). *Group exercises for adolescents*. Newbury Park, CA: Sage.

Carvalho, A. M. A., Smith, P. K., Hunter, T., & Costabile, A. (1990). Playground activities for boys and girls: Developmental and cultural trends in children's perceptions of gender differences. *Play and Culture, 3,* 343–347.

Cashden, S. (1988). *Object relations therapy*. New York: W.W. Norton.

Cass, V. (1979). Homosexual identity formation: A theoretical model. *Journal of Homosexuality, 4,* 219–235.

Castro-Martin, T., & Bumpass, L. (1989). Recent trends and differentials in marital disruption. *Demography, 26,* 37–51.

Center for Epidemiologic Studies Depression Scale (CES–D). (1977). Developed by NIMH. (Available from NIMH, 6001 Executive Boulevard, Room 8184, MSC 9663 Bethesda, MD 20892–9663.)

Centers for Disease Control and Prevention. (2000). CDC Growth Charts: United States. Retrieved November 6, 2001 from <http://www.cdc.gov/growth charts>.

Chambers, J. H., & Ascione, F. R. (1987). The effects of prosocial and aggressive videogames on children's donating and helping. *Journal of Genetic Psychology, 148*, 499–505.

Children's Defense Fund. (2001). *The state of America's children yearbook 2001*. Retrieved November 5, 2001 from <http://www.childrensdefense.org/key-facts.htm>.

Cicchetti, D., & Aber, J. L. (1986). Early precursors to later depression: An organizational perspective. In L. Lipsett & C. Rovee-Collier (Eds.), *Advances in infancy* (Vol. 4, pp. 81–137). Norwood, NJ: Ablex.

Cicchetti, D., & Howes, P. W. (1991). Developmental psychopathology in the context of the family: Illustrations from the study of child maltreatment. *Canadian Journal of Behavioural Sciences, 23*, 257–281.

Cicchetti, D., & Manly, J. T. (1990). A personal perspective on conducting research with maltreating families: Problems and solutions. In E. Brody & I. Sigel (Eds.), *Family research journeys: Vol. 2. Families at risk* (pp. 87–133). Hillsdale, NJ: Erlbaum.

Cicchetti, D., & Olsen, K. (1990). The developmental psychopathology of child maltreatment. In M. Lewis & S. Miller (Eds.), *Handbook of developmental psychopathology* (pp. 261–279). New York: Plenum.

Cicchetti, D., & Rizley, R. (1981). Developmental perspectives on the etiology, intergenerational transmission, and sequelae of child maltreatment. *New Directions for Child Development, 11*, 31–55.

Clark, E. V. (1983). Meanings and concepts. In J. H. Flavell & E. M. Markman (Eds.), *Handbook of child psychology: Vol. 3. Cognitive development* (4th ed., pp. 787–840). New York: Wiley.

Clark, R., Anderson, N., Clark, V., & Williams, D. (1999). Racism as a stressor for African Americans. *American Psychologist, 54*, 805–816.

Coie, J., Miller-Johnson, S., Terry, R., Maumary-Gremaud, A., & Lochman, J. (1996, November). The influence of deviant peers on types of adolescent delinquency. Symposium conducted at the meeting of the American Society of Criminology. Chicago.

Collins, W. A., Sobol, S. K., & Westby, S. (1981). Effects of adult commentary on children's comprehension and inferences about a televised aggressive portrayal. *Child Development, 52*, 158–163.

Coopersmith, S. (1967). *The antecedents of self-esteem*. San Francisco: Freeman.

Corbett, K., Gentry, C., & Pearson, W. (1993). Sexual harassment in high school. *Youth and Society, 25*(1), 93–103.

Corey, G. (2001). *Theory and practice of counseling and psychotherapy* (6th ed.). Belmont, CA: Wadsworth.

Cotton, C. R., & Range, L. M. (1996). Suicidality, hopelessness, and attitudes toward life and death in clinical and nonclinical adolescents. *Death Studies, 20*, 601–610.

Cowan, C. P., & Cowan, P. A. (1992). *When partners become parents*. New York: Basic Books.

Cowan, C. P., Cowan, P. A., Heming, G., Garrett, E., Coysh, W. S., Curtis-Bole, H., & Boles, A. J., III. (1985). Transition to parenthood: His, hers, and theirs. *Journal of Family Issues, 6*, 451–481.

Crockenberg, S. B. (1986). Are temperamental differences in babies associated with predictable differences in care-giving? *New Directions for Child Development, 31*, 53–74.

Crockenberg, S. B., & Acredolo, C. (1983). Infant temperament ratings: A function of infants, or mothers, or both? *Infant Behavior and Development, 6*, 61–72.

Crose, R. (1990). Reviewing the past in the here and now: Using gestalt therapy techniques with life review. *Journal of Mental Health Counseling, 12*, 279–287.

Cross, W. (1991). *Shades of Black*. Philadelphia: Temple University Press.

Darville, D., & Cheyne, J. A. (1981). Sequential analysis of response to aggression: Age and sex effects. Paper presented at the biennial meeting of the Society for Research in Child Development, Boston.

Davis, N. (1999). Resilience. Working paper for Substance Abuse and Mental Health Administration Center for Mental Health Services Division of Program Development, Special Populations and Projects Special Development Branch.

Dean, A., Malik, M., & Richards, W. (1986). Effects of parental maltreatment on children's conceptions of interpersonal relationships. *Developmental Psychology, 22*, 617–626.

Dekovic, M., & Janssens, J. M. A. M. (1992). Parents' child-rearing style and child's sociometric status. *Developmental Psychology, 28*(5), 925–932.

DeLoache, J. S. (1987). Rapid change in the symbolic functioning of young children. *Science, 238*, 1556–1557.

DeLoache, J. S. (1989). The development of representation in young children. In H. W. Reese (Ed.), *Advances in child development and behavior* (Vol. 22, pp. 1–39). New York: Academic Press.

DeLoache, J. S., Kolstad, V., & Anderson, K. N. (1991). Physical similarity and young children's understanding of scale models. *Child Development, 62*, 111–126.

Dempster, F. N. (1981). Memory span: Sources of individual and developmental differences. *Psychological Bulletin, 89*, 63–100.

Denham, S., & Grout, L. (1992). Mothers' emotional expressiveness and coping: Relations with preschoolers' social–emotional competence. *Genetic, Social, and General Psychology Monographs, 118*, 73–101.

DiLalla, L. F., Mitchell, C. M., Arthur, M. W., & Pagliocca, P. M. (1988). Aggression and delinquency: Family and environmental factors. *Journal of Youth and Adolescence, 17*, 233–246.

Dishon, T., McCord, J., & Paulin, F. (1999). When interventions harm. *American Psychologist, 54*(9), 755–764.

Dishon, T. J., Patterson, G. R., Stoolmiller, M., & Skinner, M. L. (1991). Family, school, and behavioral antecedents to early adolescent involvement with anti-social peers. *Developmental Psychology, 27*, 172–180.

Dodge, K. A. (1986). Social information-processing variables in the development of aggression and altruism in children. In C. Zahn-Waxler, E. M. Cummings, & R. Iannotti (Eds.), *Altruism and aggression: Biological and social origins*. New York: Cambridge University Press.

Dodge, K. A., Bates, J. E., & Pettit, G. D. (1990). Mechanisms in the cycle of violence. *Science, 250,* 1678–1683.

Donaldson, M. (1978). *Children's minds.* London: Fontana/Croom Helm.

Donaldson-Pressman, S., & Pressman, R. (1994). *The narcissistic family.* San Francisco: Jossey-Bass.

Donnelly, B. W., & Voydanoff, P. (1991). Factors associated with releasing for adoption among adolescent mothers. *Family Relations, 40,* 404–410.

Dornbusch, S. M., Carlsmith, J. M., Bushwall, S. J., Ritter, P. L., Leiderman, H., Hastdorf, A. H., & Goss, R. T. (1985). Single parents, extended households, and the control of adolescents. *Child Development, 56,* 326–341.

Dryfoos, J. (1990). *Adolescents at risk: Prevalence and prevention.* New York: Oxford University Press.

Dunham, P., & Dunham, F. (1992). Lexical development during middle infancy: A mutually driven infant–caregiver process. *Developmental Psychology, 28,* 414–420.

Dunn, J., Bretherton, I., & Munn, P. (1987). Conversations about feeling states between mothers and their young children. *Developmental Psychology, 23,* 132–139.

Eaton, W. O., & Enns, L. R. (1986). Sex differences in human motor activity level. *Psychological Bulletin, 100,* 19–28.

Eckerman, C. O., & Stein, M. R. (1990). How imitation begets imitation and toddlers' generation of games. *Developmental Psychology, 26,* 370–378.

Egan, G. (1990). *The skilled helper: A systematic approach to effective helping.* Pacific Grove, CA: Brooks/Cole.

Egeland, B., Jacobvitz, D., & Sroufe, L. A. (1988). Breaking the cycle of abuse. *Child Development, 59,* 1080–1088.

Eisenberg, N. (1988). The development of prosocial and aggressive behavior. In M. E. Lamb & M. H. Bornstein (Eds.), *Developmental psychology: An advanced textbook* (pp. 461–495). Hillsdale, NJ: Erlbaum.

Eisenberg, N. (1992). *The caring child.* Cambridge, MA: Harvard University Press.

Eisenberg, N., Cialdini, R. B., McCreath, H., & Shell, R. (1987). Consistancy-based compliance: When and why do children become vulnerable? *Journal of Personality and Social Psychology, 52,* 1174–1181.

Eisenberg, N., & Murphy, B. (1995). Parenting and children's moral development. In M. H. Bornstein (Ed.), *Handbook of parenting: Vol. 4. Applied and practical parenting* (pp. 227–257). Hillsdale, NJ: Erlbaum.

Eisenberg, N., Murray, E., & Hite, T. (1982). Children's reasoning regarding sex-typed toy choices. *Child Development, 49,* 500–504.

Eisenberg, N., & Mussen, P. (1989). *The roots of prosocial behavior in children.* Cambridge: Cambridge University Press.

Eisenberg, N., Shell, R., Pasternack, J., Lennon, R., Belber, R., & Mathy, R. M. (1987). Prosocial development in middle childhood: A longitudinal study. *Developmental Psychology, 23,* 712–718.

Eisenberg, N., & Strayer, J. (1987). Critical issues in the study of empathy. In N. Eisenberg & J. Strayer (Eds.), *Empathy and its development* (pp. 3–13). Cambridge: Cambridge University Press.

Eisenberg, N., Tryon, K., & Cameron, E. (1984). The relation of preschoolers' peer interaction to their sex-typed toy choices. *Child Development, 55,* 1044–1050.

Eisenberg, N., Wolchik, S. A., Hernandez, R., & Pasternak, J. F. (1985). Parental socialization of young children's play. *Child Development, 56,* 1506–1513.

Eisenberg-Berg, N., & Geisheker, E. (1979). Content of preachings and power of the model/preacher: The effect on children's generosity. *Developmental Psychology, 15,* 168–175.

Eitel, S. (1996). *Examining outcomes of sexual harassment in high school and college students.* Unpublished doctoral dissertation (UMI No. 9627313), University of Rochester.

Elkind, D. (1967). Egocentrism in adolescence. *Child Development, 38,* 1025–1034.

Elkind, D. (1991). Development in early childhood. *Elementary School Guidance & Counseling, 26,* 12–21.

Erikson, E. H. (1963). *Childhood and society* (2nd ed.). New York: Norton.

Erikson, E. H. (1968). *Identity, youth, and crisis.* New York: Norton.

Erikson, E. H. (1977). *Toys and reasons.* New York: Norton.

Eron, L. D. (1982). Parent–child interaction, television violence and aggression in children. *American Psychologist, 37,* 197–211.

Eron, L. D. (1987). The development of aggressive behavior from the perspective of a developing behaviorism. *American Psychologist, 42,* 435–442.

Fagot, B. I., & Hagan, R. I. (1991). Observations of parent reactions to sex-stereotyped behaviors: Age and sex effects. *Child Development, 62,* 617–628.

Fagot, B. I., & Leinbach, M. D. (1989). The young child's gender schema: Environmental input, internal organization. *Child Development, 60,* 663–672.

Fairbairn, W. (1954). *An object relations theory of the personality.* New York: Basic Books.

Fantuzzo, J. W., DePaola, L. M., Lambert, L., Martino, T., Anderson, G., & Sutton, S. (1991). Effects of interparental violence on the psychological adjustment and competencies of young children. *Journal of Consulting and Clinical Psychology, 59,* 258–265.

Farrington, D. P. (1991). Childhood aggression and adult violence: Early precursors and later-life outcomes. In D. J. Pepler & K. H. Rubin (Eds.), *The development and treatment of childhood aggression* (pp. 5–29). Hillsdale, NJ: Erlbaum.

Feeley, N., & Gottlieb, L. (1988–1989). Parents' coping and communication following their infant's death. *Omega, 19,* 51–58.

Fein, G. (1987). Affective themes in the pretense of master players. Paper presented at the biennial meeting of the Society for Research in Child Development.

Fein, G., Johnson, D., Kosson, N., Stork, L., & Wasserman, L. (1985). Sex stereotypes and preferences in the toy choices of 20-month-old boys and girls. *Developmental Psychology, 11,* 527–528.

Field, D. (1987). A review of preschool conservation training: An analysis of analyses. *Developmental Review, 7,* 210–251.

Field, T. (1994). Psychologically depressed parents. In M. H. Bornstein (Ed.), *Handbook of parenting: Vol. 4. Applied and practical parenting* (pp. 85–99). Hillsdale, NJ: Erlbaum.

Folkman, S., Chesney, M., McKusick, L., Ironson, G., Johnson, D., & Coates, T. (1991). Translating coping theory into an intervention. In J. Eckenrode (Ed.), *The social context of coping* (pp. 239–260). New York: Plenum.

Fowler, J. W. (1981). *Stages of faith.* San Francisco: Harper & Row.

Frankel, V. (1963). *Man's search for meaning.* New York: Simon & Schuster.

Freud, A. (1946). *The psychoanalytic treatment of children.* London: Imago.

Freud, A. (1965). *The psycho-analytical treatment of children.* New York: International Universities Press.

Freud, S. (1900). *The interpretation of dreams. Standard Edition* 4: 150–151. London: Hogarth Press.

Freud, S. (1905). *On psychotherapy. Standard Edition* 7: 257–268. London: Hogarth Press.

Freud, S. (1914). *On narcissism. Standard Edition* 14: 69–102. London: Hogarth Press.

Freud, S. (1949). *An outline of psycho-analysis.* (James Strachey, Trans.). New York: Norton. (Originally published 1940.)

Freud, S. (1953). The relation of the poet to daydreaming. In *Collected papers.* London: Hogarth Press.

Friedrich, L. K., & Stein, A. H. (1992). Prosocial television and young children: The effects of verbal labeling and role playing on learning and behavior. *Child Development, 46,* 27–36.

Fromm-Reichmann, F. (1950). *Principles of intensive psychotherapy.* Chicago: University of Chicago Press.

Fukuyama, M. (1990). Taking a universal approach to multicultural counseling. *Counselor Education and Supervision, 30,* 6–17.

Furstenberg, F. F. (1988). Child care after divorce and remarriage. In E. M. Hetherington & J. D. Arasteh (Eds.), *Impact of divorce, single-parenting, and stepparenting on children* (pp. 245–261). Hillsdale, NJ: Erlbaum.

Furth, H. G., & Kane, S. R. (1992). Children constructing society: A new perspective on children at play. In H. McGurk (Ed.), *Childhood social development: Contemporary perspectives* (pp. 149–174). Hillsdale, NJ: Erlbaum.

Garfinkel, I., & McLanahan, S. S. (1986). *Single mothers and their children: New American dilemma.* Washington, DC: The Urban Institute Press.

Garmenzy, N. (1981). Children under stress: Perspectives on anecdotes and correlates of vulnerability and resistance to psychopathology. In A. I. Rahin, A. M. Barclay, & R. A. Zuker (Eds.), *Further explorations in personality* (pp. 196–270). New York: Wiley.

Garmenzy, N., & Rutter, M. (Eds.). (1983). *Stress, coping, and development in children.* New York: McGraw-Hill.

Garvey, C. (1990). *Play.* Cambridge, MA: Harvard University Press.

Garvey, C. (1991). *Play* (2nd ed.). Cambridge, MA: Harvard University Press.

Gazda, G. (1989). *Group counseling.* Boston: Allyn & Bacon.

Gelman, R. (1969). Conservation acquisition: A problem of learning to attend to relevant attributes. *Journal of Experimental Child Psychology, 7,* 167–187.

Gelman, R. (1972). The nature and development of early number concepts. In H. W. Reese & L. P. Lipsitt (Eds.), *Advances in child development and behavior.* New York: Academic Press.

Gelman R., & Baillargeon, R. (1983). A review of some Piagetian concepts. In J. H. Flavell & E. M. Markman (Eds.), *Handbook of child psychology: Vol. 3. Cognitive development* (4th ed., pp. 167–230). New York: Wiley.

Gerbner, G., Gross, L., Signorelli, N., & Morgan, M. (1986). Television's mean world: Violence. Profile No. 14–15. Philadelphia: Annenberg School of Communications, University of Pennsylvania.

Gibson, R. C. (1995). Promoting successful and productive aging in minority populations. In L. A. Bond, S. J. Cutler, & A. Grams (Eds.), *Promoting successful and productive aging* (pp. 279–288). Thousand Oaks, CA: Sage.

Gilligan, C. (1977). *In a different voice: Women's conceptions of self and morality.* Cambridge, MA: Harvard University Press.

Gilligan, C. (1982). *In a different voice: Psychological theory and women's development.* Cambridge, MA: Harvard University Press.

Gladding, S. (1997). *Group work* (3rd ed.). Upper Saddle River, NJ: Merrill.

Gloger-Tippler, G. (1983). A process model of the pregnancy course. *Human Development, 26,* 134–148.

Golan, N. (1981). *Passing through transitions: A guide for practitioners.* New York: Free Press.

Goldman, R. K., & King, M. J. (1985). Counseling children of divorce. *School Psychology Review, 14,* 280–290.

Goldstein, J. (Ed.). (1994). *Toys, play, and child development.* Cambridge: Cambridge University Press.

Gottschalk, L. (1988). Narcissism: Its normal evolution and development and the treatment of its disorders. *American Journal of Psychotherapy, 42*(1), 4–27.

Gould, R. (1978). *Transformations: Growth and change in adult life.* New York: Simon & Schuster.

Greif, G. L. (1985). *Single fathers.* Lexington, MA: Heath.

Gringlas, M., & Weinraub, M. (1995). The more things change: Single parenting revisited. *Journal of Family Issues, 16,* 29–52.

Gross, J., & McCaul, M. E. (1991). A comparison of drug use and adjustment in urban adolescent children of substance abusers. *The International Journal of the Addictions, 25,* 495–511.

Grusec, J. E., Saas-Kortsaak, P., & Simutis, Z. M. (1978). The role of example and moral exhortation in the training of altruism. *Child Development, 49,* 920–923.

Hafen, B., Karren, K., Frandsen, K., & Smith, L. (1996). *Mind/body health.* Boston: Allyn & Bacon.

Haight, W. L., & Miller, P. J. (1993). *Pretending at home.* Albany: State University of New York Press.

Halford, G. S. (1990). *Children's understanding: The development of mental models.* Hillsdale, NJ: Erlbaum.

Hanna, F., Hanna, C., & Keys, S. (1999). Fifty strategies for counseling defiant, aggressive adolescents: Reaching, accepting, and relating. *Journal of Counseling and Development, 77,* 395–404.

Hartmann, H. (1964). *Essays on ego psychology.* New York: International Universities Press.

Hartup, W. (1996). The company they keep: Friendships and their developmental significance. *Child Development, 67,* 1–3.

Haskett, M. E., & Kistner, J. A. (1991). Social interactions and peer perceptions of young physically abused children. *Child Development, 62,* 979–990.

Havighurst, R. J. (1961). Successful aging. *The Gerontologist, 1,* 8–13.

Havighurst, R. J. (1972). *Developmental tasks and education.* New York: McKay.

Hawkins, J., Catalano, R., & Miller, J. (1992). Risk and protective factors for alcohol and other drug problems in adolescence and early adulthood: Implications for substance abuse prevention. *Psychological Bulletin, 112,* 64–105.

Hay, D. F., & Murray, P. (1982). Giving and requesting: Social facilitation of infants' offers to adults. *Infant Behavior and Development, 5,* 301–310.

Hays, P. (1995). Multicultural applications of cognitive-behavior therapy. *Professional Psychology: Research and Practice, 26,* 309–315.

Hays, P. (1996). Addressing the complexities of culture and gender in counseling. *Journal of Counseling & Development, 74,* 332–337.

Hazan, C., & Shaver, P. (1987). Romantic love conceptualized as an attachment process. *Journal of Personality and Social Psychology, 52,* 511–524.

Helms, J. (Ed.). (1990). *Black and white racial identity.* New York: Greenwood Press.

Hersch, P. (1999). *A tribe apart.* New York: Ballantine.

Hetherington, E. M. (1988). Parents, children, and siblings six years after divorce. In R. Hinde & J. Stevenson-Hinde (Eds.), *Relationships within families* (pp. 311–331). Cambridge: Cambridge University Press.

Hetherington, E. M. (1989). Coping with family transitions: Winners, losers, and survivors. *Child Development, 60,* 1–14.

Hetherington, E. M. (1991). Families, lies, and videotapes. *Journal of Research on Adolescence, 1,* 323–348.

Hetherington, E. M. (1993). An overview of the Virginia longitudinal study of divorce and remarriage with a focus on early adolescence. *Journal of Family Psychology, 7,* 39–56.

Hetherington, E. M., & Clingempeel, W. G. (1992). Coping with marital transitions: A family systems perspective. *Monographs of the Society for Research in Child Development, 57* (2–3, Serial No. 227).

Hetherington, E. M., Law, T. C., & O'Conner, T. G. (1992). Divorce: Challenges, changes, and new chances. In F. Walsh (Ed.), *Normal family processes* (2nd ed., pp. 208–234). New York: Guilford.

Hetherington, E. M., & Parke, R. D. (1993). *Child psychology: A contemporary viewpoint* (3rd ed.). New York: McGraw-Hill.

Hetherington, E. M., & Stanley-Hagan, M. M. (1995). Parenting in divorced and remarried families. In M. H. Bornstein (Ed.), *Handbook of parenting* (Vol. 3, pp. 233–254). Hillsdale, NJ: Erlbaum.

Hetherington, E. M., Stanley-Hagan, M. M., & Anderson, E. R. (1989). Marital transitions: A child's perspective. Social issue: Children and their development: Knowledge base, research agenda, and social policy application. *American Psychologist, 44,* 303–312.

Hobbs, F., & Lippman, L. (1990). Children's well-being: An international comparison. International Population Reports Series (Series P95, No. 80). Washington, DC: U.S. Government Printing Office.

Hoffman, M. L. (1982). Development of prosocial motivation: Empathy and guilt. In N. Eisenberg (Ed.), *The development of prosocial behavior* (pp. 281–313). New York: Academic Press.

Hoffman, M. L. (1987). The contribution of empathy to justice and moral judgment. In N. Eisenberg & J. Strayer (Eds.), *Empathy and its development* (pp. 47–80). Cambridge: Cambridge University Press.

Hoffman, M. L. (1988). Moral development. In M. H. Bornstein & M. E. Lamb (Eds.), *Developmental psychology: An advanced textbook* (2nd ed., pp. 497–548). Hillsdale, NJ: Erlbaum.

Hoffman, M. L. (1991). Developmental counseling for prekindergarten children: A preventive approach. *Elementary School Guidance & Counseling, 26,* 56–65.

Hohenshil, T. H., & Hohenshil, S. B. (1989). Preschool counseling. *Journal of Counseling and Development, 67,* 430–431.

Holden, G. W., & Ritchie, K. L. (1991). Linking extreme marital discord, child rearing, and child behavior problems: Evidence from battered women. *Child Development, 62,* 311–327.

Holmes, T. H., & Rahe, R. H. (1967). The social readjustment rating scale. *Journal of Psychosomatic Research, 11,* 213–218.

HON. (2001). *Health on the Net: Mother and child glossary.* Retrieved October 19, 2001 from <http://www.hon.ch/Dossier/MotherChild>.

Hosie, T. W., & Erk, R. R. (1993, January). ACA reading program: Attention deficit disorder. *American Counseling Association Guidepost, 35,* 15–18.

Howes, C., Phillips, D. A., & Whitebook, M. (1992). Thresholds of quality: Implications for the social development of children in center-based child care. *Child Development, 63,* 449–460.

Howes, P. W., & Cicchetti, D. (1993). A family/relational perspective on maltreating families: Parallel processes across systems and social policy implications. In D. Cicchetti & S. L. Toth (Eds.), *Child abuse, child development, and social policy* (pp. 249–299). Norwood, NJ: Ablex.

Huesmann, L. R., Eron, L. D., Lefkowitz, M. M., & Walder, L. O. (1984). The stability of aggression over time and generations. *Developmental Psychology, 20,* 1120–1134.

Huesmann, L. R., Guerra, N. G., Zelli, A., & Miller, L. (1992). Differing normative beliefs about aggression for boys and girls. In K. Bjorkquist & P. Niemele (Eds.), *Of mice and women: Aspects of female aggression.* Orlando, FL: Academic.

Hug-Helmuth, H. (1921). On the technique of child analysis. *International Journal of Psychoanalysis, 2,* 287.

Huston, A. C. (1983). Sex-typing: In E. M. Hetheringon (Ed.), *Handbook of child psychology: Socialization, personality, and social development* (Vol. 4, pp. 387–463). New York: Wiley.

Huston, A. C., & Alvarez, M. M. (1990). The socialization context of gender role development in early adolescence. In R. Montemayor, G. R. Adams, & T. P. Gullotta (Eds.), *From childhood to adolescence: A transitional period?* (pp. 156–181). Newbury Park, CA: Sage.

Huston, A. C., Donnerstein, E., Fairchild, H., Feshbach, N. D., Katz, P. A., Murray, J. P., Rubinstein, E. A., Wilcox, B. L., & Zuckerman, D. (1992). *Big world, small screen: The role of television in American society.* Lincoln: University of Nebraska Press.

Huston, A. C., McLoyd, V. C., & Coll, C. (Eds.). (1994). Children and poverty (special issue). *Child Development, 65*(2).

Inhelder, B., & Piaget, J. (1958). *The growth of logical thinking from childhood to adolescence.* New York: Basic Books.

Ivey, A., Ivey, M., & Simek-Morgan, L. (1997). *Counseling and psychotherapy: A multicultural perspective* (4th ed.). Boston: Allyn & Bacon.

Ivey, A., Pedersen, P., & Ivey, M. (2001). *Intentional group counseling.* Belmont, CA: Wadsworth/Thompson Learning.

Izard, C. E. (1977). *Human emotion.* New York: Plenum.

Janssens, J. M. A. M., & Gerris, J. R. M. (1992). Child rearing, empathy, and prosocial development. In J. M. A. M. Janssens & J. R. M. Gerris (Eds.), *Child rearing: Influence on prosocial and moral development* (pp. 57–75). Amsterdam: Swets & Zeitlinger.

Jones, F. R., Morgan, R. F., & Tonelson, S. W. (1992). *The psychology of human development* (3rd ed.). Dubuque, IA: Kendall/Hunt.

Kalter, N. (1990). *Growing up with divorce*. New York: The Free Press.

Karylowski, J. (1982). Doing good to feel good versus doing good to make others feel good: Some child-rearing antecedents. *School Psychology International, 3*, 149–156.

Katz, P. (1990). The first few minutes: The engagement of the difficult adolescent. In S. Feinstein (Ed.), *Adolescent psychiatry*. Chicago: University of Chicago Press.

Kaufman, J., & Zigler, E. (1989). The intergenerational transmission of child abuse. In D. Cicchetti & V. Carlson (Eds.), *Child maltreatment: Theory and research on the causes and consequences of child abuse and neglect* (pp. 129–150). New York: Cambridge University Press.

Kernberg, O. (1975/1995). *Borderline conditions and pathological narcissism*. Northvale, NJ: Jason Aronson.

Kissman, K., & Allen, J. A. (1993). *Single-parent families*. Newbury Park, CA: Sage.

Klaus, M., & Kennell, J. (1982). *Parent–infant bonding*. St. Louis: C. V. Mosby.

Klein, M. (1955). The psychoanalytic play technique. *American Journal of Orthopsychiatry, 25*, 223–237.

Klein, M. (1975). *Envy and gratitude and other works: 1946–1963*. New York: Dell.

Knight, S. (1994). Elementary-age children of substance abusers: Issues associated with identification and labeling. *Elementary School Guidance & Counseling, 28*, 274–284.

Kohlberg, L. (1966). A cognitive-developmental analysis of children's sex-role concepts and attitudes. In E. E. Maccoby (Ed.), *The development of sex differences*. Stanford, CA: Stanford University Press.

Kohlberg, L. (1967). Moral and religious education and the public schools: A developmental view. In T. R. Sizer (Ed.), *The role of religion in public education*. Boston: Houghton-Mifflin.

Kohlberg, L. (1969). *Stages in the development of moral thought*. New York: Holt, Rinehart & Winston.

Kohlberg, L., & Wasserman, E. R. (1980). The cognitive developmental approach and the practicing counselor: An opportunity for counselors to rethink their roles. *The Personnel and Guidance Journal, 58*(9), 602–605.

Kohut, H. (1971). *The analysis of the self*. New York: International Universities Press.

Kohut, H. (1977). *The restoration of the self*. New York: International Universities Press.

Kohut, H. (1984). *How does analysis cure?* Chicago: University of Chicago Press.

Kohut, H., & Wolf, E. (1978). The disorders of the self and their treatment: An outline. *International Journal of Psychoanalysis, 59*, 413–425.

Kovacs, M. (1992). Children's Depression Inventory (CDI). (Available from Multi-Health Systems [MHS, Inc.], 65 Overlea Blvd., Suite 10, Toronto, Ontario M4H1P1, Canada.)

Krebs, D., & Sturrup, B. (1982). Role-taking ability and altruistic behavior in elementary school children. *Journal of Moral Education, 11*, 94–100.

Kuziel-Perri, P., & Snarey, J. (1991). Adolescent repeat pregnancies: An evaluation study of a comprehensive service program for pregnant and parenting black adolescents. *Family Relations, 40*, 381–385.

Lamborn, S. D., Mounts, N. S., Steinberg, L., & Dornbusch, S. M. (1991). Patterns of competence and adjustment among adolescents from authoritative, authoritarian, indulgent, and neglectful families. *Child Development, 62*, 1049–1065.

Landreth, G. (1991). *Play therapy: The art of the relationship*. Muncie, IN: Accelerated Development.

Lange, G., & Pierce, S. H. (1992). Memory-strategy learning and maintenance in preschool children. *Developmental Psychology, 28*, 453–462.

Lee, R. (1988). The reverse self-object experience. *American Journal of Psychotherapy, 42*(1), 416–424.

Lee, V. E., Burkham, D. T., Zimiles, H., & Ladewski, X. (1994). Family structure and its effect on behavioral and emotional problems in young adolescents. *Journal of Research on Adolescence, 4*, 405–437.

Lee, V. E., Chroninger, R., Linn, E., & Chen, X. (1996). The culture of sexual harassment in secondary schools. *American Educational Research Journal, 33*(2), 283–417.

LeFrancois, G. (1993). *The lifespan* (4th ed.). Belmont, CA: Wadsworth.

Lempers, J. D., Clark-Lempers, D., & Simons, R. (1989). Economic hardship, parenting, and distress in adolescence. *Child Development, 60*, 25–39.

Lempers, J. D., Flavell, E. R., & Flavell, J. H. (1978). The development in very young children of tacit knowledge concerning visual perception. *Genetic Psychology Monographs, 95*, 3–53.

Levinson, D., Darrow, C., & Klien, E. (1978). *The seasons of a man's life*. New York: Knopf.

Levy-Shiff, R. (1999). Fathers' cognitive appraisals, coping strategies, and support resources as correlates of adjustment to parenthood. *Journal of Family Psychology, 13*, 554–567.

Liebert, R. M., & Sprafkin, J. (1988). *The early window: Effects of television on children and youth* (3rd ed.). New York: Pergamon.

Lipsey, M. (1992). Juvenile delinquency treatment: A meta-analytic inquiry into the variability of effects. In T. D. Cook, H. Cooper, D. S. Corday, H. Hartman, L. V. Hedger, R. J. Light, T. A. Louis, & F. Musteller (Eds.), *Meta-analysis for explanation: A casebook* (pp. 83–125). New York: Russel Sage.

Loevinger, J. (1976). *Ego development*. San Francisco: Jossey-Bass.

LoGerfo, M. (1980). Three ways of reminiscence in theory and practice. *International Journal of Aging and Human Development, 12*, 39–48.

Long, N., Forehand, R., Fauber, R., & Brody, G. (1987). Self-perceived and independently observed competence of young adolescents as a function of marital conflict and recent divorce. *Journal of Abnormal Child Psychology, 15*, 15–27.

Lowenthal, M., Chiriboga, D., & Thurnber, M. (1975). *Four stages of life*. San Francisco: Jossey-Bass.

Lytton, H., & Romney, D. M. (1991). Parents' differential socialization of boys and girls: A meta-analysis. *Psychological Bulletin, 109*, 267–296.

Maccoby, E. E. (1984). Socialization and developmental change. *Child Development, 55*, 317–328.

Maccoby, E. E. (1988). Gender as a social category. *Developmental Psychology, 24*, 755–765.

Maccoby, E. E. (1990). Gender and relationships: A developmental account. *American Psychologist, 45*, 513–520.

Maccoby, E. E., Buchanan, C. M., Mnookin, R. H., & Dornbusch, S. M. (1993). Postdivorce roles of mothers and fathers in the lives of their children. *Journal of Family Psychology, 7*, 1–15.

Maccoby, E. E., & Jacklin, C. N. (1980). Sex differences in aggression: A rejoinder and reprise. *Child Development, 51*, 964–980.

Maccoby, E. E., & Martin, J. A. (1983). Socialization in the context of the family: Parent–child interaction. In P. H. Mussen (Series Ed.) & E. M. Hetherington (Vol. Ed.), *Handbook of child psychology: Vol. 4. Socialization, personality, and social development* (4th ed., pp. 1–101). New York: Wiley.

Maccoby, E. E., & Mnookin, R. H. (1992). *Dividing the child: Social and legal dilemmas of custody.* Cambridge, MA: Harvard University Press.

MacLean, P. D. (1985). Brain evolution relating to family, play, and the separation call. *Archives of General Psychology, 42,* 405–417.

MacLennan, B., & Dies, K. (1992). *Group counseling and psychotherapy with adolescents* (2nd ed.). New York: Columbia University Press.

Madsen, M. C. (1967). Cooperative and competitive motivation of children in three Mexican sub-cultures. *Psychological Reports, 20,* 1307–1320.

Madsen, M. C., & Lancy, D. F. (1981). Cooperative and competitive behavior: Experiments related to ethnic identity and urbanization in Papua New Guinea. *Journal of Cross-Cultural Psychology, 12,* 389–409.

Madsen, M. C., & Shapiro, A. (1970). Cooperative and competitive behavior of urban Afro-American, Anglo-American, Mexican-American, and Mexican village children. *Developmental Psychology, 3,* 16–20.

Mahler, M. (1968). *On human symbiosis and the vicissitudes of individuation.* New York: International Universities Press.

Mahler, M., Pine, M., & Bergman, A. (1975). *The psychological birth of the human infant.* New York: Basic Books.

Malekoff, A. (1997). *Group work with adolescents.* New York: Guilford.

Martin, C. L., & Halverson, C. F., Jr. (1981). A schematic processing model of sex-typing and stereotyping in children. *Child Development, 52,* 1119–1134.

Martin, C. L., & Halverson, C. F., Jr. (1983). The effects of sex-typing schemas on young children's memory. *Child Development, 54,* 563–574.

Martin, C. L., & Halverson, C. F., Jr. (1987). The role of cognition in sex-role acquisition. In D. B. Carter (Ed.), *Current conceptions of sex roles and sex typing: Theory and research* (pp. 123–137). New York: Praeger.

Martin, C. L., Wood, C. H., & Little, J. K. (1990). The development of gender stereotype components. *Child Development, 61,* 1891–1904.

Martin, D., & Martin, M. (1992). *Stepfamilies in therapy: Understanding systems, assessment, and intervention.* San Francisco: Jossey-Bass.

Masterson, J. (1993). *The emerging self.* New York: Brunner/Mazel.

McBurnett, K., Lahey, B. B., & Pfiffner, L. J. (1993). Diagnosis of attention-deficit disorders in *DSM-IV*: Scientific basis and implications for education. *Exceptional Children, 60,* 108–117.

McCollum v. CBS. (1988). 202 Cal. App. 3d 989, 997, 249 Cal. Rptr. 187, 191. Retrieved January 27, 2001 from <http://www.mtsu.edu/~lburriss/block>.

McCord, J. (1978). A thirty-year follow-up of treatment effects. *American Psychologist, 33,* 284–289.

McCord, J. (1981). A consideration of some effects of a counseling program. In S. E. Martin, B. Sechrest, & R. Redner (Eds.), *New directions in the rehabilitation of criminal offenders* (pp. 394–405). Washington, DC: The National Academy of Sciences.

McCord, J. (1986). Instigation and insulation: How families affect antisocial aggression. In D. Olweus, J. Block, & M. Radke-Yarrow (Eds.), *Development of antisocial and prosocial behavior: Research, theories, and issues* (pp. 343–384). Orlando, FL: Academic Press.

McCord, J., & Tremblay, R. E. (1992). *Preventing antisocial behavior: Interventions from birth through adolescence.* New York: Guilford.

McGlauflin, H. (1998). Helping children grieve at school. *Professional School Counseling, 1,* 46–49.

McGrath, M. P., & Power, T. G. (1990). The effects of reasoning and choice on children's prosocial behavior. *International Journal of Behavioural Development, 13,* 345–353.

McGurk, H. (1992). *Childhood social development: Contemporary perspectives.* Hillsdale, NJ: Erlbaum.

McLanahan, S., & Booth, K. (1989). Mother-only families: Problems, prospects, and politics. *Journal of Marriage and the Family, 51,* 557–580.

McLaughlin, J., Miller, P., & Warwick, H. (1996). Deliberate self-harm in adolescents: Hopelessness, depression, problems, and problem solving. *Journal of Adolescence, 19,* 523–532.

McLoyd, V. C., & Wilson, L. (1991). The strain of living poor: Parenting, social support, and child mental health. In A. C. Huston (Ed.), *Children in poverty: Child development and public policy* (pp. 105–135). Cambridge: Cambridge University Press.

Meadows, S. (1993). *The child as thinker: The development and acquisition of cognition in childhood.* New York: Routledge.

Menke, J., & McClead, R. (1990). Perinatal grief and mourning. *Advances in Pediatrics, 37,* 261–283.

Meyer-Bahlburg, H. F. L., Feldman, J. F., Cohen, P., & Ehrhardt, A. A. (1988). Perinatal factors in the development of gender-related play behavior: Sex hormones versus pregnancy complications. *Psychiatry, 51,* 260–271.

Middleton, J., & Quirk, T. (1990). Grief and loss. In K. Buckley & N. Kulb (Eds.), *High-risk maternity nursing manual* (pp. 20–22). Baltimore: Williams & Wilkins.

Miller, J. B. (1976). *Toward a new psychology of women.* Boston: Beacon Press.

Miller, K., Zylstra, R., & Standridge, J. (2000). The geriatric patient: A systematic approach to maintaining health. *American Family Physician, 61,* 1089–1104.

Moller, L. C., Hymel, S., & Rubin, K. H. (1992). Sex typing in play and popularity in middle childhood. *Sex Roles, 26,* 331–353.

Moore, B., & Eisenberg, N. (1984). The development of altruism. In G. Whitehurst (Ed.), *Annuals in child development* (Vol. 1, pp. 107–174). New York: JSI Press.

Morgan, J. (1994). Beareavement in older adults. *Journal of Mental Health Counseling, 16,* 318–326.

Morganett, R. S. (1994). *Skills for living: Group counseling activities for elementary students.* Champaign, IL: Research Press.

Muro, J. J., & Dinkmeyer, D. C. (1977). *Counseling in the elementary and middle schools.* Dubuque, IA: W. C. Brown.

Murray, F. B. (1981). The new conservation paradigm. In I. Siegel, D. Brodzinsky, & R. Golinkoff (Eds.), *New directions in Piagetian research and theory.* Hillsdale, NJ: Erlbaum.

Myers, J. E. (1989). *Adult children and their aging parents.* Alexandria, VA: American Counseling Association.

Myers, J. E., & Schwiebert, V. L. (1996). *Competencies for gerontological counseling.* Alexandria, VA: American Counseling Association.

Myrick, R. D. (1993). *Developmental guidance and counseling: A practical approach* (2nd ed.). Minneapolis: Educational Media Corporation.

Nakamichi, M. (1989). Sex differences in social development during the first four years in a free-ranging group of Japanese monkeys, Macaca fuscata. *Animal Behaviour, 38,* 737–748.

National Center for Health Statistics. (1991). Advance report of final marriage statistics: 1988. In *Monthly vital statistics report, 39* (12, Suppl. 2, pp. 1–20). Hyattsville, MD: Public Health Service.

National Institute on Aging. (2001). *Age Page: Health information.* Retrieved November 1, 2001 from <http://www.nia.nih.gov/health/agepages.htm>.

Nelson, J., Lott, L., & Glenn, H. S. (1993). *Positive discipline A–Z: 1001 solutions to everyday parenting problems.* Rocklin, CA: Prima Publishing.

Nettlebeck, T., & Vita, P. (1992). Inspection time in two childhood age cohorts: A constraint or a developmental function? *British Journal of Developmental Psychology, 10,* 180–197.

Neugarten, B. (1979). Time, age and the life cycle. *American Journal of Psychiatry, 139,* 887–895.

Neukrug, E. (1999). *The world of the counselor.* Pacific Grove, CA: Brooks/Cole.

Newman, B. M., & Newman, P. R. (1995). *Development through life: A psychosocial approach* (6th ed.). Pacific Grove, CA: Brooks/Cole.

O'Brien, M., & Huston, A. C. (1985). Development of sex-typed play behavior in toddlers. *Developmental Psychology, 21,* 866–871.

Oliver, R., & Fallat, M. (1995). Traumatic childhood death: How well do parents cope? *The Journal of Trauma, 39,* 303–308.

Olweus, D. (1979). Stability of aggressive reaction patterns in males: A review. *Psychological Bulletin, 86,* 852–875.

Olweus, D. (1980). Familial and tempermental determinants of aggressive behavior in adolescent boys: A causal analysis. *Developmental Psychology, 16,* 644–660.

Olweus, D. (1982). Development of stable aggressive reaction patterns in males. In R. Blanchard & C. Blanchard (Eds.), *Advances in the study of aggression* (Vol. 1). New York: Academic Press.

Orestein, P. (1978). Introduction: The evolution of Heinz Kohut's psychoanalytic psychology of the self. In *The search for the self* (Vol. 1, pp. 1–106). New York: International Universities Press.

Orestein, P., & Kay, J. (1990). Development of psychoanalytic self-psychology: A historical-conceptual overview. In A. Tasman, S. M. Goldfinger, & C. A. Kaufmann (Eds.), *Annual Review of Psychiatry 1990* (Vol. 9). Washington, DC: American Psychiatric Press.

Osman, A., Downs, W. R., Kopper, B. A., Barrios, G. X., Baker, M. T., Osman, J. R., Besett, T., & Linehan, M. M. (1998). The reasons for living inventory for adolescents (RFL-A): Development and psychometric properties. *Journal of Clinical Psychology, 54,* 1063–1078.

Paisley, P. O., & Hubbard, G. T. (1994). *Developmental school counseling programs: From theory to practice.* Alexandria, VA: American Counseling Association.

Palmore, E. B. (1995). Successful aging. In G. L. Maddox (Ed.), *Encyclopedia of aging: A comprehensive resource in gerontology and geriatrics* (2nd ed., pp. 914–915). New York: Springer.

Parke, R. D., & Slaby, R. G. (1983). The development of aggression. In P. H. Mussen (Series Ed.) & E. M. Hetherington (Vol. Ed.), *Handbook of child psychology: Vol. 4. Socialization, personality, and social development* (pp. 547–641). New York: Wiley.

Parker, R. J. (1994). Helping children cope with divorce: A workshop for parents. *Elementary School Guidance & Counseling, 29,* 137–148.

Parsons, J. E. (1982). Biology, experience, and sex-dimorphic behaviors. In W. R. Gove & G. R. Carpenter (Eds.), *The fundamental connection between nature and nurture* (pp. 137–170). Lexington, MA: Lexington Books.

Parten, M. B. (1932). Social participation among preschool children. *Journal of Abnormal and Social Psychology, 27,* 243–269.

Patterson, G. R. (1982). *Corrective family process.* Eugene, OR: Castalia.

Patterson, G. R., DeBaryshe, B. D., & Ramsey, E. (1989). A developmental perspective on antisocial behavior. *American Psychologist, 44,* 329–335.

Patterson, G. R., Dishon, T., & Yoerger, K. (1999). Adolescent growth in new forms of problem behavior: Macro- and micro-peer dynamics. Manuscript submitted for publication.

Payne, F. (1980). Children's prosocial conduct in structured situations and as viewed by others. *Child Development, 51,* 1252–1259.

Pearl, R. (1985). Children's understanding of others' need for help: Effects of problem explicitness and type. *Child Development, 56,* 735–745.

Pederson, P. (1991). Multiculturalism as a generic approach to counseling. *Journal of Counseling and Development, 70,* 6–12

Peppers, L., & Knapp, R. (1980). *Motherhood and mourning a perinatal death.* New York: Praeger.

Perls, F. (1969). *Gestalt therapy verbatim.* Moah, UT: Real People Press.

Perry, D. G., Bussey, K., & Freiberg, K. (1981). Impact of adults' appeals for sharing on the development of altruistic dispositions in children. *Journal of Experimental Child Psychology, 32,* 127–138.

Perry, D. G., Perry, L. C., & Boldizar, J. P. (1990). Learning of aggression. In M. Lewis & S. M. Miller (Eds.), *Handbook of developmental psychopathology* (pp. 135–146). New York: Plenum.

Perry, D. G., Perry, L. C., & Weiss, R. J. (1989). Sex differences in the consequences that children anticipate for aggression. *Developmental Psychology, 25,* 312–319.

Perry, W. (1970). *Forms of intellectual and ethical development in the college years: A scheme.* New York: Holt, Rinehart & Winston.

Peterson, J. L., & Zill, N. (1986). Marital disruption, parent–child relationships, and behavior problems in children. *Marriage and the Family, 48,* 295–307.

Piaget, J. (1929). *The child's conception of physical causality.* New York: Harcourt, Brace, & World. (Original work published 1926.)

Piaget, J. (1952a). *The child's conception of number.* London: Humanities Press.

Piaget, J. (1952b). *The origins of intelligence in children.* New York: International Universities Press.

Piaget, J. (1954). *The construction of reality in the child.* New York: Basic Books.

Piaget, J. (1962). *Play, dreams and imitation in childhood* (C. Gattegno & F. M. Hodgson, Trans.). New York: Norton. (Original work published 1945.)

Piaget, J. (1963). *The origins of intelligence in children.* New York: Norton.

Piaget, J. (1967). *Six psychological studies.* New York: Vintage Books.

Piaget, J., & Inhelder, B. (1969). *The psychology of the child* (H. Weaver, Trans.). New York: Basic Books.

Pianta, R., Egeland, B., & Erickson, M. F. (1989). The antecedents of child maltreatment. In D. Cicchetti & V. Carlson (Eds.), *Child maltreatment: Theory and research on the causes and consequences of child abuse and neglect* (pp. 203–253). New York: Cambridge University Press.

Picariello, M. L., Greenberg, D. N., & Pillemer, D. B. (1990). Children's sex-related stereotyping of colors. *Child Development, 61,* 1453–1460.

Pill, C. J. (1990). Stepfamilies: Redefining the family. *Family Relations, 39,* 186–193.

Power, T. J., & DuPaul, G. J. (1996). Attention-deficit hyperactivity disorder: The reemergence of subtypes. *School Psychology Review, 25,* 284–296.

Pratt, C., & Bryant, P. E. (1990). Young children understand that looking leads to knowing (so long as they are looking into a single barrel). *Child Development, 61,* 973–982.

Progress Report on Alzheimer's Disease. (2000). Retrieved November 1, 2001 from <http://www.alzheimers.org/pubs/prog00.htm>.

Pulkkinen, L. (1982). Self-control and continuity in childhood delayed adolescence. In P. Baltes & O. Brim (Eds.), *Lifespan development and behavior* (Vol. 4, pp. 64–107). New York: Academic Press.

Purcell, P., & Stewart, L. (1990). Dick and Jane in 1989. *Sex Roles, 22,* 177–185.

Radke-Yarrow, M., & Zahn-Waxler, C. (1983). Roots, motives, and patterns in children's prosocial behavior. In J. Reykowski, J. Karylowski, D. Bar-Tal, & E. Staub (Eds.), *Origins and maintenance of prosocial behaviors.* New York: Plenum.

Radke-Yarrow, M., & Zahn-Waxler, C. (1984). Roots, motives, and patterns in children's prosocial behavior. In J. Reykowski, J. Karylowski, D. Bar-Tal, & E. Staub (Eds.), *The development and maintenance of prosocial behaviors: International perspectives on positive morality* (pp. 81–99). New York: Plenum.

Radke-Yarrow, M., Zahn-Waxler, C., & Chapman, M. (1983). Prosocial dispositions and behavior. In P. H. Mussen (Series Ed.) & E. M. Hetherington (Vol. Ed.), *Handbook of child psychology: Vol. 4. Socialization, personality, and social development* (pp. 469–545). New York: Wiley.

Ramirez, M., III. (1991). *Psychotherapy and counseling with minorities.* New York: Pergamon.

Renaud, J., Axelson, D., & Birmaher, B. (1999). A risk–benefit assessment of pharmacotherapies for clinical depression in children and adolescents. *Drug Safety, 20*(1), 59–75.

Rice, M. E., & Grusec, J. E. (1975). Saying and doing: Effects on observer performance. *Journal of Personality and Social Psychology, 32,* 584–593.

Riegel, K. (1975). Adult life crises: A dialectic interpretation of development. In N. Datan & L. Ginsberg (Eds.), *Life-span developmental psychology: Normative life crises.* New York: Academic Press.

Robinson, B., & Bradley, L. J. (1998). Adaptation to transition: Implications for working with cult members. *Journal of Humanistic Education and Development, 36,* 212–221.

Rogers, C. (1951). *Client-centered therapy.* Boston: Houghton-Mifflin.

Rogers, C. (1986). Client-centered therapy. In I. Kertash & A. Wolf (Eds.), *Psychotherapist's casebook theory and techniques in practice of modern therapies* (pp. 197–208). San Francisco: Jossey-Bass.

Rogosch, F. A., Cicchetti, D., Shields, A., & Toth, S. L. (1995). Parenting dysfunction in child maltreatment. In M. H. Bornstein (Ed.), *Handbook of parenting* (Vol. 4, pp. 127–159). Hillsdale, NJ: Erlbaum.

Ruble, D. N. (1987). The acquisition of self-knowledge: A self-socialization perspective. In N. Eisenberg (Ed.), *Contemporary topics in developmental psychology* (pp. 243–270). New York: Wiley-Interscience.

Ruble, D. N., Balaban, T., & Cooper, J. (1981). Gender constancy and the effects of sex-typed televised toy commercials. *Child Development, 52,* 667–673.

Rushton, J. P. (1980). *Altruism, socialization, and society.* Englewood Cliffs, NJ: Prentice-Hall.

Rutan, S. (1993). Psychoanalytic group psychotherapy. In H. I. Kaplan & B. J. Saddock (Eds.), *Comprehensive group psychotherapy* (4th ed.). Baltimore: Williams & Wilkins.

Salmela-Aro, K., Nurmi, J., Saisto, T., & Halmesmaki, E. (2000). Women's and men's personal goals during the transition to parenthood. *Journal of Family Psychology, 14,* 171–186.

Santrock, J. W., & Siterle, K. A. (1987). Parent–child relationships in stepmother families. In K. Posley & M. Ihinger-Tallman (Eds.), *Remarriage and step-parenting: Current research and theory* (pp. 135–154). New York: Guilford.

Scheidlinger, S. (1985). Group treatment of adolescents: An overview. *American Journal of Orthopsychiatry, 55,* 102–111.

Schimpf, M., & Domino, S. (2001). Implications of the Human Genome Project for obstetrics and gynecology. *Obstetrical and Gynecological Survey, 56,* 437–443.

Schlossberg, N. (1984). *Counseling adults in transition.* New York: Springer.

Schlossman, S., & Cairns, R. B. (1993). Problem girls: Observations on past and present. In G. Elder, Jr., J. Modell, & R. D. Parke (Eds.), *Children in time and place.* New York: Cambridge University Press.

Schneider, W., & Pressley, M. (1989). Memory development between two and twenty. New York: Springer-Verlag.

Seeman, T. E. (2000). *Successful aging: Fact or fiction?* Retrieved November 2, 2001 from <http://www.aging.ucla.edu/fallcmeeting2000.html>.

Seeman, T. E., Lusignolo, T., Albert, M., & Berkman, L. (2001). Social relationships, social support, and patterns of cognitive aging in healthy, high-functioning older adults: MacArthur studies of successful aging. *Health Psychology, 20,* 243–255.

Seifert, K. L., & Hoffnung, R. J. (1987). *Child and adolescent development.* Boston: Houghton-Mifflin.

Shaffer, D., & Craft, L. (1999). Methods of adolescent suicide prevention. *Journal of Clinical Psychiatry, 60*(Suppl. 2), 70–74.

Shaffer, D., Fisher, P., & Dulkan, M. K. (1996). The NIMH Diagnostic Interview Schedule for Children version 2.3 (DISC-2.3): Description, acceptability, prevalence rates and performance in the MECA study. *Journal of the American Academy of Child and Adolescent Psychiatry, 35*(7), 865–877.

Shaffer, D., Gould, M. S., Fisher, P., Trautment, P., Moreau, D., Kleinman, M., & Florey, M. (1996). Psychiatric diagnosis in child and adolescent suicide. *Archives of General Psychiatry, 53,* 339–348.

Shantz, C. U. (1987). Conflicts between children. *Child Development, 58,* 283–305.

Shantz, C. U., & Hartup, W. W. (1992). Conflict and development: An introduction. In *Conflict in child and adolescent development.* Cambridge: Cambridge University Press.

Shapiro, A., Gottman, J., & Carrere, S. (2000). The baby and the marriage: Identifying factors that buffer against decline in marital satisfaction after the first baby arrives. *Journal of Family Psychology, 14,* 59–70.

Sheikh, J. I., & Yesavage, J. A. (1986). Geriatric depression scale (GDS): Recent evidence and development of a shorter version. *Clinical Gerontology, 5,* 165–172.

Shell, R., & Eisenberg, N. (1990). The role of peers' gender in children's naturally occurring interest in toys. *International Journal of Behavioral Development, 13,* 373–388.

Siegal, M. (1991). *Knowing children: Experiments in conversation and cognition*. Hillsdale, NJ: Erlbaum.

Siegler, R. S. (1991). *Children's thinking* (2nd ed.). Englewood Cliffs, NJ: Prentice-Hall.

Sigelman, C. (1999). *Life-span development* (3rd ed.). Pacific Grove, CA: Brooks/Cole.

Singer, D. G., & Singer, J. L. (1990). *The house of make-believe: Children's play and developing imagination*. Cambridge, MA: Harvard University Press.

Singer, M. (1978). Therapy with ex-cult members. *Journal of the National Association of Private Psychiatric Hospitals, 9*, 14–19.

Smith, H. (2001). *Why religion matters*. San Francisco: HarperCollins.

Springer, C., & Wallerstein, J. S. (1983). Young adolescents' responses to their parents' divorces. In L. A. Kurdek (Ed.), *Children and divorce: New directions for child development* (pp. 15–28). San Francisco: Jossey-Bass.

St. Clair, M. (1989). *Object relations and self-psychology*. Monterey, CA: Brooks/Cole.

Stanard, R. P. (2000). Assessment and treatment of adolescent depression and suicidality. *Journal of Mental Health Counseling, 22*, 204–217.

Stein, N. (1995). Sexual harassment in school: The public performance of gendered violence. *Harvard Educational Review, 65*(2), 145–162.

Steinberg, L. D. (1990). Interdependence in the family: Autonomy, conflict, and harmony in the parent–adolescent relationship. In S. S. Feldman & G. R. Elliott (Eds.), *At the threshold: The developing adolescent* (pp. 255–276). Cambridge, MA: Harvard University Press.

Stepfamily Association of America. (1989). *Stepfamilies stepping ahead: An eight-step program for successful family living*. Lincoln, NE: Stepfamilies Press.

Stern, D. (1985). *The interpersonal world of the infant*. New York: Basic Books.

Stierman, E. (1987). Emotional aspects of perinatal death. *Clinical Obstetrics and Gynecology, 30*, 352–361.

Stoelb, M., and Chiriboga, J. (1998). A process model for assessing adolescent risk for suicide. *Journal of Adolescence, 21*, 359–370.

Stone, W. (1992). The place of self-psychology in group psychotherapy: A status report. *International Journal of Group Psychotherapy, 42*, 350–353.

Strayer, F. F., Wareing, S., & Rushton, J. P. (1979). Social constraints on naturally occurring preschool altruism. *Ethology and Sociobiology, 1*, 3–11.

Sue, D., & Sue, D. (1990). *Counseling the culturally different: Theory and practice*. New York: Wiley.

Sugarman, S. (1987). *Piaget's construction of the child's reality*. Cambridge: Cambridge University Press.

Suito, N., & Reifel, S. (1992, May). Gender differences in Japanese and American sociodramatic play. Paper presented to the International Council for Child's Play, Paris.

Sullivan, H. (1953). *The interpersonal theory of psychiatry*. New York: Norton.

Tangney, J. P. (1991). Moral affect: The good, the bad, and the ugly. *Journal of Personality and Social Psychology, 61*, 598–607.

Tannenbaum, L., Neighbors, B., & Forehand, R. (1992). The unique contribution of four maternal stressors to adolescent functioning. *Journal of Early Adolescence, 12*, 314–325.

Teti, D. M., & Ablard, K. A. (1989). Security of attachment and infant–sibling relationships: A laboratory study. *Child Development, 60*, 1519–1528.

Thompson, C., & Rudolph, L. (1983). *Counseling children*. Monterey CA: Brooks/Cole.

Thompson, R. (1996). *Counseling techniques*. Philadelphia: Accelerated Development Press.

Thompson, R. (1998). *Nurturing an endangered generation*. Philadelphia: Accelerated Development Press.

Tomasello, M. (1990). The role of joint attentional processes in early language development. *Language Sciences, 10,* 69–88.

Trevarthen, C. (1989, Autumn). Origins and directions for the concept of infant intersubjectivity. *Society for Research in Child Development Newsletter,* 1–4.

Trickett, P. K., Aber, J. L., Carlson, V., & Cicchetti, D. (1991). Relationship of socioeconomic status to the etiology and developmental sequelae of physical child abuse. *Developmental Psychology, 27,* 148–158.

Trickett, P. K., & Susman, E. J. (1988). Parental perceptions of childrearing practices in physically abusive and nonabusive families. *Developmental Psychology, 24,* 270–276.

U.S. Department of Commerce, Bureau of the Census. (1992a). Households, families, and children: A 30-year perspective. In *Current population reports* (Series P23, No. 181). Washington, DC: U.S. Government Printing Office.

U.S. Department of Commerce, Bureau of the Census. (1992b). Studies in marriage and the family: Married couple families with children. In *Current population reports* (Series P23, No. 162). Washington, DC: U.S. Government Printing Office.

U.S. Department of Commerce, Bureau of the Census. (1994). More education means higher career earnings. *Statistical Brief SB/94–17.* Washington, DC: U.S. Government Printing Office.

U.S. Department of Commerce, Bureau of the Census. (1997). Child custody, divorced families, 1997. In *Current population reports.* Retrieved April 12, 2002 from <http://www.gocrc.com/research/spgrowth.html>.

U.S. Department of Health and Human Services. (2001). *Mental health, culture, race and ethnicity.* Rockville, MD: Author.

Valliant, G. (1977). *Adaptation to life.* Boston: Little, Brown.

Vernon, A. (1999). *Counseling children and adolescents* (2nd ed.). Denver: Love Publishing.

Virginian-Pilot. Race and the brain. November 15, 2000, p. 4.

Visher, E. B., & Visher, J. S. (1988). *Old loyalties, new ties.* New York: Brunner/Mazel.

Vitaro, F., Tremblay, R., Kerr, M., Pagani, L., & Bukowski, W. (1997). Disruptiveness, friends' characteristics, and delinquency in early adolescence: A test of two competing models of development. *Child Development, 68,* 676–689.

Vygotsky, L. S. (1934). *Thought and language.* Cambridge: Massachusetts Institute of Technology Press.

Vygotsky, L. S. (1978). *Mind in society: The development of higher mental processes.* Cambridge, MA: Harvard University Press. (Original work published 1930, 1933, 1935.)

Vygotsky, L. S. (1987). *The collected works of L. S. Vygotsky* (R. W. Rieber & A. S. Carton, Trans.). New York: Plenum Press. (Original work published 1934, 1960.)

Wallerstedt, C., & Higgens, P. (1996). Facilitating perinatal grieving between the mother and the father. *Journal of Obstetric, Gynecologic, and Neonatal Nursing, 25,* 389–394.

Wallerstein, J. S. (1984). Children of divorce: Preliminary report of a ten-year follow-up of young children. *American Journal of Orthopsychiatry, 54,* 444–458.

Wallerstein, J. S. (1989, January 23). Children after divorce: Wounds that don't heal. *The New York Times Magazine,* pp. 19–21, 41–44.

Wallerstein, J. S., & Kelly, J. B. (1974). The effects of parental divorce: The adolescent experience. In E. J. Anthony & C. Koupernik (Eds.), *The child in his family: Children at psychiatric risk* (Vol. 3). New York: Wiley.

Wallerstein, J. S., & Kelly, J. B. (1975). The effects of parental divorce: Experiences of the preschool child. *Journal of the American Academy of Child Psychiatry, 14,* 600–616.

Wallerstein, J. S., & Kelly, J. B. (1976). The effects of parental divorce: Experiences of the child in later latency. *American Journal of Orthopsychiatry, 46,* 256–269.

Wallerstein, J. S., & Kelly, J. B. (1980). *Surviving the breakup.* New York: Basic Books.

Walrond-Skinner, S. (1986). *Dictionary of psychotherapy.* New York: Routledge & Kegan Paul.

Wannan, G., & Fombonne, E. (1998). Gender differences in rates and correlates of suicidal behaviour amongst child psychiatric outpatients. *Journal of Adolescence, 21,* 371–381.

Waters, E. (1990). The life review: Strategies of working with individuals and groups. *Journal of Mental Health Counseling, 12,* 270–278.

Wegener-Spohring, G. (1989). War toys and aggressive games. *Play and Culture, 2,* 35–47.

Weinraub, M., Clemens, L. P., Sockloff, A., Ethridge, T., Gracely, E., & Myers, B. (1984). The development of sex-role stereotypes in the third year: Relationships to gender labeling, gender identity, sex-typed toy preference, and family characteristics. *Child Development, 55,* 1493–1503.

Weinraub, M., & Gringlas, M. B. (1995). Single parenthood. In M. H. Bornstein (Ed.), *Handbook of parenting* (Vol. 3, pp. 65–88). Hillsdale, NJ: Erlbaum.

Weiss, B., Dodge, K. A., Bates, J. E., & Pettit, G. S. (1992). Some consequences of early harsh discipline: Child aggression and a maladaptive social information processing style. *Child Development, 63,* 1321–1335.

Weissman, M. M., Wolk, S., Goldstein, R. B., Moreau, D., Adams, P., Greenwald, S., Klier, C., Ryan, N. D., Dahl, R. E., & Wickramaratne, P. (1999). Depressed adolescents grow up. *Journal of the American Medical Association, 28,* 1707–1713.

Welfel, E., Danzinger, P., & Santoro, S. (2000). Mandated reporting of abuse/maltreatment of older adults: A primer for counselors. *Journal of Counseling and Development, 78,* 284–292.

Wellman, H. M. (1988). The early development of memory strategies. In F. E. Weinert & M. Perlmutter (Eds.), *Memory development: Universal changes and individual differences.* Hillsdale, NJ: Erlbaum.

Werker, J. F., & Lalonde, C. E. (1988). Cross-language speech perception: Initial capabilities and developmental change. *Developmental Psychology, 24,* 672–683.

Werner, E. (1992). *Vulnerable but invincible: A longitudinal study for resilient children and youth.* New York: McGraw-Hill.

Werner, E., & Smith, R. (1992). *Overcoming the odds: High-risk children from birth to adulthood.* Ithaca, NY: Cornell University Press.

Wetzel, R., & Brown, N. (2000). *Student-generated sexual harassment in secondary schools.* Westport, CT: Praeger.

White, B. L., & Watts, J. (1973). *Experience and environment: Major influences on the development of the young child.* Englewood Cliffs, NJ: Prentice-Hall.

Whiting, B. B., & Edwards, C. P. (1988). *Children of different worlds: The formation of social behavior.* Cambridge, MA: Harvard University Press.

Whiting, B. B., & Whiting, J. W. M. (1975). *Children of six cultures: A psychological analysis.* Cambridge, MA: Harvard University Press.

Wilkes, T., Belsher, G., Rush, A., Frank, E., et al. (1994). *Cognitive therapy for depressive adolescents.* New York: Guilford.

Wilson, B. J., & Gottman, J. M. (1995). Marital interaction and parenting. In M. H. Bornstein (Ed.), *Handbook of parenting: Vol. 4. Applied and practical parenting* (pp. 33–55). Hillsdale, NJ: Erlbaum.

Wilson, C., & Nettlebeck, T. (1986). Inspection time and the mental age deviation hypothesis. *Personality and Individual Differences, 7,* 669–675.

Wilson, C., Nettlebeck, T., Turnball, C., & Young, R. (1992). IT, IQ, and age: A comparison of developmental functions. *British Journal of Developmental Psychology, 10,* 179–188.

Winnicott, D. (1951). Transitional objects and transitional phenomena. In *Collected Papers: Through pediatrics to psycho-analysis* (pp. 129–144). London: Tavistock.

Winnicott, D. (1960). *Maturational processes.* New York: International Universities Press.

Winnicott, D. (1962). Ego integration in child development. In *Maturational processes* (pp. 56–63). New York: International Universities Press.

Winnicott, D. (1971). *Playing and reality.* London: Tavistock.

Wolfelt, A. D. (1983). *Helping children cope with grief.* Muncie, IN: Accelerated Development.

Wolfelt, A. D. (1988). *Death and grief: A guide for clergy.* Muncie, IN: Accelerated Development.

Worden, J. W. (1991). *Grief counseling and grief therapy: A handbook for the mental health professional.* New York: Springer.

Yalom, I. (1980). *Existential psychotherapy.* New York: Basic Books.

Yalom, I. (1995). *The theory and practice of group psychotherapy* (4th ed.). New York: Basic Books.

Zahn-Waxler, C., & Kochanska, G. (1990). The origins of guilt. In R. Thompson (Ed.), *Nebraska symposium on motivation: Vol. 36. Socioemotional development* (pp. 183–258). Lincoln: University of Nebraska Press.

Zahn-Waxler, C., Radke-Yarrow, M., Wagner, E., & Chapman, M. (1992). Development of concern for others. *Developmental Psychology, 28,* 126–136.

Zill, N. (1991, Winter). U.S. children and their families: Current conditions and recent trends, 1989. *SRCD Newsletter,* pp. 1–3.

Zill, N., Morrison, D. R., & Coiro, M. J. (1993). Long-term effects of parental divorce on parent–child relationships, adjustment, and achievement in young adulthood. *Journal of Family Psychology, 7,* 1–13.

Zuravin, S. J. (1989). Severity of maternal depression and three types of mother-to-child aggression. *American Journal of Orthopsychiatry, 59,* 377–389.

Index

About the Authors

RADHA J. HORTON-PARKER is an associate professor of counseling at Old Dominion University in Norfolk, Virginia. She is a National Certified Counselor (NCC) and National Certified School Counselor (NCSC). Her specialities include lifespan development, counseling theories and techniques, and counseling children and adolescents in school settings. Dr. Horton-Parker received her doctorate in counselor education from the University of Virginia and is the past president of the Virginia Association for Spiritual, Ethical, Religious, and Values Issues in Counseling and the former editor of the *Virginia Counselors Association Journal* and the Virginia Counselors Association newsletter, *The Relator*. In addition, she is a former member of the editorial review board of *Elementary School Guidance and Counseling* and is currently serving on the editorial review board of *Counseling and Values*. Her recent publications include articles on helping parents develop prosocial behavior in children, on training school counselors in professional development schools, and on using rituals to strengthen relationships and promote healing.

NINA W. BROWN is a professor of counseling at Old Dominion University in Norfolk, Virginia. She received her doctorate from The College of William and Mary and teaches masters and doctoral courses in counseling at ODU. Dr. Brown is the author of five books on group counseling: *Teaching Group Dynamics: Process and Practice*; *Group Counseling for Elementary and Middle School Children*; *Expressive Processes in Group Counseling*; *Psychoeducational Groups*; and *Creating High Performance Classroom Groups*. She is also the author of *The Destructive Narcissistic Pattern*; *Children of the Self-Absorbed*; *Whose Life Is It Anyway*; and *Working with the Self-Absorbed*. Dr. Brown co-authored the books, *Peer-Generated Sexual Harassment in the Secondary School* and *Student Development and Student Learning at a Distance*.